Women in History

by

Alice H. Deck

ISBN: 978-0-7596-3167-0 (sc)
ISBN: 978-0-7596-3166-3 (e)

Print information available on the last page.

This book is printed on acid-free paper.

1st Books rev: 01/26/2021

Table of Contents

Suffrage Facts Around the World

Women obtained the right to vote in the following countries on the dates indicated:

DATE	COUNTRY	COMMENT
1838	Pitcairn Island	Universal Suffrage granted
1883	New Zealand	Women obtain the vote – the first nation to do so.
1891	Isle of Man	Women's suffrage granted
1902	Commonwealth of Australia	Women's suffrage granted
1906	Aland	Women's suffrage granted
	Republic of Finland	Universal suffrage granted
1908	Republic of Iceland	Women given right to vote
1913	Kingdom of Norway	Women get equal voting rights
1914	Norfolk Islands	Women's suffrage granted
1915	Kingdom of Denmark	Women granted the vote
	Faero Islands	Women's suffrage granted
1916	Christmas Island	Women's suffrage granted
1917	Federal Republic of Russia	Women obtain the vote
1918	Commonwealth of Canada	Women granted the vote
	England	Women over 30 get vote and can sit in Parliament
	Georgia	Women's suffrage granted
	Germany	Women granted the vote
	Grand Duchy of Luxembourg	Women's suffrage granted
	Republic of Austria	Women's suffrage granted
	Republic of Czechoslovakia	Women given the vote
	Republic of Estonia	Women's suffrage granted
	Republic of Latvia	Women's suffrage granted
	Republic of Poland	Women granted the vote
1919	Austria	Women given right to vote
	Azarbaijan	Women's suffrage granted
	Belgium	Women given the vote
	Grand Duchy of Luxembourg	Women given right to vote
	Jamaica	Women's suffrage granted
	Kingdom of the Netherlands	Women obtain the vote
	Republic of Ireland	Women given right to vote
	Republic of Kenya	Women's suffrage granted
	Kingdom of Sweden	Women given the vote
	Ukraine	Women given right to vote

	United Republic of Tansania	Women's suffrage granted
1920	Albania	Women given right to vote
	Slovakia	Women given right to vote
	United States of America	19th Amendment passed grants women the right to vote
1921	State of Mongolia	Women's suffrage granted
	Georgia	Women's suffrage granted
1922	Azerbaijan	Women given right to vote
	Lithuania	Women given right to vote
	Republic of Armenia	Women's suffrage granted
	Republic of Kazakhstan	Women's suffrage granted
	Republic of Uzbekistan	Women's suffrage granted
	Tajikistan	Women's Suffrage granted
1924	Saint Lucia	Women's suffrage granted
	Tajikistan	Women's suffrage granted
1927	Arab Republic of Egypt	Women's suffrage granted
	Turkmenistan	Women given right to vote
1929	Ecuador	Women given right to vote
	Republic of Fiji	Women's suffrage granted
	Romania	Women given right to vote
1930	Republic of Moldova	Women's suffrage granted
	Republic of South Africa	White women given the vote
	Turkey	Women given right to vote
1931	Chile	Women given right to vote
	Spain	Women get the vote
	Democratic Socialist Republic of Sri Lanka	Women granted the vote
	Portugal	Women given right to vote
1932	Federal Republic of Brazil	Women granted suffrage
	Republic of Maldive Islands	Women's suffrage granted
	Kingdom of Thailand	Women get the vote
	Republic of Uraguay	Women given right to vote
1934	Republic of Cuba	Women granted right to vote
1935	Union of Myanmar (Burma)	Women's suffrage granted
1936	Republic of Kiribati	Women's suffrage granted
1937	Republic of Bulgaria	Women's suffrage granted
	Republic of the Phillipines	Women given right to vote
1838	Uzbekistan	Women given right to vote
1939	Republic of Bolivia	Women's suffrage granted
	Republic of El Salvador	Women granted right to vote

1941	Republic of Indonesia	Women granted suffrage
	Republic of Panama	Women given right to vote
1942	The Domenican Republic	Women's suffrage granted
1944	Bermuda	Women's suffrage granted
	Cayman Islands	Women's suffrage granted
	Jamaica	Women given right to vote
	Republic of Albania	Women's suffrage granted
1945	France	Vote extended to women
	Guyana	Women given right to vote
	Republic of Italy	Vote extended to women
	Japan	Vote extended to women
	Republic of Croatia	Women's suffrage granted
	Republic of Senegal	Women given right to vote
	Slovenia	Women given right to vote
	Togo	Women given right to vote
	Vietnam	Vote extended to women
1946	Republic of Benin	Women's suffrage granted
	Burkina Faso	Women's suffrage granted
	Central African Republic	Women's suffrage granted
	Guatemala	Women given right to vote
	Islamic Republic of Mauritania	Women given right to vote
	Korea	Women given right to vote
	Nouvelle Caledonie	Women's suffrage granted
	Macedonia	Women given right to vote
	Republic of Djibouti	Women's suffrage granted
	Republic of Liberia	Women's suffrage granted
	Republic of Madagascar	Women's suffrage granted
	Republic of Togo	Women's suffrage granted
	Trinidad and Tobago	Women given right to vote
	United Republic of Cameroon	Women's suffrage granted
	Venezuela	Women granted right to vote
	Yugoslavia	Women given right to vote
1947	Argentina	Women given right to vote
	Bangledesh	Women's suffrage granted
	Kingdom of Nepal	Women's suffrage granted
	Peoples Republic of China	Universal suffrage granted
	Republic of Balau	Women's suffrage granted
	Republic of Comoro Islands	Women's suffrage granted
	Republic of India	Women's suffrage granted
	Republic of Malta	Women given right to vote
	Republic of Marshall Islands	Women's suffrage granted

	Republic of Mauritius	Women's suffrage granted
	Singapore	Women given right to vote
1948	Greenland	Women's suffrage granted
	Kingdom of Belgium	Full women's suffrage granted
	Republic of Algeria	Women's suffrage granted
	Republic of Seychelles	Women given right to vote
	Republic of South Korea	Women obtain right to vote
	Republic of Suriname	Women given right to vote
	State of Israel	With formation of state, women receive full suffrage
1949	Falkland Islands	Women's suffrage granted
	Principality of Monaco	Women's suffrage granted
	Republic of Bosnia	Women's suffrage granted
	Republic of Chile	Women granted voting rights
	Republic of China	Women get the vote
	Republic of Costa Rica	Women's suffrage granted
	Republic of Ghana	Women given right to vote
	Republic of Niger	Women's suffrage granted
	Syrian Arab Republic	Women given right to vote
	Taiwan	Women's suffrage granted
	The Cocos Islands	Women's suffrage granted
1950	India	Women granted right to vote
	Republic of Haiti	Women obtain right to vote
1951	Antiqua and Barbados	Women's suffrage granted
	Commonwealth of Domenica	Women's suffrage granted
	State of Grenada	Women given right to vote
	Federation of Saint Christopher and Nevis	Women's suffrage granted
	Saint Vincent and Grenadines	Women's suffrage granted
1952	Greece	Women's suffrage granted
	Republic of Ivory Coast	Women's suffrage granted
	Republic of Lebanon	Women granted right to vote
1953	Hungary	Women given right to vote
	Kingdom of Bhutan	Women's suffrage granted
	Republic of Guyana	Women's suffrage granted
	Republic of Sudan	Women's suffrage granted
	United States of Mexico	Women win right to vote
1954	Aruba	Women's suffrage granted
	Belize	Women's suffrage granted
	Federal Republic of Nigeria	Women obtain right to vote
	Nederlandse Antillen	Female suffrage granted
	Republic of Columbia	Women get the vote

1955	Kingdom of Cambodia	Women's suffrage granted
	Republic of Ethiopia	Women's suffrage granted
	Republic of Honduras	Women's suffrage granted
	Republic of Nicaragua	Women obtain right to vote
	Republic of Peru	Women get the vote
1956	Benin	Women given right to vote
	Comoros	Women given right to vote
	Democratic Republic of Laos	Women's suffrage granted
	Egypt	Women given right to vote
	Islamic Republic of Pakistan	Universal suffrage granted
	Mali	Women given right to vote
	Mauritius	Women given right to vote
	Republic of Gabon	Women's suffrage granted
	Republic of Congo	Women given right to vote
	Republic of Tunesia	Women's suffrage granted
	Democratic Republic Somalia	Women given right to vote
1957	Federation of Malaysia	Women's suffrage granted
	Fiji Islands	Women's suffrage granted
	Zimbabwe	Women given right to vote
1958	Burkina Faso	Women given right to vote
	Chad	Women given right to vote
	Guinea	Women given right to vote
	Republic of Sierra Leone	Women's suffrage granted
	Somaliland	Women's suffrage granted
1959	Kingdom of Morocco	Women's suffrage granted
	Republic of Cyprus	Women's suffrage granted
	Republic of San Marino	Women's suffrage granted
	Sultanate of Brunei	Women's suffrage granted
	Tunisia	Women given right to vote
	United Republic of Tanzania	Black's suffrage granted
1960	Cyprus	Women given right to vote
	Kingdom of Tonga	Women's suffrage granted
	Republic of Malawi	Women given right to vote
	Republic of Zaire	Women's suffrage granted
	Republic of Zambia	Women's suffrage granted
	Tonga	Women given right to vote
1961	Commonwealth of The Bahamas	Women's suffrage granted
	Republic of Burundi	Women's suffrage granted
	Republic of Botswana	Women's suffrage granted
	Republic of Paraguay	Women granted voting Rights
	Republic of The Gambia	Women's suffrage granted

	Rwanda	Women given right to vote
	Sierra Leone	Women given right to vote
1962	Commonwealth of Australia	Aborigines granted suffrage
	Northern Mariana Islands	Women's suffrage granted
	Republic of Uganda	Women's suffrage granted
	State of Kuwait	Women's suffrage granted
	Zambia	Women given right to vote
1963	Equatorial Guinea	Women's suffrage granted
	Fiji	Women given right to vote
	Islamic Republic of Iran	Women's suffrage granted
	Kenya	Women get the vote
	Republic of Libya	Women granted right to vote
1964	Federated States Micronesia	Women's suffrage granted
	Gibraltar	Women's suffrage granted
	Papua New Guinea	Women given right to vote
	Republic of Afganistan	Women's suffrage granted
	Republic of Iraq	Women's suffrage granted
	Sudan	Women's suffrage granted
1965	Bostwana	Women given right to vote
	Kingdom of Leshoto	Women's suffrage granted
	Niue	Female suffrage granted
1966	Jordan	Women's vote added to its Constitution
	Republic of Namibia	White women granted suffrage
	Republic of Nauruo	Women's suffrage granted
1967	Anguilla	Universal suffrage granted
	Kiribati	Women given right to vote
	Republic of Ecuador	Women's suffrage granted
	Tuvalu	Women given right to vote
1968	Kingdom of Swaziland	Women's suffrage granted
	Nauru	Women given right to vote
1969	Zanzibar	Female suffrage granted
1970	Principality of Andorra	Women's suffrage granted
	Yemen Arab Republic	Women given right to vote
1971	Switzerland	Women obtain right to vote
1972	Bangladesh	Women given right to vote
1973	Republic of Guinea Bissau	Women's suffrage granted
1974	Solomon Islands	Women given right to vote
1975	Cape Verde Islands	Women's suffrage granted
	Cook Islands	Women's suffrage granted
	Republic of Angola	Women's suffrage granted
	Republic of Mozambique	Women's suffrage granted
	Republic Sao Tome e Principe	Women's suffrage granted

1976	Macau	Women's suffrage granted
1979	Palau	Women given right to vote
1980	Iraq	Women given right to vote
1984	Principality of Liechtenstein	Women given right to vote
	Republic of South Africa	Coloured & Indians given vote
1986	Central African Republic	Women given right to vote
1989	Independent State of Samoa	Women's suffrage granted
	Republic of Nambia	Suffrage granted to all
1994	Republic of South Africa	Blacks given the vote
	Sultanate of Oman	Universal suffrage granted
1997	Saharan Arab Democratic Republic	Women's Suffrage granted
1999	State of Quatar	Women's Suffrage granted

African Women

ANGOLA

1624
Mbande Zinga
She became Queen in 1624 and appointed women to all government offices. When the Portuguese broke the peace treaty, she led her largely female army against them and inflicted terrible casualties while also conquering nearby kingdoms in order to build a strong enough confederation to drive the Portuguese out of Africa.

1978
Maria de Jesus Haller
In 1978, she was appointed ambassador to Sweden, the first woman ambassador in her country.

BENIN

1939
Colette Agossou Houeto
(1939-)
A teacher by profession, she became Director of Benin's National Institute of Training and Research into Education in 1977. From 1986-1991, she worked in the BAD program, a project which aimed at integrating women into the country's' growth and expansion development program.

1980
Bernardine do Regio
In 1980, she was appointed ambassador to Nigeria, the first woman ambassador in her country. From 1992 to 1994, she was ambassador to Canada.

1990
Veronique Ahayo Ahogo
In 1990 she became Minister of Labor and Social Affairs. She was appointed ambassador to Canada in 1994.

1995
Grace d'Almeida Adamon
In 1995, she became Minister of Justice and Legislation, Keeper of the Seals.

BOTSWANA

1970
Gaositwe Kpgalwa Tipe Chiepe
(1926 -)
In 1970, she was appointed ambassador to United Kingdom, Germany, France, Norway, Denmark, European Communities and Nigeria, the first female ambassador of her country. She was later Minister of Foreign Affairs.

1999
Margaret N. Nasha
A former TV journalist and civil servant, she was appointed ambassador to United Kingdom in 1991. She became Minister of Local Government in 1999.

BURKINA FASO

1942
Aminata Salambere Ouedraogo
(1942 -)
She was Secretary General FESPA (1981-84), Secretary of State for Culture (1987-92) and in 1992 became Director General of Culture and Communication of the Agency of Cultural and Technical Cooperation in Paris.

Noelie Victoire Kone Tou
(1950 -)
She was Economic Councilor and Director of International Financial Relations from 1975-85. In 1990, she became Minister of Trade and Community Supplies, in 1991, Minister, Secretary General of the Government and in 1992, Economic Advisor to the President.

1985
Maimouna Ouattara
In 1985, she was appointed ambassador to Ghana, the first woman ambassador in her country.

1987
Alice Solange Kaboret Tiendrebeogo
She was Secretary of State of Social Action in 1987, Minister of Basic Education and Mass Aphabetisation in 1988, Minister of Water Supply in 1995 and Minister of Women's Promotion in 1997.

1995
Bona Ouandaogo Maiga
In 1995, she became Minister of Social Welfare and Family. Previously, she was President of the Burkina Red Cross.

Vivianne Yolande B. Compaore Ouedraogo
She was Director General of International Cooperation in the Ministry of Foreign Affairs from 1994-95 and Minister Delegate of Public Works, Housing and Town Planning from 1995-96. In 1997, she became Minister of Regional Integration.

1997
Juliette Yeredon Yameogo Bonkoungou (1954 -)
In 1997, she became Chairman of the Economic and Social Council, which is the supreme advisory body of the President. She is a former Judge and head of the Broadcasting Corporation.

Anne Konate
Between 1990-99, she was Ambassador to Denmark, Sweden, Norway, etc. She became Minister Delegate of Economic Development in 1999.

BURUNDI

1993
Sylvie Inigi
In 1993, she became Premier Minister. During the Civil War the President was killed and, as the highest-ranking person, she became De-Facto Acting President.

1994
Julie Ngiriye
She was Minister of Social Affairs From 1987-93 and was appointed Ambassador to Sweden, Denmark, Finland, Norway and Iceland in 1994, the first female ambassador of her country.

1993
Sylvie Kinigi (1952 -)
From 1993-94, she was Premier Minister and as such was Head of the Economic Planning Office in the President's Office. When the president was killed, she as the highest-ranking person was De-Facto Acting President. She joined the Burundi's Commercial Bank after her resignation.

CAPE VERDE ISLANDS
1962
Carmen Pereira
Since 1962, she was a member of the African Party for Independence of Guinea-Bissau and Cape Verde. She was the only femal member of the 24-member Comite Executivo da Luta. Between 1973-84, she was Deputy President of Assembleia Nacional Popular Vice-President and President of the Assebleia Nacional and Minister in Guinea Bissau from 1984-89.

1992
Maria Helena Nobre de Morais Querido Semedo
She was Secretary of State for Fisheries (1992-93), Minister for Fisheries,

Agriculture and Rural Development (1993-95) and Minister of the Sea (1995-98). In 1998, she became Minister of Tourism, Transport and Marine Affairs.

1996
Ana Paula Almieda
She was Secretary of State for Administration and Administrative Reform from 1996-98, and Secretary of State of Employment, Training and Social Integration.

2000
Januaria Mareira
In 2000, she became Minister of Justice and Internal Integration.

CAMEROON
1935
Delphine Zanga Tsogo
(1935 -)
Apart from her professional activities as a nurse and author, her political career has been exceptional. In 1965 she was elected a Member of Parliament and has been Minister for Social Affairs since 1975. She is one of the 1st African women to reach top positions in world of politics.

1937
Isabelle Bassang-Akouma-Manneyeng (1937 -)
In 1987, she became Minister of Health. She has been ambassador to European Economic Council, Belgium, The Netherlands and Luxembourg since 1989.

1938

Therese Kuoh Moukoury (1938-)
President of the 'Union des femmes africaines et malgaches' (Union of African and Madagascan Women), she worked for international organizations or with African governments as an authority on social communication.

1950

Werewere Liking (1950 -)
She is a prolific author who has written in every genre. Her literary career is based on the Ki-Yi Mbock initially movement for the rebirth of African arts, for the birth of a contemporary Panafrican culture and for the coming together and recognition of the cultures of the Black world.

1954

Monique Bessomo (1954 -)
She has a State Diploma in Ergotherapy and currently works in the National Centre for the rehabilitation of the handicapped.

1955

Stella Irene Virginie Engama (1955 -)
She has a Masters and DEA in Law. In 1990, she founded the "Foundation Universelle Stella Engoma" for culture, education and sport.

1982

Simone Mairie
She was Appointed ambassador to the United Nations in 1982, the first woman ambassador in her country.

1983

Marie Therese Assiga Ahanda
A professional chemist, she worked for Science faculty at Yaounde. In 1983, she was a delegate to the Cameroonian National Assembly.

1993

Chulong Someara
In 1993, she became Deputy Governor of the National Bank of Cambodia.

CENTRAL AFRICAN REPUBLIC

1855

Natelegie (1855-1900)
Queen of the Nzakara of the Central African Republic, she was the first woman of her people to be acclaimed chieftain in her own right.

1975

Elizabeth Domitien
First Prime Minister of her country, she was appointed in 1975 by the ruler Jean Bedel Bokassa, who had himself crowned Emperor in an elaborate ceremony in 1977. She was essentially without power in this newly created post.

1995

Simone Bodemou
She was elected President of Central African Republic Red Cross and in 1995 became Secretary General of the Government.

Domenique Guerematchi

In 1995, she became Secretary of State of Foreign Affairs.

COMORO ISLANDS

1991

Mahamed Sittou Radhadat

(1952 -)

She was Secretary of State for Population and Women's Affairs (1991-92), High Commissioner responsible for Women's Affairs (1992-93), and Minister of Social Affairs, Employment and Labor (1993-94). In 1995, she became Minister of Social Affairs, Employment and Works.

1996

Soiffat Said Bourhan

She was Minister-Delegate in charge of Economy and Trade from 1996-98.

CONGO

1940

Cecile Ivelyse Diamoneka

(1940-)

A teacher, she has been a member of the National Council of the Congolese National Union of Writers, Artists and Artisans. In 1991, she became Director of Spiritual and Religious Affairs at the Ministry for Culture.

1944

Clementine Faik Nzujo

(1944 -)

She has a doctorate in African Studies from the University of Paris III, La Sorbonne Nouvelle. She has taught Linguistics, oral literatures and African cultures at the Catholic University of Louvain in Belgium since 1981. Her research and scientific publications are in the field of oral literatures, African symbolic systems and links between cultures.

1985

C. Ecomband

In 1985, she was appointed ambassador to Guinea, the first woman ambassador in her country.

DJBOUTI

1990

Kadidja Abeba

In 1990, she became Deputy Head of State and President of the Court of Appeal.

1999

Hawa Ahmad Yousouf

She became Minister-Delegate by the Premier Minister in charge of the Promotion of Women, Family Well-Being and Social Affairs in 1999.

EQUATORIAL GUINEA

1978

Christina Ndjombe Ndjangani

She was Minister of Women's Planification from 1978-83.

1991

Teresa Efua Asangono

She was Minister of Women and Social Affairs (1991-94) and Minister-Delegate of Foreign Affairs and Cooperation (1998-99).

1999

Evangelina Filomena Oyo Ebule
She became Vice-Minister of Justice and Religion in 1999.

ETHIOPIA

1850

Taytu Betul (1850-1918)
In 1889, she became Empress of Ethiopia. During her reign she she administered large holdings of land, led troops in battle, negotiated peace treaties and established and named the modern capital of Addis Ababa.

1929

Youdith Imre (1929 -)
In 1971, she became Deputy Minister of Foreign Affairs and was the leader of the Ethiopian delegation to the Non-Aligned Nation's Conference. She was appointed ambassador to Denmark, Sweden, Norway, Finland and Iceland in 1975.

1995

Weizer Almaz Meko
In 1995, she became Speaker of the Yefedereshn Mekir Bet (Council of the Federation).

1999

Fatuma Roba
In 1999, she wins her third Boston Marathon in three years becoming only the second woman in history to accomplish that feat. She is the first African woman to win the race.

GABON

1982

Honorie Dossou-Naki
From 1982-88, she was Deputy Minister of Foreign Affairs and since 1995, ambassador to France.

Pauline Nyingone
In 1982, she was Secretary of State of Justice and Keeper of the Seals and in 1994, Gouveneur de la Province d'Estvaire.

1987

Jeanne Nzao-Mabike
In 1987, she was appointed ambassador to Senegal, the first woman ambassador of her country.

1992

Angele Ondo
In 1992, she became Minister of Communication, Post and Telecommunication and Government Spokeswoman. From 1992-93, she was Minister for Social Affairs and Relations with Assemblee Nationale.

1997

Yolande Bike
Former Deputy Minister of Education, Sport and Women, she has been ambassador to United Nations in Geneve since 1997.

2000

Angelique Ngoma
From 1997-2000, she was Secretary of State of Social Affairs. In 2000, she became Minister of Family and Women's Advancement. After

2000, the government had no Secretaries of State.

GAMBIA

1982
Louise N'Jie
In 1982, she became Minister of Youth, Sport and Culture, second in the Cabinet. From 1988-92, she was Minister of Social Security and Health.

1991
Ruth Adjue Sowe
In 1991, she was appointed ambassador to Benelux, France, Germany, European Communities and Union.

1992
Amie Bensouda
She became Solicitor General and Legal Secretary in 1992. From 1994-95, she was Acting Minister of Justice.

1993
Mariam Alaba Mbonge
From 1993-94, she was Parliamentary Secretary of External Affairs.

1996
Aisatou N'jie-Saidy
She became Secretary of State of Social Welfare, Health and Women's Affairs in 1996 and Vice President in 1997.

1998
Fatou Bensouda
She became Attorney General and Secretary of Justice in 1998.

1999
Therese Ndong-Jatta
In 1999, she became Secretary of State of Education. Prior to her appointment, she was director of higher education.

GHANA

1921
Peggy Appiah (1921 -)
She started collecting and writing children's books about Ashanti's old and complex culture. Most of her storybooks are about village and forest life, animals and birds.

1940
Ama Ata Aidoo (1940 -)
An important and vocal figure in the struggle for Ghanian national liberation, she is also an outspoken proponent for women's liberation. As a writer, she has written two plays, two novels, a collection of short stories, two collections of poetry as well as numerous essays on African literature and the status of women in African society.

1950
Annie Jiagge
In 1950, she became the first female Judge in Ghana. She became chairman of the United Nations Commission on the Status of Women in 1960.

1958
Efua Sutherland (1924-)
She founded the Ghana Drama Studies and the Ghana Society of Writers in 1958 and

subsequently established schools in upper and middle Ghana as well as one of the schools at the University of Ghana. Author who in her works captures the essence of African culture while practicing it in a contemporary setting.

1961
Suzanna Al-Hassan
From 1961-63, she was Deputy Minister of Education and from 1963-67, Minister of Social Affairs. In 1993, she was a member of the National Defense Council.

1969
Gloria Amon Nikoi
In 1969-74, she was Deputy Chief of Mission to the United Nations and from 1981, Chairman of the Bank of Housing and Construction.

1970
Bertha Amohoo-Neiser
In 1970, she was appointed ambassador to Denmark, the first female ambassador of her country.

1980
Esther Afua Ocloo
A pioneering leader since the time of Ghana's independence, she is a highly successful entrepreneur, industrialist, philanthropist, international leader and the first woman to receive the Africa Prize for Leadership. She was founder and first national president of the Federation of Ghana Industries, the first female

executive chairman of the Ghana National Food and Nutrition Board and founder of the Ghanaian chapter of the International Federation of Business and Professional Women. In 1980, she became first chairman of the Board of Women's World Banking, which provides guarantees for women who cannot provide collateral so that they are eligible for a bank loan.

1982
Ama Ata Aidoo (1942 -)
Since this African woman author's play "*Dilemma of a Ghost*" was performed in 1964 at the University of Ghana, she has been an important and vocal figure in the struggle for Ghanaian national liberation and an outspoken proponent for women's liberation. She published her novel "*Sister Killjoy*" in 1977, which expressed an African woman's cultural shock in the country. She became Secretary of Education in Ghana in 1982.

Joyce Aryee
From 1982-85, she was Minister of Information and in 1988 became Minister of Democracy in the Office of the Premier Minister.

1988
Theresa Owusu
From 1988-92, she was Deputy Minister of Fuel and Power when she became Deputy Minister of Energy.

1993

Christine Amooko-Noamah

From 1993-97, she was Minister of Environment, Science and Technology. In 1998, she became Minister of Lands and Forestry.

Teresa Owusu

From 1993-98, she was Deputy Governor of Bank of Ghana.

1997

Gertrude S. Aboagye

(1947 -)

A specialist in cattle production and animal breeding, she worked with the Animal Genetics Resource Group at FAO headquarters in Rome in 1997. This program has a country-based global infrastructure to help countries design, implement and maintain comprehensive national strategies for the management of their animal genetic resources. She hopes that her involvement in developing a global animal genetic resources management program will help Ghana and other countries reach a goal they all share - to improve the productivity of their national livestock.

1999

Margaret Clarke-Kwestie

A former ambassador, she became Minister without Portfolio in 1999.

1956

Koumanthio Zeinab Diallo

(1956 -)

She is an agricultural engineer, poet and a member of the International Committee of Women Writers.

1972

Jeanne Martin Cisse (1926 -)

She served as Guinea's first female delegate to the United Nations from 1972-76 and was the first woman to preside over the United Nations Security Council. In 1964, she was Deputy President of Assemblee Nationale and from 1975-84, she was Minister of Social Affairs.

1988

Hadja Achia Bah Diallo

Between 1988-90, she was Secretary of State for Pre-University Education, from 1990-92 Minister of Education and Minister of Secondary Education from 1994-97.

1994

Josephine Leno Guilano

From 1994-96, she was Minister of Labor and Social Affairs. She was a member of the Transitional Committee for National Recovery from 1992-96.

1996

Saran Daraba

She was Minister of Social Affairs and Promotion of Women and the Child from 1996-2000.

2000

Camara Hadja Mawa Bandoura

A former ambassador to the United Nations, she became Minister of Foreign Affairs in 2000. Her official title is Minister to the presidency charged with Foreign Affairs.

IVORY COAST

1980

Hortense Aka-Anguih

From 1980-94, she was Vice President of the Assemblee Nationale and from 1984-90 Minister for Women's Affairs.

1985

Ekilda Liyonda

In 1985, she was appointed ambassador to Belgium, the first woman ambassador of her country. She became Minister of Foreign Affairs in 1987 and Minister of Information and The Press in 1988.

1988

Daniele-Marie-Ablane Akissi Boni-Claverie

She was Director of National Television between 1988-94 and Minister of Communication from 1994-99.

1994

Safiatou Francoise Ba-N'Daw

From 1994-98, she was Minister-Delegate of Economic Infrastructure charged with Energy and Transports. In 1999, she became Minister of Energy.

1996

Liliana Marie-Laure Ba

In 1996, she was appointed ambassador to Denmark, Finland and Norway.

KENYA

1907

Elspeth Huxley (1907 -)

Author of more than 30 books about the land where she spent her childhood, she is known as the chronicler of colonial Kenya. She had difficulty publishing her book *Red Strangers* because she wrote about the terrible genital mutilation of girls and women which is part of the Kikuyu culture.

1930

Grace Ogot (1930 -)

A nurse and midwife, she became an announcer for BBC in Kenya, a member of parliament, a United Nations delegate and a member of UNESCO. She is also an author of short stories and novels that examine the problems in transition from colonial to modern culture.

1938

Asenath Bole Odaga (1938 -)

A prolific Kenyan writer of children's literature, she spent most of her childhood among the Luo - an ethnic group in western Kenya. She has published children's material in both English and Luo and many of her stories have moral teachings. She served as chairperson of the Children's Literature Association of Kenya in 1988.

1940
Wangari Maathai (1940 -) Environmental and Human rights activist, she organized the planting of trees in the Green Belt movement and organized victims of violence in the Kenyan war. She is the first woman to earn a Ph.D. and chair a department at the University of Nairobi.

1966
Grace Ogat (1930-) She has worked as a midwife and served as a community relation's officer. In 1966, she published her first novel The Promised Land in which she wove witchcraft and folklore into her plot.

1976
Margaret Wambui Kenyatta Former mayor of Nairobi, from 1976-86 she was permanent representative to the United Nations Environmental Program in Nairobi.

1977
Wangari Muta Maatai In 1977, she founded the Green Belt Movement of Kenya, one of the world's most successful programs to combine community development and environmental protection. The goal of the movement is to curtail the devastating social and environmental effects of deforestation and desertification. In recent years, Maathai has evolved from one of Africa's leading environmentalists to one of Kenya's most visible political dissidents as she tries to reform the political process so that government addresses the concerns of ordinary Kenyans.

1978
Julia Ojiambo From 1978-89, she was Minister of Housing and Social Services.

1984
Asenath Bole Odaga A prolific writer in both Dholuo and English, she has written plays, children's stories and a number of well-received novels. In 1984 she published works on Kenyan oral literatures including *Yesterday's Today: The Study of Oral Literature* published.

1982
L. Marita Atebe In 1982, she became Assistant Minister of Agriculture.

1994
Tegla Laroupe In 1994, she became the first African woman to win a major marathon – finishing the New York City Marathon in 2:27:37. She ran the fastest women's marathon ever when she won the 1998 Rotterdam Marathon in 2:20:47.

1997

Agnes Ndetei

She was Assistant Minister of Education from 1997-98.

LESHOTO

1939

Qmamoshebi Kabi (1939 -)

She was Minister of Transport and Communication from 1996-98 and Minister of Women, Environment, and Youth in 1998-99.

1977

Marion Likhapa Sehiabo

In 1977, she was appointed ambassador to United Kingdom, Austria, Belgium, France, West Germany, Italy, Sweden, Netherlands and Switzerland, the first female ambassador of her country.

1995

Khauhelu Deborah Rasitapole

She was Minister of National Treasures from 1995-96 and Minister of Trade and Industry from 1996-98.

1999

Nitlhi Matsamai

Deputy Speaker from 1996-99, she became Speaker of the National Assembly in 199.

LIBERIA

1916

Edith Mai Willes Padmore (1916 -)

Special Assistant to the President from 1963-71, she became Minister of Health and Social Security in 1972.

1939

Ellen Johnson-Sirlaf

She was Secretary of State of Finance from 1972-73 and 1977-79. In 1980, she was president of the National Bank. From 1994-97, she was African Director of the United Nations Development Program. She is Leader of the Unity Party since 1997 as well as 1997 presidential candidate.

1940

Ruth Perry (1940 -)

In 1996, she became Acting President and leader of the government. A former senator, she was Chairman of the Council of State during the final stage of the civil war which had plagued the country for decades.

1969

Angie Brooks-Randolph (1928 -)

Attorney and diplomat, she became president of the International Federation of Western Lawyers in 1964. In 1969, she became President of Liberia – the first female president of an African nation. From 1967-68 she was President of the United Nations Trusteeship Council administering Nauru, Papua New Guinea and the Pacific Islands Territories and in 1976 the 2nd woman president of the United Nations General Assembly. She became Judge of the Supreme Court in 1997.

1981

Hanna Abedou Bowen Jones

Former Minister of Health and Social Security, she was appointed ambassador to the United Nations in 1981. She was Vice-President (1982-84) and President (1984) of the General Assembly of the United Nations.

Veronica Peagor

In 1981, she was Deputy Minister of State without Portfolio in Ministry of Presidential Affairs.

1985

McLeod Darpoh

She was Minister of Commerce, Industry and Transport from 1985-87 and Minister of Post and Telecommunication from 1987-90.

1991

Amalie Ward

Between 1991-95 and 1998-99, she was Minister of Economy and Planning and in 1999 became Minister of Commerce and Industry.

1996

Victoria Refell

In 1996, she became Deputy Chairman of the Council of State (Vice-President).

1999

Neh Rita Sangai Dukuly-Tolbert

Former Ambassador to France, Switzerland and Luxembourg, she became Ambassador to the United Nations in 1999.

1977

Giselle Rabesahala

Between 1977-91, she was Minister of Revolutionary Art and Culture. She has been Co-leader of Congres de l'independence du Madagaskar since 1995.

1986

Charlotte Arrissoa Rafenomanjato

A writer, poet, essayist and translator, she is President of the Indian Ocean Writers Society. Her play *Le prix de la Paix* (The Price of Peace) was awarded the Radio France International prize in 1986, adapted for the screen and presented at the Festival of African Films in Montreal in 1988.

1994

Therese Ravao

Between 1994-95, she was Minister of Population, Youth and Sports and Secretary of State in charge of Population from 1995-97.

1995

Michele Ratsivalaka

She was Secretary of State in the Premier Minister's Office in charge of Housing and the Fight Against Poverty from 1995-96.

1997

Lila Ratsifandrihamanana

In 1997-98, she was Minister of Scientific Research and became Minister of Foreign Affairs in 1998.

MALAWI

1966

Jean M. Mlanga

She was Parliamentary Secretary to the President from 1966-74.

1994

Edda E. Chitalo

In 1994-96, she was Minister of State for Women's and Children's Affairs in the Cabinet and Minister of Physical Planning and Surveys from 1996-97. She has been Minister of State in the Office of the President and in the Cabinet responsible for Human Resources Management and Development since 1997.

1997

Joyce Banda

An influential advocate for improving the quality of life in Malawi by empowering thousands of women to become economically self-reliant, she won the 1997 Africa Prize. She founded the National Association of Business Women of Malawi in order to boost the status of all women - by giving them access to credit, training, information, markets and appropriate technology. Women entrepreneurs have moved progressively up the economic ladder from trading to small business to village industries and small-scale manufacturing.

1998

Alice Sumani

From 1998-99, she was Deputy Minister of Transport and Civil Aviation and became Deputy Minister of Natural Resources in 1999.

1999

Lillian Pratel

She was Minister of Health and Population from 1999-2000 and Minister of Foreign Affairs and International Co-operation in 2000.

2000

Lyna Tambala

Former Deputy Minister of Agriculture, in 2000 she became Deputy Minister of Home Affairs and Internal Security.

MALI

1912

Aoua Keita (1912-1980)

She was militant in the ranks of the Rassemblement Democratique Africain (RDA) [the African Democratic Assembly] in 1946, which was influential in all of the French colonies in Africa. In 1958, she was elected to the political office of the Sudanese Union of the RDA, where she was the only woman. In 1959, she was elected a Member of Parliament in the legislative elections and played a major political role until Modibo Keita's downfall.

1952
Bernadette Sanou Dao
(1952 -)
One of the top poets in Burkina, she has written children's stories, novellas and poems in French as well as the national language "Jula". In 1986, she was Minister for Culture and in 1991 she set up the GUIMBI (women's savings bank/credit society.

1957
Aicha Fofana (1957-)
She studied languages at the Sorbonne and is currently a translator and English/German bilingual interpreter.

1980
Gakou nee Natou Niang
From 1980-85 and 1988-91, she was Minister of Information and Telecommunications.

1993
Fatou Haidara
From 1993-94, she was Minister of Employment and Cottage Industry, Vocational Training and Private Initiatives Promotion and Minister of Cottage Industry and Tourism from 1994-97.

Madina Ly-Tall
In 1993, she was appointed ambassador to France and Spain, the first female ambassador of her country.

1994
Sy Kadiatou Sow
She was Minister of Foreign Affairs, Malians Abroad &

African Integration from 1994-95 and Minister of Town Planning and Housing from 19995-98.

1998
Hassane Barrey
From 1998-2000, she was Minister of Relations with Political Institutions and Parties.

2000
Zakyatou Oaulett Halatine
In 2000, she became Minister of Cottage Industry, Handy-Crafts and Tourism.

Bouare Fily Sissoko
In 2000, she became Minister of the State Domains and Ground Tax.

MAURITANIA
1971
Toure Aissata Kane
A feminist politician in Islamic Mauritania, she was first woman to achieve cabinet rank in her country when she was appointed Minister for the Protection of the Family and for Social Affairs from 1971-78.

1987
Abdelerahman Khadija Mint Ahmed Aiche
From 1987-90, she was Minister of Industry in the first civil government after the military dictatorship, which lasted from 1978-87. In 1994, she became Secretary of State for Women.

1997
Diye Ba
In 1997, she became Minister of Health, Social Solidarity and Human Services.

1998
Mantata Mint Adeid
In 1998, she became Minister of Women's Affairs.

MAURITIUS

1975
Radhamanay Roonoosarny
In 1975-76, she was Minister of Women's Affairs, Prizes and Consumer's Affairs.

1982
Shirin Aumeuruddy-Cziffranin
She was Minister of Justice and Attorney General, Minister of Women's Rights and Family Affairs from 1982-83. Between 1993-96, she was appointed Ambassador to France and Spain.

1989
Ghislaine Henry
In 1989-93, she was appointed Ambassador to France, the first female ambassador of her country.

1995
Marie-Therese Joceline Minerve
She was Minister of Social Security and National Solidarity from 1995-98.

1996
Marie-France Roussetry
Former Minister of Civil Service and Employment, she has been Ambassador to France and Spain since 1996.

MOZAMBIQUE

1980
Frances Victoria Velho Rodrigues
She was Ambassador and Director in the Foreign Ministry of International Economic Relations (1980-95) and Ambassador to Belgium, France, The Netherlands and the European Union (1985-98). Since 1998, she has been Vice-Minister of Foreign Affairs and Cooperation.

1988
Maria dos Anjos Rosario
From 1988-92, she was Secretary of State for Technical and Professional Education.

1991
Salome Milagre Machinassane Moiane
She became Vice-Minister of Foreign Affairs in 1991. Since 1997, she has been a member of Presidium of Assemblea da Republica.

1992
Graca Simbine Machel
The 1992 Africa Prize honors her dedication to educating the people of Mozambique and for leading an organization devoted to the children of her war-torn country. She has been a major force in increasing literacy and schooling in Mozambique.

1993
Luisa Dias Diogo
In 1993-95, she was Director of Budget in Ministry of Planning and Finance and became Minister of Planning and Finance in 2000.

1995
Acuenca da Costa Duarte
From 1995-99, she was Minister of Social Action Coordination. She became Vice-Minister of Justice in 1999.

1998
Celina Cossa
Founder of the General Union of Agricultural Cooperatives, she won the 1998 Africa Prize for Leadership for the Sustainable End of Hunger. The cooperatives, comprised of 95% women, produce food for member and their families and are generating a surplus that enables them to supply the markets in Maputo, the Mozambican capital.

2000
Lidia Maria Ribeiro Arthur Brito
In 2000, she became Minister of Higher Education, Science and Technology.

NAMIBIA

1950
Michaela M.E.K.H. Hubschle
Deputy Whip of SWAPO in the House of Representatives (1990-95), she became Deputy Minister of Prisons and Correctional Service in 1995.

1983
Margaret Jacobsohn
In 1983, she co-founded a program to assist rural communities to link social and economic development to the conservation of the region's spectacular wildlife and other natural resources. She is now providing support to communities wishing to form conservancies as the areas designated for wildlife use in Namibia are expanding considerably. In addition, communities are earning income and rural jobs are being created via the establishment of natural resource related enterprises.

1989
Netumbo Ndaitwali
She was Deputy Minister of Foreign Affairs (1989-96), Head of the Department of Women in the Office of the President (1996-2000) and Secretary General of SWAPO since 1996. In 2000, she became Minister of Women's Affairs.

1991
Tonata Lilja Itenge-Emvula
She was ambassador to Sweden, Norway, Denmark, Finland and Iceland from 1991-95, the first woman ambassador of her country.

1996
Pendukeni Timvula Ithana
Former Minister of Youth and Sport, she became Minister of Land, Resettlements and Rehabilitation in 1996.

1997

Saara Kuugongelwa

In 1997, she became Cabinet Member and Director-General of the National Planning Commission.

NIGER

1951

Hima Mariama (1951 -)

Former Director-General of Ministry of Culture and Conservator-General, she became Secretary of State of Women's and Children's Promotion in 1996. From 1996-97, she was Minister of Social Development, Population and of Women's Promotion and Children's Protection.

1974

Garba Sidikou

In 1974, she became Deputy Minister of Youth, Sport and Culture.

1989

Aissata Moumouni

She was Minister of Social Affairs and Women (1989-91), Minister of National Education (1996-99) and Minister of State (1997-99).

1996

Diallo Dissa Abdoulaye

From 1996-99, she was Minister of Tourism and Crafts and Minister charged with relations with the assemblies.

2000

Ossey Mirelle

In 2000, she became Minister of Labor and Modernization of the Administration.

NIGERIA

1533

Amina Sarauniya Zazzua

(1533-1610)

As Queen of Zazzua and leading warrior of Zazzua calvalry, she expanded the domain of Zazzua to its largest size ever during her reign. Her main focus was not on annexation of neighboring lands but on forcing local rulers to accept vassal status and permit Hausa traders' safe passage. She is credited with popularizing the earthen city wall fortifications, which became characteristic of Hausa city-states since then.

1536

Amina (1536-1573)

She ruled the Hausa Empire and extended its boundaries to the Atlantic coast, founded cities and personally led her army of soldiers into battle.

1907

Hajiya Ma'daki

She was the driving force behind the establishment of schools for girls in Nigeria in 1907.

1931

Flora Nwapa (1931-1993)

With *Efuru* published in 1966, she became the first Nigerian woman to have a novel published in English and the first African woman to publish in London. The novel deals with the oppression of women in Nigerian society. In the late 1970s she set up her own press and publishing company.

1932
Adaora Lily Ulasi (1932 -)
Descended from the Royal House of Nnewi, she worked as a journalist and editor of a woman's magazine. She pioneered the detective novel in Nigeria.

1937
Remi Adeeji (1937 -)
A well-known academic and author, she has been a leading campaigner for enhanced literacy and has occupied a number of posts in Nigerian public life. For a time, she was editor of *Book Bird*.

1944
Buchi Emecheta (1944 -)
Her books deal with the portrayal of African women and show what it means to be a woman and a mother in Nigerian society. The theme of her 2nd book, *Second Class Citizen*, is one of vehement animosity at the gender discrimination often found in the culture of her people.

1950
Eka Esu-Williams (1950 -)
An immunologist, she founded the Society of Women Against AIDS in Africa for the purpose of educating girls and women about this disease and instructing them in safe sex practices. In SWAA workshops, women also learn about self-esteem and how to be in better control of their lives.

1976
Flora Nwapa
In 1976, she founded the first book publishing company in Nigeria run by a woman.

1979
Chief Adenike Ebun Oyagbola
In 1979, she became Minister of National Planning.

1982
Chief Bisi Ogunleye
She is a pioneer in the economic empowerment of women, a gifted advocate for their full participation in policy and decision making and a long-time leader in the fight to free her country from poverty, malnutrition, hunger, environmental degradation and injustice. In 1982, she founded the Country Womens Association of Nigeria, which is known for its women-designed programs in credit, agriculture and small business development. Her inspired leadership grows out of her tenacity and vision that rural women possess the desire, capability and commitment to work to improve their own lives and their communities.

1987
Maryam Ibrhim Babangida
She turned her traditionally ceremonial post as first lady into a potent force for women's rural development in Nigera. In 1987, she founded the Better Life Programme for the Rural Woman which seeks to empower women's social, economic and political status using programs in adult education, primary health, agriculture, trade, crafts and food processing. Also, she campaigned vigorously for women's participation in elections and government and voter turnout in 1989 showed greatly increased women's participation.

1995
Judith Sefi Attah
She was Ambassador to UNESCO (1982-86), Permanent Secretary of Science and Technology (1986-87), Director General of the Foreign Ministry (1987-90) and Ambassador to Italy, Greece and Cyprus (1990-95). In 1995, she became Minister of Women's Affairs and Social Welfare.

1996
Chioma Ajunwa
She caused one of the biggest upsets of the Olympics when she gave Nigeria their first Olympic women's long jump title in 1996.

1998
Laraba Gambo Abdullahi
From 1998-99, she was Minister of Women's Affairs. Since 1999, she has been vice-chancellor of the University of Abuha.

1999
Kenna Chikwe
She was Minister of Transport from 1999-2000 and became Minister of Aviation in 2000.

RHODESIA

1919
Doris Lessing (1919 -)
Her novels and short stories address Women's problems with independence. Much of her later work is set in Southern Africa and are concerned with the racial situation in Rhodesia and conflicts inherent between intellectual pursuits and political activism.

RWANDA

1964
Madeleine Ayinkamiye
From 1964-65, she was Minister of Social Affairs and Public Health.

1992
Pauline Nyirama-Suhuko
She was Minister of Women and Family from 1992-94. She was charged with genocide and crimes against humanity (among other rape) by the United Nations War Crimes Tribunal in 1999, the first woman ever.

Agathe Uwilingiyimana
From 1992-93, she was Minister of Education and became Premier Minister in 1993. She was murdered with her family in civil war between the Hutus and Tutsies.

1993
Agness Ntamaabyaliro
Former Minister of Commerce, Industry, Mines and Artisans, she became Minister of Justice in 1993.

1998
Beatrice Sebatware Panda
In 1998, she became Minister of State for Interior, Communal Development and Resettlement.

2000
Sylie Zayinabo Kayitesi
She became Minister of State of Lands, Human Resettlements and Environmental Protection in 2000.

SAO TOME & PRINCIPE

1930
Clara Boscagli (1930 -)
She was Minister of State of Public Works (1974-76), Minister of State of the Interior (1976-78) and Secretary of State of Finance and Budget (1986-90).
Between 1979-84, she was Secretary General of Partito Democratico Cristiano.

1954
Faustia Simona Morganti
She was Minister of State of Culture and Education from 1978-92. Since 1995, she is Ambassador in the Ministry to France, Denmark, Sweden, Norway, etc.

1975
Maria do Nascimenta Graca Amorin
Between 1975-78, she was Ambassador to France and Portugal. From 1978-85, she was Minister of Foreign Affairs and a member of the Politburo from 1984-96.

Alda Graca d'Espirito Santo
She was Minister of Culture and Education (1975-78), Minister of Information and Social Affairs (1978) and President of the Asembleia Popular Nacional (1978-91). As President of the National Assembly, she was Deputy Head of State.

1983
Emma Rossi
She was Minister of State of Health and Social Affairs (1983-86), Minister of State of Justice, Culture and Education (1992-94) and Minister of State of Territory, Environment and Agriculture (1994-97). Since 1997, she has been political coordinator of Partito Social Reformanista in the Consiglio Grande e Generale.

1991
Alda Bandeira Tavares Vaz da Conceicao
In 1991, she became Minister of Foreign Affairs, in 1992

Minister of Cooperation and a Presidential Candidate in 1996.

1996
Fernanda de Azeuedo Roncon
She was Minister of Health, Family and Women's Status from 1996-97.

1999
Maria Pires de Carvalho Silveira
In 1999, she became Governor of Bank Central de Sao Tome e Principe.

SENEGAL
1920
Aline Sitoe (1920-1944
Queen of the Diola of Senegal, she is exiled by the French for her anticolonial policies and for turning her people against the French.

1926
Annette Mbaye d'Erneville (1926 -)
She obtained a diploma in journalism and radio and works as a program director at the broadcasting studio in Senegal. In 1957, she launched a new journal entitled *Femmes de Soleil*.

1929
Mariama Ba (1929-1981)
In 1980, she obtained the Noma Prize for her first novel, *"Une si longue lettre"*.

1937
Amina Sow Mbaye (1937 -)
Author and teacher, she was appointed headmistress of the ENR ecole d'application in Saint-Louis. She later became the first qualified female basketball umpire in Senegal. In 1991, she became the Regional President of the Senegalese Federation of Women's Associations.

1951
Aminata Mbengue Ndiaye (1951 -)
Between 1988-95, she was Chargee de Mission in the Cabinet of the President and Mayor of Louga since 1997. From 1995-2000, she was Minister of Women, Child, Family and Welfare.

1953
Mariama Ndoye Mbengue (1953 -)
In 1982 she obtained a doctorate in French language and literature. She has worked as a Curator at the Etnographic Museum of the 'Institut fondamental d'Afrique Noire' in Dakar and also manages the fashion business "Sapiane".

1973
Absa Claude Diallo
In 1973, she was appointed Ambassador to UNESCO, the first woman ambassador of her country. From 1993-97, she was ambassador to Denmark and in 1997 Ambassador to the United Nations in Geneve.

1978
Caroline Diop Faye
She was Minister of Social Affairs (1978-81), Minister-Delegate by the Premier Minister (1981-83) and Minister of State (1982-83), third in cabinet. Between 1971-84, she was Deputy President of the National Assembly.

1982
Raymonde Konte
In 1982, she became Chief of Special Secretariat of the President. The Special Secretaries were second in command in the ministry.

1991
Mata Sy Dallo
From 1991-92, she was Vice-Minister by the President for Immigration. Since 1995, she has been Vice-President of the Assemblee Nationale.

1993
Aminata Tall Sall
Between 1993-95, she was Member of the Bureau of National Assembly and High Court Judge. In 1995, she became Minister-Delegate of Technical Education and Professional Training, Minister of Communication in 1998-2000 and Minister of Family and National Solidarity in 2000.

1995
Marie-Louise Corea
Former Director of the Minister of Public Works, she became Minister of Scientific Research and Technology in 1995 and Minister of Employment and Labor in 1998.

1997
Mame Younousse Dieng
In 1997, she wrote one of the first Senegalese novel in Wolof entitled "Aawo bi". She has also translated the Senegalese national anthem into Wolof at the time of Senegal independence and writes poetry in that language.

1998
Abibatou Mbaye
From 1998-2000, she was Minister-Delegate in the Premier Ministers Office in charge of African Economic Integration.

2000
Mame Madior Boye
She had a long career as Magistrate before her appointment as Minister of Justice and Guardian of the Seals in 2000.

SEYCHELLES

1943
Danielle Marie-Madeleine Jorre de St. Jorre (1943-97)
Between 1994-90, she was Undersecretary in the Ministry of Foreign Affairs and Planning. From 1993-97, she was Minister of the Environment.

1983
Giovinela Gonthier
She was ambassador to the United Nations and United

States from 1983-87 and to the European Union from 1987-97.

1986
Rita Sinon
She was Minister of Home Affairs from 1986-90 and Minister of Foreign Affairs and Economic Planning from 1990-97.

1990
Sylvette Frichot Pool
In 1990-93, she was Minister of Information, Culture and Youth and Minister of Education and Sport in 1993-94. Between 1981-90, she was Chief Coordinator of the Seychelles People's Front.

1993
Jacqueline Dugasse
In 1993-96, she was Minister of Agriculture and Fisheries, in 1996-97 Minister of the Sea and Transport and Minister of Health in 1997.

1997
Nollie Alexander
In 1997, she became Minister of Administration, Economic Planning, Environment, and Information.

2000
Ernesta Dolor
In 2000, she became Minister of Agriculture and Marine Resources.

SIERRA LEONE
1962
Ella Koblo Gutama
In 1962, she was Minister of State and from 1962-67 Minister without Portfolio.
1981
Agnes Ben Davis
From 1981-85, she was Permanent Secretary of Ministry of the Interior and Minister of State of Food Affairs in 1985.

1991
Emma Simb
She became Deputy Minister of Agriculture, Forests and Fisheries in 1991.

1994
Christiana Thorpe
She was Deputy Secretary for Foreign Affairs in 1994 and International Cooperation and Secretary of State for Foreign Affairs in 1995.

1996
Shirley Yema Gbiyama
Former Ambassador to Senegal, she was Minister of Tourism and Culture (1996-97) and Minister of Foreign Affairs and International Cooperation (1997-98).

Therese Koroma
She was Deputy Minister in the Office of the Vice-President from 1996-97 and Deputy Minister of Trade and Industry in 1999.

1997
Kula Samba
Member of the Military Junta which took power in a military coup d'etat in 1997, she became Minister of Social Welfare, Children and Gender from 1997-98.

SOUTH AFRICA

1855
Olive Schreiner (1855-1920)
In 1883, she wrote *The Story of an African Farm*, which represents her early awareness of the struggles faced by women in her native country. The book was translated into five languages. She wrote *Women and Labour* in 1911.

1889
Sarah Millin (1889-1968)
She published her first book *The Dark River* in 1919. Her beliefs in white supremacy and apartheid served as the foundation for the plots in all her novels.

1914
Ellen Kuzwayo (1914 -)
In addition to her resistance to apartheid, she has developed a reputation to the rights of women in South Africa. She has been an influential force behind the movement for equality of rights for men and women under the law and has participated in a number of programs to improve living conditions.

1922
Elsa Joubert (1922 -)
She writes mostly in Afrikaans although some of her major works have since been translated into English and a number of other languages. *Poppie*, her best-known novel, was first published in English in 1980. She wrote in an overtly critical manner of the apartheid system's brutality and of the way in which this in turn diminished the Afrikaners as a people.

1937
Bessie Emery Head (1937 -)
Novelist and short story writer, she described the contradictions and shortcomings of African society, both white and black, that often treats women as "dead things".

1940
Mantombazana E. Tshabalala-Msimang (1949 -)
From 1996-99, she was Deputy Minister of Justice and became Minister of Health in 1999.

1949
Gill Marcus (1949 -)
Between 1988-96, she was Deputy Secretary of Information of the ANC and Deputy Minister of Finance from 1996-99. Since 1999, she has been Deputy Governor of the National Reserve Bank.

1956

Dorthy Nyembe (1930-)
In 1956, she was the first woman to lead Natal women in protest against the South Africa government's policy of apartheid. She devoted her life to the cause of equality for blacks in her country.

1976

Mamphela Ramphele
Doctor and activist, she founded the Zanempilo Health Clinic in King William's Town in 1976.

1989

Cecilia Johanna Schmidt
In 1989, she was appointed Ambassador to Austria, the first female ambassador of her country.

1991

Nadine Gordimer (1923 -)
She resented and resisted the pressure to conform to the white supremacist attitudes embodied in the system of apartheid, has been active politically most of her life and has often written about the relationships among white radicals, liberals and blacks in South Africa. In 1991, she was awarded the Nobel Prize for Literature.

1996

Mamphela Ramphele (1947 -)
In 1996, she was appointed vice-chancellor of the University of Cape Town. She is the recipient of numerous prestigious national and international awards, including three honorary doctorates acknowledging her scholarship and contribution to the development of South Africa. Also, she is director of the Institute for Democracy in South Africa's Public Information Centre and Chairperson of the Independent Development Trust.

1999

Penny Heyns
She breaks the world swimming record in the 100-meter breaststroke and the 200-meter event twice in 1999.

Gail Marcus
In 1999, she became Deputy Governor of South African Reserve Bank.

SWAZILAND

1926

Fanny Friedman (1926)
She has been Director of Medical Service in the Ministry of Health (1972-79), Member of the House of Assembly (1983-87) and Minister of Health (1987-93).

1990

Mary Madzandza Kanya
In 1990, she was appointed Ambassador to Canada, the first female ambassador of her country.

1996

Phetsile Kholekile Dlamini-Nkomo
In 1996, she became Minister of Health and Social Services.

1998
Stella Hope K. Lukkele
She became Minister of
Housing and Urban Development
In 1998.

TANZANIA
1956
Amina Salem Ali (1956 -)
Between 1985-88, she was
Minister of Finance, Economy
and Planning and Minister of
State for International
Cooperation in the Ministry
of Foreign Affairs in 1988.

1960
Louise Jilek-Aall
In 1960, Dr. Jilek-Aall
founded the "Mahenge Epilepsy
Clinic" where patients and
their families received
education about epilepsy and
its treatment. During the 36
years the clinic has been
operating, the general
attitude towards epilepsy has
improved considerably and
many of the well controlled
patients have been accepted
back into their families and
are able to live a close to
normal life.

1961
Titi Mohammed
She was one of the first
female MP's elected in 1961
and became Deputy Minister
for Health in 1962.

1963
Dorah Bantu (1941 -)
Tanzanian economist and
political scientist, she
became Tanzania's first woman

Foreign Service officer in
1963.

1973
Julia Manning
In 1973, she becomes the
first woman High Court Judge
in East and Central Africa.

1975
Lilly Monze
She was Deputy Minister of
Finance in 1975 and Minister
of Economic and Technical
Cooperation in 1976.

1990
Naila Lazaro Kiula
She was Minister of Works,
Public Utilities, Roads and
Construction from 1990-92 and
Minister of Works, Transport
and Communication from 1992-
95.

Gertrude Ibengwe Mwongola
Between 1990-93, she was
Ambassador to India, 1993-95
Secretary General for United
Nations Women's Conference
and Special Representative of
the Secretary General of the
United Nations on Women's
Development since 1996.

1995
Zakia Hamdan Meghji
In 1995-97, she was Minister
for Health and became
Minister of National
Resources and Tourism in
1997.

TOGO

1978

Biyemi Kekeh

From 1978-81, she was Minister of Social Affairs, Health and Women. In 1981, she was appointed Ambassador to Cuba and in 1982 to the United Nations, the first female ambassador of her country.

Bibi Yao Savi de Tore

She was Minister of Justice and Keeper of the Seals from 1978-82.

1981

Massan Dagadze

In 1981, she was Minister of Relations with Parliament in Office of the President.

1993

Regine Were Gazaro

From 1993-94, she was Minister of Social Affairs, National Solidarity and Human Rights.

1997

Atcha Tcha-Gouni Ati

She was Secretary of State of the Premier Minister in charge of Planning and Territorial Development in 1997-99.

1998

Hodeminou Dero

Since 1998, she has been Minister-Delegate at the Premier Minister's Office in charge of Relations with the Parliament and the European Union.

Essivi Florence Djokpe

She became Minister-Delegate at the Premier Minister's Office in charge of Economic Reform and Modernization of Administration in 1998.

Fayadowa Nukotchi

In 1998, she became Secretary of State of Companies and the Development of the Free Trade Zone.

UGANDA

1940

Barbara Kimenye (1940 -)

Well-known children's literature author in East Africa, her books has been used in elementary schools around East Africa for a long time. She has also worked as a journalist and columnist for the Daily Nation newspaper.

1954

Wandira Speciosa Kazibwe
(1954 -)

Africa's most senior female politician, the Ugandan Vice-President (and a doctor) has brought credibility to President Yoweri Museveni's government and shored up his stubborn tribal base against threats from northerners. Her influence derives from her membership of the Musoga tribe and her prominence in Ugandan intellectual circles. As she is not a member of any military council, her role in government is largely symbolic but her prominence as a female politician on the world's most sexist continent has raised the prospect of a female president in Africa.

1966
Princess Elizabeth Bagaya
In 1966, she became the first African woman allowed to practice law in an African country.

1975
Bernadette Olowo
A diplomat, she became the first female Ambassador to the Vatican in 1975. Her appointment broke a 900-year old tradition that kept female envoys out of the Holy See.

1987
Miriam R. Kategaya Matembe
She was Secretary for Mass Mobilization and Education in the Kampala Resistance Council from 1987-89. She became Minister Attached to the Office of the President responsible for Ethics and Integrity in 1998.

1988
Victorie Sekitoleko
In 1988, she became Minister of Agriculture and Minister of Natural Resources, Forests and Fisheries in 1991.

1994
Wandira Speciosa Kagibwe
Former Deputy Minister of Industry, she became Vice President of the State and Government in 1994.

1996
Jane Frances Kuka
She became Minister of State of Gender (1996-98), Minister of State of Culture in Ministry of Gender (1998-99) and Minister of State for Disaster Preparedness and Refugees in 1999.

1998
Hajati Syda Namirembe Bbumba
From 1998-98, she was Minister Attached to the Office of the President responsible for Economic Monitoring. In 1999, she became Minister of Energy and Minerals.

1999
Jovina Ayuma Akaki
In 1999, she became Minister of State for Tourism, Wildlife and Antiquities.

Sara Kiyingi
She was Minister of State of the Elderly and Disabilities in Ministry of Gender, Labor and Social Development from 1999-2000 and Minister of State of Internal Affairs in 2000.

ZAIRE
1966
Lusibu Z. N'Kanza
In 1966, she became Minister of State for Social Affairs of Zaire.

1983
Bintou' A-Tshabola
In 1983, she was appointed ambassador to Austria, the

first woman ambassador in her country.

ZAMBIA

1966
Princess Nakatindi
In 1966, she became the first female Member of Parliament in Zambia.

1969
Lombe Phyliss Chibesakunda
(1944 -)
A lawyer and diplomat, she was the first woman to serve as state advocate in her country's Ministry of Legal Affairs. She was Ambassador to United Kingdom, the Netherlands and the Vatican from 1977-81 and later Minister of Justice and high court judge.

1977
Chamba Gwendoline G. Konie
In 1977, she was Ambassador to the United Nations and in 1992 to Belgium, European Union and Germany.

ZIMBABWE

1862
Nehande (1862-1898)
A priestess of the MaShona nation of Zimbabwe, she became a military leader of her country when the British invaded her country. She led a number of successful attacks but was eventually captured and executed.

1959
Tsitsi Dangarembga
(1959 -)
A successful film director, her first novel *Nervous Condiitions* was awarded the Commonwealth Writers Prize in 1988. It was the first novel to be published in English in Zimbabwe by a black woman.

1993
Lilie Chitauro
She was Ambassador to Canada from 1993-98.

Amina Hughues
Former Deputy Minister, she was Ambassador to Denmark, Norway, Sweden and Finland in 1993.

ZANZIBAR

1981
Manical Mastura Ali Salem
From 1981-83, she was Minister of Culture and from 1983-90 Minister of Health.

1990
Amina Slem Ali
Former Member of the Central Cabinet, she became Minister of Finance from 1990-96 (2nd in the cabinet) and Minister of Treasury in 1996.

1997
Asha Bakari Hamad
In 1997, she became Minister of Women and Children's Affairs.

Arabian Women

ALGERIA

1982
Zhor Ounissi

She became Secretary of State for Social Affairs in 1982 and the first woman cabinet minister since independence was achieved in 1962.

1991
Hassiba Boulmerka

In 1991, she became the first woman from an Arab nation to win world track championship with her gold medal in the 1500 meters at the Tokyo world track and field championships. At the 1992 Olympic Games in Barcelona, she won gold in the 1500 meter. She is one of seven athletes directly elected to the IOC Athlete's Commission by the athlete's in the 1996 Olympic Games in Atlanta.

EGYPT

400
Hypatia of Alexandria
(370-415)

Her scientific inventions include the hydrometer, the plane astrolabe and several methods of distillation. She was the first woman to make a contribution to the development of mathematics. Her *Arithmetica* was a 13-volume definitive study of algebra. She lectured on mathematics and philosophy, in particular teaching the philosophy of Neoplatonism.

1904
Umm Kulthum (1904-1975)

The most popular and treasured musician in the Middle East of this century, her songs are still heard frequently over the entire Arab world. Her style was influenced by Western popular music of her time, but is firmly and dominantly based upon traditional classical Arab music.

1910
Huda Shaarawi (1879-1947)

In 1910, she opened a school for girls where she focused on teaching academic subjects rather than practical skills. She was the first to remover her veil in public in 1923 in defiance of the restrictive tradition and helped form the Egyptian Feminist Union which campaigned for various reforms to improve women's lives including increasing women's educational opportunities and improving health care.

1913
Aishah Abd al-Rahman
(1913 -)

After receiving her Ph.D. in 1950, she became Professor of Arabic Literature at the University College for Women of the Ain Shans University. In addition to teaching, she wrote fiction as well as biographies of early Muslin women, including the mother, wives and daughters of the Prophet Muhammad.

1920
Huda Sh'arawi

In 1920, she became head of an organization of women teachers and established a woman's union.

1929
Nawal El Saadawi (1929 -)

Egyptian doctor, author and feminist, she set out to liberate the mind of the Arab woman, her sexuality, legal position and liberate them economically from male dominance. She has had her works published in Lebanon as they were banned in her native Egypt.

1933
Jehan Sadat (1933 -)

Over the years she has fulfilled her desire to participate in the destiny of her people by her efforts status of women in Egypt. her accomplishments include the establishment of a woman's emancipation, education and training society known as the Talla Society and the founding of a city where handicapped war veterans can live with their families and assist in the reconstruction of Kasar El Einy Hospital, the first hospital for modern medicine built in the Mediterranean in over 150 years.

1956
Dori'a Schafiq (1910-1975)

An Egyptian feminist educated at the Sorbonne, she founded Bint-E-Nil (Daughters of the Nile) in the 1940s, a women's rights organization in Cairo, Egypt. She was instrumental through this group in gaining the vote for women in her country in 1956.

1959
Aisha Abdel Rahman
(1920 -)

She was the first woman to research the women surrounding the prophet, Mohammed. Between 1959-66, she published three books about Mohammed's wives, daughters and mother.

1960
Aisha Rateb (1928-)

In 1960, she became the first professor of international law at the University of Cairo. She became Minister of Social Affairs in 1971.

1965
Karimah Al-Said

First woman to serve as Minister of Education in the Egyptian government, she believed in women's education.

1970
Aminah Al-Said (1914-)

She was the first woman to be elected to the Egyptian Press Syndicate Executive Board. A journalist concerned with feminist issues, she is the editor of "Hawa", a woman's weekly magazine that has the largest foreign circulation of any Arabic paper.

1972
Nawal El Saadawi (1930 -)
Trained as a physician, she was the first woman in Egypt to call for revolutionary changes in the position of Egyptian women within the family and as wage earners. In 1982, she founded the Pan-Arab Women's Organization.

1988
Laila Iskandar Kamel
She introduced innovative social and environmental projects to the garbage collectors, which have been largely informal educational models of learning in the context of recycling. She became the Volunteer Field Director for the Rag Recycling Center at the Association for the Protection of the Environment in 1988, which has pioneered many projects in the garbage collector community.

JORDAN

1951
Queen Noor of Jordan
(1951 -)
During her marriage to King Hussein, she played a mediating role and promoted international exchange and understanding of Middle Eastern politics, Arab-Western relations and current global issues at world affairs organizations, international conferences and academic institutions. In Jordan, she initiates, directs and sponsors projects and activities, which respond to specific national needs in the areas of mother and child health car, education, women's development, environmental protection, culture, and public architecture and planning. After the death of King Hussein in 1999, she was entrusted with the establishment and chairmanship of the King Hussein Foundation which is dedicated to give meaningful expression to King Hussein's vision and legacy of humanitarian interests that include: democracy and peace, education and leadership, environment and health.

1969
Laurice Hlass
A career diplomat, she was appointed ambassador for Jordan in 1969 and represented Jordan at three sessions of the United Nations General Assembly.

1980
Inamal al-Mufti
She was Minister of Social Affairs from 1980-82.

1984
Laila Abdul Hamid al-Shariff
From 1984-85, she was Minister of Information and later a Senator.

1993

Rima Khalaf Hneidi

She was Minister of Trade and Industry from 1993-95 and Minister of Planning from 1995-98. In 1999, she became Deputy Premier Minister and Minister of Planning but resigned in 2000 becaue of disagreement with the Premier Minister about the economic policies.

2000

Taman al-Ghul

In 2000, she became Minister of Social Development.

KUWAIT

1990

Rasha Al-Sabah

She was Deputy Representative to the United Nations from 1990-94.

1991

Sheika Rasha as-Sabakh

From 1985-91, She was Vice-Rector of the University of Kuwait and in 1991 became Undersecretary of Higher Education.

1993

Nabila Al-Mulla

In 1993, she was appointed ambassador to South Africa and Zimbabwe, the first female ambassador of her country.

1997

Amal Hamad

She became undersecretary of Information in 1997.

1999

Sara Al-Duweisan

She became undersecretary of Planning in 1999.

LEBANON

1925

Etel Adnan (1925 -)

A poet, painter and essayist, her novel *Sitt Marie Rose* has been published in six languages worldwide and is considered a classic of Middle Eastern literature.

1983

Sameera E. Hanna-Al-Daheer

In 1983 and 1999, she was appointed Ambassador to Japan, the first woman ambassador of her country.

LIBYA

1989

Fatima Abkul Abd al-Hafiz Mukhtar

She was Minister of Education from 1989-94.

1992

Fatima Magami

In 1992, she was appointed Ambassador to Ghana, the first female ambassador of her country.

Salma Ahmed Rashed

From 1992-94, she was Assistant Secretary for Women and Secretary in the General Secretariat of the General Peoples' Congress for Women's Affairs from 1994-95, Deputy Chief of Government. Since 1996, she has been the first woman Ambassador to the League of Arab Nations.

1995

Fawziya Bashir al-Shalababi

Between 1995-2000, she was Secretary for Information, Culture and Jamhariri (Mass) Mobilization. In 2000, she became Secretary of the General People's Committee for Information, Culture, Jamhariri and Tourism.

MOROCCO

1965

Princess Lalla Aisha

Princess Aisha, sister of King Hassan of Morocco, was made Ambassador to London from 1965-69 and Italy and Greece from 1969-75.

1940

Fatima Mernissi (1940 -)

A feminist sociologist and former professor at the University of Mohammed V, she is the most interesting Arab intellectual now being published in a European language.

1943

Aziza Bennaki (1943 -)

In 1981, she was Doyenne of the Faculty of Letters and Humanities of the Mahamedia University. From 1994-97, she was High Commissioner for Handicapped and was appointed Ambassador to UNESCO in 1999.

1959

Mme H. E. Anegay

In 1959, she became the first Moroccan woman representative to the United Nations General Assembly.

1981

Aziza Bennaki (1943 -)

In 1981, she was Doyenne of the Faculty of Letters and Humanities of the Mahamedia University and became High Commissioner for Handicapped from 1994-97. She became Ambassador to UNESCO in 1999.

1984

Nawal al-Mautawakil

In 1984, she won the first Olympic gold medal of her country. Former civil servant in the ministry, she became Secretary of State of Youth and Sport in 1997.

1994

Amina Benkhadra

She was Director of the Management of Mines (1994-97) and Secretary of State of Energy and Mines (1997-98).

1997

Zouyklikha Nasiri

Former Director of Assurance in the Ministry of Finance, she was Secretary of State of Social Affairs from 1997-98.

1998

Aicha Belarbi

In 1998, she became Special Minister and Secretary of State of Foreign Affairs in charge of co-operation.

Nezha Chekrouni

From 1998-2000, she was Secretary of State of Social Development in charge of the Handicapped and became Minister-Delegate in charge of the Condition of Women, Protection of the Family, Childhood and Integration of the Handicapped in 2000.

OMAN

1995

Rajiha bint Abdul Ameer Bin Ali

In 1995, she became Deputy Minister for Development in Ministry of National Economy.

1997

Thuwaibah bint Ahmad Bin Isa Al-Barwani

She became Deputy Minister for Social Affairs in Ministry of Social Affairs, Labor and Vocational Training in 1997.

1999

Khadija bint Hassan bin Salman al-Luweti

She was appointed Ambassador to The Netherlands in 1999, the first woman ambassador of her country.

PALESTINE

1940

May Sayigh (1940 -)

She obtained a BA in Sociology from Cairo University. She was the President of the Union of Palestinian Women and has been very active in the cause of Palestinian women. She has published a number of poetry collections and a prose account of the 1982 Israeli invasion of Lebanon in "*The Siege*".

1991

Hanan Mikail-Ashrawi (1946 -)

Between 1991-93, she was spokesperson of the Palestinian Delegation during the Peace Negotiations and again at the Camp David Peace Negotiations in 2000. From 1996-98, she was Minister of High Education and in 1998 became Minister of Tourism and Archaeology.

Leila Shahid

Former Ambassador to Ireland, she became Ambassador to The Netherlands and Denmark from 1991-93 and Ambassador to France since 1993.

QATAR

1996

Sheika Ahmed Al-Mahmond

In 1996, she became Under Secretary of the Ministry of Information and Culture.

SAHARAN ARAB REPUBLIC

1982

Nema Ould al-Joumani

She was Minister of Health from 1982-85.

1999

Mariem Salek H'Mada

In 1999, she became Minister of Culture and Sport.

SAUDIA ARABIA

1967

Iffat (1910-)

Wife of King Faisal, she founded the College of Education in 1967, an institute designed to train girls as teachers.

1977
Salwa Salel
In 1977, she was manager of a branch of the Khalij Commercial Bank where women depositors could remove their veils and complete their own transactions.

SUDAN

1972
Fatima Abd el-Mahoud
In 1972, she became Deputy Minister of Social Welfare, Youth and Sport. From 1975-79, she was Minister of Social Welfare.

1981
Nekanura Manok
Between 1981-83, she was Regional Minister of Health and Social Welfare in the High Executive for the Southern Region.

1995
Ihsan Abdallah el-Ghabshawi
From 1995-96, she was Minister of State of the Interior and Commissioner for Refugees and from 1996-98 Minister of Health.

1998
Agnes Lukudo
Former Governor of Bah-al-Jaba l, she was Minister of Public Services and the Labor Forces from 1998-2000.

SYRIA

1976
Naja Al-Attar
From 1976-2000, she was Minister of Culture and from 1994-2000, Minister of Guidance.

1986
Mary Roy
She is a crusader for equal property rights for Syrian Christian women. In 1986, in response to a court case she initiated, the Supreme Court ruled that daughters were entitled to an equal share in their father's estate. She also founded the Corpus Christi school, which offers a liberal, Western-leaning education.

1988
Siba Naser
In 1988, she was appointed Ambassador to Belgium, The Netherlands, Luxembourg and the European communities, the first woman ambassador of her country.

1992
Salimah Sanqar
Former professor and Dean of Faculty of Education at the University of Damascus, she was Minister of Higher Education from 1992-2000.

2000
Baria al-Qudsi
In 2000, she became Minister of Labor and Social Affairs.

TUNISA

1949
Nabiha Gueddana (1949 -)
She was Secretary of State of Social Development (1987-92) and Secretary of State of

Women and Family by the
Premier Minister (1992-95).

1973
Saida Agrebi (1945-)
Tunsian health director, she
became director of field
workers for the Tunisian
family planning agency.

1992
Nezina Mehoud
From 1992-93, she was
Secretary of State of Social
Development and Minister of
Family and Women's Affairs
(1993-95). Since 1996, she
has been Ambassador to
Norway.

1993
Zeinouba Khomsi Maaref
In 1993, she was appointed
Ambassador to Malta, the
first female ambassador of
her country.

1997
Aissa Hidoussi
In 1997, she became Minister
of State in charge of
Reconstruction and Public
Enterprises and Secretary of
State in charge of Public
Management in 1998.

YEMEN

1991
Amat Al-Ali'im As-Asooswa
She was Undersecretary of
Information from 1991-99 and
was appointed Ambassador to
The Netherlands, the first
female ambassador of her
country in 2000.

Asian Women

AFGANISTAN

1965

Kobra Nourzai

She became Public Health Minister of Afghanistan in 1965 - the first woman in the cabinet.

1979

Anahita Ratebezad (1928 -)

A former minister in the government, she was appointed ambassador to Yugoslavia in 1979, the first woman ambassador of her country. In 1980, she became Minister of Education.

BANGLADESH

1980

Tahmina Khan Dolly

In 1980, she was appointed ambassador to Sri Lanka, the first woman ambassador in her country.

1991

Begum Khaleda Zia

She became Prime Minister in 1991. Since then, she has sought to give special attention to the role of women in Bangladeshi society - a task made more difficult by heightened fundamentalist activity. To date, she has had little success.

BHUTAN

1990

Ashi Sonam Chhoden Wangchuk

A member of the royal family, she became Minister of Finance In 1990-91 and 1996-97. She is Chairman of Royal Insurance Corporation since 1975, of Druk Air Corporation from 1980, of the National Women's Association from 1981, of Royal Civil Service Commission and Royal Monetary Authority since 1982.

BURMA

1928

Daw Tee Tee Luce

An activist, she founded orphanages and schools in Rangoon for abandoned boys in 1928.

1959

Tee Tee Luce

In 1959, she received the Ramon Magsaysay Award Foundation's Public Service Award for her work with wayward and abandoned boys.

1960

Daw Khin Kuy

In 1960, she was appointed ambassador to India, the only female ambassador of her country.

1988

Aung San Suu Kyi (1948 -)

An impressive and charismatic woman in Asia, she is a champion of the democratic movement and helped found the National League for Democracy in 1988 that won a landslide victory two years later. She was awarded the Nobel Peace Prize in 1991. The military refused to honor the results.

In 1989 she was placed under house arrest for leading a pro-democracy uprising. She is the most potent symbol of the struggle for democracy under Southeast Asia's most reviled regime.

CHINA

625

Wu Zetian (625-705)
She was the only female in Chinese history to rule as emperor. She had scholars write biographies of famous women in a campaign to elevate the position of women. Everyone one had to compete for government positions by taking exams thus setting the practice of government run by scholars. During her reign, she was also fair to the peasants, lowering taxes, strengthening public works and raising agricultural production.

1600

Ng Nui
A nun in the famed Shoolin Temple (legendary for its boxing abilities), she developed wu shu, the Chinese national martial art during the Ming Dynasty in the 1600s.

1875

Qiu Jin (1875-1907)
A poet and revolutionary, she started publishing a woman's magazine in which she encouraged women to gain financial independence through education and training in various professions. She worked for the overflow of the Manchu government and upon her death, became a symbol of women's independence.

1893

Wu Yi Fang (1893 -?)
She was the first and only woman college president in China before communism and the first woman to head the National Christian Council.

1902

Bing Xin (1902 -)
She was the first Chinese woman to become a successful writer in the 20th Century. She began to publish in 1919 and is known for both her poetry and prose, for her work for children as well as for adults. Her subjects include the problems of being a woman and social oppression.

1917

Han Suyin (1917-)
Writer and physician, she writes fiction and nonfiction on modern Chinese and Asian subjects. She wrote *Selected Writings on Politics, Culture and Society* in 1990. Her autobiography is a great way to study the history of modern China.

1920

Jingyu Ziang (1895-1928)
A feminist revolutionary, she was cofounder of the Chinese Communist Party in 1920 in Hunan province. In 1922, she became the first director of

the Communist Party Women's Department. A friend of Mao Zedong, leader of the Communist revolution in China, and other important Chinese Communist leaders, she was arrested and executed during Xiang Kai Shek's anti-Communist campaign in 1928.

1930
Chen Li
She became China's first major general in 1930. She later led Communist troops against the Nationalists forces.

1933
Wei Feng-Ying (1933-)
Machinist, by 1965 over 80% of the technical processes in her workshop were automated and she had more than 400 technical innovations to her credit.

1941
Dai Qing (1941-)
She trained as a guided-missile engineer but soon after graduating during the Cultural Revolution was sent to the countryside. Now a freelance journalist but she is not permitted to publish outside China. She remains a strong critic of the Three Gorges Dam project, which plans to dam the Yangtze River forcing the evacuation of more than one million people. Her book about the dam was banned.

Wu Yi (1941-)
As Minister of Foreign Trade, she is the most influential woman in China. In true socialist style, she worked for 25 years in the oil industry. At one time, she was both a bulldozer operator and in charge of explosives.

1950
Ma Huidi (1950 -)
She has taken part in many programs concerning the relation between science, technology and society since 1992, and written many papers about science, culture and education. Although feminism is limited to philosophy and literature in China, she believes that women's liberation plays a part in people progressing and in societies developing throughout the world. The nature of feminism is that it awakens people to women's intrinsic value.

1975
Zhengying Qian (1923-)
One of China's first female engineers, she was the first woman to become Minister of Water Conservation in 1975 in Beijing. Her authority was broadened in 1982, and she became first woman in her country to serve as Minister of Water Conservation and Power.

1977
Chen Muhua
A Chinese politician, she became Minister of Economic

Relations with Foreign Countries in 1977 and is named to the Politburo - one of only two women members of that body. In 1987, she became President of People's Bank of China.

Zeng Xiaoying

China's first woman orchestra director, she became head conductor at Beijing's Central Opera Theatre in 1977.

1979
Deng Xuesong

In 1979, she was appointed ambassador to The Netherlands and in 1982 to Denmark.

1983
Wu Wenying (1932 -)

A Chinese textile worker and politician, she was the first woman to head the largest textile industry in the world. She became her government's Minister of the Textile Industry in 1983 in Beijing. In 1985-86, she led textile delegations to Germany, Belgium, New Zealand, Burma, Britain and Bulgaria.

1987
Yue-Sai Kan (1949-)

In 1987, she produced One World, the first western-style magazine format broadcast in China.

1992
Zhang Shan

Chinese skeet shooter, she is the first woman to earn gold medal in a mixed shooting event.

HONG KONG

1937
Elizabeth Chi-lieh Wong-Chien (1937 -)

In 1982, she became Commissioner for Culture, Deputy Secretary of Assessment Office for Taxation in 1984 and Deputy Secretary of Culture and Municipal Services in 1986. From 1990-94, she was Secretary of Health and Welfare.

1941
Anson Chan (1941-)

She became Chief Secretary and Deputy Governor of Hong Kong in 1993, the first Chinese - and first woman - to hold the colony's second-highest position.

1975
Fanny M. Cheung

Since 1975, she has been active in promoting rights of and services for women and the disabled in Hong Kong. She spearheaded the War on Rape campaign and founded the first community women's center. She has been actively involved in supporting psychiatric rehabilitation for twenty years. Her research interests include gender roles, violence against women, personality assessment and psychopathology among Chinese. She was awarded Badge of Honour in 1986, appointed Justice of

Peace in 1988 and in 1997 was awarded the Honour of Officer of the Most Excellent Order of the British Empire.

1991
Emily Lau (1953 -)
In 1991, she was the first and only woman directly elected to the Legislative Council. She describes Hong Kong's Chinese-dominated future as a nightmare from which Britain should rescue millions who hold limited British passports.

1995
Denise Yue Chung-yee
She was Secretary of Trade and Industry from 1995-98, and in 1999 became Secretary of the Treasury.

1997
Rita Fan Hsu Lai-tai
From 1997-98, she was President of the Provisoral Legislative Council, which was set up by the Chinese before they took over the administration of the Region. In 1998, she became President of the Legislative Council.

2000
Sandra Lee
Former representative of the Special Autonomous Region of Hong Kong in London, she became Secretary of Economic Services in 2000.

INDIA

1498
Mira Bai (1498-1547)
A legend in India, her odes to Krishna are still regarded with awe.

1830
Lakshmi Bai (1830-1858)
The Rani of a principality called Jhansi in northern India, she led an uprising against a takeover of her homeland by the British. She became a heroine and a symbol of resistance to the British rule.

1879
Sarojini Naidu (1879-1949)
A passionate advocate for India, she was among the most visible leaders of pre-independent India. She became the first Indian woman to be president of the Indian National Congress in 1925. She became governor of the United Provinces in 1947 – the first woman to be appointed a state governor.

1886
Anandibai Joshee
In 1886, she became the first Hindu woman and the first Indian woman to earn a medical degree.

1889
Rajkumari Amrit Kaur, Princess of Kapurthala (1889-1964)
She was Minister of Health from 1947-57 and a member of Rayja Sabha, the Upper House, from 1957-64.

1894

Cornelia Sorabji (1866-1954)
In 1894, she became India's first woman law graduate though she was not allows to practice until 1923.

1900

Vijava Lakshmi Pandit (1900 -)
National leader, politician and diplomat, she was one of the most influential women of the 20th century but little recognized in the US. She served as Ambassador to the US, Mexico and USSR. In 1953, she was the first woman president of the UN general assembly.

1905

Anna Chandy (1905 -)
She was the first woman in India and the second in the world to reach a high state court judgeship. In 1928, she was admitted to the bar, became the first woman judge in India in 1937 and was appointed to the state high court in 1959.

Rokeya Sakkawat Hossain
An Indian author, she publishes the short story *Sultana's Dream* in 1905. It is a utopian work about a country where the men, to keep their destructive tendencies in check, are kept in purdah while the women move about freely.

1919

Abala Bose (1865-1951)
In 1919, she established the Nari Shiksha Samiti, which was dedicated to the education of women throughout India. She introduced the Montessori system of education in India in 1920. She worked throughout her life on behalf of education for women in her country and advocated school reform and innovative teaching. She also founded several educational and relief organizations and supported self-defense training for women.

1923

Urmila Eulie Chowdhury (1923 -)
She was first woman to qualify as an architect in Asia and to be Chief Architect of an Indian state. The focus of her work was all types of public buildings for government, hotels, shopping centers, parks, housing, and jails.

1926

Tarakeshewari Prasad Sinha (1926 -)
From 1952-58, she was Deputy Minister of Economic Affairs and from 1958-66 Deputy Minister of Finance. She became Secretary of Congress in 1979.

1937

Anita Desai (1937-)
Her published works include short stories, children's books and eight novels. She

received the Guardian Award for Children's Fiction for *The Village by the Sea* in 1982 and the 1978 National Academy of Letters Award for *Fire on the Mountain*.

1948
Vijaya Lakshimi Pandit

From 1948-61, she was Ambassador to Soviet Union, United States, Mexico, United Kingdom, Ireland and Spain. She also was Delegate to and President of the General Assembly of the United Nations and Governor of an Indian State.

1951
Meena Alexander (1951 -)

Her nomadic life involved speaking many languages – Malayalan, English, Arabic, Hindi, and French. She has written several books of poetry, novels and a book of memoirs. As a writer, she is particularly interested in "fault lines", the areas of fracture between one cultural tradition and another.

1953
Vijaya Pandit

An Indian diplomat, she became the first woman president of the United Nations General Assembly in 1953. She was imprisoned three times in the struggle to free India from British rule.

1957
Violet Alva (1908-1969)

From 1957-62, she was Minister of State for Home Affairs and in 1969 Acting Chairman of Rayjiah Shaba. The Vice-President of the Republic is Chairman of the Upper House; when he/she acts as President, the Deputy Chairman becomes acting Chairman of the House.

1961
Manorama Pandey

She was Parliamentary Secretary of Finance and General Administration from 1961-66 and Minister of State from 1972-74.

1972
Kiran Bedi (1949 -)

She is one of the most well known and controversial officers of the Indian Police Service ever since she became the very first woman in the IPS in 1972. She has worked in various aspects of modern day policing in India, including narcotics, traffic, VIP security and most notably, as head of Tihar, Asia's largest prison system. While at Tihar, she worked to reform the conditions of the prisoners, especially its women.

1974
Sarojini Mahishi (1927 -)

She was Minister of State for Law, Justice and Company Affairs (1974-76). From 1984-85 and 1986-88, she was

Vice-President of the Rayja Sabha.

1976
Manorama Bhalla
She was Ambassador to Peru (1976-78), Denmark (1982-87), Kenya (1987-89) and Spain (1990-95).

1978
Susham Bedi
She began writing in 1978 when her first story was published in the literary magazine Kahani. Since then she has written three novels all of which deal with the cultural dilemmas of Indians living in the West.

1980
Kumudben Joshi
From 1980-82, she was Deputy Minister of Information and Broadcasting and from 1982-84, Deputy Minister of Health and Family Welfare.

1985
Sushila Rohatgi (1921 -)
Former Minister of State of Finance, she became Minister of State with independent charge of Culture and Education (1985-86) and Minister of State of Power, Energy, Petroleum and Natural Gas (1986-88).

1988
Krishna Sahi
She was Minister of State of Water Resources (1988-89), Minister of State of Industrial Relations and Heavy Industry (1991-95) and

Minister of State of Civil Supplies (1995-96).

1991
Margaret Alva
Former Minister of State of Parliamentary Affairs, she became Minister of State with independent charge of Personnel, Public Grievances and Pensions from 1991-96.

Kumari Mamata Banerjee
From 1991-93, she was Minister of State of Human Resources Development for Youth Affairs, Sports, Women and Child Development. In 1999, she became Minister of Railways, fourth in the Cabinet.

1992
Deepa Dhanraj
An Indian filmaker, she directs *Something Like a War* about family-planning experiments conducted on Indian women.

1994
Ammu Joseph
A freelance journalist, media analyst and editorial consultant, she co-authored a book entitled *Whose New? The Media and Women's Issues* in 1994 and is currently completing another book on Indian women in journalism.

1998
Maneka Gandhi
Former Minister of State of Program Implementation, she became Minister of State with independent charge of welfare

from 1998-99. She became
First Minister of State with
independent charge of Social
Justice and Empowerment In
1999.

1999
Sushree Uma Bharati
(Sadhui Uma Shree Bhatari)
As a Hinduistic nun, her
title is Sushree. She was
Minister of State of Human
Resources (1998-99) and
became Minister of State with
independent charge of Tourism
in 1999.

Vasundhra Raje
Former Minister of State of
External Affairs, in 1999 she
became Minister of State with
independent charge of Agro
and Rural Industries, Small
Scale Industries, as well as
Personnel, Public Grivances
and Pension, Atomic Energy
and the Department of Space.

INDONESIA

1904
Ibu Dewi Sartika
(1884-1942)
An educator, she establishes
the first girls' school in
Indonesia in 1904. It
teaches chiefly domestic
skills, reading and writing.

1912
Sitti Rohanda
She published the first
feminist magazine in Sumatra
in 1912.

1943
Tutty Alawiyah (1943 -)
Rector of the As-Syafi-iyah
Islamic University, she
became State Minister of
Woemen's Affairs from 1998-
99.

1946
Maria Ulfah Santoso
She became Indonesia's first
female Minister of Social
Affairs in 1946.

1949
Ani Manoppo
Indonesia's first woman
lawyer, she became Dean of
the law faculty of Medan in
1949.

**Siti Hardiyanti Rukmana
Suharto** (1949 -)
She is one of the most
powerful infrastructure
developers in the world's 4th
most populous country with
business interests including
toll roads, television,
banking, publishing and
telecommunications. She holds
a key executive post in
Golkar, the ruling political
organization, and is thought
to be jockeying for a future
ministerial post or the vice-
presidency.

1959
Laili Rosad
She became Indonesia's first
female ambassador for Belgium
and Luxembourg in 1959 and
Austria in 1967.

1988
Haryati Subardio (1928 -)
Former Director General for Culture in Ministry of Education and Culture, she became Minister of Social Affairs from 1988-93.

1998
Dewi Fortuna Anwar
In 1998-99, she was Assistant Minister of Foreign Affairs and Spokesperson of the President. She became spokesperson for Habibie after Suharto was forced to step down after the mass demonstrations caused by the economic crisis.

1999
Miranda S. Goeltom
In 1999, she became Deputy Governor of the Bank of Indonesia.

Kofifah Inder Parawangsa
(1965 -)
An academic, she was first Vice President of the House of Representatives prior to her appointment to the cabinet. In 1999, she became State Minister of Women's Empowerment.

IRAN

1902
Fatima Sayyah (1902-)
An Iranian educator, she was Tehran University's first female professor and Iran's first female representative to the UN. In 1945, she became editor of the women's magazine *Zanane Iran*.

1905
Mohtaram Eskandari
A feminist, she founded Iran's first women's organization, the Union of Patriotic Women in 1905. It's first meeting was dispersed by religious leaders who tied the women to trees and burnt some of them alive.

1921
Shahnaz A'lami (1921 -)
A poet and teacher, she also wrote biographical sketches and critical work on women's role in Persian Literature.

1933
Forugh Farrokhzad
(1933-1967)
She published three books of poems, *The Captive*, *The Wall* and *Rebellion*. Her poems express the hidden feelings and emotions of the Iranian women. Her poetic vision has continued to be one of the achievements of modernism in Persian poetry.

1958
Parvin Birjandi
An Iranian educator, in 1958 she became the first Dean of Women at the University of Iran.

1971
Farrokchroo Parsa
Politician, she was one of the first six women in the Iranian Parliament. In 1971, she became the first female cabinet minister when named Minister of Education.

She was executed in 1979 for her feminist views.

1977
Mehrangiz Dolatshahi
From 1977-79, she was Ambassador to Denmark, the first female ambassador of her country.

1995
Shahla Habibi
She was Presidential Advisor on Women's Affairs from 1995-99.

1997
Masoumeh Ebtekar (1961 -)
In 1997, she became Vice-President and Minister of Environmental Protection.

ISRAEL
1890
Rosa Ginossar (1890-?)
She was the first woman to practice law in Israel.

1917
Ruth Dayan (1917-)
In 1955 while an official at the Israeli Labor Ministry, she became head of Maskit, a center for encouraging and marketing handicrafts.

1948
Golda Meir (1906 -)
She was part of the People's Council signing the vital proclamation establishing the State of Israel in 1948. Her commitment to her land and her people was the paragon of human dedication. She was Minister of Labor from 1949-1956. During her time as Foreign Minister (1956-1965) she had the opportunity to work with the cooperative agricultural and urban planning programs between Israel and Africa. In 1969, she was nominated by the Labor Party to be Prime Minister of Israel, which position she held until her retirement in 1974.

1949
Sara Levi-Tanai
In 1949, she founded the provisional Iubal Dance Co of Israel bringing folk dance traditions to high art.

1959
Ofra Haza (1959-2000)
A traditional folk singer, she was Israel's best known female singer. She also won a Grammy Award for her performance in the Hatvika theater group and was runner-up in the 1983 Eurovision song contest.

1965
Shulamit Aloni (1931-)
An ardent feminist, she is pushing for better working conditions for women and better childcare for working mothers. She was elected to the Knesset in 1965 and founded and was Chairman of the Civil Rights Party (1973-95). In 1966, she was named chair of the Israeli Consumer Council. She became Minister of Communication, Science and Art from 1993-96.

1978

Golla Cohen

In 1978, she co-founded and has been co-leader of the Tehiya Zionist Revival Movement. She was Secretary of State of Science from 1990-92.

1983

Sara Doron

She was Minister without Portfolio (1983-84) and Chairman of the Likut Knesset-Group (1988-92).

1992

Ora Namir (1930 -)

Former officer in Israel Defense Forces during the War of Independence, she became Minister of Environment (1992-93) and Minister of Labor and Social Affairs in (1993-96). She was appointed Ambassador to China in 1996.

1999

Dalia Izhik (1952 -)

She was a former Deputy Mayor of Jerusalem in charge of education and became Minister of the Environment in 1999.

JAPAN

978

Murasaki Shikibu (978-1026)

She is one of her country's greatest writers and author of the world's first novel, *The Tale of Genji* that paints a charming and accurate picture of Japanese court life in the Heian period.

1563

Hosokawa Gracia (1563 -?)

She was Japan's first saint. Her life of sacrifice and endurance in maintaining her faith was rewarded when the Vatican made her a saint in 1862.

1770

Tani Kankan (1770-1799)

A Japanese bunjin artist and devoted Buddhist, she painted over 1,000 pictures of the bodhisattva Kannon, as well as numerous images of landscapes, figures, birds and flowers.

1791

Otagaki Rengetsu

(1791-1875)

Japanese waka poet and potter, she published the poetry collection *Rengetsu Shikubu nijo waka shu* in 1868 and often inscribed her poems on her pottery. She was also a Buddhist nun and a student of swordfighting and jujutsu.

1837

Okuhara Seiko (1837 -?)

A Japanese artist, in 1874 she co-founded an art society, Hankansha.

1847

Katsushika Oi

A Japanese artist, she illustrated the *E-iri nichiyo onna choho-ki* in 1847, an encyclopedia for women that gave advice on behavior, traditional values, health, pregnancy, cosmetics, cooking, sewing, weaving, poetry, music, calligraphy and games.

1854
Utako Shimodo (1854-1934)
After a short marriage, she devoted herself completely to education for women and became their champion. She also helped establish the Court-sponsored Peer's School for Girls and a school that taught crafts and fostered artistic skills. She helped many schools open doors to women and lectured and taught on the benefits of educating women. She wrote more than 80 books on education, hygiene, literature, and poetry.

1868
Yosano Akiko (1868-1942)
A graduate of the Sakai School for women where she was the foremost poet, she evolved into a social critic. In her writing, she openly criticized the government and to foster social changes and rights for women.

1875
Shoen Uemura (1875-1949)
She was the first woman recipient of the Order of Culture, Japan's highest award for cultural achievement. Portraits of women were her favorite theme, which she painted with children as graceful dancers. She felt that women possessed a quiet but determined will.

1883
Kageyama Hideko (1863-1927)
She devoted her life to the plight of women in near feudal Japan. In 1883, she opened a school for women, which is later closed because of its liberal policies.

1886
Raicho Hiratsuka
(1886-1971)
In 1911, she founded the bluestocking magazine, *Seitou* – its first edition boldly called for women's rights. After World War II she focused her energy on world peace.

1893
Fusaye Ichikawa (1893-1981)
Japanese politician and feminist, she founded the New Women's Association in 1920 which successfully fought for women's right to attend political meetings. After World War II, she became head of New Japan Women's League, which secured the vote for women in 1945. She served in the Japanese Diet where she continued to press for an end to bureaucratic corruption.

1900
Yoshioka Yayoi
She opens the country's first medical school for women in 1900.

1905
Hatsuko Endo
In 1905, she opened a bridal "grooming parlor" in the Ginza in Tokyo and became a

pioneer in a new and much needed industry. With study and research, she learned makeup techniques, including how to use and apply new cosmetics to flatter all faces. Since World War II, the firm bought and made wedding kimonos and rented them to brides.

1907
Kinue Hitomi (1907-1931)
Japan's foremost woman athlete, she wins two gold medals at the second World Women's Games in 1926.

1909
Sachiko Hashimoto (1909 -)
She was the first volunteer in the formation of the Japanese Red Cross. Her efforts earned her the first Jean Henri Dunant Red Cross Award to any Japanese. She took special pains to help children and youth of the country, starting programs to help both their minds and bodies to recover from the effects of war and to help them find direction.

1924
Kobo Abe (1924-1993)
Japanese novelist and poet, she wrote *The Woman in the Dunes* in 1965.

Tetsu Yasui (1870-1945)
A Japanese educator, she became the 1st female college president in Japan when she became president of Tokyo Women's Christian University in 1924.

1927
Kono Yasui
A botanist, in 1927 she becomes the first Japanese woman to earn a Ph.D. in science.

1941
Yoriko Kawguchi (1941 -)
Former Minister in the Embassy in Washington and leader of a company, in 2000 she became Minister of Environment.

1945
Keiko Ochiai (1945 -)
A writer, translator and feminist, she started Crayon House, a bookstore specializing in children and women's literature. Her essays, *A Spoonful of Happiness*, are stories of young women living in the big city.

1948
Kondo Tsuruyo
From 1948-54, she was Vice-Minister of Foreign Affairs. In 1962, she became Minister of State and Director General of the Science & Technology Agency.

1956
Hanae Mori
A Japanese fashion designer and the first designer of Western-style clothes, she opened her first store in Tokyo in 1956.

1967
Yoshi Katsurada

A Japanese mathematician, she became the first woman full professor at Hokkaido University.

1968
Michiko Ishumure

In 1968, she began a nationwide movement against politicians with her book *Kukai Jodo*, which documents the nervous system, disorders caused by the dumping of mercury into the bays.

1972
Ariyoshi Sawako

Novelist, she published *Kokotsu no Hito* in 1972 about the plight of senior citizens.

1973
Jochiko Mibuchi

Judge Mibuchi, as head of the Niiyata Court of Family Affairs, becomes the first woman head of a Japanese court.

Katsuko Sarahashi

Scientist, she became head of the Meteorological Research Institute's geochemistry laboratories in 1973.

1975
Junko Tabei (1939 -)

In 1975, she became 1st woman to climb Mount Everest, the world's highest mountain. Since then, she became 1st woman to have climbed the tallest mountain on each of the seven continents in 1992.

1976
Sakado Ogada

In 1976, she became Japan's first female diplomat of ministerial rank.

1980
Nobuko Takahashi

In 1980, she becomes Japan's first female ambassador when she is posted to Denmark.

1986
Ryoko Aakamatsu

Between 1986-89, she was Ambassador to Venezuela and Uruguay. In 1993, she became Minister of Education.

1989
Mayumi Mariyama

In 1989, she became Minister of State and Director General of Enviroment. Formerly, she was Parliamentary Vice-Minister of Foreign Affairs, Chairman of the Foreign Affairs Committee and Director General of Labor.

Sumiko Takahara (1934 -)

She was Minister of State of Economy and Planning from 1989-90. Since 1997, she has been Ambassador to Sweden and Estonia.

1993
Takako Doi (1929 -)

She was elected the 68th speaker of Japan's House of Representatives in 1993. A former law professor, she was chairman of the Japanese Socialist Party from 1986 to 1991, becoming the party's only celebrity when she led a group of politically inexperienced housewives to victory in the 1989 elections to the Upper House.

1994
Chiaki Mukai
Heart surgeon and first Japanese woman in space, in 1994 she spent 15 days doing scientific experiments aboard a US spacecraft.

1999
Kayoko Shimizu (1936 -)
Former civil servant who entered politics as Member of House of Councilors in 1989, she became Minister of the Environment from 1999-2000.

2000
Chikage Ogi (1933 -)
Former Vice-Minister in the Directorate General of Science & Technology, in 2000 she became Minister of Construction and Director General of the National Land Agency.

KIRIBATI

1971
Tereki Russell
She was the first female MP from 1971-78 and Minister of Public Health from 1975-77.

1991
Maragaret Baaro
In 1991, she became Permanent Secretary of Foreign Affairs.

LAOS

1987
Pany Yathotou
In 1987, she was Cabinet Member and Governor of the Central Bank.

1997
Onecham Thammovong
In 1997, she became Vice President of the National Assembly and the first woman in any state office in government or parliament. She is also President of the Lao Women's Organization.

1998
Sengchanh Souklaseum
In 1998, she was appointed Ambassador to Philippines, the first woman ambassador of her country.

MACAU

1991
Ana Maria Siqueira Basto Perez
She was Undersecretary (Minister) of Social Affairs and Health from 1991-97.

1992
Anabela Sales Ritchie
From 1992-99, she was President of the Legislature.

1999
Florinda de Rosa Silva Chan
In 1999, she became Secretary for Administration and Justice, the highest-ranking official below the chief executive.

MALAYSIA

1970
Prema Lucas (1970 -)
Singer, she wrote and performed all the songs in her album as well as the backing vocals and part of the guitar works. She is also a spokesperson on social causes such as wife battery and child abuse.

1973
Tan Sri Fatimah binti Abdul Majid Hashiim
A Malaysian politician, in 1973 she became the first woman to hold a cabinet-level position in her country when she was appointed to serve as Minister for Social Welfare.

1977
Rafidah binti Aziz
In 1977-90, she was Minister of Trade and Industry and in 1990 became Minister of International Trade and Industry.

1980
Hajjah Rahmah binti Osman
From 1980-84, she was Deputy Minister of Information and from 1984-87, Deputy Minister of Transport.

1981
Shariffah Dora binti Datuk Seyd Mohamed
Former Welfare Officer of the Johar Government, she was Parliamentary Secretary of Land and Regional Development from 1981-82 and Deputy Minister by Premier Minister from 1982-86.

1982
Napisah Omar
She became the first female member of the Dewan Raky (House of Representatives) in 1982 and was Minister of National Unity and Social Development from 1990-95.

1992
Siti Zaherah binti Saulaiman
In 1992-97, she became Deputy Minister of Public Works and Enterprises and in 1997-99 Deputy Minister of Health.

1995
Rafia Salim
In 1995, she became Assistant Governor of Bank Negara Malaysia.

1997
Shahnzat binti Abdul Jalil
She was Parliamentary Secretary of Youth and Sport from 1997-99 and Deputy Minister in the Office of the Prime Minister since 1999.

MONGOLIA

1940
Yanjmaa Nemendeyen Suhbaatar (1893-1963)
A member of the Presidium of the Little Khural (1940-50) and of the People's Great Khural (1950-62), she became Acting Head of State and Acting Chairperson of the Presidium of the Great Khural from 1953-54.

1980
Damdiny Beljinnyam
In 1980, she was appointed Ambassador to United Nations

in Geneve, the first woman ambassador of her country.

1987
Pagbajabyn Nymadawa
She was Deputy Minister of Health from 1987-90 and Minister of Health from 1990-91.

1998
Tuya Nyam-Osoriyon
Minister of Foreign Affairs from 1998-2000, she was appointed Acting Premier Minister in 1999 when her predecessor resigned.

NEPAL

1950
Punya Praua Dhungana
In 1950, she found the All Nepal Women's Organization – a group, which supported education for women.

1959
Dwarka Chand Thakumrani
She was Deputy Minister of Health and Local Government from 1959-61.

1982
Bhadra Kumari Ghale
In 1982, she was Cabinet Member and Minister of State for Labor and Social Welfare.

1989
Bindheswari Shah
In 1989, she was appointed Ambassador to India, the first female ambassador of her country.

1990
Sahana Pradham
In 1990-91, she was Minister of Industry and Trade, in 1996-97 Minister of Forests and Soil Conservation and Minister of Women and Welfare since 1997.

1991
Sailaja Acharya (1944 -)
She is a longtime member of the Nepali Congress Party leadership as Vice President and from 1999 as 4th member. Between 1991-93, she was Minister of Agriculture and Forests and in 1998 became Deputy Prime Minister and Minister of Water Resources.

1996
Sahana Pradhan
In 1996, she became Nepal's Minister of Industry and Commerce for the interim government.

PAKISTAN

1935
Nafis Sadik (1935 -)
As head of the United Nations Fund for Population Activities, she is the first Muslim woman to hold such a high position in an international organization. A strong believer in women's equality, she has guided policy on improving the status of women in developing countries while fighting to contain the population explosion.

1952
Zeb-Un-Nirsa Hamidullah
In 1952, she became publisher and editor of the magazine Mirror.

1954
Liaquat Ali Kham (1905-)
Politician and active feminist, she was the first Muslim woman to serve as ambassador when she was named Ambassador to Belgium and the Netherlands in 1954.

Maleeha Lodhi (1954 -)
Her journalistic career spanned 8 years in which she edited two of Pakistan's major English daily newspapers. She was the 1st woman in all of Asia to be the editor of a daily paper and became Pakistan's 16th Ambassador to the United States in 1994.

1963
Yasmeen Lari (1943 -)
In 1963 she became first woman architect of Pakistan and in 1969 she was appointed by the government of Pakistan to report on housing for industrial workers. She was president of Institute of Architects from 1980-83.

1973
Begum Liaquat Ali Khan
Pakistani politician and women's leader, she became the first Muslim woman ambassador. In 1973, she became Governor of Sind province, the first woman to govern a province.

1975
Shahzada Saaedur Rashid Abbasi
She was Minister of State of Science from 1975-76 and Technology and Minister of State of Tourism from 1976-79.

1986
Asma Jahangir (1953 -)
She is one of Pakistan's foremost lawyers and a leading advocate of women's rights. In 1982, she founded the Women's Action Forum to promote legal reform. In 1986, she started the Human Rights Commission and serves as co-chairperson. She does not believe in laws like the blasphemy law, capital punishment, and laws against women and in favor of child labor.

1988
Benezir Bhutto (1953-)
In 1988 she was sworn in as Prime Minister of Pakistan becoming the first woman to head the government of an Islamic State. She emphasized the need to put an end to the divisions in Pakistani society since assuming the office of Prime Minister - including discrimination between men and women and has launched a nationwide program of health and education reform. During the preceding decade of political struggle, she was arrested on numerous occasions for her dedicated leadership of the Pakistan People Party. She received

the Bruno Kreisky Award for Human Rights in 1988 and the Honorary Phi Beta Kappa Award from Radcliffe in 1989.

1992
Seyda Abida Hussain
She was appointed Ambassador to United States between 1992-93. In 1996-97, she became Minister of Education, Science and Technology in transitional government and from 1997-99 Minister of Population, Welfare, Women's Development, Social Welfare, Environment, Special Education, and Minister of Local Government and Rural Government.

1999
Attiya Inayatullah
After a number of years as representative to UNESCO, she as one of 4 civilians appointed to the Security Council which ruled the country with the military after a military coup. From 1999-2000, she was Member of the National Security Council (Supreme Civilian governing body) and in 2000 became Minister of Social Welfare, Women Development, and Special Education.

SOUTH KOREA

634
Queen Sondok
In 634, she became sole ruler of Sillia and the first female ruler of the kingdom. She built the "Tower of the Moon and Stars" considered the first observatory in the Far East. Her respect as a ruler was reinforced by the ancient tradition of female shamanism, which was prominent in Korea.

1504
Sin Saimdang (1504-1551)
Korean artist noted for her paintings of grapes and grasshoppers, she was also a poet, embroider, calligrapher and scholar of Confucian literature and history.

1563
Ho Nansolhon (1563-1589)
Korean scholar and poet, she was author of about 140 poems in Korean and Chinese. She was one of the greatest writers of kasa, a genre somewhere between prose and lyric poetry in which verses are composed of pairs of four-syllable phrases.

1887
Meta Howard
A Methodist missionary, she opens Korea's first women's hospital in 1887.

1898
Soon Chan Park (1898-1983)
One of the principle figures in Asian feminism, she founded and became the first president of the Korean National Women's Association

1905
Yi Li-chong
A Korean businesswoman, she starts a store near Auguk-dong in 1905 to demonstrate

that women can be economically independent.

1934
Sung-kook Jeon (1934 -)
She was appointed at consular and secretariat, Asian Affairs Bureau, the Ministry of Foreign Affairs in 1952. She showed distinguished activities in the diplomatic field when she was stationed in Japan as Korean vice-consul in 1962.

1948
Yim Yong-Shin
In 1948, she was Minister of Trade and Industry, in 1949 the first female MP and in 1954 a vice-presidential candidate. She was the founding Chairman of Women's Party in 1952.

Mo Yun-Suk
In 1948, she was Special Ambassador and Leader of the Delegation to United Nation's General Assembly meeting in Paris.

1952
Park Hyun-sook
She was one of the first four women of the South Korean Legislative Assembly and twice a member of the National Assembly. From 1952-54, she was Minister without Portfolio.

1957
Lee Tai Young
Korea's first woman lawyer, she opens the Korean Legal Aid Center for Family

Relations where she helps women often assisting them in getting divorces.

1963
Helen Kim
In 1963, she received the Ramon Magsaysay Award Foundation's Public Service Award for her role in the emancipation and education of Korean women.

1988
Cho Kyung-hee
In 1988, she was Minister of the Second Ministry of Political Affairs and from 1989-90, Secretary of State for Political Affairs.

1995
Kim Jong-sook
She was Second Minister of State for Political Affairs from 1995-97. Since 1997, she has been Chairman of the Committee of the Women's Affairs and member of the Presidium of the National Assembly.

1996
Lee In-ho
In 1996, she was appointed Ambassador to Finland.

1998
Yun Ho-chung
She was Chairwoman of the Special Presidential Commission on Women's Affairs from 1998-99.

SRI LANKA

1939
Suvimalee Karunaratna
(1939 -)
She wrote a television script *The Journey*, which was televised in 1982 by Rupavahini, the National Television Network of Sri Lanka. In 1993 her first novel *Lake Marsh* was published. The theme of the novel has to do with lethargy, corruption and ethnic strife, which bedevil Sir Lankan society today.

1952
Sunila Abeysekera (1952 -)
She has worked on women's rights and human rights issues in Sri Lanka and in the South Asia region for over 20 years as an activist and scholar. Since 1992, she has been working with the Global Campaign for Women'' Human Rights focusing on the issue of mainstreaming women's human rights concerns within the international human rights system.

1960
Sirimavo Bandaranaike
(1916 -)
She became the world's first female Prime Minister when her party, the Sri Lanka Freedom Party, won the general election in 1960. In 1972, she promoted the new constitution, which proclaimed a republic and changed the country's name to Sri Lanka. She became Prime Minister again in 1994, and became the first woman to succeed a woman through a democratic process.

1966
Lorani Senarathna
In 1966, she was appointed Ambassador to Ghana, the first woman ambassador of her country.

1975
Irangani Manele Kamangara Abeysejera
Between 1975-90, she was appointed Ambassador to Thailand, Austria, Germany and Switzerland.

1977
Irene Wimala Kannangara
She was Minister of Shipping, Aviation and Tourism from 1977-82 and Minister of Rural Development from 1982-86.

1984
Maureen Seneviratne
A writer of short stories and essays, she is deeply committed to the struggle for children's rights and against sex tourism – including publishing *The Sexual Exploitation of Children in Sri Lanka* in 1984. *Mists on a Lake*, a collection of short stories, won two Sri Lankan awards for best English fiction in 1985.

1986
Kumari Jayawardena
She is an author of several books including Feminism and Nationalism in the Third World, which was chosen for

the Feminist Fortnight Award in Britain in 1986 and cited by MS. Magazine in the US in 1992 as one of the 20 most important books of the feminist decades. The book reconstructs the history of women's rights movements in Asia and the Middle East from the 19th Century to the 1980's. It is widely used in Women's Studies programs around the world.

1994
Srimani Athulathmudali

Between 1994-97, she was Minister of Transport, Highways, Environment and Women's Affairs.

Chandrika Kumaratunge

(1948 -)

In 1994, she was elected Prime Minister – and later President. She pledged to seek an end to Sri Lanka's political violence. She has drawn international praise for seeking to end the 13-year war with the Tamil Tigers through a radical devolution plan. One day she may be remembered as the person who finally put an end to her country's years of civil war.

Punykante Wijenaike

Writer of short stories and novels, her fiction has been taught in university courses in Britain, Australia and other countries. The tyranny of a community or group toward its weaker members is a recurrent them in her

writings. In 1994, her latest novel *Amulet* was the winner of a literary prize for the best Sri Lankan book in English.

1997
Hema Ratnayeke

In 1997, she was Minister of Women's Affairs and in 2000 became Minister of Health and Indigenous Medicine.

1998
Sumithra Priyangani Abeweera

She became Deputy Minister of Internal and External Commerce and Food in 1998.

TAIWAN
1979
Shirley Kuo Wang-jung

(1930 -)

Between 1979-88, she was Deputy Governor of the Central Bank of China, the National Bank of Taiwan. In 1988-90, she was Minister of Finance and Minister of State from 1990-98 and 1999-2000.

1992
Annette Hsiu-lien Lu

Feminist and dissident, she is an author, publisher and founder of Taiwan's National Organization for Women. In 1992, she is elected to the Taiwans Legislative Yuan and becomes Vice President in 2000.

1993
Helen Lin Cheng-Chih

Between 1993-96, she was Director General of Women's Affairs of the Control

Committee of Kuomingtang and from 1996-2000, Chairman of the Council of Cultural Planning and Development.

1995
Cao Yang-Ching
She was Director General of the Department of National Treasury in the Ministry of Finance from 1995-96 and became Chairman of the Council for Fair Trade in 1996.

2000
Chung Chin (1953 -)
Former Executive Director in a publishing company, she became Cabinet Member and Government Spokesperson and Director General of Information Office in 2000.

Lin Geng-mei (1961 -)
Professor of journalism, she became Chairman of the National Youth Commission in 2000.

THAILAND
1909
Kunying Pierra Vejjabul (1909 -)
Physician, she worked for the Thai public health department and established Pierra Maternity and Child Welfare Foundation. In spite of death threats and attempts on her life, she also campaigned against prostitution and polygamy.

1961
Nilawan Pintong
In 1961, she received the Ramon Magsaysay Award Foundation's Public Service Award for developing civic enterprises that give woman a new and creative role in Thailand.

1962
Pierra Hoon Vijjabu
In 1962, she is the first female physician of Thailand. Under her influence, the Thailand government outlawed prostitution.

1968
Kritaya Archavanitkul
She is a demographer with the Institute for Population and Social Research at Mahidol University in Thailand, which conducted its first project in 1968. Her work focuses on Thai populations, with studies ranging from the country's unique internal migration patterns to determinants impacting a child's continuation on to secondary school. Currently, she is conducting research on the trafficking of girls and women and the expansion of Thailand's sex trade.

1973
Tuenjai Deetes
She is a social activist who has been working in community development since 1973. She has also promoted sustainable agricultural development and forest conservation awareness among tribal peoples of

Thailand. Through providing information to the hill area people and allowing them to make their own choices, she has succeeded in bringing many improvements to the hill area while supporting the rights and wisdom of the indigenous people.

1981
Kanitha Wicliencharoen

In 1981, she opened the first battered women's shelter in Thailand.

1989
Saisuree Chutikul

From 1989-92, she was Minister in the Office of the Premier Minister and Special Advisor of the Premier on Women and Social Affairs from 1992-95.

1993
Suchira Hiranprueck

In 1993, she was appointed Ambassador to Russia, the first female ambassador of her country.

Charatsri Teepirat

Interior Ministry official, she becomes the first woman to govern a province in Thailand in 1993.

1996
Royal Princess, Somdetceh Phra Debaratanarajasuda Chao Fa Maha Chakri Sirindhorn of Thailand (1955 -)

She has acted as Regent on several occasions and is one of the King's closest advisors. In 1996, she was appointed General, Admiral and Air Chief-Marchal and in 1997 averted a military coup d'etant during her father's illness.

1998
Tanya Sirivedhin

In 1998, she became Deputy Governor of Bank of Thailand.

TURKEY

1506
Mihri Hatun (1506 -?)

She is considered the first major poet of Turkey. The Russians finally published her poems in the 1960's.

1859
Mary Mills Patrick (1850 -?)

She was founder and president of the Istanbul College for Women.

1912
Halide Adivar (1883-1964)

Teacher and writer for a liberal newspaper, she wrote articles on women's right to emancipation and education. In 1912, she wrote two books *Handan* and *Yeni Turan* advocating women's rights.

1920
Safieh Ali

In 1920, she is the first female medical doctor in her country.

1958
Nuzhet Gokdogen

Turkish astronomer, she becomes head of the observatory at Istanbul University in 1958.

1982
Filiz Dincimen

She was appointed Ambassador to The Netherlands in 1982, the first woman ambassador of her country.

1991
Imren Aykut (1940 -)

In 1991 and 1996, she was Minister of State by Premier Minister and from 1997-99 Minister of Environment.

Lale Aytaman

A university professor, she became Turkey's first woman provincial governor in 1991.

1993
Tansu Ciller (1947 -)

After she became Turkey's first woman Prime Minister in 1993, she persuaded the West she was Turkey's only answer to Islamic fundamentalism, and the European Union rewarded her with a long-coveted customs union agreement. But while she has been tough on the downtrodden Kurds, she has had less success fighting 150% inflation. As Prime Minister her achievements include a loosening of restrictions on Turkish political life and running a successful campaign to bring at least some of Central Asia's oil through Turkey.

1996
Isialy Saygin (1946 -)

In 1996, she became Minister of Tourism and Minister of State in charge of Women's Affairs from 1997-99.

VIETNAM

1938
Nguyen Thi Kim

In 1938, this Vietnamese feminist and communist published "the Woman Question" attacking both sexism and colonialism.

1966
Nguyen Thi Hau

In 1966, she is inaugurated as Mayor of Dalat – the highest post every held by a woman in her country in modern times.

1987
Nguyen Thi Binh

A symbol of the woman's role in the "Resistance War", she was head of the Provisional Revolutionary Government at the Paris peace talks. From 1969-76, she was Minister of Foreign Affairs, Minister of Education from 1976-87 and the Vice-President of Vietnam since 1987.

Central American/Caribbean Women

ANGUILLA

1994
Marjorie Connor
In 1994, she became Clerk of the House of Assembly.

1999
Yvonne Maginley
She became Deputy Governor General and Ambassador-at-Large in 1999.

ANTIGUA

1948
Althea Romeo-Mark (1948-)
Teacher and poet, she has published four collections of poems and have had poems published in various journals. She has received an award from the Virgin Islands Council on the Arts and a poetry award from Cuyahoga Writers Workshop.

1964
Novelle Richards
In 1964, she became President of the Senate.

1992
Deborach-Mae Lowell
In 1992, she was appointed ambassador to Canada, the first woman ambassador in her country.

1994
Millicent Percival
In 1994, she became Co-Deputy Head of State and President of the Senate.

ARUBA

1989
Alicia A. Tromp-Yarzagargay
From 1989-93, she was Minister Plenipotentiary in the Netherlands and from 1993-94 Minister of Finance responsible for Public Works and Public Health.

1994
Lili G. Beke-Martinez
She was Minister of Social Affairs, Culture and Sport in 1994 and Minister of Public Health from 1994-98. In 1998, she became Minister of Economic Affairs and Tourism.

1998
N. R. van Lis-Donata
In 1998-2000, she was Deputy Minister Plenipotenciary in the Netherlands and is Director of the Arubahuis in Amsterdam.

BAHAMAS

1921
Doris Louise Johnson
In 1979, she became Acting Governor General. She was previously Minister without Portfolio and leader of the Government in the Senate.

1956
Theresa Maria Moxey-Ingraham (1956 -)
In 1999, she became Minister of Agriculture, Commerce and Industry.

1968
Doris Louise Johnson
(1921-1983)
She was Minister without Portfolio and Leader of the Government in the Senate (1968-69, Minister of Transport (1969-72) and President of the Senate from 1973-83. In 1979, she was Acting Governor General.

1979
Patricia E. Ridgers
In 1979, she was appointed ambassador to Canada and Charge d'affires to the United States. She became Under Secretary in the Ministry of Foreign Affairs in 1988.

1986
Margaret McDonald
In 1986, she was appointed ambassador to the United States.

1992
Janet Gwennet Bostwick
In 1992, she became Minister of Housing and Labour and in 1995 Minister of Women's Affairs.

Roma Italia Johnson
From 1992-97, she was Deputy Speaker of the House of Representative and in 1997 Speaker of the House.

1994
Marion Bethel
She was awarded the Casa de las Americas Prize for her book of poetry, *Guanahani, My Love* in 1994. Her writing has appeared in The Massachusetts Review and other journals.

1997
Geneva Rutherford
She became Deputy President of the Senate in 1997.

BARBADOS

1927
Maizie Baker-Welch (1927 -)
She became Parliamentary Secretary of Education and Culture in 1985 and Parliamentary Secretary of Civil Service, Labor, Industrial Relations, Public Works and Community Development & Sports in the Office of the Prime Minister in 1994.

1975
Cyralene Gale
In 1975, she was appointed ambassador to Canada, the first woman ambassador of her country.

1976
Bille Antoniette Miller
(1944 -)
In 1976, she became Minister of Health and Insurance; in 1994, Deputy Premier and Minister of Foreign Affairs and in 1999, she became Minister of Foreign Trade.

1990
Ruth Nita Barrow
(1915-1996)
In 1990, she became first woman governor of Barbados and a representative of Queen Elizabeth II of England. The

older sister of Prime Minister Errol Barrow, who led Barbados to independence from Britain in 1966, she represented Barbados at the United Nations from 1986-1990.

1998
Lois Marie Brown-Evans
(1927 -)
In 1998, she became Minister of Legislative Affairs and in 1999 Attorney General. She was the first female official Leader of the Opposition anywhere in the Commonwealth.

BELIZE

1981
Elmira Minita Gordon
In 1981, she became Governor General. During 1970-77, she was Commissioner of Belize City.

1986
Janet Gibson
In 1986, she campaigned for the establishment of Hol Chan Marine Reserve, the first reserve of its kind in Central America. Her ability to introduce the concept and practice of long-term strategic planning has aided in the conservation of other marine ecosystems in Belize. In addition, she has been instrumental in the expansion and strengthening of Belize's integrated Coastal Zone Management program, which attempts to guarantee the conservation of outstanding marine biodiversity and the sustainable use of the country's coastal resources.

1989
Ursula H. Barrow
She was appointed Ambassador to the UN in 1989 and to United Kingdom, Germany, France and European Union in 1993.

Jane Usher
She was Speaker of the House of Representatives from 1989-93.

1993
Carla Barnett
From 1993-96, she was Deputy Governor of the Central Bank of Belize.

CAYMAN ISLANDS

1991
Sybil McLaughlin
From 1991-94, she was Speaker of the Legislative Assembly and Minister of Education from 1994-98.

1997
Cindy Bush
She became Governor of Cayman Island Currency Board in 1997.

COSTA RICA

1930
Carmen Naranjo (1930 -)
She served as ambassador and cabinet minister in the social democratic government. In 1970, she published her political writing on her work and national liberation.

1959
Angela Acuna Braun
She was appointed ambassador to the Organization of American States in 1959.

1964
Maria de Chittenden
She was appointed ambassador to the United Kingdom in 1964.

1978
Elizabeth Odio Benito
In 1978, she became Minister of Justice and Attorney General. She was vice-rector of the University of Costa Rica, Ambassador to the United Nations in Europe and, Judge of the International Tribunal in the former Yugoslavia in 1993.

1986
Rosemary Karpinsky Doder de Morillo
In 1986, she became President of Asamblea Legislativa. She was appointed ambassador to Spain and France in 1994.

1994
Maureen Clark
In 1994, she became Minister of the Interior and Police and a Member of the Cabinet Affairs Team.

CUBA

1814
Gertrudis Gomez de Avelaneda (1814-1873)
Cuban author, she was best known for her abolitionist novel *El Mulato Sab*.

1903
Aida de Acosta
She piloted a dirigible over Paris in 1903 just months before the Wright Brothers fly at Kitty Hawk, NC.

1922
Carilda Oliver Labra (1922-)
She received the coveted National Prize for poetry in 1950 for her popular and notorious book, *"At the South of My Throat"*.

1936
Lydia Cabrera (1900-1991)
In 1936 she published *Contes negres de Cuba*, a collection of African-Cuban stories and records of traditional African-Cuban customs and beliefs. She dedicated her life to the recording and creative interpretation of the virtually unexplored African-Cuban heritage.

1944
Nancy Morejon (1944-)
She is the most successful and widely translated black Cuban woman poet of the post-revolutionary period. She was the first black woman poet in Cuban's history given the opportunity to publish widely. Her most renowned and widely translated poems are those which foreground the black Cuban women participating in the long struggle for personal and collective freedom.

1948

Alicia Alonso (1921 -)

Dancer and choreographer, she formed the Alicia Alonso Company in 1948, which grew into a national ballet company for Cuba. As a dancer she was famous for several roles particularly the title role in Giselle.

1952

Maria Gomez Garbonell

In 1952, she became Minister without Portfolio. She was one of the first female members of the House of Representatives in 1936 and later a Senator.

1960

Vilma Espin (1930-)

She founded and was the first head of the Federation of Cuban Women. The group was designed to fight illiteracy and to increase women's political involvement. She later worked as Ministry of Food in Fidel Castro's government.

Argelia Velez-Rodriguez

(1936 -)

Obtained her degree in Mathematics from University of Havana in 1960 in the fields of differential equations and astronomy and was the first Black woman to receive a doctorate in mathematics. Her dissertation was on "Determination of Orbits Using Talcott's Method".

1961

Luisa Gonzalez

Methodist minister, children's book author and literature professor, she co-founded Alfalit in 1961, which encourages literacy in Latin American countries.

1962

Blanca Diaz Collazo

In 1962, she was appointed ambassador to Columbia, the first woman ambassador in her country.

1970

Haydee Santamaria

(1931 -)

A Cuban revolutionary leader, she was the first female president of the Latin American Organization of Solidarity in 1970. She was instrumental in the 1959 overthrow of the government of the Cuban dictator, Fulgencio Batista (1901-1973).

1988

Maria de los Angeles Folorez Prida

She was Ambassador and Deputy Permanent Representative to the United Nations From 1988-90.

1993

Isabel Allende Karon

In 1993, she became Deputy Minister of Foreign Affairs. She was appointed Ambassador to Portugal from 1989-93.

1997

Mara Mercedes Esciredo Olazabal

In 1997, she became President of the Provincial Assembly of the People's Power.

DOMENICA

1907

Minerva Bernardino

(1907-1998)

A Dominican feminist, she was one of four women to sign the United Nations charter in 1945. She went on to head the UN Inter-American Commission on Women, and fought throughout her life for women's and children's rights.

1908

Phyllis Shand Allfrey

(1908-1986)

In 1958, she became Minister of Labour and Social Affairs. She was minister in the government of the West Indies Federation, which lasted from 1958-62.

1980

Mary Eugenia Charles

(1919 -)

She became the first woman lawyer on this island in 1949 and co-founded the Dominica Freedom Party, which helped Dominica win independence from Great Britain in 1978. First woman elected Prime Minister of Dominica in 1980 (re-elected in 1985 and 1990) and first woman to hold the post of Prime Minister in the Caribbean region. In 1983, she encouraged the United

State's invasion of Grenada to prevent Cuban infiltration of that island. Her primary concern is to improve the lives of the citizens and is determined to preserve the island's ecology and national identity. Dominica's motto, in Creole, is *Apres Bondie, c'est la Ter* (After God, the Earth).

Marie Davies-Pierre

She had been clerk of the house since 1965. In 1980, she became Speaker of the House and as such was Deputy Head of State.

1985

Marciella H. Mukasa

In 1985, she was appointed Ambassador to United States, the first female ambassador of her country.

1990

Neva Edwards

She became Speaker of the House of Representatives in 1990and was former President of the Domenican National Council of Women.

EL SALVADOR

1952

Nidio Diaz (1952 -)

She was a revolutionary fighter for Salvadorian freedom from military rule and activist for women's rights. In 1985, she was named President of the "Melida Anayo Montes" Salvadorian Union for Women Liberation. Diaz was later appointed to Political -

Diplomatic Commission of Frente Farabunda Marti de Liberacion Nacional in 1987.

1974
Maria Julia Castillo Rodas
From 1974-81, she was Subsecretary of Health and became President of Asembleia Legislativa in 1982.

1978
Claribel Algeria (1924-)
One of Central America's foremost poets, she has published 15 collections of poetry since 1948. She was awarded the Casa de las America's prize in 1978 for *Sobrevivo*.

1989
Ana Cristina Sol Midence
(1945 -)
From 1989-93, she was Ambassador to France, Belgium, Portugal, European Union and UNESCO and from 1993-97 to the United States. She became Commissioner for State Modernization in 1997.

1994
Gloria Saiguero Gross
She was President of Asamblea Nacional from 1994-95.

GRENADA
1961
Cynthia Byroe
She became Minister of Social Affairs In 1961 and Minister of Social Affairs, Culture and Community Development in 1967.

1976
Marie-Jo McIntyre
In 1976, she was appointed Ambassador to UN and Canada.

1979
Phyllis Coard
In 1979, she became Minister of Communication and Minister of State for Women.

1984
Joan Purcell
In 1984, she became Minister of Labor and Women. From 1995-99 she was Minister of Information, Caicos and Petit Martinique Affairs. In 1998, she was leader of the National Democratic Congress and candidate for the post of Prime Minister.

1990
Margaret Necklers
In 1990, she became President of the Senate.

1993
Shirley Mathlin
In 1993, she became Permanent Secretary of External Affairs, Caicom Affairs and Political Unification, one of two Permanent Secretaries.

1999
Claris Charles
In 1999, she became Minister of State in the Office of the Prime Minister with special responsibility for Information and Minister of Agriculture, Forestry, Lands and Fisheries.

GUATEMALA

1541
Dona Beatriz de la Cueva de Alvarado
She was appointed Acting Govenor in 1541 and was killed by an exploding volcano after two weeks rule.

1953
Ana Isabel Perez de Lobo
(1953 -)
She was Secretary of the High Court of Justice from 1986-87 and Minister of Culture and Sport from 1987-91.

1959
Francisca Fernandez Hall-Zuniga
She was Ambassador to Israel from 1959-75 and to Costa Rica from 1975-79.

1978
Ruth Chicas Redon de Sosa
In 1978, she became Minister of Welfare.

1981
Hilda Yolanda Morales
The President appointed her Secretary of Social Welfare in 1981.

1985
Ana Catalina Reyes Soberanis
From 1985-90, she was Minister of Labor and Social Affairs and in 1991 was Presidenta of Congreso Nacional. In 1999, she was a presidential candidate.

1992
Rigoberta Menchu (1957 -)
A Quiche Indian, who had no rights of citizenship in Guatemala, she was an activist in the United Peasant Committee's fight for rights of the indigenous people. In 1984, she wrote her autobiography, which together with her campaign for social justice brought international attention to the conflict between the indigenous Indians and the military government of Guatamala. In 1992 she was awarded the Nobel Peace Prize and used the money to set up a foundation to continue the fight for human rights of the indigenous people.

1993
Antonieta de Bonilla
In 1993, she became Vice President of the Banco de Guatemala.

1994
Arabella Castro Quinonez de Comparini
From 1994-95 and 1997-98, she was President of Congresso de la Republica.

HAITI

1946
Claudette Werleigh (1946 -)
She was Minister of Foreign Affairs and Religion from 1993-95 and Premier Minster from 1995-96.

1962

Lucienne H. Estine

She was Ambassador to Belgium from 1962-76, the first woman ambassador of her country.

1989

Maryse Penette

In 1989, she was Charge d'Affaires in Belgium and in 1991 Ambassador to Belgium, Luxembourg and the European Union. She became Secretary of State for Tourism in 1995.

1990

Ertha Pascal-Trouillol

(1944 -)

The first woman to sit on the Supreme Court of Haiti, she became provisional President for a year in 1990.

1991

Myrtho Celestine-Saurel

Former Director-General in Ministry of Youth & Sports, she became Minister of Labor and Social Affairs in 1991 and Minister of Education in 1995.

1994

Edwidge Danicat

She published *Krik? Krak* and *Breath, Eyes, Memory*. In 1994 she won a Pushcart Prize for a story in the Caribbean Writer and was a recipient of the Canute A. Brodhurst Prize for fiction.

1995

Therese Goulloteau

From 1995-96, she was Minister of Women's Affairs and Women's Rights.

1999

Michaelle Amedee Gedeon

In 1999, she became Minister of Public Health and Population.

HONDURAS

1962

Albertina Bernhard de Zelarya

In 1962, she was appointed Ambassador to Columbia and from 1976-80 to Ecuador, the first woman ambassador of her country.

1986

Sonia Canales Gonzales de Mendieta

Former Vice-Minister of Culture, she was ambassador to Guatemala and to Mexico from 1986-92. In 1989, she was vice-presidential candidate of the Liberal Party.

1993

Guadelupe Jerezano Mejio

In 1993, she became 3rd Executive Vice-President in Honduras.

Maritza Salinas

She was Subsecretary of Public Works, Transport and Housing from 1993-97.

1998

Mari Marta Diaz

In 1998, she became cabinet member and Director of Women's Affairs.

1999

Gladys Caballero de Arevalo

She became 2nd Executive Vice-President of her country in 1999.

Silvia Xiomara Gomez de Caballero

In 1999, she became Minister of Natural Resources and Environment.

JAMAICA

1953

Rose Agatha Leon (1919-1999)

She was Minister of Health and Labor (1953-60) and Minister of Local Government (1972-76).

1957

Mary Seacole (1805-1881)

A Jamaican healer, she published her autobiography in 1957 describing her greater successes with traditional healing methods.

1962

Edith Nelson

She became Jamaica's first female general secretary of a labor union in 1962.

1970

Esme M. Grant

She became Parliamentary Secretary of Labor and National Insurance in 1970.

1974

Lucille Mathurin Maric

In 1974, she was appointed Vice-Ambassador to the United Nations. From 1975-78, she was Ambassador to Cuba and from 1992-96 Ambassador to the United Nations.

1979

Marjorie Taylor

From 1979-96, she was Special Assistant to the Prime Minister. In 1999, she became Ambassador and Special Envoy for Children.

1980

Mavis Gilmour-Petersen

(1926 -)

Former Parliamentary Secretary of Health and Environment, she became Minister of Education (1980-86) and Minister of Social Security and Consumer Affairs (1986-87).

1983

Jeanette Grant-Woodham

She was Vice President from 1981-83 and became President of the Senate in 1983.

1987

Patricia Mohammed

She received her M. Sc. in Sociology from the University of the West Indies with her dissertation on *"Women and Education in Trinidad and Tobago, 1838-1980"*. She has written extensively on feminism, feminist theory, gender relations in Caribbean society, gender-based violence and feminist epistemology and the study of masculinity.

1989
Portia Lucretia F. Simpson-Miller
From 1989-91 and 1993-99, she was Minister of Labor, Social Welfare and Sports. In 1999, she became Minister of Tourism, Entertainment and Sports. Three times she has been acting Prime Minister.

1992
Donna Scott-Bhoorasingh
Former Deputy President of the Senate, she was Permanent Secretary of Information and culture from 1992-94.

1994
Patricia Durrant
She was Permanent Secretary of Foreign Affairs from 1994-97, and was appointed Ambassador to the United Nations in 1997.

Maxine Henry-Wilson
In 1994, she became Minister without Portfolio in the Office of the Prime Minister and Leader of the Government Business in the Senate and in 2000, she became Minister of Information.

1997
Lorna Goodison
She is the author of *Tamarine Season*, *I am Becoming my Mother* and *Heartease* and won the 1997 Daily News Prize. Her work is widely published and translated into many languages.

Violet Neilson
She was Deputy Speaker of the House from 1991-95 and became Speaker of the House of Representatives in 1997.

MARTINIQUE
1989
Euzhan Palcy
She undertook her first filmmaking venture in Martinique in 1974 creating a film out of her own drama, *La Messagere*. In 1989, she is the first black woman filmmaker to have directed a feature-length Hollywood film, "*A Dry White Season*".

MEXICO
1651
Sor Juana Inez de la Cruz
(1651-1695)
She was a nun in Mexico City who, as a scholar, observed the stars, composed music and painted. She claimed that science and knowledge will strengthen faith in God not weaken it.

1902
Amalia de Cxastillo Ledon
(1902-1986
She was Ambassador to Sweden From 1954-58, Ambassador and Head of the Delegation to the International Atomic Energy Organization from 1964-70 and to Austria in 1967.

1907
Frida Kahlo (1907-1954)
She is the quintessential autobiographical artist of the 20th century. Using *retablo*, a traditional art

form that depicted saints or miracles, she transforms the usual religious theme into a depiction of exotic beauty, feminine strength and Mexican cultural identity.

1920
Elena Garro (1920-)
She began her career as a journalist subsequently writing novels, short stories and plays. Her first novel *Los Recuerdos del porvenir* published in 1963 is central to understanding the development of contemporary Mexican fiction in general and of Mexican women writing in particular. The work explores the magical and the fantastic as they co-exist with objective dimensions of reality.

1925
Rosario Castellanos
(1925-1974)
Much of her work was in Indian theater groups and the Indigenous Institute of San Cristobal tried to traverse the distance between the pre-Columbian and the European cultural traditions of Mexico. Her poetic vision was determined in large part by the Mexican Indian's mystical understanding of the interconnectedness of all life. She died in a freak household accident in Tel Aviv while serving as Mexico's Ambassador to Israel.

1930
Maria Luisa Mendoza
(1930 -)
She has been journalist, essayist, novelist television commentator and congresswoman for the State of Guanajuato at the LIII Legislatura. She received the Magda Donato Prize for her novel *Con el, conmigo, con nostros tres* in 1971 and received prize of the Secretaria de Educacion Publica for the best television commentary about addiction in 1973.

1951
Coral Bracho (1951 -)
A poet, she won the Premio Nacional de Poesia de Aguascalientes in 1981 for her book *El ser que va a morir*. She has collaborated with the magazines Punto de Partida, La Gaceta del Fondo de Cultura Economica, La mesa Ilena and La Cutura en Mexico.

1954
Carmen Boullosa (1954 -)
A poet, dramatist and narrator, she worked in the Colegio de Mexico as editor of the Diccionario del Espanol en Mexico. In 1983, she founded the Editorial Workshop "Tres Sirenas". She won the Premio Xavier Villaurrutia for her novel *Antes* in 1989.

Maria de Los Angelos Moreno Uriegas (1954 -)
In 1999, she became President of the Republic and President of the Senate.

1957
Flor Garduno (1957 -)
She is one of Mexico's leading photographers and the most classic in art photography. Her themes include Native Latin American cultures, portraits, still life and landscapes.

1961
Ifignea Martinez Hernandez
From 1961-65, she was Subsecretary of Revenues and from 1983-84, Subsecretary of Agrarian Reform. She was Ambassador and Deputy Permanent Representative to United Nations from 1980-92.

1964
Martha Chavez Padron de Velazques (1925 -)
She was Director General in the Ministry of Agriculture between 1964-67, and from 1967-70, Advisor of the President. She was Judge in the Supreme Court from 1985-94.

1976
Maria Emilia Tellez Bentoit (1921 -)
She was Subsecretary of External Relations for International Cooperation from 1976-82 and had a number of diplomatic posts on sub-ambassador level.

1976
Rosa Luz Alegria Escamilla (1949 -)
Between 1976-80, she was Subsecretary of Budget and in 1980 became Secretary of Tourism, the first female member of Cabinet.

1977
Aida Gonzales Martinez
She was Ambassador in charge of International Labor Organizations from 1977-79 and Official Mayor of the Secretariat of External Relations from 1979-88.

1980
Carmen Moreneo Toscano de Del Cueto
Between 1980-88, she was Representative to a number of United Nations Committees (from 1982 with rank of Ambassador), from 1989-94 Ambassador to Costa Rica and 1995-98 Ambassador to the Organization of American States. In 1998, she became Subsecretary of Foreign Affairs for United Nations, Africa and Middle East.

Maria del Rosario Valles Gonzales
She was Subsecretary of the Treasury and Public Credit for Tax Inspection from 1980-82.

1988
Rosario Ibarra de Piedra
In 1988, she became Mexico's first woman candidate for President.

1989
Rosario Green Macias de Heller (1941 -)
She was appointed Ambassador to East Germany (1989-90), Subsecretary of Foreign Affairs for Latin America, Cultural Affairs and International Cooperation (1992-94), Deputy Secretary General of the United Nations for Political Affairs (1994-98) and Secretary of Foreign Affairs in 1998.

1992
Laura Esquivel
Author of *Como Agua para chocolate*, the best-selling novel in Mexico in 1989 The novel has been translated into 29 languages. She later wrote the screenplay for *Like Water for Chocolate*, which won 11 Ariel Awards from the Mexican Academy of Motion Pictures.

1995
Maria Guadelupe Lopez Breton
In 1995, she became President of the Camera de Senadores and in 1998 Prosecretary of the Senate.

NEDERLANDSE ANTILLEN
1971
Lucinda Elona da Costa Gomez-Matheeuws (1929 -)
From 1971-76, she was Vice President of the National Volkepartij, Minister Presidente (Premier Minister) and Minister of General Affairs, Foreign Affairs and Defense in 1977 and since 1995, Member of the Raad van Advies (the Council of Advisors).

1984
Maria Liberia-Peters (1941 -)
Former Lieutenant-Governor of Curacau, she became Minister Presidente, Minister of General Affairs and the Interior, Minister of Health and Environment from 1984-86 and Minister Presidente, Minister of General Affairs and Interior from 1988-93.

1994
Simona E. Strauss-Maarsera
She was Minister of Welfare, Development, Cooperation, Women's and Humanitarian Affairs between 1994-98, and Chairman of the Parliamentary Committee of Health and Environment and Vice-Chairman of the Committee of Education, Women, Youth and Welfare since 1998.

1996
Beatriz J. Dorau-Scoop
From 1996-98, she was Minister Health and Environment, Welfare, Gender and Humanitarian Affairs.

1999
J. van Lis Donata
In 1999, she became Minister Plenipotentiary in the Hauge.

NICARAGUA
1950
Olga Nunez de Sasallow
In 1950, she is the first woman in Nicaragua to get a law degree. She was also

Nicaragua's first female
Deputy Minister of Education.

1972
Gioconda Belli
Her poems appeared in several
Latin American publications.
In 1972, she was awarded the
prestigious Marino Fiallos
Gil Prize for Poetry of the
Universidad Autonoma of
Nicaragua for her first book,
Sobre la Grama.

1979
Rita Delia Caso Montenegro
From 1979-96, she was
appointed Ambassador to
United States and Canada, the
first female ambassador of
her country.

1982
Lea Guido
In 1982, she becomes first
woman president of the Pan-
American Health Organization.

1987
Nora Astorga-Gadea
(1944-1988)
Former commander in the civil
war, she became Deputy
Minister of Foreign Affairs
from 1984-86 and Ambassador
to the United Nations and
United States from 1986-88.

1990
Violeta Barrios de Chamorro
(1929 -)
Between 1979-90, she was
publisher of the opposition
newspaper, La Prensa. When
the revolutionary Sandinista
party was defeated, she was
elected President of war-torn
Nicaragua in 1990. With
international help, she put
an end to the decade-long
Contra war, but living
conditions in Nicaragua
remain among the poorest in
Latin America.

1995
Julia de la Cruz Mena Rivera
In 1995, she became and Vice-
President of the Asamblea
Nacional and Vice-President
from 1995-97. She was the
first woman to serve as
deputy to a female president/

PANAMA
1958
Nora Arosemena de Batinovich
(1958 -)
Former Director General for
Foreign Relations of the
Ministry of Labor, she was
Vice Minister of Labor and
Social Affairs from 1993-94,
Vice Minister of Housing from
1999-2000 and became Vice
Minister of Education in
2000.

1970
Emilia Arosemena Vallarino
From 1970-93, she was
appointed Ambassador to
Mexico, the first female
ambassador of her country.

1984
Balbina Herrera Arauz
Between 1984-89, she was
Mayor of San Migel and from
1994-95 President of Asambeia
de Ligaladores.

1994
Noberta Tejades
From 1994-98, she was Vice Minister of Finance and Taxes and was appointed Secretary General of the Regional Government of Panama City in 1999.

1998
Mirei Endam
She became Administer General of the National Authority of the Environment in 1998-99, a newly established authority in the cabinet.

Mariela Sagel
In 1998-99, she became Minister of Government and Justice and first in the Cabinet after the president and the two vice-presidents.

1999
Doris Rosas de Mata (1938 -)
Former Ambassador to Spain, she was Minister of Education in 1999.

Mireya Moscoso Rodrigez
In 1999, she became President of Panama.

SAINT CHRISTOPHER & NEVIS
1974
Constance V. Mitcham (1947 -)
Between 1974-76, she was Chief Magistrate of the British Virgin Islands. In 1994, she became Minister of Health, Labor and Women's Affairs.

1991
Laurine Fenton
In 1991, she was appointed Ambassador to Canada for the Organization of Eastern Caribbean States.

SAINT LUCIA
1974
Heraldine Rock
She was Minister of Housing, Local Development, Local Government and Social Affairs, Groups Needs, Cooperatives, the Provident Fund and Water from 1974-81.

1981
Sylvia Burton
In 1981-84, she was Minister of Housing, Local Development and Local Government & Social Affairs.

1992
Lorraine Williams
She became the first female senator in 1992. From 1992-97, she was Attorney General and Minister of Legal Affairs. In 1997, she became Minister of Health, Human Service, Family Affairs and Women.

1997
Sonia Johnny
In 1997, she was appointed Ambassador to Organization of American States (OAS) and the United States, the first female ambassador of her country.

Menissa Rambally (1976 -)
From 1997-2000, she was Parliamentary Secretary of

State of Civil Aviation and Financial Services and Tourism. In 2000, she became Minister of Civil Aviation and Tourism.

TRINIDAD & TOBAGO

1919
Pearl Primus (1919-1994)
Graduate student of health education and psychology, she was prevented from obtaining a laboratory job by racial prejudice. In 1941, she won a scholarship and began a long career that sought to counteract racism with Afrodiasporic performance culture. She popularized African American, African and Caribbean dance styles internationally.

1939
Mona James
In 1939, she became the first native-born barrister in Trinidad.

1961
Isabella U. Teshea
From 1961-63, she was Parliamentary Secretary of Local Government for Health, Water and Sanitation. In 1970-71, she was appointed Ambassador to Ethiopia and Zambia, in 1974-77 Ambassador to Guyana and from 1975-76 Ambassador to Senegal.

1972
Marilyn Gordon
She was Parliamentary Secretary for Better Village Program (1972-76), Minister in the Ministry of Industry and Trade (1978-79), Minister of Transport (1979-82) and Minister of Culture, Sport and Youth (1981-85).

1980
Annette Auguste des Iles
She was appointed Ambassador to Venezuela, Columbia and Peru from 1980-85, Ambassador to Ecuador resident in Venezuela in 1985 and in 1992 Ambassador to the United Nations. From 1986-89, she was Permanent Secretary of External Affairs and Trade.

1986
Pamela Nicholson
Between 1986-91, she was Minister of Public Utilities and Settlements.

1991
Occah Seapaul
She was Speaker of the House of Representatives from 1991-95.

1995
Kamla Persad-Bissessar
(1952 -)
From 1995-96, she was Attorney General (2nd in the Cabinet), Minister of Legal Affairs from 1996-99 and became Minister of Education in 1999.

1996
Vimala Tota-Mahara (1956 -)
She was Parliamentary Secretary in the Ministry of Agriculture, Land and Marine Resources from 1996-99, and became Minister in the Ministry of Health in 1999.

European Women

ALAND

1909

Anni Blomqvist (1909-1990)
Her first book, *I Stormens Spar*, was published in 1966 and was followed by several others depicting the harsh and gentle nature and life of fishermen of Aland Islands. She then published a series of books about a fisherman's wife named Maja, which was made into a television series. The books presented Aland from the standpoint of a woman, who had to struggle not against the hard nature but also inside a patriarchal society.

1934

May Valborg Flodin (1934 -)
She was Member of the Landskabsstyrelse for Social Affairs and Health from 1980-81 and 1984-91, Vicelandtrad (Deputy Chief of Government) from 1988-91 and member of the Nordic Council from 1991-95.

1980

Gunnevi Nordman (1935 -)
She was Member of the Landskabsstyrelse for Culture and Education in 1980-88, Vicelandtrad (Deputy Chief of Government) in 1984-88, Chairperson of the Law Committee in 1988-91 and 1st Vice-Chairperson of the Landsting (Parliament) in 1991-95.

1995

Gun Carlsson
From 1995-99, she was Minister of Social Affairs, Health, Environment and Equality and in 1999 became Minister of Education and Culture.

Lotta Wickstrom-Johanson
She is Chairperson of the Justice Committee and since 1995, Member of the Speaker's Conference.

ALBANIA

1910

Agnes Gonxha Bojaxhiu (Mother Teresa) (1910-1997)
In 1948, Mother Teresa founded the Missionaries of Charity – an order whose members must pledge vows of poverty, obedience, chastity and service to the poor. In 1952, she founded the Kalighat Home for the Dying in Calcutta. Under her guidance, a leper colony was established near the city of Asansol. In 1971, Pope Paul VI honored Mother Teresa by awarding her the first Pope John XXIII Peace Prize. In 1979, she received her greatest award, the Nobel Peace Prize.

1972

Eleni Selenica
Between 1972-89, she was Vice President of the Supreme Court. From 1975-82, she was Vice-president of the Kuvendit Popullor (National Assembly).

1982
Emine Guri (1945 -)
She became 1st Vice-president of the Kuvendit Popullor (National Assembly) from 1967-79, Member of the Council of State from 1979 and Vice-President of the Republic from 1982-89.

1993
Suzana Faja
In 1993, she was appointed ambassador to Poland, the first woman ambassador in her country.

1995
Rexhina Bajraktari
From 1995-96, she was Deputy Governor of the Bank of Albania.

1996
Margarita Qirko
She became Deputy Speaker of the People's Assembly in 1996.

1998
Lijana Bsjati
In 1998, she was appointed ambassador to the United States.

ANDORRA

1960
Bibiana Rossa Miro Torres (1960 -)
From 1979-89, she was Public Prosecutor/judge and in 1995 became one of the first two female mayors of the country.

1993
Mertxel Mateu I Pi
In 1993, she was appointed ambassador to France, Belgium, The Netherlands and Luxembourg and European Union, the first woman ambassador of her country.

ARMENIA

1948
Sira Seza
Writer and journalist, she began publishing a magazine Young Armenian Women in 1948.

1975
Rema Kh. Svetlova
In 1975, she became Deputy Premier Minister and Vice Chairman of the Supreme Soviet from 1975-89.

1991
Sevad Sevan
In 1991, she was appointed ambassador to Bulgaria, the first woman ambassador of her country.

AUSTRIA

1717
Maria Teresa (1717 -?)
One of the great rulers of Europe, she governed the Austrian Hapsburg empire from 1740 to 1780. She used her administrative skills to consolidate powers into a central government, instituted taxation of the church and nobility rather than just the people and started compulsory education.

1759
Maria Theresia von Paradis (1759 -)
Although blind from birth, this Austrian pianist, organist, composer and singer

wrote organ music and light opera. She founded a music school for girls in Vienna.

1810
Fanny Eissler (1810-1884)
In 1941, she introduced Austrian folkdances to the United States especially the tarantella.

1869
Adeherd Popp (1869-1939)
Founder of the Socialist Women's Movement, she dedicated her life to women's issues, socialism and served as a elected official in the Austrian government.

1871
Olga Rudel-Zeynek (1871-1948)
She was Chairperson of the Bundesrat (Federal Assembly) from 1927-29 and in 1932. The Bundesrat, Federal Council, is the Upper House.

1890
Marianne Beth (1890-?)
She was the first woman to receive a doctorate of law in Austria. She specialized in international law and gained a reputation for her liberal and feminist views.

1892
Liane Zimbler (1892-1987)
She was the first woman in Austria to be awarded an architect's license. The focus of her work was interior design.

1900
Marie Ebner-Eschenbach
In 1900, she became the first woman to receive an honorary doctorate from the University of Vienna.

1905
Bertha von Suttner
(1843-1914)
Austrian novelist and pacifist, she gave Alfred Nobel the idea for the Peace Prize and became the first woman to win it in 1905.

1925
Helene Deutsch
(1884-1982)
A pioneering psychoanalyst, she was the first woman to serve as director of the Vienna Psychoanalytic Institute from 1925 to 1933.

1926
Ingeborg Bachmann
(1926-1973)
Writer of poetry, radio-plays and short stories, her most famous radio-play "*Der gute Got van Manhattan*" was first performed in 1958 and won a prize the next year. She also wrote several librettos for Henze and an opera based on Kleist.

1940
Heidi Pataki (1940-)
Essayist and film critic, she was one of the earliest activists in the Austrian women's movement. One of the keenest observers and sharpest critics of contemporary society, she is well known for

her satirical provocative poetry that unites language experimentation with social criticism.

1959
Ingeborg Bachmann
An author, she becomes the first professor of poetics at the University of Frankfort in 1959.

Johanna Mondschein
In 1959, she was appointed ambassador to Norway, the first woman ambassador in her country.

1966
Grete Rehor (1910-1972)
An Austrian politician, in 1966 she was the first woman to serve in her country's government when she was appointed Minister of Social Administration. In 1970, she was honored for her lifetime of service with the Grand Medal of Honor of the Republic of Austria.

1966
Johanna Nestor
She was appointed ambassador to India and Sri Lanka in 1966, to Israel in 1972 and to Ireland in 1979.

1973
Annemarie Proell Moser
An Austrian skier, she wins the World Cup downhill championship in 1973 and wins eleven consecutive downhill competitions.

1990
Maria Schaumayer
In 1990, she became Governor of the Austrian National Bank.

Heide Smith
She became President of the Nationalrat (National Assembly) in 1990. As the 2nd Vice President of the National Council, she was part of the collective vice-presidency of the Republic.

1991
Anna Elisabeth Hasselbach
She was Vice President of the Bundesrat from 1996-99 and President in 1991, 1996 and 2000. Title of the presiding officer was changed from Chairman to President in 1988.

AZERBAIJAN
1963
Tira Aza-Kyzy Tairova
She became Minister of Foreign Affairs in 1959 and Deputy Premier Minister in 1963.

1990
Elmia Mikael-Kysy Kafarova
Former Acting Head of State, she became President of the Supreme Soviet in 1990-92.

1993
Elenora Gousseinova
In 1993, she was appointed ambassador to France, the first woman ambassador of her country.

1994
Lala-Shovket Hajiyeva
Between 1994-95, she was appointed Ambassador to the United Nations.

BELARUS

1994
Nina Nikolaevna Mazai
In 1994, she was appointed ambassador to France and in 1996 to Spain, the first woman ambassador of her country.

1997
Tamara Dudko
She became Vice President of the Upper Council of the Republic in 1997.

BELGIUM

1710
Maria Anna de Camargo
(1710-1770)
A ballet dancer, she is said to be responsible for the shortening of the traditional ballet skirt which allowed more complicated steps to be seen. She is also one of the first celebrities to lend her name to merchandizing shoes and wigs.

1846
Marie Popelin (1846-1913)
In 1905, she becomes the first president of the Council of Belgian Women.

1888
Marie Popelin
She is the first woman law graduate in Belgium in 1888, but is refused admission to the bar on the grounds of her sex.

1915
Bertha di Vito-Delvaux
(1915 -)
She composed 8 operas, several concertos, 9 ballets and many symphonic compositions and songs. In 1938, she taught at the Conservatoire Royal de Liege and won many awards including Grand Prix de Rome in 1943.

1916
Martha Bol Poel
(1877-1956)
A Belgian feminist, she was the first woman to organize secret news correspondence service during the German occupation of Belgium during World War I. During the 1920's, she became a leading figure in the women's movement in Belgium.

1930
Jacqueline Fontyn (1930 -)
Composer, she won the Grand Prix de Rome for composition in 1959 as well as numerous other awards. Her works are played extensively in Europe.

1932
Luce Irigaray (1932-)
Psychoanalyst and philosopher, the central concern of her work was women's desire and women's language. Her first book *Le langage des dements* published in 1973 discusses the relationship of demented people to language, which according to her is similar to that of women.

1949
Anne-Marie Lizin-Vanderpeeten
(1949 -)
She was Minister of the Economy (1972-73), Secretary of State of Foreign Affairs for "Europe 1992" (1988-92) and Secretary of State of External Trade for European Affairs (1992-95).

1953
Marie Gevers
In 1953, she became the first woman president of Brussels University's law school.

1965
Marguerite De Reimacker-Legot
She was Secretary of the House of Representatives from 1961-65 and was appointed Minister of Family and Housing in 1965, - the first woman to serve as a minister in her country's government.

1968
Elizabeth Malaise
In 1968, she is the first woman appointed director of the Belgian National Bank.

1971
Chantal Akerman (1950-)
In 1971, her first film *Blow Up My City* was critically acclaimed as one of the outstanding avant-garde films of the day. She is much admired by feminists for her dramatic portrayal of the drudgery of women's work and lives as well as their sexuality.

1973
Edmonde Dever
In 1973, she was appointed ambassador to Sweden, to Austria in 1978 and to the UN in 1981.

1977
Ilya Prigogine
She won the Nobel Prize for Chemistry in 1977.

Rika de Backer-Van Ocken
In 1977, she became Belgium's first woman minister for Flemish Cultural Affairs.

1980
Cecile Goor-Eyben
Former Vice President of the Senate, in 1980 she became Minister of the Brussel Region (Chief Minister) and from 1980-85 was Secretary of State for Brussel.

1981
Edmonde Dever
She was appointed Ambassador to the United Nations in New York from 1981-88.

Nora Staels-Dompas
Between 1981-85, she was Vice President of the Council of Europe and in 1988 became Vice President of the Senate.

1989
Magda de Galan
She was Mayor of Forest (1989-91), Minister of Social Affairs and Health of French Community (1991-93), Minister of Social Solidarity, Health and Environment (1993-94) and Minister of Social Affairs

(1994-99). Since 1999, she has been President of the Regional Parliament of Brussel.

1993
Ingrid Daubechies
(1954 -)
In 1984, she received her Ph.D. in physics from Free University Brussels. A leading authority on wavelet theory, she constructed a class of wavelets that were identically zero outside a finite interval in 1987. In 1984, she received the Louis Empain Prize for Physics which is awarded once every five years to a Belgian scientist on the basis of work done before age 29.

1994
Laurette Onckelinx
She was Premier and Minister of Social Solidarity, Health and Environment of the French Community from 1994-99. Since 1999, she is Federal Deputy Premier and Minister of Labor.

1995
Magda G. H. Aelvoet (1954 -)
In 1995, she was appointed Minister of State, an honorary title given for life. From 1995-99, she was Vice-Chairman of the Green Group in the European Parliament and in 1999, became Minister of Consumer Protection, Health and Environment.

BOSNIA
1395
Dowager Queen Jelena Gruba of Rama
She reigned from 1395-98 and was probably the only woman to rule in her own name since the Slavs came to the Balkans.

1992
Tatjana Ljugic-Mijatovic
From 1992-96, she was a Member of the Presidency and Council of Ministers. Since 1997, she was Ambassador to Austria and to United Nations in Vienna.

Sadzida Silaidzic
In 1992, she was appointed ambassador to Pakistan, the first female ambassador of her country.

1996
Mirsada Jahic
In 1996, she became Chief of Cabinet of the Prime Minister.

Seada Curcic-Selimanic
She was Deputy Minister of Finance from 1996-98.

BULGARIA
1812
Tonka Tihovitza Obretenova
(1812-1893)
She is known as "Babe Tonka", the mother of the revolution that helped free Bulgaria from the Turks. Active in many fronts from carrying supplies to foiling military traps, in 1872 she was a member of the revolutionary committee.

1886
Dora Petrova Gabe
(1886-1983)
One of Bulgaria's foremost women poets, her first collection of poems *Temenugi* was published in 1908. She wrote many poems and short stories for children. Also, she edited *Biblioteka za malkitz* and the journal *Prozorce*.

1893
Elisaveta Bagryana (1893-)
Poet, she was a major contributor to the influential journal *Zlatorog* in the 1920's. Much of her works relate to landscapes of her homeland. The cycle *Seismograph of the Heart* appeals for tenderness as opposed to mechanistic modern culture.

1936
Ekaterina Yakoba Marinova
(1936 -)
She was Deputy Minister of Agriculture (1971-79), Deputy Minister of Internal Trade and Public Service (1982-84), Deputy Minister of Production and Trade with Consumer Goods (1984-86), and Consul General to Leningrad/Saint Petersburg (1986-90).

1947
Tsola Nicheva Draoycheva
(1894-1989)
In 1947, she became Minister of Post, Telegraphs and Telephones. She was Member of Council of State from 1974-84.

1949
Stela Dmitrova Blagoeva
In 1949, she was appointed ambassador to USSR and Finland, the first woman ambassador of her country.

1966
Svetla Daskolova (1921 -)
She was Deputy President of Narodno Subranie (National Assembly) in 1962 and became Minister of Justice in 1966.

1992
Dlaga Nikolova Dimitrova
A poet and dissident, she became vice president of Bulgaria in 1992. Her works, which were sometimes banned by the old communist regime, defended the rights of Turkish residents of Bulgaria.

1993
Albena Simeonova
One of her most successful and novel initiatives to date has been the creation of the "Ecological Inspectorates" at the local level. Even though she is not a lawyer, she formulated community environmental regulations. She persuaded environmental groups in Bulgaria to come together in an association called Green Parliament in 1993. She helped establish the Green Justice Association in 1997, which works together with local authorities to create environmental legislation.

1995

Irena Georgieva Bokova

(1952 -)

From 1995-97, she was Deputy Minister of Foreign Affairs for European Integration and Advisor of the Ministry of Foreign Affairs in 1997. She was presidential candidate in 1996.

CROATIA

1952

Djurdja Knezevic (1952 -)

She has been active in the women's movement and other organizations in Croatia for more than 20 years. She was one of the coordinators of the first and most active feminist organization "Women and Society" in 1977. She founded Women's Infoteka in 1992 and publishes *Bread and Roses* - the only feminist magazine in Croatia.

1967

Savka Dabcevic Kucar (1923 -)

She was Premier Minister from 1967-69, Leader of Communist Party in Croatia from 1969-70 and presidential candidate in 1992. She was dismissed as Communist Party Leader because her views were too liberal.

1985

Ema Derossi-Bjelajac

(1926 -)

In 1985, she became President of the Presidency.

1991

Ljerka Mintas Hodak

From 1991-92, she was Head of Croatian Office with the European Union Monitoring Mission in Zagreb. In 1993, she became Deputy Premier Minister of Maritime Affairs, Transport and Communication and in 1995, was Advisor to the Premier Minister in charge of maritime affairs. She became Minister of European Integration from 1998-2000.

1992

Anamarija Besker

In 1992, she was appointed ambassador to the UN in Vienna.

Vesna Girardi Jurkic

In 1992, she became Minister of Education, Culture and Sport. Since 1995, she has been Ambassador to France.

1995

Marina Dropulic Martulovic

Former Deputy Mayor of Zagreb, she became Minister of Ecology, Urban Development, Construction and Housing from 1995-96.

1997

Spomenka Cek

In 1997-98, she was Assistant Minister of Foreign Affairs and in 1998, was appointed Ambassador to United Nations in Geneve.

1998

Marija Kastelan Macan

She was Assistant Minister of Development and Reconstruction for Scientific Research and Projects from 1998-99.

1999

Milena Benini Getz

She is editor of the bilingual Croatian literary e-zine NetPens and editor-in-chief of Croatian Weekly Economic Bulletin, a weekly overview of economic events in Croatia. Her novel, *Children of Chaos and Eternity* won the SFera Award in 1999 as the best Croatian SFF-novel.

2000

Mirjana Mladieno

She became Deputy Minister of European Integration and also Head of the Office for European Integration in 2000.

CYPRUS

1960

Stella Soulitou (1920 -)

A transport pilot of RAF Women Auxillary Service, she became Minister of Justice, Social Affairs and Culture in 1960. Since then, she has been Law Commissioner (1970-84) and Attorney General (1984-1988).

1993

Myra Y. Kleopas

She was appointed ambassador to China in 1993, the first woman ambassador of her country.

CZECHOSLOVAKIA

1609

Rebecca Tiktinca

In 1609, she was the first woman to publish in Yiddish her book on religion and religious duties.

1786

Magdalena Dobromila Rettigova

(1786 - 1845)

She was the earliest female Czech writer who is generally known. Today she is remembered for her Cook Book, which was published in 1826.

1820

Bozena Nemcová

(1820-1862)

The most famous female Czech writer, she wrote poetry, fairy tales and short stories. Her book, *Babicka* published in 1855, is the most venerated Czech book and was translated into more that 100 languages.

1845

Klementina Hanucová

(1845-1918)

One of the first female sports' teachers, she lead a gymnastic club of ladies and young ladies. After 1884, she worked on special orthopedic training for girls.

Františka Plaminková

(1845-1942)

A politician, a Senator, and a teacher, she founded penská národní rada (National Council of Women) and penské domovy (a pension for single ladies).

1847

Eliska Krasnohorska

(1847-1926)

She edited the first Czech women's journal *"Women's Letters"*, helped to found the first girls' gymnasium (high school) and wrote numerous works of lyric poetry and social and literary criticism. In addition, she is remembered for her children's literature and opera librettos.

1852
Anna Bayerova (1852-1924)
She studied in Switzerland to become one of the first female physicians in Czechoslovakia.

1907
F. Plamnikoua
In 1907, she founded the Czech Committee on Women's Suffrage.

1920
Marie Leopoldine Deutch
(1882-1979)
She became the first woman member of parliament in 1920.

1915
Vitezslava Kapralova
(1915-1940)
First female conductor, she wrote her first composition as a 9-year old.

1921
Milada Petoíková
(1895-1985)
In 1921, she became the first female Czech architect. She built the Činoherní klub in Prague, which, before World War II, was the seat of a woman's organization.

1947
Ludmila Jankovcov
In 1947, she is named Industry Minister for Czechoslovakia – the first woman in her country to hold a cabinet post.

1988
M. Novakova (1941-)
She received prize of the Czech Ministry of Culture in 1989 and diploma of the Prague International Assembly of Architects in 1989. The focus of her work was reconstruction of interiors, exhibitions and galleries. She represented Czechoslovakia at the International Union of Women Architects.

1990
Hanna Sevelkova
In 1990, she was appointed Ambassador to Denmark.

DENMARK
890
Thyra, Queen of Denmark
She led her army against the Germans who invaded Sleswick and Jutland. Around 890, she built the Danneverke, a great wall which was Denmark's major defense for centuries and portions of are still in existence.

1353
Margaret of Denmark
(1353-1411)
In 1387 she became ruler of Denmark and led her armies, which took control of key cities and fortresses, eventually forcing the Swedes and Norwegians to withdraw from Denmark. She was elected Queen of Norway in 1388; the following year she was offered the Swedish throne. In 1397, she forged the Calmar Union, uniting the three nations under a single monarchy and

becoming the most powerful ruler in Scandinavian history.

1850
Natalie Zahle (1827 -?)
In 1850, she founded the first Danish school for girls.

1885
Karen Blixen (1885-1962)
One of Denmark's great writers, she wrote in English and Danish. She drew inspiration for her books from the Bible, the Arabian Nights and the Icelandic sagas. Her books include *Seven Gothic Tales, Out of Africa* (which was made into a movie) as well as her collections of stories *Winter Tales* and *Last Tales*.

Isak Dinesen (1885-1962)
Short-story writer, her stories, set in the past are pervaded with an aura of supernaturalism, incorporate the themes of Eros and dreams.

1902
Marie Bregendahl
(1867-1940)
In 1902, she published her first book *At the Sickbed of Lars* that showed a profound understanding of the harshness of the lives of the people.

Helga Pedersen (1911-1980)
Her career in government included Personal Secretary of the Minister of Justice, City Court Judge, Minister of Justice and Police, Judge in the Court of Appeals and High Court Judge. In 1972, she became first woman Judge at the Court for Human Rights of The Council of Europe.

1918
Nina Bang (1866-1928)
She was elected after the passage of women's suffrage in 1918 and served in Denmark's first Social Democratic government, the first woman to serve as a member of the Landsting (the upper house) in Denmark's Parliament. She became Minister of Education in 1924. An economist, historian and journalist, she also worked on behalf of the League of Nations.

1924
Ellen Osiier
She was the first woman to win an Olympic gold medal in individual foil fencing at the 1924 Olympic games in Paris, France, the first year this event was open to women.

1940
Dorrit Willumsen
(1940 -)
In 1981, she received the Danish Academy Major Award for Literature, the first woman to do so. Her novels *Marie* and *Clothed in Purple* give powerful accounts of women's struggle to find a place in the world. In 1997, she received the Nordic Council Prize for Literature for *Bang*, a biographical novel about the author Herman Bang.

1952
Pia Tafdrup (1952-)
She made her literary debut in 1981 and has published eight collections of poetry, written two plays and edited two anthologies of contemporary Danish poetry. English versions of her poems have appeared in more than 40 literary journals in the UK, the US and Canada. Her work has also been translated into Swedish, Spanish, German, French, Italian, Russian, Macedonian, Rumanian, Slovakian, Turkish and Arabic.

1960
Pia Gjellerup (1960 -)
In 1993, she became Minister of Justice and Police, 1993-98 Deputy Chairman of the Finance Committee and 1998 Minister of Business and Industry.

1955
Bodil Begtrup
From 1955-73, she became Ambassador to Iceland, European Council, Switzerland and Portugal.

1963
Ella Jensen (1907 -)
In 1963, she is elected head of the Tobacco Workers Union, making her the first woman in Denmark to chair a dual-sex labor union.

1972
Margrethe II (1940 -)
When she succeeded her father to the throne in 1972, she became Denmark's first Queen since 1000 AD. The right of female succession was only established in 1953. Her role as Queen is merely ceremonial and she spends most of her time with her family and working on her profession, archeology.

1995
Bodil Nyboe Andersen
(1941 -)
One of the few female Central Bank heads in industrialized world, she is a staunch defender of the Danish krone, adopting an unpretentious, no-nonsense approach to her job as manager of a small but wealthy Scandinavian nation's monetary system. When appointed governor of the Danish Central Bank in 1995, she vowed to continue its steady exchange rate and low inflation policies. She has spent her working life in finance and economics, notably as professor of money and banking at Copenhagen University.

Ritt Bjerregaard
(1942 -)
Too unDanish, colorful and controversial to fulfil her dream of becoming Denmark's first female premier, she was sent to Brussels as European Union environment commissioner in 1995. As such, she was responsible for nuclear policy and later confronted the French on their tests in the South Pacific.

1997

Britta Caroc Schall Holberg

As Owner of the Estate Hagenskov, she was appointed Hafjaegermester/Chasseur to the Royal Court by Queen Margrethe in 1997, a courtesy title given to Landowners in 1997. She was one of two first women to be given the title.

1999

Helle Degn

She was President of the Parliamentary Assembly of the Organization for Security and Cooperation in Europe (OSCE) from 1998-2000.

ESTONIA

1886

Hella Marie Wuolijoki

(1886-1954)

She was born in the southern part of Estonia in a district known as the birthplace of Estonian nationalism. Her first play *Talu* lapsed was printed in Estonia in 1912 and performed at the Estonia Theatre in Reval.

1917

Marie Under (1883-1980)

Poet and distinguished translator, she claims to be Estonia's real national poet. Her first collection of poems *Sonetid* was published in 1917 and the public was surprised by the overt eroticism of her poetry. Her themes range from nature and pantheism to biblical legends. She has received a number of literary prizes and has been repeatedly nominated for the Nobel Prize.

1944

Olga Lauristin

In 1944, she became Minister of Social Security.

1967

Meta Jangolenka-Vannas

From 1967-69, she served as Vice-President.

1969

Andra Veideman

In 1969, she became Minister of Public Service/Consumer Protection. She became Minister without Portfolio for European Affairs in 1999.

1980

Leida Perps

In 1980, she graduated from Agricultural School and devised techniques for efficient milking and meticulous procedures for monitoring cow nutrition.

1992

Mauri Lauristi

Former Vice-Chairman, she was Minister of Social Affairs from 1992-94.

Lehte Soot-Hainsalu

From 1992-93, she was a Member of the Presidium and Chairman of the Finance Committee.

1999

Signe Kivi

Professor of the Estonian Academy of Arts, she became Minister of Culture in 1999.

Merle Pajula
In 1999, she was appointed Ambassador to the United Nations in New York.

FAERO ISLANDS

1978
Karin Kjolbro
In 1978, she one of the two first female assembly members and from 1980-90 the only woman.

1984
Jongero Purkhus
From 1984-89, she was Minister of Finance, Environment and Trade and Minister of Economy, Statistics, Transport and Justice from 1989-91. She later worked as Assistant Secretary of Budget in the Ministry of Economy.

1991
Marita Peterson (1940 -)
She was Minister of Justice, Education, Culture and Church Affairs (1991-93), Premier Minister and Minister of External Relations, the Underground, Administration and Public Wages (1993-94) and Chairman of the Assembly (1994-95). Since 1998, she has been substitute member of the Danish Folketing.

FINLAND

1833
Larin Paraske (1833-1904)
A rune singer, her repertoire, which is the truest and most complete example of southern Karelian folksong including epic, lyric, wedding and chain runes, demonstrated that even when subordinated and under difficult circumstances women have been able to create a culture out of their own experiences.

1844
Minna Canth (1844-1897)
The first Finnish author to describe women's position in society, she was also the first Finnish social realist. Her most famous plan *Papin Perhe* depicted crisis in a bourgeois family and *Tyomiehen Vaimo* revealed in Dickensian light the misery of a poor wife, her husband's alcoholism and the evils of prostitution.

1863
Sophie Mannerheim
(1863-1928)
A famous nurse, she is known as the pioneer of modern nursing in Finland. She was appointed head nurse of Helsinki Surgical Hospital and later elected President of the Finnish Nurses' Association. She was also elected President of the International Council of Nurses and co-founded the Children's Hospital in Helsinki as well as the Mannerheim League for Children's Welfare.

1871
Maila Talvio (1871-1951)
She was a Finnish writer whose novels often served as an indicator of moods in the country. During her career, she wrote nearly 50 works – plays, novels, short stories, speeches, and non-fiction. In

protest against increasing Russian suppression (Finland was a Grand Duchy under Russian rule) she joined other Finnish artists and politicians writing patriotic articles in 1893. She passionately defended Poland under Russian oppression and Baltic neighbors and devoted time in the preservation of local arts and crafts.

1874
Lilli Porthan (1874-1967) Finnish teacher and children's book writer, her fairy tales represent the romantic tradition, which concentrated on wonders and adventures. In 1952 she received the Nuorten Kirja (children's book) award.

1875
Anni Emilia Swan (1875-1958) Writer and translator, she wrote mainly for children. Folk tales from around the world combined with realistic elements with fantasy influenced her fairy tales. In 1907, she was editor of the juvenile magazine *Paaskynen* and translated into Finnish works by Lewis Carroll, James Fenimore Cooper, etc.

1878
Aino Kallas (1878-1956) A writer, she gained fame as a novelist and short story writer. A number of her works were adapted for the stage and some of them were made into operas. She also participated with her writings to the struggles of Estonian people to free themselves from foreign domination.

1880
Maria Jotuni (1880-1943) Novelist, playwright, one of the classic feminist authors in Finland; she often showed society from a woman's point of view. She also wrote aphorisms and children stories. Her most important novel Huojuva *Talo*, published in 1963, depicts a destructive marriage where the husband psychologically and physically tortures his wife at home. In 1995 it was adapted into a 5-part television drama.

1886
Hella Maria Wuolijoki (1886-1954) Writer and playwright, in 1937 she wrote *Juurakon Hulda*, which was the basis for the Oscar-winning film, *The Farmer's Daughter*. Her best-known work is family saga *Niskavuori*, which depicts the power, struggles between old women and young men and women generations from the 1880s to the 1940s. She worked as director of Carelia Timer Co in 1923 and in 1931 was chairman of the board of Suomen Nafta, an oil company.

1895
Katri Ingman (1895-1971) A Finnish writer and translator, who worked as a notary and financial manager. She was among the first feminist authors who depicted

in her books independent women living on their own conditions. Her novels portray women who must choose between social acceptability or loneliness.

1899
Lucina Hagman
In 1899, she founded Helsinki's Finnish New School and served as its director until 1958.

1907
Helvi Hamalainen
(1907-1998)
She was awarded the Finlandia Prize for Literature in 1988 for her collection of poems *Sukupolveni Unta*. Although some of her novels contain historical subject matter, most of her works depict village society and its reaction to various social and psychological changes.

1913
Aale Maria Tynni
(1913-1997)
A poet and translator, in 1957 she edited and translated into Finnish a comprehensive anthology of European poetry ranging from the Middle Ages to the present day entitled Tuhat Laulujen Vuotta.

1914
Marika Tove Jansson (1914 -)
Writer-illustrator, she wrote children's books in Swedish, the language of the educated Finn. Her books about the Moomintrolls have been translated into 34 different languages and sold worldwide. In 1994, she received the Great Prize of the Swedish Academy for outstanding achievement.

1916
Eila Pennamen
(1916 - 1994)
She was one of the most significant female novelists in Finland after World War II. In the 1950s she published historical novels, such as *Pyha Birgitta*, which depicted the medieval Swedish mystic, and *Valon Lapset*, which focused on the birth of the Quaker movement in 17th century England. Her major work from the 1970s was the *Tampere* trilogy, which portrayed lower middle-class life from the late 19th century to the stormy social changes of the General Strike of 1905 and to parliamentary reform.

1917
Miini Sillanpaan
(1917-1996)
A journalist and one of the most influential political figure in Finland in the early 20th century, she was a Member of Parliament during 1907-47. As Finland's first female member of the government as Minister of Social Affairs, she paid special attention to the conditions of women who worked and took care of their children alone.

1927
Miina Sillanpaa
(1866-1952)
A journalist and one of the most influential political figures in Finland in the early 20th century, she was a member of Parliament during 1907-1947 and the first female member of Social Affairs in Finland in 1926. She is remembered particularly for her commitment to improving the social conditions of working class women and single parents.

1935
Armi Ratia
Designer and entrepreneur, she established her own weaving company in 1935.

1951
Anneli Kariina Taina (1951 -)
In 1995, she was 2nd Minister of Environment for Housing and from 1995-99, Minister of Defense.

1958
Tynne Leivo-Larson (1902 -)
Between 1945-56, she was Deputy Mayor of Helsinki and in 1958, became Vice Premier Minister and Minister without Portfolio. She was Ambassador to Norway and Iceland from 1958-66.

1964
Inkeri Antilla (1916 -)
In 1964, she became director of the Institute of Criminology at Helsinki University. She became chairman of the Finnish Commission on Women's Rights and head of the Commission on Sexual Crimes in 1966.

1966
Inkeri Antilla
A Finnish criminologist, she becomes chairman of the Finnish commission on women's rights and head of the commission on sexual crimes.

1970
Margit Eskman
In 1970, she was Minister in the Office of the Premier Minister and from 1971-72, Second Minister of Finance (Taxation).

1973
Helvi Linnea Spilia (1915 -)
In 1973, she becomes assistant secretary-general of the United Nations, the highest post held by a woman to date.

1977
Pirkko Annikki Tyolajarui
In 1977, she became Finland's Minister of Social Affairs and Health.

1983
Eeva Kuuskaski-Vikatmaa
From 1983-87 and 1991-92, she was Minister of Health and Social Affairs. She was an independent presidential candidate in 1994, but resigned in protest of the party's economic policy.

1987
Anja Helena Pesola
She was Minister of Health and Social Affairs from 1987-91

and Director of the Social
Insurance Institution since
1990.

1990
M. Elisabeth Rehn (1935 -)
From 1990-95, she was Minister
of Defense and from 1991-95
Minister of Equality. She was
Assistant Secretary General of
the United Nations (1995-99),
United Nations Commissioner
for Human Rights in the former
Yugoslavia (1995-98), United
Nations Representative and
Special Coordinator in Bosnia-
Herzegovina (1998-99) and the
Personal Representative of the
Secretary General responsible
for Police and other
Operations.

1991
Hannele Pokkala (1952 -)
From 1991-94, she was Minister
of Justice. Since 1995, she
was Governor of Lapland, the
most northern county of the
country.

1992
Sirkka Hamalainen
(1939 -)
In 1992, she became governor
of the Bank of Finland. She
was chosen to calm the
situation after economic
storms and seen off her
predecessor. Her straight talk
about Finland's difficult
economic times has increased
her popularity and established
her as the country's most
influential woman.

1995
Sinikka Monkare (1947 -)
From 1995-99, she was Minister
of Social Affairs and Health
and Minister in the Ministry
of Environment, from 1999-2000
Minister of Labor and in 2000
Minister of Industry and
Trade.

1996
Kiirsti Lihtonen
Former Ambassador to Namibia
and Tanzania, she became
Understate Secretary of
Foreign Affairs in 1996.

1999
Siv Hellen
In 1999, she became Vice
President of Nordic Investment
Bank.

2000
Tarja Kaarina Halonen (1943 -)
She was a member of Parliament
(1979-2000), Chairman of the
Social Affairs Committee and
Member of the Presidium of the
Parliament (1984-87, Minister
of Nordic Cooperation (1989-
91) and Minister of Justice
(1990-91). From 1995-2000, she
was Minister of Foreign
Affairs and as such Chairman
of the Council of Ministers of
the European Union. In 2000,
she became President.

FRANCE

1364
Christine de Pisan
(1364-1431)
One of France's first
professional writers, she is
popularly known as the first
person ever to be self-

supporting through writing alone. Her poem, "*Song in Honor of Joan of Arc*", was her last poem and the only one to celebrate Joan during Joan's lifetime.

1492

Marguerite of Navaree
(1492-1549)
She was author of letters, poetry, a spiritual guide entitled *The Mirror of the Sinful Soul* and *The Heptameron*. Many consider her to be the mother of the French Renaissance.

1525

Louise Labe (1525-1566)
She was a skilled equestrian and archer who fought on horseback for the Dauphin against Spain. She was nicknamed "la belle Amazone" for her fighting ability.

1563

Louyse Bourgeois
(1563-1636)
Midwife, she was the first person to treat anemia with iron and her observations established undernourishment as the cause of anemia.

1565

Marie Le Jars de Gournay
(1565-1645)
She produced an impressive body of writings in subject areas spanning from poetic treatises to political pamphlets to a novel. She actively advocated education for woman, which equals that of men.

1665

Elisabeth Jacquet de La Guerre
(1665-1729)
Harpsichord player and composer, she was the world's first female musician. Her earliest published works date from 1687 and her first book of harpsichord pieces (*Pieces de Clavessin*) particularly demonstrates her taste for improvisation.

1759

Nicole-Reine Lepaute
(1723-1788)
In 1759, she begins work at the Paris Observatory, where she will do important work on the movements of the sun, moon, and plants including a monograph about Venus and calculation for a solar eclipse.

1773

Marie Anne Victoire Bolvin
(1773-1847)
She was trained as an obstetrician and was the first woman to invent a pelvimeter and vaginal speculum.

1791

Olympe de Gouges
French feminist and founder of a famous radical political group, The Club des Tricoteuses, she writes her *Declaration of the Rights of Women and Citizeness* in 1791.

1790

Louise Felicite de Keralio
(1758-1821)
Translator, journalist, biographer and author, she

founded the first political newspaper run by a woman, the *Journal d'Etat et due Citoyen* in 1790.

1791
Olympe de Gouges
A leader of the women revolutionaries, she protested in 1791 by issuing her Declaration of the Rights of Women and Citizenesses. She argued that if women could die on the scaffold they should be able to vote for the government in power.

1795
Henriette d'Angeville
(1795-1871)
A French mountaineer, she made 21 ascents in 25 years and at the age of 69, climbed Oldenhorn in the Alps wearing a hoopskirt. In 1838, she became the first woman to organize an ascent of Mont Blanc.

1796
Marie Lachapelle (1796-1821)
An obstetrician, she devised a method of shortening labor. Among her most noted innovations was the immediate repair of perineum that is torn during delivery. If her modern methods had been followed, thousands of women's lives would have been saved. Her 3-volume book *Pratique des Accouchements* summarized 40,000 childbirths.

1798
Genevieve Labrosse
In 1798 she was the first woman to parachute jump from a balloon.

1805
Madeleine Sophie Blanchard
In 1805, she soloed in a gas-powered balloon. She made her living as a balloonist. In 1810, she became Chief of Air Services and performed at royal functions.

1814
Marie Boivin
A midwife, she became co-director of the General Hospital for Seine and Oise and received an order of merit from the King of Prussia in 1814.

1822
Rosa Bonheur (1822-1899)
She was one of the most renowned animal painters in history. *Sheep by the Sea* illustrates her lifelong interest in portraying farm animals authentically, reinforcing her commitment to direct observation from nature - a principle she adhered to throughout her life.

1832
Jeanne Villepreux-Power
(1794-1871)
A naturalist, she was the first to create and use aquariums for experimentation in aquatic environments in 1832. She wrote several books including "*Guida per la Sicilia*", a brilliant and

erudite inventory of the environment of Sicily. She was known throughout Europe for her works on the Argonauta argo shell.

1846
Anne Pauline Crepin
In 1846, she took out a patent for a circular saw, which is the present day bandsaw. It revolutionized the technique for thin cutting wood and particularly veneers.

1849
Jeanne Deroin (1810-1894)
A French socialist, she becomes the first woman to run for the National Assembly in 1849.

1873
Sidonie Gabrielle Colette (1873-1954)
Novelist, she was the first woman president of Goncourt Academy and officer of French Legion of Honor.

1874
Madeleine Pelletier (1874-1939)
A French militant feminist and physician, she was the first woman in France licensed to practice in a mental hospital and also performed illegal abortions. She was also the editor of La Suffragiste.

1888
Jeanne Chauvin (1862-1926)
She is the first Frenchwoman to graduate with a law degree in 1888.

1899
Suzanne Rachel Flore Lenglen (1899-1938)
French tennis player, whose popularity in the 1920s helped establish women's tennis as a spectator sport. She became celebrated for her tennis apparel, which exposed her forearms and calves. In 1926, she became one of the first tennis players to turn professional and later opened a tennis school.

1907
Vera Maria Atkins (1907-2000)
At the outbreak of World War II, she joined the WAAF and became assistant to Colonel Maurice Buckmaster at the French Section of the Special Operations Executive. This section is credited with shortening the war by six months. After the war, she was involved in fostering Anglo-French relations and keeping alive the spirit of the Resistance. In 1987, she was appointed a Commandant of the Legion d'honneur. She inspired the character of Miss Moneypenny in the James Bond stories.

1908
Simone de Beauvoir (1908-1986)
A French writer, she was at the center of an influential intellectual movement and the fight against oppression. She participated in the French Resistance movement against Nazi occupation during World War II (1939-1945) and wrote

about the experience in her novel *The Mandarins*. A major figure in the feminist movement, her study of the status of women in *The Second Sex* is regarded as a classic statement of liberation.

1910
Marie-Madeline Fourcade
(1910-1989)
A leader/commander of French Resistance during World War II, she was the only woman head of alliance network.

1919
Adrienne Bollard
In 1919, she became first French pilot to fly across the Andes in a single engine plane.

1923
Yvonne Choquet-Bruhat (1923 -)
In 1979, she became the first woman elected to the French Academy of Sciences in its 300-year history. She worked in the area of mathematical physics.

1928
Agnes Varda (1928 -)
A still photographer, she went into motion pictures and became one of the most honored women directors of her country. Her work is considered the vanguard of French New Wave film.

1937
Nadia Boulanger (1887-1979)
One of the most influential music teachers in the 20th Century and the first woman to conduct symphony orchestra in London in 1937, she performed and recorded baroque and Renaissance music, which helped to revive their popularity. She premiered Stravinsky's concerto for wind instruments in Washington, DC in 1938.

1945
Marthe Ricard (1889-1982)
A French feminist, who worked for the French secret service during WWI and for the Resistance during WWII, she was the first woman to campaign successfully against prostitution in France. She worked to rid her nation of legalized prostitution, which she felt exploited women as slaves. Her efforts resulted in closure of Paris brothels in 1945 and in legislation against prostitution throughout France in 1946.

1947
Germaine Peyrolles
In 1947, she was the first woman to preside over the French National Assembly.

1951
Francoise Gilot
Throughout her life, she has combined artistic talent with academic achievement. She expressed herself through painting and other art forms and her work was acclaimed internationally by 1945. From 1946 to 1953, she worked with Picasso and Henri Matisse, learning, teaching and sharing the wealth of their tremendous

talent. Since 1951, she has had one-woman shows in every major gallery in the world.

1955
Bernadette Perrin-Riou (1955 -)
A mathematician, she was awarded the AMS Ruth Lyttle Satter Prize in 1999 in recognition of her number theoretical research on p-adic L-functions and Iwasawa theory.

1957
Jacqueline Thome-Patenotre
She became Undersecretary of State for Reconstruction and Housing in 1957 and from 1960-65, Vice-President of the Assemblee Nationale.

1967
Helene Ahrweiler (1916 -)
French scholar and expert on Byzantine social history, she became the first woman to head Sorbonne's history department and the first woman to become president of the Sorbonne in Paris from 1976 until her retirement in 1981.

1968
Marie-Madeleine Diensch
In 1968, she became Secretary of State for Education and from 1968-76 Secretary of State for Social Affairs and Health. She was appointed Ambassador to Luxembourg in 1976.

1974
Francoise Giroud (1916 -)
A French journalist and politician, she was the first person to serve the French government as Secretary of State for Women's Affairs, a position to which she was appointed in 1974.

Simone Veil (1928 -)
The popular former health and social affairs minister is a champion of women's right, giving her name to France's abortion laws which she steered through parliament in 1974. She later trained as a lawyer and became the first president of the European Parliament from 1979-82. She remains a passionate defender of her humanist beliefs. In 1993, she became Minister of State (Deputy Premier) and Minister of Housing, Social Affairs, Health and Development of Cities.

Alice Saunier-Seite (1925 -)
In 1976, the French Cabinet appointed her the first female Secretary of State for Universities.

Christiane Scriviner (1926 -)
Between 1976-78, she was Secretary of State of Trade for Consumers' Protection and from 1989-95 European Communities Commissioner for Taxes, Revenue Harmonization and Consumer Policies.

1980
Henriette Magna
An engineer, she co-patented a computer data carrier for recording information in 1980.

1981
Yvette Roudy
In 1981, she became Secretary of State for Women's Rights.

1982
Martina Kempf (1958 -)
In 1982, she designed a fast lightweight voice recognition system. It was used in voice-controlled wheelchairs and surgical microscopes by 1986.

1983
Georgina Dufoix (1943 -)
From 1983-84, she was Secretary of State of Family, Population and Immigration and from 1984-86, Minister of National Solidarity and Social Affairs.

Francoise Barre-Sinoussi
(1938 -)
In 1983, this brilliant French research scientist was the woman responsible for identifying HIV and for discovering its role in the Aids virus. Head of the Retrovirus Biology Unit at the Pasteur Institute in Paris, Dr. Barre-Sinoussi has been awarded one of the French Republic's highest honours – the Chevalier de l'Ordre National de Merite.

1984
Simone Rozes
She was President of the Court of Appeals from 1984-88.

1986
Nicole Catanla
She was Secretary of State for Education (1986-88), Deputy Mayor of Paris (1989-95) and Vice-President of the Assemblee Nationale (1993-97).

1988
Catherine Trautmann (1952 -)
In 1988, she was Secretary of State for Seniors and Handicapped and from 1989-97 Mayor of Strassbourg.

1989
Anne Marie Couderc (1950 -)
In 1989-95, she was Deputy Mayor of Paris for Properties and Environment and Secretary of State by the Premier Minister for Employment in 1995.

1991
Edith Cresson (1934 -)
In 1981, she was appointed the first female Minister of Agriculture and when she was appointed Prime Minister of France in 1991, she became first woman in the history of France to hold this position. During her time in office, she drew attention and controversy for her outspoken attacks on Japanese businesses while battling French prejudice against women in politics. From 1995-99, she was Commissioner of the European Union for Science, Research,

Education and Youth. In 1999, she caused the downfall of the Commission when she refused to step down after it was learned that she was responsible of nepotism and mismanagement.

1994
Christine Jean

In 1980, the government planned to construct dams on the Loire, which would have flooded scenic, gorges, drowned a traditional village and altered the ecology of the entire valley downstream. Christine Jean crusaded to save the Loire by rallying the small opposition groups along the river into one strong national organization – SOS Loire Vivante, which, under her leadership, was able to provide constructive, unified opposition to the dam scheme. Finally, in 1994, she achieved a resounding victory.

Ariane Obolensky

She was Vice President of the World Bank from 1994-99.

Christine Ockrent (1945 -)

Nicknamed "la Reine", the powerful French journalist crowned her glittering media career in 1994 when she was made editor of L'Express, the French news magazine. She is highly respected for her serious approach and her courteous but tough interviewing techniques.

1993
Francoise de Veyrinas (1943 -)

From 1993-95, she was Deputy Mayor of Toulouse charged with Social Affairs. In 1995, she became Secretary of State for Difficult Neighborhoods by the Minister of Integration.

1995
Colette Codaccioni (1943 -)

In 1995, she became Minister of Solidarity between the Generations, Family and Women's Affairs.

1997
Domenique Voyonet

Presidential candidate in 1995, she became Minister of Environment and Physical Planning in 1997.

1998
Nichole Pery

From 1997-98, the Premier Minister charged her with the Mission for Languages and Regional Cultures. She became Secretary of State of Women's Rights and Professional Education in 1998.

GEORGIA

1957
Zinadia A. Kuadhadze

From 1957-59 she was Minister of Trade, Deputy Premier Minister from 1957-62, and Secretary of the Presidium from 1962-76.

1963
Irena Sarishvili-Chaturia (1963 -)

From 1992-99, she was a member of the Presidium of the Head

Committee of the Supreme Council and from 1994-99 Leader and Group Chairman of the National Democratic Party in Parliament. She became Deputy Premier Minister in 1993.

1993
Nino Otorovna Chkhobadze
(1966 -)
In 1993, she became Deputy Minister of National Resources and Environmental Protection and in 1995 Minister of National Resources and Environment. She was Deputy Minister of Trade and Foreign Economic Relations from 1998-99.

1998
Lana Gogoberidge
From 1998-99, she was Ambassador to the Council of Europe.

1999
Tamar G. Berushashvili
(1962 -)
From 1999-2000, she was Minister of Trade and Foreign Economic Relations.

GERMANY

1099
Hildegard (1099-1179)
Abbess of St. Rupert at Bingen-am-Rhine, she was the most prolific writer of the middle ages. She also wrote music and developed the plain chant into the Gregorian chant. Much of what she wrote is in mystical terms yet her ideas are modern. Her ideas on universal gravitation are correct and pre-date Newton's by several centuries.

1607
Anna Maria van Schurman
(1607-1678)
German scholar and author of theological works and an Ethiopian grammar, she studied Asian languages at Utrecht University.

1647
Maria Sibylla Merian
(1647-1717)
She is described as one of the very best botanical and natural life artists of her time. Merian produced a 3-volumne catalogue of flower engravings titled *Neues Blumen Buch* and published a 3-volumne set of insect paintings between 1679-1717. These books revolutionized zoology and botany because the insects were drawn from direct observation. She traveled to Surinam in South America where she was one of the first Europeans to observe and make notes of the local people and their customs in 1699. The publication of *Metamorphosis insectorum Surinamsium* in 1701 consisted of detailed paintings of the plants and insects of Surinam.

1715
Dorothea Erxleben
(1715-1762)
She became the first woman to earn a full medical degree from a German university, when she graduated from the University of Halle with King

Frederick's authorization in 1754. In 1749, she published *Rational Thoughts on Education of the Fair Sex.*

1750
Caroline Herschel
(1750-1848)
In 1786, she became the first woman to discover a comet and undertook the recataloging of Flamsteed's stellar catalog, which was published by the Royal Society in 1798. In 1846, the King of Prussia awarded her the Gold Medal for Science.

1797
Annette Elisabeth von Droste-Holschoff (1797 -?)
One of Germany's great poets of the era, her poem had bold imagination and strong lyrical tones with metric freedom. Her novella *The Jews' Beech Tree* published in 1842 is recognized as a landmark.

1814
Josepha Siebold
A German physician, she becomes the first woman in Germany to earn a doctorate in obstetrics in 1814.

1849
Luise Otto-Peter
(1819-1895)
She founded a movement urging women to participate in government and to demand equality in 1849.

1867
Kathe Kollwitz (1867 – 1945)
One of the most influential and famous German printmakers of the 20th century, she starkly depicted the plight of the poor and denounced the atrocities of war. She devoted herself to describing the human condition.

1868
Lida Gustava Heymann (1868 -?)
A noted feminist and peace advocate, she was one of the founders of the German women's suffrage movement.

1869
Henriette Pagelson
After obtaining her degree in the United States, she returns home to become the first woman dentist in Germany in 1869.

1873
Gertrude Baumer (1873-1954)
Leader of the German feminist movement, she became president of the League of German Women's Associations in 1910. She also edited the newspaper *Die Frau.*

1876
Paula Modersohn-Becker
(1876-1907)
A German painter, she is best known for her lyrical self-portraits and studies of children and old peasant women. She also produced still lifes and landscapes.

1885
Karen Horney (1885-1952)
Psychiatrist, she founded the neo-Freudian school of psychoanalysis based on the conclusion that neuroses are the result of emotional conflicts arising from childhood experiences and later disturbances in interpersonal relationships.

1888
Berta Benz
In 1888 she became the first woman to drive on a 60-mile trip cross-country in Germany in a motor-wagon (a 3-horse-power car with solid rubber tires).

1900
Agnes Hacker
In 1900, she became the first female physician hired by the Berlin police force.

1901
Lily Braun (1865-1916)
As an unorthodox Marxist, she campaigned against patriarchy and capitalism. In her 1901 book, *Die Frauenfraga*, she expressed her strong feminist views by asserting that the political economy rested on female labor.

1904
Hilde Bruch (1904 -)
Psychiatrist, she is best known for her work on eating disorders and wrote *The Golden Cage: The Enigma of Anorexia Nervosa* in 1978.

1905
Ruth Moufang (1905-1977)
In 1937, she became the first German woman with a doctorate employed as an industrial mathematician at the Krupps Research Institute. She published several papers on theoretical physics and helped create a new mathematical specialty in the algebraic analysis of projective planes that drew on a mixture of geometry and algebra.

1908
Merlitta Bentz
She created the drip coffee maker in 1908 in Germany. It is used today in 150 countries worldwide. Two-thirds of American coffee drinkers use the drip preparation method she created.

1910
Countess Marion Donhoff (1910-)
The publisher of Die Zeit, Germany's most influential liberal weekly, she has contributed strongly to the formation of Germany's Ost Politik – Bonn's opening of Eastern Europe. She helped establish the key think-tank known as the German Society for Foreign Policy. Her many articles and books deal with either aspects of German foreign policy or are biographical.

1928
Helene Mayer
She won the gold medal for fencing in the 1928 Amsterdam Olympics.

1929
Irmgard Flugge-Lotz
(1905 -)
In 1929, she obtained a doctorate from University of Hanover for a thesis on the mathematical theory of heat. Her contributions spanned a lifetime and included solving differential equations on the distribution of lift on wings, research in numerical methods to solve boundary layer problems in fluid dynamics and automatic control theory which made possible the development of jet aircraft. Her work involved finite difference methods and the use of computers.

1932
Kathe Kollwitz (1867-1945)
Artist and sculptor, she chose serious, tragic subjects with strong social or political content. After her son was killed in battle in 1914, she began a sculpture in granite, which was erected in Flanders as a memorial to all the young men killed in the war in 1932. Also, in 1928, she became the first woman to be elected to the Prussian Academy of Arts.

1932
Hannah Reitsch
In 1932, she began soaring and went on to become one of the first people to cross the Alps in a glider. As the world's first female test pilot and helicopter pilot, she flew everything the Third Reich had and went on to set more than 40 altitude and endurance records in motorless and powered aircraft in her lifetime. She was the only woman ever to be awarded the Iron Cross and Luftwaffe Diamond Clasp.

1937
Rita Sussmuth (1937 -)
As speaker of the German Parliament, she is the second most important person in the republic after the president. She champions women's causes, pleads for softer drug policy and addresses the problem of Aids and the family dilemmas of the country's 4-million unemployed.

1944
Erika Emmerich (1944 -)
President of the German Automobile Manufacturers Association, she is the first woman to head one of the most powerful industrial lobbies in Germany. Scarcely a week goes by without her urging the Government to lower wage costs and cut company taxes to make Germany more competitive.

1948
Petra Kelly (1948-1992)
Environmental activist, she was elected to the German parliament as a representative of the Green Party.

Christina von Braun
(1948 -)
A cultural theorist, author and filmmaker, she has created 50 documentary films and TV specials on cultural history themes, numerous books and interchange between the history of ideas and gender changes, in film and mediatheory, just as in the history of anti-Semitism.

1956
Charlotte Auerbach (1899 -)
Discoverer of mustard gas and expert on mutagens, she published *Genetics in the Atomic Age* in 1956.

1957
Ruth Moufang (1905-1977)
Because she was a woman, Hitler's minister of Education would not allow her to teach the mostly male student body. She therefore became first German woman with a doctorate in Mathematics to work as industrial mathematician. In 1946, she was finally able to accept a teaching position at the University of Frankfurt where, in 1957, she became the first woman in Germany to be appointed a full professor. She helped to create a new mathematical specialty in the algebraic analysis of projective planes that drew upon a mixture of geometry and algebra.

1958
Eleonora Straimer
She was appointed Ambassador to Yugoslavia from 1958-69,

the first female ambassador of her country.

1964
Geraldine Mock
A German pilot, she became the first woman to complete a solo flight around the world in 1964.

1972
Annemarie Renger (1919 -)
She became the first woman president of the West German Bundestag, the second highest political office in the nation.

1974
Eleonora Smid
She was appointed Ambassador to Guinea and Sierra Leone from 1974-78. In 1981, she became Acting Ambassador to Ivory Coast.

1988
Heffa Schucking
Highly effective in influencing environmental policy, she prepared the now-famous Rainforest Memorandum in 1988, which documented the country's responsibility for rainforest destruction and called for an end to German funding of destructive activities in primary forests. In 1992, she founded Urgewald, a small organization that effectively challenges the conventional development model and provides concrete support to local communities fighting destructive projects in the Third World. In 1995, the organization of Urgewald

succeeded in stopping plans to build a dam in one of the last ecologically intact valleys in the Himalayas – the Arun Valley in Nepal.

1995
Christiane Nusslein-Volhard
(1942-)
She was co-recipient of Nobel Prize in Medicine in 1995 for discoveries concerning the genetic control of early embryonic development.

GREECE
1083
Anna Comnena (1083-1153)
She is considered the world's first female historian and a major source of information about the reign of her father Alexius I. Her works are full of details of daily life at court and the deed of her family. In 1138, she began serious work on *Alexiad*, a 15-volumne history of her family, the Comneni.

1847
Soteria Aliberty
(1847-1929)
Teacher and feminist, she founded the first feminist association called Ergani Athena. She was the first person to compile biographies of Greek women entitled *Biographies of Greek Women* which was published in the 1880's.

1861
Callirhoe Parren
(1861-1940)
A leading figure in Greek feminism, she started publishing *Efimeris ton Kyrion* (Ladies Newspaper) in 1887, the first feminist publication in Greece exclusively edited by women. Its campaign for women's rights resulted in the first successful protective legislation for women. In 1889, she published *Women's History*.

1872
Kalliopi Kehajia
An educator and feminist, she established the Society for Promoting Women's Education in 1872.

1896
Angelique G. Panayodatou
In 1896, she was the first woman to graduate from the medical school of the University of Athens. She wrote a history of hygiene among the ancient Greeks.

1920
Maria Svolou
As inspector of labor in the Ministry of Economics, she was the first person to reveal the appalling working and housing conditions of the poor women. She took great interest in working class women and struggled to improve their situation.

Avra Theodoropoulou
(1880-1963)
She was founder of the League for Women's Rights in Athens, Greece, in 1920. A committed feminist, she did much in her country to further equal rights for women. In 1911, she founded the School for Working Women in Athens.

1925
Melina Mercouri
(1925-1944)
She won international fame as actor before becoming Minister of Culture for Greece's first socialist government. She increased arts funding and tried to retrieve the Elgin Marbles from England.

1937
Loula Anagnostaki (1937-)
Playwright, her first play *Dianyktereuse* dealt with the different feelings of 2 people of different generations.

1956
Lina Tsaldaris (1897 -?)
In 1956, she was named Welfare Minister, the first woman in the Greek cabinet.

1981
Maria Kyproatako-Perraki
She was Deputy Minister of Health and Welfare from 1981-85.

1982
K. Kokkta
In 1982, she became the first woman manager of the Bank of Greece.

1987
Elizabeth Papazoi
She was appointed Ambassador to Cuba from 1987-92, the first woman ambassador of her country.

1989
Dora Bakoyiannis
She was an elected Member of Parliament in Greece and an international leader of the first order. Her dedicated and tireless efforts toward the new Democratic Party, education, equal rights and women's issues have earned her a place of honor in the hearts of the people. She overcame the traditional role of women in Greek society to achieve great strides not only for her country but also for people throughout the world. The policies and changes she has initiated have affected and will continue to affect the lives of people throughout the world.

GREENLAND

1686
Gertrud Rask Egede
(1686-1758)
Missionary and nurse, she had a ship named after her and appeared on a Greenland stamp.

1943

Agnete Johanne Davidsen (1943 -)
She was Minister of Social Condiitons (1983-84, Deputy Mayor (1991-93) and Mayor (1993) of Nuuk (the Capital) and member of the Landsting (1995-97).

1953

Elisabeth Johansen (1917-1993)
From 1953-75, she was Member of the Landsrad and from 1971-75 President-by-Age.

1956

Marianne Jensen (1956 -)
She was Mayor of Ililussat/ Jakobshavn, member of the Landstinget since 1995 and Minister of Environment and Health from 1995-99.

1984

Henriette Rasmussen (1950 -)
From 1984-95, she was Member of the Landsting and its Vice-Chairman from 1987-91. In 1995, she became Advisor to the United Nations High Commissioner for Human Rights and Advisor of International Labor Organization (ILO) for Aboriginal Affairs in 1996.

1995

Benedikte Thorsteinson (1950 -)
Former Deputy Mayor of Qaqortoq, she became Minister of Social Affairs and Labor in 1995.

1999

Lise Skifte Lennert (1948 -)
Former headmaster of a school in Nuuk, she became Minister of Culture, Education and Research in 1999.

HUNGARY

1863

Emmuska Orczy (1863-1947)
She is best known as the author of the *Scarlet Pimpernel*, which was published in 1905. She also wrote a series of detective stories that were more successful - the first detective novel *The Old Man in the Corner* was published in 1909.

1880

Margit Kaffka (1880-1918)
Feminist and pacifist, she is Hungary's first great female writer. Her pioneer work explored the inner psychology of her protagonists and her female heroes often reject traditional roles but are frustrated by the lack of alternatives for women.

1892

Therese Benedek (1892-1977)
She became a psychoanalyst and developed a lifelong interest in the psychology of women. She published five important books including Psychosexual Functions in Women in 1952.

1899

Kate Seredy (1899-1975)
As author of children's books, her writing is charming and sensible but her art is some of the most beautiful in

children's illustration. She has written and illustrated over 10 books. Her most famous is *The White Stag*, which won the Newberry Award in 1938.

1905
Rozsa Peter (1905-1977)
Founder of recursive function theory, she made major contributions to mathematical theory and worked to increase opportunities in mathematics for girls and young women. She became a contributing editor of the *Journal of Symbolic Logic* in 1937, and wrote a book, *Playing with Infinity*, in 1943, a discussion of ideas in number theory and logic. In 1951, she published a monograph, Recursive Function that earned her the states Kossuth Award. In 1976, she published *Recursive Functions in Computer Theory*.

1907
Anna Hajinal (1907-1976)
Hungarian poet and author of 13 books, she translated Shakespeare into Hungarian and co-founded a Budapest literary magazine in the 1930's.

1918
Rosika Schwimmer
(1877-1948)
A Hungarian feminist and pacifist, she was the world's first female ambassador. She was appointed to serve her country as Ambassador to Switzerland in 1918. In 1926, she founds the Hungarian Feministrak Egesulte, a feminist-pacifist organization instrumental in many of Hungary's social reforms including suffrage. She was nominated for the Nobel Peace Prize in 1948.

1934
Ilona Elek
The World Foil Champion in 1934, 1935 and 1951 and she was the only woman to win two Olympic gold medals in fencing - 1936 and 1948. She won an Olympic silver medal in 1952 at age 45.

1950
Joboni Magda
From 1950-58, she was Deputy Minister of Education and Director General of the National Library from 1958-89.

1952
Margit Korondi
A Hungarian athlete, she was the first woman to win an Olympic gold medal in 1952 in vault gymnastics in Helsinki, Finland – the first year this event was open to women.

1958
Benke Valerie
Former President of the Radio/TV Corporation, she became Minister of Education and Culture from 1958-61. In 1967, she was Member of the President's Council.

1963
Vass Metzker Erzebet
She was President of the Orszagule from 1963-67. As President of the National

Assembly, she was Deputy Head of State.

1973
Ilona Burka
At 20, she becomes Hungary's youngest Member of Parliament in 1973.

1982
Ferencne Nyitrai
In 1982, she became State Secretary for the Central Office of Statistics.

1990
Tade Alody
From 1990-91, she was Deputy Secretary of Foreign Affairs. In 1991, she became Ambassador to Greece and to United Kingdom in 1995.

Botos Katalin
She became State Secretary of Finance in 1990 and was Minister without Portfolio of the Bank System from 1990-93.

Fluckne Papacsay Edith
From 1990-94, she was Deputy State Secretary of Justice and Administrative State Secretary of Justice from 1994-98.

1992
Laszlone Tarjan
In 1992, she became Political State Secretary of Environment and Rural Development.

1994
Csiha Judith
She was Political State Secretary of Justice (1994-96) and Minister without Portfolio

with responsibility for privatization (1996-98).

1999
Hankiss Agnes
In 1999, she became Government Commissioner and State Secretary for Europalia.

ICELAND
1239
Joreior Hermundardottir I Miojumdal (1239-?)
Her visionary poetry written in Old Norse was a mirror of the apprehension and political tension characteristic of her time – the decline of the Icelandic republic. It also represents the largest body of work attributed to any single women in the Old Norse period.

1856
Briet Bjarnhedinsdottir
(1856-1940)
In 1907, she founded the Icelandic Women's Association.

1910
Auour Audens (1910 -)
Former Mayor of Reykjavik, she became Minister of Justice and Church Affairs from 1970-72.

1930
Ragnhilour Helgadottir
President of the Neori Deild from 1961-62 and 1974-78, she was President of the Nordic Council from 1975-76. She was Minister of Education from 1983-85 and Minister of Health, Social Affairs and Communication from 1985-87.

1953
Valgreour Sverrisdottir
(1953 -)
Former Vice-President of the Nordic Council, she became Minister of Trade and Industry in 1999.

1961
Siv Fredleifsdottir (1961 -)
In 1999, she became Minister of Environment and Nordic Cooperation.

1980
Vigdis Finnbogadottir (1930 -)
In 1980, she was elected President of Iceland, the world's first democratically elected female president. Her fight for the culture and language of Iceland has silenced conservative critics who maintained that a divorced mother could not run a country. She served as Chairman of Alliance Francaise and has given lectures abroad on Icelandic culture. In 1972, 9 years after her divorce, she adopted a daughter - this was one of the first adoptions by a single person in Iceland. Since 1976, she has been member of Advisory Committee on Cultural Affairs of the Nordic Council.

1983
Salome Borleisdottir
In 1983, she became President of the Upper House of the Albing and in 1991 President of the Albing and member of the collective vice-presidency of the Republic.

1990
Guorun Helgarsdottir
From 1990-92, she was Member of the Vice-presidency and President of the High Court. She has been the only female High Court Judge since 1986.

1991
Sigriour Aios Snaeuvarr
From 1991-96, she was Ambassador to Sweden and Finland, the first woman ambassador of her country.

1995
Ingibjorg Palmadottir (1949 -)
Former Deputy Mayor of Akranes, she was Minister of Health and Social Welfare from 1995-99 and became Minister of Health in 1999.

2000
Sigriour Ann Boroardottir
In 2000, she became President of the Nordic Council.

IRELAND
1530
Grace O'Malley (1530-1603)
She was a famous pirate, seafarer, trader and chieftain in Ireland in the 1500's. Her strength and leadership saw that her clan were mostly unaffected by the spread of English rule throughout Ireland. During her lifetime, she also had been able to preserve the old Gaelic way of life.

1550
Graine Ni Maille (1550-1600)
She was an Irish princess who commanded a large fleet of war galleys, which wreaked havoc on the English navy, shipping, and coastal towns.

1800
Maria Edgeworth (1767-1849)
Author, in 1800 she publishes *Castle Rackrent* that condemns the rapacious absentee landlords who keep the Irish peasantry in poverty.

1820
Mary Anne Sadlier
(1820-1903)
She wrote 60 volumes of work – from domestic novels to historical romances to children's catechisms. In *Life in Galway*, she was one of the first fiction writers to address the Irish Famine. Her novels also narrate the Trans-Atlantic voyage west of millions of immigrants.

1822
Frances Power Cobbe
(1822-1904)
She was involved in various philanthropic causes including the schooling of the poor and the treatment of girls in workhouses. From the 1860's, she was a committed feminist, writing on such areas as wife battering and the exclusion of women from the vote. She was a devoted anti-vivisectionist from the 1870's, campaigning energetically against the use of life animals in scientific research.

1847
Alice Stopford Green (1847 -)
Historian, she proved the Irish had a rich culture before English rule. An ardent supporter of Irish independence, she was a member of the first Irish Senate.

1852
Lady Isabella Augusta Gregory
(1852-1932)
Playwright and folklorist, in 1902 she published her translations of some of the native Irish epics in *Cuchulain of Muirthemne*. In 1920, she published her serious folklore study *Visions and Beliefs in the West of Ireland* which earned her the epithet "mother of folklore".

1858
Katherine Tynan (1858 -?)
A prolific writer, she wrote over 105 popular novels, twelve collections of short stories and innumerable newspaper articles apart from two anthologies, five plays, seven books of devotion and one book about her beloved dogs. Some of her fiction champions the rights of women, as do many of her later newspaper articles.

1866
Mrs. Seumas Macmanus
(Anna Johnston) (1866-1902)
Writer of prose and verse, she began publishing in 1881 and contributed to most of the Irish magazines and newspapers of her time and to Harper's Magazine, The New York

Criterion, The Century and other American periodicals.

1873
Peig Sayers (1873-1958)
She was the first person to record over 400 Irish stories and folksongs.

1896
Mairead Ni Ghrada
(1896-1971)
She was the first major woman playwright in the Irish language and author of school textbooks and children's books in Irish. Her many plays in Irish were aimed at the conditions of her time. Known to the Irish public at large as a radio broadcaster, she was the first female broadcaster in either Britain or Ireland.

1903
Kathleen Lonsdale
(1903-1971)
She received many honors for her work as crystallographer, physicist and chemist. Her scientific work included theory of space groups, divergent beam x-ray photography of crystals and diffuses x-ray single crystal reflection. In 1956 she became Dame Commander of British Empire and President of the International Union of Crystallographers.

1912
Mary Lavin (1912–1996)
Generally acknowledged as one of Ireland's greatest short story writers, her stories while of their time carried subtle social commentaries. Her first collection of stories, *Tales from Bective Bridge* won the James Tait Black memorial prize in 1943. She published a total of 13 collections of short stories and two novels.

1920
Elis Dillon (1920-1994)
At first she wrote children's books in Irish and English, then novels and detective stories. Her work was translated into 14 languages. In 1973, she wrote a large historical novel about the road to Irish independence in the 19th and 20th centuries, *Across the Bitter Sea*, which was an instant bestseller.

1932
Edna O'Brien (1932 -)
A novelist and short-story writer, much of her writing is concerned with the position of women in society, their lack of fulfillment and the repressive nature of their upbringing.

1950
Josephine McNeill
In 1950-55, she was appointed Ambassador to The Netherlands, the first female ambassador of her country.

1967
Susan Jocelyn Bell Burnell
(1943-)
She constructed and operated an 81.5-megaherz radio telescope while at Cambridge,

to study interplanetary scintillation of compact radio sources. For the first time in the history of radio astronomy, a large area of the sky had been repeatedly surveyed with an extremely sensitive radio telescope tuned to meter wavelengths. Her subsequent discovery in 1967 of the first pulsar ranks as an important milestone in the history of astrophysics. Pulsars represent rotating neutron stars that emit brilliant flashes of electromagnetic radiation at each revolution like beacons from a lighthouse.

1973
Mary Tinney
An Irish diplomat, she became ambassador to Sweden in 1973.

1976
Mairead Corrigan (1944 -)
In 1976, she founded the Northern Irish Peace Movement and was awarded the Nobel Peace Prize for trying to bring peace to Northern Ireland.

Eileen Gray (1879-1976)
A professional architect and designer, she was the first Irish female designer to be the subject of a retrospective exhibition at the Victoria and Albert Museum in London in 1976.

1977
Marie Geoghegan Quinn
In 1977-79, she became Minister of State of Industry and Energy, Ireland's first woman parliamentary secretary. She was Minister of the Gaeltacht (Gaelic or Irish speaking areas) in 1979-81 and Minister of State of the Taoiseach (Prime Minister) with responsibility as Coordinator of Government Policy and for European Questions.

1982
Tras Horan
She was Chairperson of the Senate and member of the collective vice-presidency of the country from 1982-83 and Vice-President from 1983-87.

1986
Avril Doyle (1949 -)
Former Mayor of Wexford, she was Minister of State of Finance and Environment from 1986-87 and Minister of State of the Deputy Premier, Finance, Transport, Energy and Communication from 1994-97 with responsibility for Consumers of Public Services.

1989
Mary Harney
From 1989-92, she was Minister of State of Environment and in 1997 she became Deputy Premier and Minister of Enterprises and Employment and Minister of Trade.

1990
Mary Robinson (1944 -)
Former Professor of Law, she was President of Ireland from 1990-97. She had outstanding qualifications and has worked

in the area of human rights with special expertise in constitutional and European human rights law. Since 1997, she was appointed Assistant Secretary General and United Nations High Commissioner of Human Rights. She will assume principal responsibility for the human rights machinery throughout the United Nations system.

1993
Margaret Maccurtain
A Dominican Sister, she was the prioress of Sion Hill Convent. In 1993, she won the award of the Eire Society of Boston Gold Medal for her research into the history of Irish women. She campaigned for the abolition of corporal punishment in schools, speaks out publicly against domestic violence and on behalf of birth control, founded the first community college in Ireland and was an outspoken fighter against Apartheid and gave impassioned speeches on human rights.

1997
Mary McAleese (1951-)
She was appointed Director of the Institute of Professional Legal Studies, which trains barristers and solicitors for the legal profession in Northern Ireland in 1987. From 1993-97, she was Prochancellor of University of Belfast. In 1997, she was inaugurated as the 8th President of Ireland, the first person from Northern Ireland and British citizen to be elected president of Ireland.

1997
Liz O'Donnell
In 1997, she was Minister of State of Foreign Affairs with special responsibility for Overseas Development Assistance and Human Rights.

Mary Wallace
She was Minister of State of Justice, Law Reform and Equality with special responsibility for Equality and Disabilities in 1997.

ITALY
1236
Bettina Gozzadini
She was appointed to the Chair of Law at the University of Bologna in 1236.

1469
Laura Cereta (1469-1499)
An ardent feminist, her letters include many feminist issues in addition to the issues of contemporary Italian humanism. A staunch defender of women, she discussed the oppression of women in marriage, the right of women to education in the arts and sciences and women's contribution to history and culture.

1490
Properzia de Rossi
(1490-1530)
She was first known for her complex miniature sculptures using an unorthodox medium of

apricot, peach or cherry stones. Later she was commissioned to decorate the altar of Santa Maria del Baraccano and produce a marble sculpture for the church of San Pedro in Bologna.

1532
Sofonisba Anguissola
(1532-1625)
Educated as a painter, she became a celebrated portrait painter at the court of Phillip II of Spain. She was the first important woman artist of the Renaissance, and the first female painter to enjoy international reputation.

1552
Lavinia Fontana (1552-1614)
The first woman painter to have had a successful artistic career, she did not just produce portraits or still life's but small and large scale biblical and mythological works with many figures, including make and female nudes. She also painted public altarpieces, a rare distinction for a woman artist.

1555
Moderata Fonte (1555-1592)
A feminist broadside, her best-known work, *The Worth of Women*, deserved wider recognition. She used a popular literary style, the dialogue, to breathe new life into the defense genre by injecting new issues, new arguments and new characters into the drama.

1581
Francesca Caccini (1581 -?)
Noted Italian musician, her *Primo Libro* published in 1618 was the most extensive collection of songs by a single composer to that date. Her opera *La liberazione du Ruggiero dall'isola d'Alcina* was performed in 1625 and is considered the first opera composed by a woman.

1593
Artemisia Gentileschi
(1593-1652)
She was known as one of the most important Italian Baroque painters, especially known for her skilful use of strong contrasts of light and dark and her powerful images of women characters from the Old Testament. She became the first woman elected to the Academy of Design.

1638
Elisabetta Sirani
(1638-1665)
A professional painter and engraver by age 17, she completed approximately 170 paints, 14 etchings, and a number of drawings. One of her paintings "Virgin and Child" was featured on the Christmas stamp issued by the United States in 1994. It was the first time that an historical work by a woman artist was depicted on a Christmas stamp.

1645

Elena Lucrezia Cornaro Piscopia (1645-1684)
Venetian noblewoman, she becomes the first woman to earn a Ph.D. in 1678. She is related to the former Queen of Cyprus.

1675

Rosalba Carriera (1675-1757)
She pioneered the new genre of portraits done in pastel. She began her career painting snuffboxes, but her skill as a portrait artist made her famous all over the continent. She was elected to the Academie Royale in 1720.

1718

Maria Gaetana Agnesi (1718-1799)
A child prodigy, she spoke six languages by age 11. Her mathematical textbook *Istituzioni analitiche* was published in 1784 and became famous throughout Italy.

1837

Francesca Alexander (1837-1917)
Artist and author, she kept elements of Tuscany and northern Italian folk culture alive in her works.

1854

Catrina Scarpellini
In 1854, She organized the Meterological Ozonometric station in Rome and discovered a comet. In 1872, Italy struck a gold medal honoring her work in statistics.

1856

Matilde Serapo (1856 -?)
Noted novelist, she founded the Neapolitan daily newspaper Il Giorno.

1905

Maria Cinquini-Cibrario (1905-1992)
Her work and research as a mathematician helped to achieve the classification of linear partial differential equations. She is credited with solving the Coursat problem for hyperbolic nonlinear equation of the second order.

1907

Maria Montessori (1870-1952)
She was first woman in Italy to earn a medical degree. In 1907 she opened her first nursery school, "Casa dei Bambini" in San Lorenze. Her ideas are the basis of today's preschool and daycare programs. In 1915, the first Montessori nursery school was opened in the United States but the method was not widely used until the 1950's.

1926

Grazia Deledda (1871-1936)
She was a writer whose study of Sardinian folklore and the man-earth mythical cycle helped her express ancient Bronze Age Sardinia. In 1926, she was awarded the Nobel Prize in Literature for her idealistically inspired writings, which with clarity picture life on her native

island and with depth and sympathy deal with human problems in general.

1930
Oriana Fallaci (1930 -) Writer and journalist, her interviews with national leaders were collected in *"Interviews with History"* in 1976.

1944
Cecilia Danieli (1944 -) She called the "Iron Lady" of Italy because of her success in building her family's steel business into an international power. In 1980, she became Managing Director of the business.

1950
Ilda Boccassini (1950 -) Most famous frontline magistrate of Italy, she tracked down and brought to trial the alleged Mafia killers of the crimefighter and folk hero Giovanni Falcone. The Cosa Nostra blew her up in May 1992.

1958
Maria-Teresa de Filippis In 1958, she was the first woman to compete in a European Grand Prix auto race.

1959
Irene Pivetti (1959 -) She became the youngest speaker of the Italian Parliament in 1992. She rules the largely male Parliament with an iron hand and is contemptuous of male pomposity

and chauvinism, arguing that the obsession with her looks, dress and private life would not exist if she were a man.

1969
Tina Anselmi In 1969, she became the first woman to serve in the Italian cabinet.

1972
Leonilde Iotti (1926-1999) She was Vice-President of the Camera dei Diputati (Chamber of Deputies) from 1972-79 and President from 1979-92. As President of the Chamber of Deputies, she was 3rd in the state hierarchy after the President and President of the Senate. In 1997-99, she was Vice President of the Council of Europe.

1979
Maria Magnani Noya She was Undersecretary of Industry from 1979-80 and Trade and from 1981-82, Undersecretary of Health. In 1989-95, she became Vice President of the European Parliament.

1980
Jolanda Brunetti Goetz In 1980, she was appointed Ambassador to Burma, the first woman ambassador of her country. Since 1996, she was Ambassador to Uzbekistan.

1981
Teresita de Angelis She founded the National Association of Housewives to

work for pensions for housewives over 55 in 1981.

1983
Susanna Agnelli
She was Undersecretary of Foreign Affairs from 1983-91, Minister of Foreign Affairs from 1995-96 (2nd in the Cabinet) and Member of the European Union Troyka of Foreign Ministers from 1995-96. In 1996, she was President of the European Union Council of Ministers.

Elda Puce
In 1983, she became the first woman mayor of a major Italian city – Palermo.

1985
Patrizia Toia
Between 1985-95, she was Regional Councilor and Member of the Government for Health and Budget of Lombardia and from 1999-2000, she was Minister without Portfolio for the European Union.

1986
Rita Levi-Montalcini (1901-)
Italian biologist educated at the University of Turin who shared the 1986 Nobel Prize in physiology for contributions to the understanding of growth factors in human development. She was also cited for her discovery of the factor that promotes the growth of cells in the peripheral nervous system.

1987
Rosa Russo Jervolino (1936 -)
From 1987-89, she was Minister for Special Affairs, from 1998-99 Minister of the Interior and Minister in charge of coordination of the Civil Defense. She was a presidential candidate in 1999.

1989
Emma Bonino
Between 1989-94, she was Secretary of the Camera dei Deputati and from 1995-99 European Union Commissioner.

1991
Margarita Bonivier
From 1991-92, she was Minister of Immigration and from 1992-93 Minister of Tourism and Cultural Sights.

1992
Rossella Artioni
She was Undersecretary of Universities from 1992-93 and Undersecretary of Industry, Commerce and Artisans from 1993-94.

Liliana Ferraro (1944 -)
In 1992, she became Director-General for Criminal Affairs at the Italian Justice Ministry, becoming the first woman to hold such a senior post in the Italian civil service.

Margherita Hack
Former Director of the Trieste Astronomical Observatory, she became Director of the Inter-University Regional Center for

Astrophysics and Cosmology in Trieste in 1992, where she studies the atmospheres of stars.

1995
Susanna Agnelli (1923 -)
She was summoned to be Foreign Minister when Italy acquired a temporary "technocratic" government in 1995. She was mayor and Euro MP and served for eight years as a foreign ministry official.

KAZAKSTHAN

1959
Zaure S. Omarova
She was Deputy Premier Minister (1959-63), Deputy Chairman of the Government of Alma-Ata (1963-66) and Minister of Social Affairs (1966-80).

1966
Balzan Bultrikova
Former Minister of Social Security, she became Deputy Premier Minister for Culture and Minister of Foreign Affairs from 1966-72.

1974
Manura Mergaliovna Akhmentova
From 1974-80, she was Deputy Minister of Local Industry and in 1980 became Minister of Social Affairs.

1991
Amoral Khydarovna Arystanbekova (1948 -)
Former Minister of Foreign Affairs, she was appointed Ambassador to the United Nations from 1991-99. She was Vice-President of the 49th Session of the United Nations General Assembly from 1994-95. Since 1999, she has been Ambassador to France.

1992
Rosa B. Kutubayeva
In 1992, she became Deputy Chair of the National Bank.

1997
Aitkul Baigaziyevna Samakova
From 1997-99, she was Deputy Minister of Industry and Trade. In 1999, she became Minister without Portfolio and Chairman of the National Committee on Family and Women's Issues.

1999
Madiana B. Jarbussynova
In 1999, she was appointed Ambassador to the United Nations in New York.

KOSOVO

1921
Katarina Patrnogic (1921 -)
She was Secretary for Finance in 1950-60's and Vice President of the Assembly.

1928
Drita Dobroshi (1928 -)
In the 1970's, she was President of Chamber of Education and Culture of the Assembly.

1960
Milica Pajkovic (1921 -)
In the 1960's, she was President of the Chamber for Social Affairs and Health of the Montenegrin Assembly.

1987

Kagusha Jashari

From 1987-89, she was Chairman of the Provincial Executive Council and in 1989 Chief Secretary of the Communist Party. She was forced to resign after the first Kosovan riots about the Serbians in the republic.

1998

Verica Aleksic-Tepavcevic

In 1998, she was Provincial Secretary of Finance. She was part of the Serbian dominated administration that took over parallel to the Yugoslav attempts to force the Albanians out of the Province.

KYRGYZSTAN

1952

Sakin Bergmantrovna

From 1952-61, she was Deputy Minister of Finance and Deputy Premier Minister from 1961-80.

1982

Shakira B. Al'dasheva

She was Minister of Consumers' Protection (1982-92) and Deputy Premier Minister (1989-91).

1992

Rosa Isakovan Otunbaeva (1950 -)

She was Ambassador to United States and Canada from 1992-93, Turkey in 1994 and United Kingdom since 1996.

1995

Larisa Gutnichenko

From 1995-96, she was Minister of Justice and from 1996-98 Deputy Premier Minister for Social and Cultural Policy.

1997

Zamira Eshabmetova

In 1997, she was appointed Ambassador to the United Nations.

1998

Mira Jangaracheva (1952 -)

She was Deputy Mayor of Bishkeh from 1992-95 and Presidential Advisor of Social Affairs from 1995-96. In 1998, she became Minister of Labor and Social Welfare.

LATVIA

1861

Anna Brigadere (1861-1933)

Her masterpiece, the autobiographic history of novels (*Dieus, daba, darbs, Skarbos vejos* and *Akmenu sprosa*) has always been one of the most admired works in Latvian literature especially the first novel.

1922

Rita Kukaine (1922 -)

She graduated cum laude from the University of Latvia Faculty of Medicine in 1946. Her interests include oncovirology, immunology and virus infections. In 1962, she became Director of August Kirchenstein Institute of Microbiology and Virology, Latvian Academy of Sciences.

1926
Gertrude Enina (1926 -)
She discovered the determination method for the interference of arm co-ordination and has invented a device for the determination of the fields of vision for neurological patients and a device for the determination of the cerebrospinal liquid pressure.

1928
Irena Plavina (1928 -)
She is leading researcher at University of Latvia Institute of Solid State Physics. Her interests include photostimulated luminescence and mechanism of radiation storage in alkali halides.

1929
Aina Blinkena (1929 -)
Professor at Latvian Language Institute, University of Latvia, her interests include history of Latvian literary language. She has written many books on Latvian language over the years.

Jevgenija Shvarca (1929 -)
Her main inventions are the synthesis and application of monoethyl ethers for the extraction of boric acid from salt solutions. The synthesis of extractants has been introduced in the production of the plant "Biolar" for the analsyis of steel and nickel standard samples. Other inventions such as metal corrosion inhibitors have been introduced in 1987 in the production of microbiological preparations.

1935
Mara Skrivele (1935 -)
She is a researcher at the State Horticulture Plant Breeding and Experimental Station. Her research on the economical efficiency of fruit growing and the cultivation of intensive gardens are of particular importance now when commercial fruit-grown begins to develop in Latvia and intensive apple-gardens are being planted.

1936
Gaida Maruta Sedmale (1936 -)
Professor at the Institute of Silicate Materials, she is interested in the development of glassy high temperature coatings and research of their structure and qualities. Her main invention is enamel for the protection of niobium and her patents include enamel coating and heat reflective glass.

Regina Zhuk (1936 -)
As head of Research Group, Laboratory of Nucleic Acid Components, Latvian Institute of Organic Synthesis, her interests include drug development, synthesis of neucleoside analogues and anticancer, antiviral and immuniomodulating drug design. Her main research has been the design of two original drugs – anticancer *Ftorafur* and antiviral *Furavir*.

1942

Inara Turka (1942 -)
She is Head of the Department of Plant Protection, Faculty of Agriculture, Latvia University of Agriculture. Her interests include integrated plant protection, potato viruses, diagnostic mehtods and seed potato testing, forecasting and warning systems for plant protection and agrochemicals.

1948

Iveta Ozolanta (1948 -)
She became Vice-Rector for Science, Latvian Medical Academy in 1995. Her interests include biomaterials and biomechanics of biological tissue, of cardiovascular system and novel vascular grafts. She has patents for the method of evolution of vascular transplantat, artivical aortic heart valve and woven vascular graft.

1949

Raita Karnite (1949 -)
In 1997, she became Director of the Institute of Economics Ltd. Her interests include public finance, macroeconomic development, and economic aspects of culture and social issues. She is also a member of the Advisory Council of the National Economy to the Minister of Economy, Republic of Latvia.

Baiba Rivza (1949-)
Dean of the Faculty of Economics, Latvia University of Agriculture, her interests include European Union agricultural policy, rural development and marketing. She became President of the Latvia Academy of Agriculture and Forestry Sciences in 1991.

1952

Inna Steinbuka (1952 -)
Economist, her interests include analysis and simulation of macroeconomic development of Latvia and fiscal policy in Latvia - analysis and prospects. In 1991, she became Ministry of Finance, Republic of Latvia. Currently, she is advisor to Executive Director, International Monetary Fund.

1970

Vera Vasilevna Leonova
She was Head of the Central Committee of the Department of Industry and Transport from 1970-76 and became Chairman of the State Committee of Labor in the Council of Ministers in 1976.

1990

Vita Anda Teravda (1963 -)
From 1990-94, she was Deputy State Secretary of Foreign Ministry and Minister for State Reform from 1994-95. She turned down the post of Minister of Defense in 1995.

1991

Anna Zigure
In 1991, she was appointed Ambassador to Finland, the first female ambassador of her country.

1992
Maija Eglite
She became Director of the Institute of Occupational and Environmental Health in 1992. Her interests include heavy metals in the workplace, occupational respiratory diseases, occupational allergic diseases, and environment and small doses of ionizing radiation.

1995
Ilga Kretuse
She was Chancellor of the Siema from 1995-96. As Chairman of the Assembly, she was Deputy Head of State.

1998
Inese Vaidere
She was State Minister for Environment from 1998-99 and became Presidential Advisor on Economical and Political Affairs in 1999.

1999
Brigita Busmane
In 1999, she published *Dialectal Atlas of Latvian*, the first important effort of Latvian areal dialectology and geolinguistics with great international significance.

Vaira Vike-Freiberga
(1937 -)
Latvian politician and psychologist, she became president of Latvia in 1999 – the 1st freely elected woman president in Eastern Europe.

LIECHTENSTEIN

1955
Andrea Willi (1955 -)
Between 1987-93, she worked in the Ministry of Foreign Affairs and member of a number of international delegations, 1991 Ambassador to European Trade Organization and 1992-93 ambassador to United Nations in Geneve. In 1993, she became Regierungsratin for External Relations, Culture, Youth, Sport Family and Equal Opportunities, third in the cabinet.

1987
Andrea Willi (1955 -)
Between 1987-93, she worked in the Ministry of Foreign Affairs and was a member of a number of international delegations. In 1991, she was Ambassador to EFTA (European Trade Organization) and from 1992-93 Ambassador to United Nations in Geneve. She became Regierungsratin for External Relations, Culture, Youth, Sport, Family and Equal Opportunity in 1993, 3rd in the Cabinet.

1989
Maria Bratliner
From 1989-93, she was Vice-Regierungsratin for Economic Affairs and since 1992, she is Secretary of Vaderlandische Union.

1990
Claudia Fritsche
In 1990, she was appointed Ambassador to the United

Nations, the first female ambassador of her country.

1993
Cornelia Gassner-Mott
She was Regierungsratin for Construction and Traffic from 1993-97.

1997
Erina Frick
Since 1997, she has been Vice-Regierungsratin of Education, Environment and Transport.

LITHUANIA

1845
Julija Beniuseviciute (1845-1921)
One of the classic writers of Lithuanian realism, her novellas and short stories gave detached and critical portrayal of rural Lithuanian life at the end of the 19th and beginning of the 20th century. In addition to their literary value, her works are of ethnographic interest for the accurate depiction of folk custom and traditions in the Lithuania province of Samogita. In 1900, she became active in the Lithuanian cultural resistance movement and took part in early efforts for women's emancipation when she participated in the first Lithuanian women's conference in 1907.

1918
Jadvyga Chodakauskaite-Tubeliene
She was Deputy Chief of Mission to Switzerland from 1918-19.

1921
Marija Gimbutas (1921-1994)
An internationally recognized archaeologist whose research into early European cultures convinced her and other experts that women were revered as goddesses 6,000 to 8,000 years ago and that they presided over cultures that was free of war. She was an authority on the prehistoric incursions of Indo-European speaking people into Europe and how they changed society there. Also, she was the main advocate of the theory that languages like English, German, French, and Iranian are all related because a war-like people speaking the tongue ancestral to all Indo-European languages conquered Europe and imposed their language on the conquered. Her inter-disciplinary approach and studies created a new field – <u>archaeomythology</u>.

1929
Ona Masiotene (1883-1949)
Active on behalf of women throughout her life, she founded the Alliance of Lithuanian Women in 1905 in Vilnius. In 1917 she organized the Lithuanian Women's Freedom Association in Moscow, through which she campaigned for Lithuanian independence. In 1929, she founded and was first president of the Council of Lithuanian Women.

1939
Elvyra Kuncvciene (1939 -)
In 1991, she was Economic
Advisor of the Premier
Minister and from 1991-92
Minister of Finance.

1946
Genia Sakin
In 1946, she became the only
plastic surgeon in the Allied
armies during World War II.

1948
Vidmante Jasukaityte
(1948-)
Poet and author, she published
her first novel *Stebuklinga
patuoriu 'ole* in 1981 which
became a unique phenomenon in
Lithuanian literature. In the
book many lyrical passages
combine with a fantastic note
set in a period of fighting
for Lithuanian independence
while portraying the history
of six generations of women.

1959
**Leokaida Ivozovna Dirginskaite
Pihusenko** (1918 -)
She was Vice President from
1959-69 and 1976-89 and Deputy
Premier in charge of Culture
and Minister of Foreign
Affairs from 1960-76.

1971
Iaina B. Tatsiavichene
Between 1971-73, she was Head
of the Central Committee
Department of Trade and Public
Service and from 1973-89
Minister of Social Affairs.

1989
Kasimiera Danute Prunskiene
From 1989-90, she was Deputy
Premier and Minister of
Economy and from 1990-91
Premier Minister.

1991
Laima Liucija Andrikiene
In 1991, she was Vice Minister
of Trade and Secretary General
of the Parliament from 1992-
93. She was Minister of
European Affairs (1997-98),
Minister of Industry and Trade
(1998) and Chair of the
Presidium of the Baltic
Assembly (1998-99).

1994
Irena Degutiene (1949 -)
A medical doctor, she was
Undersecretary in the Ministry
of Health from 1994-97. In
1997, she became Minister of
Social Affairs, Labor and
Women and in 1999 Acting
Premier Minister.

Halina Kobeckaite
In 1994, she was appointed
Ambassador to Estonia, the
first female ambassador of her
country.

1996
Aldona Baransuskiene (1947 -)
In 1996, she became Minister
of Construction and Urban
Development.

LUXEMBOURG

1896
**Charlotte, Grand Duchess of
Luxembourg** (1896 -?)
As constitutional queen from
1919 to 1964, she led the

country through the difficult days of World War II and helped it develop into a modern nation.

1967
Madeline Frieden-Kinnen
She was Secretary of State of Family, Social Solidarity, Youth, Population, National Education, Culture and Religious Affairs from 1967-69 and Minister of Family, Youth, Social Solidarity, Health, Culture and Religious Affairs from 1969-71.

1970
Colette Flesh (1934 -)
She was Mayor of Luxembourg (1970-80) and Deputy Premier Minister and Minister of Foreign Affairs, External Trade, Economy, Economy of the Middle Classes and Justice (1980-84). In 1980, she was President of the Council of Ministers of the European Economic Communities and from 1997-99 Director General of the General Directorate of Translation of the European Union.

1989
Lydie Err (1949 -)
Between 1989-98, she was President of the Foreign Affairs Committee, Vice-Chairman of the European Council in 1997 and State Secretary for Foreign Affairs, Foreign Trade and Cooperation and Secretary of State of Public Works from 1998-99.

Erna Hennicot-Schoepeges
Former Mayor of Walfendange, she was President of the Assemblee Nationale from 1989-94, Minister of National Education from 1995-99 and Minister of Higher Education and Public Works in 1999.

1992
Marie-Josee Jacobs (1950 -)
From 1992-95, she was Minister of Agriculture, Viniculture and Rural Development, in 1995 Minister of Family, Women's Promotion and Disabled and Minister of Social Solidarity in 1999.

1993
Arlette Conzemius-Parroud
She was appointed Ambassador to Council of Europe From 1993-98, the first woman ambassador of her country. In 1998, she became Ambassador to United States.

1998
Sylvia Lucas
In 1998, she became Deputy Representative to the United Nations.

1999
Lydie Polfer (1952 -)
Former Mayor of Luxembourg, she became Vice-Premier Minister and Minister of External Affairs and External Trade and Minister of Public Service and Administrative Reform in 1999.

MALTA

1955
Agatha Barbara (1927 -)
She became Minister of Culture and Education (1955-58 and 1971-74), the first female member of Maltese Parliament. After a distinguished career in Maltese politics, she was elected the first female president of the Republic of Malta in 1982. She has demonstrated particular concern for social legislation and women's rights.

1970
Alice Emo-Capodolisk
She was appointed Ambassador to Portugal from 1970-75, the first woman ambassador of her country.

1995
Giovanna Debono (1956 -)
From 1995-96, she was Parliamentary Secretary of Family Affairs in the Ministry of Social Affairs and in 1998 became Minister of Gozo, an island south of Malta.

1996
Helen Dalli
She was Parliamentary Secretary to the Office of Premier Minister of Women's Rights with cabinet status from 1996-98.

Miriam Spiteri Delbono
(1952 -)
In 1996-98, she was Speaker of the House of Representatives.

MACEDONIA

1949
Vera Dosta Aceva (1919 -)
Former Mayor of Skoplje, she was Minister of Agriculture from 1949-52.

1986
Radmilla Kiprijanova-Radovanovic (1940 -)
She was Member of the Executive Council and President of the Committee for Science, Technology and Information Services (1986-90), Deputy Federal Secretary for Development of Yugoslavia (1990-92) and Vice President of the Government (1998-99). From 1994-98, she was Rector of the University of St. Cyril and Methodius in Skopje.

1990
Sofija Todorova (1947 -)
Between 1990-96, she was Minister of Development and Minister of Education and Physical Culture from 1995-98.

1998
Zlatka Popovska
Former professor and dean of the Economic Faculty of the University of Skopje, in 1998 she became Vice President of the Government, National Coordinator for Foreign Assistance, President of the Foreign System and Economic Development and President of the Committee for Financial Recovery and the Banking System.

Silvija Tomovska
In 1998, she became Deputy Minister of Urban Planning and Construction.

MOLDOVIA

1962
Olga V. Bykova
From 1962-89, she was Minister of Social Affairs and Deputy Head of the Central Committee Department of Trade and Finance.

1971
Silvia Saca
She earned a BA in Spanish language and literature from the State University of Moldova in 1971. As Project Chief of the Gender in Development Project, she is working in the direction of raising public awareness regarding women's issues among decision-makers, government officials and members of Parliament.

1991
Klaudia Melnick
In 1991, she became Deputy Governor of the National Bank of Moldova.

1992
Eugenia Mikhailova
In 1992, she was Minister of Labor and Social Affairs and Director General of the State Department for Statistics in 1997.

1994
Veronica Abramcivc
She was Director General of Inter-Ethnic Relations from 1994-98.

Zinaida Grafchim
From 1994-98, she was Vice Minister of Privatization and State Property Administration.

1996
Veronica Bacalu
In 1996, she became Deputy President of the National Bank of Moldova.

1997
Iuliana Gorea-Costin
In 1997, she was appointed Permanent Representative to the Council of Europe.

Svetlana Missticci
She became Vice Minister of Territorial Development, Public Utilities and Construction in 1997.

1998
Tatiana Stoianov
In 1998, she became Director General of National Relations and Language Functions.

MONACO

1929
Grace Kelly (1929-1982)
Her acting career was short, prolific and successful. In 1954 she won a Best Actress Oscar for her role in The Country Girl. In 1956, she married Prince Rainier and succeeded her husband as president of the Red Cross and established several charities

primarily devoted to childcare and improving the situation for Monaco's youth. The United Nations Food & Agricultural Association awarded her the Ceres medal in 1977.

NETHERLANDS

1594
Clara Peeters (1594-1657)
She was one of several women who pioneered the development of still-life painting in the early 17th century. Although she painted floral still lifes, most of her works can be categorized as flower pieces and banquet pieces depicting sumptuous displays of food and drink. She is therefore credited with the development of these two categories of still-life painting.

1609
Judith Leyster (1609-1660)
She was one of the most outstanding Dutch genre painters of the 17th century. She is best known for her joyful scenes with people from everyday life, but she also painted portraits and still lifes. Leyster became the only female member of the Haarlem painters' guild and created her self-portrait in 1635 as a presentation piece to the guild.

1738
Betje Wolff (1738 -?)
She co-wrote the first Dutch novel *Die historie van mejuffrouw Sara Burgerhart* that was published in 1782.

1853
Alexandrine Pieternella-Francoise Timme (1853 -?)
Explorer, she is best known for her investigation of the course of the Nile River.

1948
Juliana (1909 -)
She was enthroned in 1948 as Queen of the Netherlands and ruled until she abdicated in favor of her daughter Beatrix in 1980. As a conscientious and hard-working monarch, she retained the devotion of her subjects despite political controversy raised by the Spanish and German marriages of two daughters and her husband's involvement in financial scandal.

1882
Aletta Jacobs (1848-1929)
In 1882, she was the first female physician in the Netherlands and started the world's first birth control clinic. In 1894, she founded the Association for Women's Suffrage.

1892
Corrie Ten Boom (1892-1983)
Dutch evangelist, she wrote of her experiences while in a World War II concentration camp in "*The Hiding Place*" published in 1971. She was also the first woman in the Netherlands to become a licensed watchmaker.

1914
Etty Hillesum (1914-1943)
Lawyer and writer, she is remembered for "*An Interruped Life: The Diaries of Etty Hillesum, 1941-1943*". She died in Auschwitz in 1943.

1918
Fanny Blankers-Koen (1918 -)
Although she lost the decade of her athletic prime to a World War and two cancelled Olympics; she won an unprecedented 4 gold medals at the 1948 London Olympics.

1953
Georgina Ana de Waal
From 1953-57, she was State Secretary of Education, Arts and Science.

1956
Maria Z. W. Witteven
In 1956, she was appointed Ambassador to the European Council, the first female ambassador of her country.

1966
Marga A. M. Klompe (1912-1986)
She was Minister of Culture, Recreation and Social Work from 1966-71 and Minister of State from 1971-86, senior member of the Council of State.

1977
Nellie Smit-Koos
In 1977-81, she was State Secretary of Transport, Public Works and Water Management and Minister from 1982-89.

1981
Heddy D'Ancona
From 1981-82, she was State Secretary of Social Affairs and Health and from 1989-94 Minister of Well-Being (seniors, handicapped and sport), Health and Culture.

1982
E. M. Schoo (1944 -)
She was Minister without Portfolio for Development Cooperation from 1982-86. In 1989, she was appointed Ambassador to India, Nepal, and Sri Lanka.

1986
Sylvia Toth (1944 -)
She became the most powerful female industrialist in The Netherlands when she became the first Dutchwoman to lead a management buyout, taking control of Content Beheer in 1986 and floating the human resources company a year later.

1990
Yvonne M.C.T. van Rooy (1951 -)
From 1990-94, she was State Secretary of Economy, External Trade, Regional Economy and Tourism.

NORWAY

1643
Dorothe Engelbretsdatter (1643-1716)
Recognized as Norway's first women writer, her first book *Siaelens Sangoffer* was published in 1678. It was a

collection of religious poetry written in Danish.

1813
Camilla Wergeland Collett
(1813-1895)
Novelist and champion of women's rights and social justice, she brought realism to Norwegian fiction in such books as *Amtmandens D'ottre* and *I den Lange Neeter*.

1847
Agathe Backer Grondahl
(1847-1907)
Pianist and composer, she was an important performer in Norway for many years. She wrote approximately 190 songs and 120 pieces for piano as well as arrangements of more than 50 folk tunes. Of all her contemporaries, she is the composer whose songs have best stood the test of time.

1855
Camilla Collett (1813-1895)
Her first novel *The Governor's Daughters* was published anonymously in 1855. She portrayed women as victims of legal, social and marital laws in her books and demanded both legal and social equality for women.

1877
Maia Bang (1877-1940)
Violinist, she founded a music school in Oslo in 1900 where she made her debut. She is the author of several methods for violins.

1911
Christine Bonnevie
In 1911, she was the first woman admitted to the Norwegian Academy of Science.

1922
Cora Sandal (1880-1974)
She published three novels in which she traced a woman's growth to independence during her life in 1922. In her later novels and short stories, she showed concern for social realities and spoke against Nazi occupation of Norway.

1928
Sonja Henie (1912-1969)
A Norwegian figure skater and movie actress who helped increase the popularity of competitive figure skating and pioneered the use of modern costumes and choreography in figure skating. She won the gold medal for figure skating at the 1928, 1932 and 1936 Winter Olympics. From 1936 into the 1950s, she performed in popular and critically acclaimed ice shows.

Sigrid Undset (1882-1949)
In 1928, she received the Nobel Prize for Literature for her two novels depicting life in medieval Norway in the 13th Century. She combined her scholarly knowledge of history with a keen sense of psychological analysis in her works. She also entered the public debate on women's emancipation to which she was categorically critical as it was developing and of the

moral and ethical decline she felt was threatening in the wake of World War 1.

1939
Gro Harlem Brundtland (1939 -)
She served as Prime Minister of Norway for more than 10 years. Throughout her political career, she has actively promoted health issues, position of women and children's welfare. In 1983, she established and chaired the World Commission on Environment and Development for the United Nations. She is the author of numerous articles on environmental, political, and development issues.

1945
Kirsten Moe Hansteen
In 1945, she became Norway's first female minister without portfolio.

1948
Harriet Bjerrum Nielsen
(1948-)
In 1977, she received her Master's degree from the University of Oslo in Danish language, literature and pscyholinguistics and is Director of the Centre for Feminist Research at the university. Her research focuses on the gender construction differences between girls and boys and comparative studies of young girls and boys in Nordic countries.

1950
Synne Skouen (1950 -)
In 1977, she was appointed editor of a new periodical for contemporary music, Ballade and a music critic for Arbeiderbladet. In 1993, after many years as a full-time composer, she was appointed Music Director for Norwegian Broadcasting's cultural channel and promoted to Head of Culture in 1999.

1954
Cecilie Ore (1954 -)
She has made a name for herself, both nationally and internationally, as one of Norway's most interesting composers. In 1981, she recived a Netherlands national fellowship to study electro-acoustical music. At the Rostrum for electronic music in Stockholm, she was awarded first prize for composers under 35 years of age in 1988. During the years 1988-93, she wrote a series of works which all used the theme "time".

1958
Kirsten Flagstad
(1895-1962)
An opera singer, she became the first director of the Royal Norwegian Opera in 1958.

1960
Signe Ryssdal
In 1960, she became Norway's first woman counsel-at-law.

1965
Elisabeth Schweigaard Selmer
(1923 -)
She was Minister of Justice
and Police from 1965-70 and
Judge in the High Court from
1970-90.

1971
Elsa Rastad Braten
Former Member of Presidency of
the City Council of Oslo, she
became Secretary of State of
Justice in 1971.

1974
Gro Harlem Bruntland (1939 -)
From 1974-79, she was Minister
of Environmental Protection
and became Statsminister
(Prime Minister) in 1981,
1986-89 and 1990-96. In 1998,
she became Director General of
the World Health Organization
and Assistant Secretary
General of the United Nations.

Kirsten Ohm
In 1974, she was appointed
Ambassador to European
Council, the first female
ambassador of her country.

1976
Annemarie Rostvik Lorentzen
From 1976-78, she was Minister
of Family and Consumers'
Affairs and from 1978-86 was
Ambassador to Iceland.

1981
Kari Gjesteby
In 1981, she became Minister
of Trade and Shipping in the
Ministry of Foreign Affairs,
from 1986-88 State Secretary
of Foreign Affairs and from

1990-92 Minister of Justice
and Police. In 1993, she
became Director in the Norges
Bank.

Mette Kongsheim (1941 -)
Between 1981-83, she was State
Secretary of Trade and since
1996, has been Ambassador to
The Czech Republic and
Slovakia.

1984
Eldbjorg Lower (1943 -)
She was Mayor of Kongsberg
from 1984-88, Minister of
Labor and Administration from
1997-99 and Minister of
Defense from 1999-2000.

1986
Helen Bosterud (1940 -)
From 1986-89, she was Minister
of Justice and Police and
since 1993, has been Director
General of the Directorate of
Civil Defense and Emergency
Planning.

1988
Helga Hernes (1937 -)
She was State Secretary of
Foreign Affairs from 1988-89
and 1990-93. Since 1996, she
was Advisor in the Ministry of
Foreign Affairs, Ambassador
and Coordinator of Peace-
Keeping Operations and
Ambassador to United Nations
in Geneve.

Tove Liv Bestun Veirod
Between 1988-90 and since
1992, she was Head of Public
Relations of Norsk Hydro Oil
Company.

1990
Astrid Nokkelbye Heiberg
(1936 -)
Former Minister, she was
Chairman of the Norwegian Red
Cross between 1990-91 and
became President of the
International Red Cross in
1997.

1992
Grethe Faremo (1959 -)
From 1992-96, she was Minister
of Justice and Police and in
1996 became Minister of Oil
and Energy.

1993
**Marianne von den Houten
Andreassen** (1961 -)
She was State Secretary of
Foreign Affairs (1993-94) and
State Secretary of Finance and
Taxation (1994-97).

1996
Sylvia Kristin Brustad
(1966 -)
From 1996-97, she was Minister
of Children and Family and in
2000 became Minister of
Communes and Regions, Asylum
and Immigration.

Anne Holt (1959 -)
A lawyer and popular author of
criminal novels, she became
Minister of Justice and Police
from 1996-97.

1997
Hilde Frafjord (1963 -)
In 1997-2000, she was Minister
of International Development
and Human Rights and Deputy
Minister of Foreign Affairs.

Johanne Nilsen Gaup
She was State Secretary of
Municipalities and Regional
Affairs in charge of Sameian
Questions form 1997-99 and
State Secretary of
Municipalities and Regional
Affairs for Refuges from 1999-
2000.

2000
Mona Juul (1953 -)
She was State Secretary of
Foreign Affairs in 2000 and
Ambassador and Middle East
Coordinator in the Foreign
Ministry. She played an
important part in the Israeli-
Palestinian negotiations that
resulted in Oslo Agreement.

POLAND
1374
Queen Jadwiga (1374-1399)
She was crowned King of Poland
in 1384, the only woman ruler
in Poland's history and the
only head of state in Poland
declared saint by the Catholic
Church. She enjoyed great
popularity and the nobles
looked to her as their true
king as long as she lived.
Queen Jadwiga traveled on
diplomatic missions,
negotiated with German,
Muscovite and Italian princes
of the Church and helped to
establish the church in
Lithuania and a college in
Prague. She also renovated the
Krakow Academy, the oldest in
Eastern Europe and renamed it
Jagiellonian University that
became a beacon of learning in
law and theology. The Church

remembers her efforts in the founding of the bishopric of Wilno.

1690
Elizabetha Hevelius
(1647-?)
Polish astronomer, she helped her husband run Danzig observatory in 1690 and edits his *Prodromus astronomiae*, a catalogue of 1564 stars.

1840
Helena Modjeska (1840 -?)
Although she was the reigning queen of the Warsaw stage, she was barred from Poland because of her anti-Russian attitudes. Her autobiography *Memories and Impressions* was published in 1910.

1841
Eliza Orzeszkowa (1841 -?)
A highly popular novelist, she emphasized equality and justice in her novels that dissected small town life for such diverse people as Jews, fishermen and poor gentility. Her novels have been translated into many languages including English.

1842
Maria Konopnicka
(1842-1910)
Prolific poet, novelist and essayist, she touched upon many social issues besetting the society of her time and expressed ideals of democracy and patriotism. She also wrote novels for children.

1854
Anna Tomaszewicz-Dobroska
(1854-1918)
Polish physician, she was the first woman to practice medicine in Poland.

1866
Eliza Orzeskowa (1841-1910)
Author of 11 books, 5 of which were on women's rights. All of her works reflect her concern for and pride in her country. In *A Few Words About Women*, she criticized the Polish custom of socializing women needing to be dependent and docile.

1879
Wanda Landowska (1879 -?)
She received worldwide acclaim as the high priestess of the harpsichord and was the recognized authority on keyboard instruments of the 17th and 18th centuries. In 1925, she founded Ecole de Musique Ancienne for experienced musicians to learn old musical instruments and musical styles.

1881
Marian Falski (1881-1974)
Educationist, she is famous for writing the elementary book, Nauka pisania i czytania (*Learning to Write and Read*).

1885
Zofia Nalkowska (1885-1954)
In 1906 she published her first book Women which later translated into English. She wrote from a feminist

perspective and her work was noted for its technical simplicity.

1899
Ida Kaminska (1899 -?)
She was recognized as the queen of the Yiddish theatre in Poland. After World War II, she established and headed the Jewish State Theatre of Poland from 1946-68.

1900
Helena Syrkus (1900–1982)
Professor at Warsaw Polytechnic School, Faculty of Architecture, she was inducted into the Golden Book of the Warsaw Polytechnic School as an outstanding academic teacher in 1979. She is also a partner in the creation of the Polish School of Architecture. She worked for the underground during World War II and afterwards was head of the committee devoted to the rebuilding of Warsaw.

1907
Wanda Jakobowska (1907 -)
Film producer and director, she co-founded the Society of the Devotees of Artistic Film in 1929.

1909
Marian Danysz (1909 -)
Physicist, she co-discovered of hyper-nuclei and hyper-nuclear isomery.

1913
Grazyna Bacewica (1913 -)
Composer and violinist, she taught at the Lodz

Conservatory before and after World War II.

1915
Christina Granville (Countess Skarbeck) 1915-1952)
Polish spy, she was one of the most successful resistance agents in France during World War II and often when on missions to Poland and the Balkans.

Elisabeth Schwartzkopf (1915 -)
Made her debut as operatic soprano at Berlin Stadtische Oper in *Parsifal*. After World War II, she sang in Vienna State Opera, Covent Gardens in London, LaScala in Milan, the Bayreuth Festival and Salzburg Festival. She originally specialized in coloratura roles but changed to lyric soprano especially in recitals of lieder.

1917
Helena Rasiowa (1917-1994)
A mathematician, her main research was in algebraic logic and the mathematical foundations of computer science. In 1984, she introduced an important concept of inference, which led to approximate reasoning and approximate logic, which are now central to the study of artificial intelligence. As a member of the Polish Mathematical Society, she also played a major role in the mathematical life of Poland.

1918

Irena Kosmowska (1879-1949)
In 1918, she became Vice Minister of Social Welfare in Poland.

1925

Maria Dabrowska (1889-1965)
She was an acclaimed novelist and journalist in Poland. In 1925, she wrote her epic novel, *Noce I Dnie*, a saga of a family through several generations, which examined the conditions of Polish peasants and calls for land reform. It is deemed to be one the best works in Polish. Her last novel *Przygody Czlowieka Myslacego* examined life under Hitler's conquering army. She also wrote articles for Polish newspapers on political and economic reform as well as cooperative movement.

Helena Wiewiorska
(1888-1967)
In 1925, she became Poland's first woman lawyer.

1929

Anna Czekanowska-Kuklinska
(1929 -)
Musicologist and ethnographer, she applied statistical mathematical methods for analysis of folk music.

1931

Janina Spychajowa-Kurkowska
She won the women's' singles title at the first international women's archery competition in 1931 and more world titles in archery than any other man or woman in history.

1933

Janina Brzostowska (1907-1986)
She published her first novel *Bezrobatni Warszawy* in 1933, which was withdrawn from publication by censorship. It was a cry of protest of the unemployed from the depth of their physical and moral misery. Her second novel described a woman coming of age. She spent the years of German occupation working in the Polish underground.

1935

Zofina Korsak-Szczucka
(1890-1968)
In 1935, she wrote her first novel *Angel in the Dust*, which is known, for its mastery of historical fact and vivid imagery. She was imprisoned during World War II in a German concentration camp.

1936

Krystyna Chojnowska-Liskiewicy
(1936 -)
Yachtswoman and shipbuilding engineer, she was the first woman to sail around the world solo in 1978. In *Pierwsza dook o/a Swiata* she described her adventures published in 1979.

1946

Eugenia Krassowska-Jadlowska
She was State Secretary of Education from 1946-50 and State Secretary of Higher Education from 1950-65.

1951

Grazyna Bacewicz
(1909-1969)
Composer and violinist, she won the International Composers Competition with her Fourth String Quartet in 1951. She composed ballets, symphonies, concertos and violin pieces and was an author of short stories, novels and a TV play.

Sof'ja Aleksandrovna Janovskaja (1896-1966)
Polish historian of logic, she received the Order of Lenin for her work in mathematical logic in 1951.

1960

Magdalena Abakanowicz (1930 -)
A world-renowned artist, she studied at the Warsaw Academy of Fine arts and sought to escape from conventional art forms through weaving. She achieved international recognition with her monumental abstract woven fibre installations called "Abakans" in 1960. Her works in bronze including "Hand-Like Tree" which was on exhibit in Central Park, are simple in form but redolent with the power of suggestion and emotional impact.

1970

Anna Walentynowicz
Crane operator at Gdansk shipyard, she led the strike over food prices in 1970. Later she contributed to the foundation of the Solidarity labor union.

1976

Maria Milczarek
From 1976-80, she was Minister of Administration, Local Economy and Environment and in 1980 Minister of Labor, Wages and Social Affairs.

1981

Halina Bortnowska
Labor organizer, she led a steelworker's strike in Cracow in 1981.

1983

Maria Skora Regent-Lechowicz
In 1974-78, she was Judge in the Supreme Court. Former Secretary of State of Justice, she was appointed Ambassador to Sweden in 1983, the first female ambassador of her country.

1984

Helena Rasiowa (1917-1994)
Her main research was in algebraic logic and the mathematical foundations of computer science. In 1984, Rasiowa introduced the concept of inference where the basic information was incomplete. This led to approximate reasoning and approximate logics, which are now central to the study of artificial intellegence. She helped set up the journal *Fundamenta Informaticae* in 1977 and, from 1986, was an associate editor of the *Journal of Approximate Reasoning*. A member of the Polish Mathematical Society, she chaired various committee

of the Polish Ministry of Science and Higher Education.

1993
Barbara Bilda
She was Minister of Housing, Construction and Regional Planning from 1993-95 and Minister of Town and Country Planning from 1995-97.

Hanna Suchocka (1946-)
From 1991-92, she was Vice-President of the Council of Europe. In 1993, she became the first female Prime Minister in post-communist Eastern Europe and 1st Vice-Chairman of the National Security Council. Since she lost power, she has become one of the most active politicians on the centre right in Poland and is working to consolidate the conservative Catholic opposition and keep it looking towards Europe. She became Minister of Justice and Procurateur-General from 1997-2000.

Ewa Wachowichz
"Miss Poland 1993", she became Government Spokesperson from 1993-95.

1996
Wislawa Szymborska (1923 -)
She received Nobel Prize for Literature in 1996 for poetry that allows the historically and biological context to come to light in fragments of human reality. She has been described as the Mozart of poetry. Her poetry has been translated into a large number of European languages and also in Arabic, Hebrew, Japanese and Chinese.

1997
Teresa Warchalowska
From 1997-99, she was Prostate Secretary of Environmental Protection, National Resources and Forestry and Chief Inspector of Environmental Protection.

1998
Franciszka Cegielska
Chairman of the Voivodship of Pomerania and Mayor of Gdynia from 1990-98, she became Minister of Health and Social Security in 1998.

Alicja Grzeszkowiak (1935 -)
In 1998, she became Marchal of the Senate. As President of the Senate, she ranks 3rd in the hierarchy after the State President and Sejm-Marchal.

2000
Barbara Tuge-Erecinska
Former Ambassador to Sweden, she became Prostate Secretary of Foreign Affairs in 2000.

1630
Josefa de Ayala (1630-1684)
An artist whose versatility is demonstrated by the range of genres she undertook including still life studies, religious themes, portraits, and allegorical subjects. One of her surviving paintings is that of the *Marriage of Saint Catherine* now at the Museu Nacional de Arte in Antiqua, Lisbon. During her lifetime, she was elected to the Lisbon Academy.

1891
Amelia Cardia
She becomes Portugal's first woman physician in 1891.

1894
Florbela de Alma da Conceicao Espanca
(1894-1930)
Portugal's foremost woman poet, she published her first collection of poems *Livro das magoas* in 1919.

1908
Maria Helena Vieira de Silva
(1908 -)
She is renown as the most important contemporary Portuguese painter and her abstract expressionism paintings hang in major modern art museums throughout the world.

1913
Regina Quintanilha
In 1913, she becomes the first woman in Portugal to earn a law degree.

1937
Maria Teresa Horta (1937-)
An innovative and daring writer, she co-authored *Novas Carta Portuguesas* in 1972. The book, an exploration of the feelings of women about love, war, the mores of society and the erotic nature of life, was declared offensive by the government. The arrest of the authors provoked an international reaction to the dictatorship and gathered support for the feminist movement in Portugal.

1955
Elisa Maria da Costa Guimaraes Ferreira (1955 -)
Between 1996-99, she was Minister of Environment and became Minister of Planning in 1999.

1970
Maria Teresa Carcomo Lobo
When she was appointed Undersecretary of State for Welfare in 1970, she became the first woman in her country to hold a cabinet level post.

1975
Maria Manuela Margado
She was Undersecretary of State for Public Investments from 1975-76, Secretary of State of Finance from 1976-78 and Secretary of State of Taxes from 1977-78.

Maria Isabel Carmel Rosa
When appointed in 1975, she became the first woman to serve as Secretary of State for Consumer Protection in Portugal.

1978
Maria Manuela Aguiar Dias Moreia Aguiar (1942 -)
She was Secretary of State of Labor from 1978-79 and Secretary of State of Emigration and Portuguese Communities Abroad from 1980-81 and 1985-87.

1979
Maria da Lourdes-Pintasilgo (1926 -)
Ambassador to UNESCO from 1975-79, she became Portugal's first woman Prime Minister in 1979. Other posts she has held include Minister of Social Affairs, State Secretary for Social Security, Member of the European Parliament and 1989 presidential candidate. She is also President of the Inter-ministerial Commission dealing with the condition and status of women.

1984
Helena de Melo Torres Marques
Former Director General of Regional and Local Action in the Ministry, she became Secretary of State of Agriculture from 1984-85.

1992
Teresa Patricio Pinto Basto Guveira
She was Secretary of State of Environment and Natural Resources from 1992-93 and Minister of Environment from 1993-95.

1996
Leonor Coutinho Pereira dos Santos (1947 -)
She was Secretary of State of Equipment, Planning and Territorial Administration for Housing and Communication from 1996-99 and Secretary of State of Transport and Housing in 1999.

1997
Maria Jose Canatancio (1939 -)
In 1997-99, she was Secretary of State of Equipment, Planning and Territorial Administration for Regional Development.

ROMANIA
1893
Ana Rabinsohn Pauker (1893-1960)
She was responsible for the collectivization of the Agriculture in the Politburo from 1940-53. In 1944, she became Romania's first female Minister of Foreign Affairs.

1924
Elena Vacaresco
In 1924, she was appointed Ambassador to League of Nations, the first female ambassador of her country.

1930
Irma Glicman Adelman (1930 -)
Economist, she is best known for developing a system of "factor analysis" integrating

social, political and economic factors to explain economic growth in developing countries.

1940
Ileana Malancioiu (1940-)
Romanian writer and philosopher, she received a doctorate in philosophy from Bucharest University and has worked for Romanian television. She is editor of the monthly literary magazine *Viata Romaneasca* and one of the most prolific of contemporary Romanian poets.

1942
Ana Blandiana (1942-)
Since 1975, she has worked as librarian at the Institute of Fine Arts in Bucharst and has been a regular columnist in the Writer Union weekly magazine. In 1970, she was awarded the Poetry Prize of the Writer Union for *A treia taina*.

1946
Florica Bagdasar
In 1946, she became Health Minister, the first woman to hold a cabinet post.

1953
Constanta Craciun
From 1953-62, she was Chairman of the State Committee for Culture and Art, Minister of Culture from 1962-66 and Vice-President of the State Council from 1966-70.

1966
Ana Mureson
She was Minister of Industry (1966-71), Minister and President of the National Council of Women (1978) and Minister of Domestic Trade (1980-87).

1968
Lia Manoliu (1932-1998)
Romanian track and field athlete, she won a gold medal in 1968 Olympic discus throw in, the oldest woman to win gold in any Olympic track and field event. In 1990, she became 1st non-royal woman to head any national Olympic committee when she became President of Romanian Olympic Committee.

Rosa Csudor de Valerio (1894-)
At age 81, she invented and patented a new embroidery technique and the sewing machine attachment to do it.

1975
Lina Ciobanu
Former President of National Council of Women, she became Minister of Light Industry from 1975-87 and Vice President of the Council of Ministers from 1987-89.

1976
Nadia Comaneci (1961 -)
A Romanian gymnast, she became the first gymnast to receive a perfect score on the uneven bars at the 1976 Olympics. She won individual gold medals on the uneven bars and the balance beam. At the 1980

Moscow Olympics, she won individual gold medals in floor exercises and on the balance beam.

1979
Magda Filipas
From 1979-82, she was First Deputy Minister of Light Industry and was appointed Ambassador to the Philippines from 1982-89.

1980
Cornelia Filipas
She was Vice President of the Council of Ministers from 1980-82 and was appointed Ambassador to Denmark from 1982-89.

1982
Paula Prioteasa
Between 1982-86, she was Deputy Minister of External Trade for Asia and Oceans and Minister of the Food Industry in 1986 and from 1988-90.

1986
Maria Ghitulica
She was Deputy Chairman of the District Council of Olt from 1979-92, and became Vice-President of the Council of State in 1986.

1991
Virgina Mihaela Gheorghiu
(1965 -)
In 1991 and 1992, she was Government Spokesperson and became Secretary of State and Head of the Public Transport Department in 1993.

1996
Michaela Rodica Staniou
Between 1996-97, she was Secretary of State of Women's Affairs in the Ministry of Labor and Social Protection.

RUSSIA

1657
Sofya Alekseyevna (1657 -?)
Regent of Russia 1682-1689, her domestic policies were far reaching as she encouraged reform, brought in foreign ideas and developed industry. She also concluded a peace treaty with Poland that gained Russia the land east of the Dnieper River including Kiev.

1743
Princess Yekaterina Dashkova
(1743 -?)
She helped the coup d'etat that seated Catherine II, the Great, and supervised the writing of the first Russian dictionary.

1831
Madame Blavatsky
(1831-1891)
Pioneer esotericist, she introduced knowledge of eastern religions to the West including the ideas of karma and reincarnation. In 1875 she founded the Theosophical Society – its first objective was Universal Brotherhood without regard to race, creed, sex, caste, or color.

1845

Elizaveta Fedorovna Litvinova
(1845-1919)
Teacher and author, she obtained her doctoral degree in 1878 from Bern University in mathematics. She published over 70 articles on the philosophy and practice of teaching mathematics and is respected as one of the foremost pedagogues in Russia.

1850

Sofia Kurtovsky Kovalevskaya
(1850-1891)
A mathematician, she was the first woman to be admitted to Academy of Science in Russia. During her career she published 10 papers in mathematics, mathematical physics and several literary works. Many of the scientific papers were groundbreaking theories or the impetus for future discoveries.

1872

Aleksandra Mikhaylovna Kollontai (1872-1952)
Soviet political leader, diplomat, writer and activist on behalf of women's concerns, she was the first Soviet commissar of public welfare in 1917. When she was appointed Ambassador to Norway from 1923-24 and 1927-30, she became the first woman ambassador in the world. She went on to Ambassador to Mexico (1926-27), Sweden (1930-45 and was Doyene of the Corps Dilplomatique from 1942-45. As Councilor in the Ministry of Foreign Affairs

from 1945-52, she was instrumental in negotiating the Soviet-Finnish armistice of 1944.

1876

Yekaterina Vasilyevna Geltzer
(1876 -?)
Prima ballerina, she helped preserve the techniques and traditions of the Imperial Russian Ballet in the bad times following the Russian Revolution.

1882

Alexandra Exter (1882-1949)
She was a pioneer in modern abstraction whose reputation was enhanced by her brilliant innovations in the field of scenic and costume design for the Russian theatre.

1889

Anna Andreevna Gorenko
(1889-1966)
She is considered one of the finest Russian lyric poets and perhaps the finest female Russian poets of all time. Her life spanned the time between the pre-Revolutionary and post-Stalin eras of Russian history. Despite terrible persecution and censorship by the State, her poetry gave voice to the struggles and deepest yearnings of the Russian people during times of great upheaval in Russian history. Lately, she has come to symbolize for the world the power of art to survive and transcend the terrors of our century.

1896
Sof'ja Aleksandrovna Janovskaja (1896-1966)
Her work in mathematical logic was important in the development of the subject in Soviet Union. In 1959, she became the first Head of the Department of Mathematical Logic at Moscow State University. She also worked on the philosophy of mathematics and logic, the history of mathematics and published work on Egyptian mathematics.

1899
Pelageya Yakovlevna Polubarinova-Kochina
(1899 -)
She is one of the most important women in mathematics in the Soviet Union and one of its leading scientists.
Applied mathematician, she became director of the division of hydromechanics at the University of Moscow.

1901
Nina Karlovna Bari
(1901-1961)
A mathematician, she was given the Glavnauk Prize in 1926 for her explanations to various difficult problems on trigonometric functions. In 1952, she published a remarkable article on primitive functions and trigonometric series converging almost everywhere. She wrote a monograph about all kinds of problems involving trigonometric series, which has become the basic reference for all mathematicians focusing on the theory of functions and the theory of series.

1908
Nina V. Makarova (1908 -)
Russian composer with great interest in Russian and Mari folksongs, she composed ballads, choruses, symphonies and the opera "Courage".

1914
Eugenie Shakhovskaya
A Russian princess, she became the first female military pilot when she flew reconnaissance missions in 1914. She will later become a member of the Bokshevik Secret Police and chief executioner at Kiev.

1920
Olga A. Ladyzhenskaya (1920-)
Mathematician, who received her Doctorate in Mathematics-Physical Science in 1953 at Moscow State University, she worked in the general areas of linear, quasilinear and nonlinear partial differential equations of elliptic, parabolic and hyperbolic types with some theoretical applications to Navier-Stokes flow.

1923
Aleksandra Kollontaj
The first woman ambassador of her country, she was appointed Ambassador to Norway (1923-24 and 1927-30), Mexico (1926-27) and Sweden (1930-40).

1925

Sophie Piccard (1902 -)

In 1925 she received her Diploma in Mathematics and the Physical Sciences from the University of Smolensk. Her work was on research on set theory, theorems about generators and relations of abstract groups, theory of groups of finite order, introduced notion of fundamental group and P-product of groups, discovered wide and various classes of P groups, studies in linear algebra, theory of relations and history of math.

1927

Tatyana Ivanova Zaslavskaya (1927 -)

Economist and sociologist, she wrote "Novosibirsk Memorandum" in 1983, a criticism of the Soviet economic system which was one of the factors behind policy change in Russia in the late 1980s. She was personal advisor to President Gorbachev on economics and social matters and has been involved in the development of economic sociology.

1931

Sofia Gubaidulina

Her compositional interests have been stimulated by tactile exploration and improvisation with rare Russian, Caucasian and Asian folk and ritual instruments and a deep-rooted belief in the mystical properties of music. She received the Russian State Prize in 1992

and has been honored twice with the coveted Koussevitzky International Recording Award.

1938

Valentina Grizodubova (1910-1993)

She broke the long-distance record for female aviators in 1938 with her flight from Moscow to the southeastern tip of Siberia.

1942

Lt. Valeria Ivanovna Khomyakova

She was the first woman pilot in history to shoot down an enemy aircraft in 1942. She also worked as an engineer at the Frunze plant in Moscow and flight instructor at an aeroclub.

1952

Maria Gorokhavskaya

A Soviet competitor, she was the first woman to win an Olympic gold medal in gymnastics for her individual performance. She achieved this record at the games in Helsinki, Finland in 1952 – the first year this event was open to women.

1951

Monika Laura Cherinowski (1951 -)

A physician, she was commissioned in the Soviet Navy as a medical officer and became one of a very few women to serve as shipboard surgical officers. Following the disintegration of the Soviet Union, she took a research-

oriented position at a
hospital in central Russia
where she pursued her medical
interest - surgical infection
control. Her studies and
writing on the state of
infection control in Russian
hospitals have been a major
contribution to the
improvement of medical
practice in her country.

1955
Z. P. Sidorishina
Soviet aviator and navigator
of a plane designed to land on
ice floes, she became the
first woman to fly to the
North Pole in 1955.

1956
Tatyana Mitkova (1956 -)
This veteran broadcaster
earned the respect of the
Russian public when she
refused to read a sanitized
account of the attack against
Lithuanian independence
movement by Soviet troops. As
the main anchor for the
independent NTV channel's
evening news, she has again
become a thorn in the side of
the authorities for her
coverage of the war in the
breakaway republic of
Chechnya.

1957
Elena V. Kondakova (1957 -)
In 1989 she was selected as a
cosmonaut candidate. In 1994
she fulfilled her first flight
on board the spacecraft "Soyuz
TM-17" and the orbital complex
"Mir" as a flight engineer.

By 1997 she has logged over
178 days in space.

Galina Yevgenyevna Nikolayeva (1911-1963)
In 1957, she published *Bitva v
Puti*, a novel dealing in part
with the workings of the
Soviet secret police.

1963
Valentina Tereshkova (1937-)
A Russian cosmonaut, she was
the first woman in space and
the 10th human being to orbit
the earth. She was the solo
pilot of the spaceship Vostok
VI that was launched in 1963.
Before joining the cosmonaut
program, she was an amateur
parachutist. After her flight,
she continued to work as an
aerospace engineer in the
space program and worked in
Soviet politics, feminism and
culture.

1966
Eudokiia F. Karpova
Between 1966-87, she was
Deputy Premier Minister and
Head of the Central Committee
Department of Light and Local
Industry.

1973
Ludmila Touritscheva (1952 -)
Russian gymnast, she won the
gold medal in every apparatus
and in the combined exercises
at the European championships
in 1973.

1991

Artamonova Ludmila Pavlovna
(1959-)
In 1981, she graduated from Rostov Institute of Transport Communications and began work as power engineer at Ulyanovsk Railroad Branch. In 1991, she became director of "Meotida Firm" Limited Liability Partnership.

Galina Vasiljevna Starovitova
(1946-1998)
She was Presidential Advisor for Ethnic and International Relations from 1991-92. In 1992, she was candidate for Defense Minister and planned to stand for Governor of St. Petersburg in 1999 and President in 2000 but she was assassinated in 1998.

1992

Borisova Natalia Yurievna
(1959-)
A specialist in economics and insurance, she has been Director General of Askorales Joint-Stock Insurance Company. since 1992.

1994

Tatyana Parmonova
In 1994-95, she was Deputy Chairman of the Central Bank of the Federation of Russia and Member of the Council of Ministers and Chairman of the Central Bank from 1995-96.

1995

Chumakova Tatiana Samoilovna
(1947 -)
An expert in the field of the share market, in 1995, she

became president of Don Financial Public Joint-Stock Company, the largest registrar in the South of Russia. Since 1997, she has been director of South-Russian branch of self-adjustable organization of the professional participants of the market of collateral securities. She is also vice-president of Rostov Board of a "Free economic society of Russia."

1997

Stadnichenko L. Ivanovna
(1937-)
She is a professional in contemporary, theatre, historic and artistic costume design. She has been assistant professor of Fine Arts Department at Rostov Institute of Architecture since 1997. She thinks that the leading tendency of a contemporary suit is its internationalism and considers that post-modernism will be changed by a mixture and comprehension of various trends of culture both in modern and historic understanding of it.

SAN MARINO

1989

Savina Zafferani
She was appointed Ambassador to Italy from 1989-93, the first female ambassador of her country.

1999

Rosa Zafferani (1960 -)
Former Director in the Department of Finance, Budget and Programs, she was elected

to the Consiglio Grande e Generale in 1998. In 1999, she became Capitano Reggente.

2000
Maria Domenica Michelotti
Former lecturer at San Marino University, she was a Member of the Consiglio Grande e Generale since 1998. She became Capitano Reggente in 2000.

SCOTLAND
1762
Joanna Baillie (1762-1851)
Scottish poet, she published *Fugitive Verses* in 1790 and 3-volumnes of blank verse entitled *Plays on the Passions* in 1798.

1862
Helen Bannerman (1862-1946)
Illustrated letters to her children formed the basis of her first book, "*The Story of Little Black Sambo*", published in 1899, which was a huge success at the time. She wrote and illustrated nine subsequent books most of them with equally dodgy titles.

Elizabeth Sanderson Haldane (1862-1937)
Writer, she wrote a life of Descartes, edited his philosophical works, and translated Hegel. She worked for the right of women to have both an education and better working conditions. In 1920, she became the first woman Justice of the Peace in Scotland.

1866
Marion Angus (1866 – 1946)
She was an early member of Scottish PEN and contributed poetry and stories to journals. Her poetry is mainly written in the Angus dialect, depicting the "cauld east contra" she knew. The poems are short, simple and influenced by traditional ballad.

1868
Mary Somerville (1780-?)
Scottish mathematician, in 1868 she publishes *Molecular and Microscopic Science*, a summary of the latest chemical and physical research. She received a gold medal from the Royal Geographical Society in the same year. In 1812, she won a prize for a paper on Diophantine algebra.

1874
Frances MacDonald (1874-1921)
She designed architectural ornaments, metalwork, stained glass and embroidery.

1897
Naomi Mitchison (1897-1999)
Novelist, her numerous works include the historical novel "The Conquered" published in 1923 and the children's book "Snake" published in 1976.

1901
Marie Stopes (1880-1958)
She was first woman in Scotland to obtain a university certificate in 1901 and achieved a double first in

botany. In 1905, she became Britain's youngest doctor of science. During World War I, she wrote a book about feminism and marriage. In 1918, she wrote a concise guide to contraception and in 1921 founded the Society for Constructive Birth Control. That same year, she also opened the first birth control clinics in the British Empire.

1918
Muriel Spark (1918 -)
Novelist and satirist, her best known novel "The Prime of Miss Jean Brodie" was adapted to film and stage in 1961.

1923
Katherine Marjory Steward Murray (Duchess of Atholl) (1874-1960)
She became Scotland's first woman member of Parliament in 1923 and also first conservative woman to hold ministerial office on Board of Education.

1928
Thea Musgrave (1928 -)
She is a much-acclaimed Scots orchestral and chamber music composer and conductor. One of the giants of 20th century music, her works have been performed by major orchestras throughout the world.

1935
Isobel Grant
Scottish economic historian, she established the Highland Folk Life Collection in 1935 to record the disappearing traditional Scottish culture.

1959
Rona Munro (1959 -)
She is one of Scotland's most innovative young playwrights and has won a number of prizes. Her radio and television writing includes three episodes of "Dr. Who".

1999
Wendy Alexander (1963 -)
In 1999, she became Minister of Social Inclusion, Local Government and Housing with special responsibility for Equality Issues.

SERBIA
1843
Draga Dejanovi (1843-1970)
She was the leader of the Serbian feminist movement, a poet and actor. One of her most noted articles "*Are Women Capable of Being Equal with Men*" was written the year of her death.

SLOVAKIA
1855
Elena Marothy-Soltessoua (1855-1939)
One of the two earliest Slovak women novelists, she was a leader of the women's literary movement. Her stories and novels represent early realistic Slovak prose fiction conceived as part of the battle of the smaller Slavic nationalities against the political repression in the Austro-Hungarian Empire.

1905
Masa Hal'amova (1905-)
A major contemporary lyric women poet, she received the National Artist title in 1883. Her first collection of poems *Dar* published in 1928 expressed intensely her relationship to the simple facts of her small world but also emphasized the polarity of hope and disappointment.

1951
Irena Durisova
Former Member of the Presidium of Narodna Rada (National Council), she became President of Narodna Rada in 1951. From 1959-60, she was Vice Chairman of the Federal National Assembly of Czechoslovakia.

1956
Maria Sedlekova
From 1956-57, she was First Deputy Commissioner of Trade, from 1957-68 Commissioner of Trade and from 1968-78 Minister of Labor.

1978
Petronella Visnovova (1921 -)
She was Member of the Presidium of the National Council (1964-78), Chairman of the Foreign Affairs Committee (1969-78) and Member of the Presidium of the House of Nationals of the Federal Assembly of Czechoslovakia (1969-89. From 1978-86, she was Deputy Minister of Trade and Tourism.

1989
Maria Kolarikova
In 1989, she was Chairman of the Cabinet Committee of Control and from 1990-94, First Deputy Minister of Privatization and Deputy Minister of Administration of Public Properties.

1992
Katarina Tothova
From 1992-94, she was Minister of Justice and from 1994-98, Deputy Premier Minister in charge of the Legislature and Media Policy.

1994
Brigita Schmognerova
In 1994, she was Deputy Premier Minister and Minister of Economic Reform and in 1998 Minister of Finance. She was also a candidate in one of the many unsuccessful attempts by the Parliament to elect a President in 1998.

Vera Straznicka
She was appointed Ambassador to Poland and the European Council in 1994.

SLOVENIA

1962
Vida Tomsic (1913 -)
She was Provisional President of Narodna Skubscina from 1962-63 and President of Narodna Skubscina from 1974-78. At the time, the President of the People's Assembly was also "Head of State".

1963

Olga Vrabic

Former Minister without Portfolio, she became Chairman of the Chamber of Social Affairs and Health of the Federal Assembly of Yugoslavia from 1963-67.

1992

Katja Boh

Former Minister of Health, she was appointed Ambassador to Austria and the Organization of Security and Cooperation in Europe in 1992.

1994

Verica Trstenjak (1964 -)

She was Under State Secretary of Science between 1994-96 and State Secretary of Science and Technology from 1996-2000.

1996

Nevenka Cresnar-Oerger (1962 -)

After a career as academic and civil servant, she became Secretary General of the Court of Audit in 1996. She was Secretary General of the Government from 1996-2000.

SPAIN

1451

Isabella I of Castile (1451-1504)

She sponsored the voyage of Columbus', brought the Inquisition to her country and led her armies into battle early in her reign to protect her succession. She was better known as a genius at military tactics and supplying armies in the field.

1656

Luisa Ignacia Roldan (1656-1704)

Known as La Roldana, she was Spain's first woman sculptor. Her work was primarily in terra cotta. She was immensely prolific and her sculptural output includes both larger-than-life-sized as well as the uniquely small terra-cotta compositions, which became her trademark.

1726

Francoise Duparc (1726-1778)

Her paintings were influenced by the Dutch style where the subjects of paintings are based on people in everyday life. She was elected to the Academy of Marseilles in 1777.

1837

Rosalia de Castro (1837-1883)

She was noted for her use of the Galician language and folklore to express the universal in her poetry and novels. Her best-known poem published in 1863 gave a intimate image of the pain and sorrow of poetry while depicting the joy of life.

1852

Emilia Pardo Bazan (1852-1921)

Spanish novelist and critic, she was a professor of literature at the University of Madrid. She was a leading exponent of naturalism and painted vivid descriptions of both the land and people of

Galicia in her books *The Mayor of Ulloa* and *Mother Nature*.

1880
Concepcion Arenal
A Spanish social scientist and philanthropist, she published in 1880 the two-volume *La cuesion social*.

1881
Isabel de Palencia (1881 -?)
She founded the first woman's club in Madrid and edited the first woman's magazine in Spain La Dama when 52% of all Spaniards were illiterate. A member of the Spanish delegation to the League of Nations for the Republic, she was the first woman to sign a convention for Spain.

1923
Lola Flores (1923 -)
The government honored her with a special gold medal for her life's work as one of the nation's most popular flamenco dancers and film actors in 1994.

Alicia de Larrocha (1923 -)
Pianist, she is known for her masterful performances of classical and Spanish music. Her interpretations emphasize the lively, crisp rhythms of Spanish composers. In 1959, she became director of the Marshall Academy in Barcelona.

1930
Dolores Gomez Ibarruri
(1895-1989)
Spanish politician and orator, she became a member of the

Central Committee of the Spanish Communist Party in 1930. In 1936 she was elected deputy to the Spanish Cortes. With the outbreak of the Civil War in 1936, she became the Republic's most emotional and effective propagandist. After the war, she took refuge in the USSR becoming president of the Spanish Communist Party in exile. In 1977, she returned to Spain as Communist deputy for Asturias.

1933
Montserrat Caballe (1933 -)
Spain's greatest living soprano, she has revived many rare Donizetti operas both in concert and in the opera house. She has brought the world of opera to a youthful audience and has brought Zarzuela and Spanish songs to an international audience.

1936
Federica Montseny Mane
(1905 -1994)
A Spanish anarchist, who was both anti-royalist and anti-clerical in her politics, she was the first woman to serve as Minister of Health and Social Assistance in the Spanish Popular Front government from 1936-37.

Luisa Isabel Alvarez de Toledo y Maura, Duchess of Medina-Sidonia (1936 -)
She is called the "Red Duchess" for her communistic efforts on behalf of the Spanish poor, land reform and

greater civil liberties for the citizens of Spain.

1954

Alicia Koplowitz (1954 -)
Vice president and major shareholder in Spain's largest construction company, she recently published a book "*Alone with Power*" which charted the meteoric rise of the business.

1981

Soledad Beceril Bustamante Atienza (1944 -)
From 1981-82, she was Minister of Culture. In 1995, she was Mayor of Sevilla and in 2000 3rd Vice-President of the Congreso de los Dipotados.

Rosa Maria Posada Chapado
In 1981, she was Secretary of State of Information, from 1987-91, President of Parliament of the Province of Madrid and Councilor of Social Affairs and Health of Madrid since 1996.

1982

Christina Narbona Ruiz
(1952 -)
Between 1982-85, she was Deputy Councilor of Economy in Andalucia, Director General in the Ministry of Public Works and Urban Development from 1991-93 and Secretary of State of Environment and Housing from 1993-96.

1985

Maria de las Mercedes Rico Carabia
From 1985-94, she was appointed Ambassador to Costa Rica and since 1994, has been Ambassador to Italy, San Marino and Albania.

1986

Isabel Tocino Biscarolasaga
From 1986-89, she was Secretary for Women's Affairs and from 1996-99 Minister of Environment.

1987

Maria Paz Antonia Fernandez Felgueroso
Between 1987-93, she was Councilor in the Principado de Asturias and from 1993-96 Secretary of State for Prison Affairs.

1999

Loyola de Palacio del Valle-Lersundi
In 1999, she became Vice President of the European Union Commission and Commissioner for Relations with the Institutions and Commissioner of Transport.

Maria Elena Pisonero Ruiz
She was Secretary of State of Trade, Tourism, Small and Medium-sized Enterprises in the Ministry of Economy and Finance from 1999-2000.

SWEDEN

1688

Ulrika Eleanora (1688 -?)
Swedish queen whose short reign 1718-20 led to Sweden's Age of Freedom. Her wise influence was instrumental in turning the nation toward parliamentary government.

1841

Elfrida Andree (1841 -?)
The first woman telegraphist in Sweden, she was a pioneer activist of the women's rights movement, elected Cathedral organist in G'teborg and elected to Swedish Academy of Music in 1879.

1849

Ellen Key (1849 - 1926)
Writer and feminist, her book "*Pallas of Sweden*" developed advanced ideas on sex, love and marriage and moral conduct, which had wide influence.

1872

Kersten Hesselgren (1872 -?)
Sociologist, she was the first woman factory inspector and in 1921 the first woman to be a member of both houses of the Swedish Riksdag. In 1931, she introduced the subject of the legal status of women in the League of Nations.

1874

Elsa Beskow (1874-1953)
Swedish writer and artist, she was among the founders of the classic Swedish children's books. In her books, she used her own childhood experiences with carefully studied details of nature and bourgeois small town life. Central theme is the relationship between children and adult and independent initiative.

1890

Moa Martinson (1890-1964)
Novelist and journalist, she was among the pioneers who depicted the life of the landless agricultural workers in Swedish countryside. In the 1920s she became actively involved in the socialist movement and wrote for labor publications demanding better pay and living conditions for farm and factory workers.

1891

Karin Kock-Lindberg
(1891-1976)
She was the first woman member of the Swedish government. She played a prominent part in society, especially as an economics expert, and made valuable contributions in the fields of science, politics and administration.

1900

Karin Maria Boye
(1900-1941)
Poet and novelist, she became a leader of the Socialist Clarte movement. In 1931 she was the founder editor of the poetry magazine *Spektrum* to which she contributed much of her own poetry.

Selma Ottilia Lovisa Lagerlof
(1858-1940)
A Swedish novelist, whose work is rooted in legend and saga, she became the first woman writer to win the Nobel Prize in Literature in 1909. She wrote in a romantic and imaginative manner vividly evoking the peasant life and landscape of northern Sweden. In the 20's she devoted much time to women's causes and as World War II approached, she helped German intellectuals and artists escape Nazi persecution.

1914
Maria Lang (1914-1991)
A prolific Swedish mystery writer, she has also published children's books and short stories. Her works are based on the traditional puzzle-mystery of Agatha Christie although she took her subjects from hidden family secrets and conflicts, incest and other sexual traumas.

1958
Agata Rossel (1910 -)
A Swedish diplomat, she became the first woman to head a permanent delegation to the United Nations in 1958. From 1964-69, she was Ambassador to Bulgaria and Yugoslavia, Czechoslovakia from 1969-73 and Greece form 1973-76. She is remembered for her work on behalf of refugee children after World War II and for her role as champion of women's rights throughout the world.

1962
Inga Thorsson (1916-1994)
Former Mayor of Stockholm, she was State Secretary of Foreign Affairs from 1962-67 and 1970-74. From 1964-66, she was Ambassador to Israel and from 1974-82 Ambassador and Chief Negotiator by the Disarmament Negotiations in Geneve.

1968
Ingrid Garde Widemar
In 1968, she became first woman on Sweden's 24-member Supreme Court.

1976
Karen Soder (1928 -)
A Swedish politician, she was the first woman to serve as Minister of Foreign Affairs in her country when appointed by Prime Minister Thorbjorn Falldin in 1976.

1982
Anita Gradin (1933 -)
From 1982-86, she became Minister of Immigration and Equality in the Ministry of Labor and Minister of External Trade and Europe in the Ministry of Foreign Affairs from 1986-91. Between 1992-94, she was Ambassador to Austria, Slovenia, United Nations for Industrial Development and International Atomic Agency. She was European Union Commissioner of Immigration, Interior and Control and Anti-Fraud Measures in 1995-99.

Alva Myrdal (1902-1986)
She devoted most of her life trying to solve problem of nuclear armament piling up throughout the world. In 1949 she was first Swedish woman to serve as principal director of the Department of Social Sciences at UNESCO. She has written several books on need for world peace and social responsibility. In 1936 she founded and served as first Vice President of the Social Pedagogical Institute in Stockholm, which promoted progressive educational theories and reforms in childcare. Between 1955-61, she served as Sweden's first female ambassador to India. As a member of Sweden's Senate of Riksdag in 1961, she began to stress role of disarmament. In 1965 she founded the Stockholm International Peace Research Institute. She received the Nobel Prize in 1982 for continuing to clamor against aggression and terrorism.

1983
Margareta Hegart
Former State Secretary of Trade, she was Consul General of Los Angeles from 1983-89 and Ambassador to Ireland from 1989-96.

1985
Monica G.E. Andersson
She was State Secretary of Social Affairs (1985-90) and Mayor for Building and Environment in Stockholm (1991-98).

1986
Birgitta Dahl (1937 -)
Between 1983-86, she was Minister of Environment and Energy and Minister of Environment from 1986-89. In 1994, she became Speaker of the Riksdag.

1989
Karin Ahrland (1950 -)
She was Consul General in Montreal from 1989-91 and Ambassador to New Zealand, Fiji and Tonga from 1993-96.

1991
Gun Hellsvik
She was Minister of Justice from 1991-94, Chairman of the Juridical Committee of the Riksdag since 1994 and in 1999 became President of the Nordic Council.

Friherreinna Margaretha af Ugglas (1939 -)
From 1991-94, she was Minister of Foreign Affairs and in 1993 became Chairman of the Council of Ministers of the Council of Europe. Friherreinna is the equivalent to the title of Baroness.

1993
Ulla Holm
A feminist activist, her 1993 dissertation of feminist ethics and praxis was the first feminist philosophical thesis in Sweden and only the 5th by a woman in philosophy. She has been an initiator of or involved in many projects such as Nordic Network for Women in Philosophy.

1994
Lena Hall Eriksson
She was State Secretary of Labor for Refugees and Immigration from 1994-96 and Secretary General of the Department of Immigration since 1996.

1997
Crown Princess Victoria of Sweden, Duchess of Vastergotland (1979 -)
On her 18th birthday, she swore the oath on the constitution and was inaugurated as Deputy Head of State.

1998
Mai-Inge Klingwall (1946 -)
Between 1998-99, she was Minister in the Ministry of Social Affairs responsible for Social Insurance and in 1999 became Minister in the Ministry of Foreign Affairs in charge of Development, Cooperation, Immigration and Asylum Affairs.

Mona Salin
Former Vice-Statsminister and Minister of Equality, in 1998, she became Minister in the Ministry of Industry and Trade responsible for Industrial Development, Small Enterprise, Regional Development and Science assisting the Minister of Industry.

1999
Anna-Karin Kammerling
In 1999, she set a new World and European swimming record in the 50-meters butterfly with a time of 26.29 seconds.

2000
Princess Madeleine of Sweden, Duchess of Halsingland och Gastrickland (1982 -)
In 2000, she became Assistant Deputy Head of State. The youngest child of King Carl XVI Gustaf, she acts as Regent in the absence of her elder sister and brother.

SWITZERLAND

1613
Elizabeth Baulacre
(1613-1693)
Swiss entrepreneur, she built a lucrative business in gold decoration and died with the second largest personal fortune in Geneva.

1784
Aime Argand
In 1784, she patented an efficient type of oil lamp. The principle of the Argand lamp was later applied to gas lighting.

1827
Johanna Spyri (1827-1901)
She achieved international fame by writing *Heidi* and stories of life in the mountains of Switzerland. Although written in German, *Heidi* has been translated into many languages and has been made into several motion pictures.

1887
Emilie Kempin-Spyri
(1853-1901)
She became the first woman in Switzerland to qualify as a lawyer in 1887.

1934
Elisabeth Kopp
Between 1974-75, she was President of the Grossrat (Grand Council) of Zurick and Federal Councilor of Justice and Police and Deputy Councilor of Finance from 1984-89. She had to resign from the government because of a scandal of which she was later cleared in court.

1969
Elisabeth Kubler-Ross
A psychiatrist, she published her first book "*On Death and Dying*" in 1969 after years of study and research which raised the awareness of the world. She has since published nine books dealing with the natural phenomenon of dying. She has been awarded over 25 honorary doctorates from major universities and received the Modern Samaritan Award and the Ideal Citizen Award.

1972
Margit Bigler-Enggenberger
In 1972, she becomes the first woman federal court judge in Switzerland.

1973
Ingrid Elginmann
She became the first woman stockbroker in Switzerland in 1973.

1976
Elisabeth Blunschy-Steiner
(1922-)
She became the first woman president of Switzerland's National Council in 1976.

1981
Heide Lang-Agheri
She was President of the Nationairat from 1981-82 and President of Government of the Kanton of Zurich from 1994-95.

1991
Josi J. Meier
From 1991-92, she was President of the Standesrat (Council of the States).

1999
Ruth Dreifuss (1940-)
Fluent in 5 languages, she served in many governmental capacities before being appointed National Councilor of the Interior in 1992. After serving a one-year term as Vice President, she became Switzerland's first female President in 1999.

TAJIKISTAN
1974
Raisa M. Grishiha
From 1974-81, she was Minister of Trade and from 1981-89 Deputy Premier Minister.

1993

Munira Abdulloyevna Inoyatova

She was Deputy Minister of Labor (1993-94), Deputy Premier Minister (1994-96) and Minister of Education (1994-99).

1995

Larisa Smeyanova

In 1995, she became 1st Deputy Minister of Economy and Foreign Economic Relations.

1997

Latofat Nasriddnova

She was Chairman of the State Committee for Women and Family Affairs in 1997.

TURKMENISTAN

1958

Khally Nazarova

She was Deputy Minister of Public Service in 1958 and Deputy Premier Minister from 1963-65.

1975

Roza Atamuradovna Bazarova

(1933 -)

In 1975, she was Deputy Premier Minister and from 1988-90 President of the Republic.

1990

Aksotlan Toreyevna Atayeva

Former Minister of Health, she became Minister of Social Affairs from 1994-96. She was appointed Ambassador to the United Nations in 1996.

1998

Djamal Geoklenova

She was Minister of Consumer Goods from 1998-99 and became Deputy Premier Minister in charge of the Chamber of Industry and Commerce and Turkmen Statistics and Forecasts Committee and Minister of Textile Industry and Foreign Trade.

UKRAINE

1871

Ljarissa Kosac (1871-1913)

Poet, her first anthology of lyric poetry *Na Krylach Pisen* was published in 1892. In the dramatic poem Robert Bruce, her interests in the struggle for Scottish independence reflect her commitment to the struggle of Ukraine for their own national autonomy.

1885

Sonia Delaunay (1885-1979)

A textile designer of international importance, her work was included in the Exposition des Arts Decoratifs in 1925.

1911

Lesya Ukrainka (1871-1913)

She first wrote traditional and patriotic poems but in 1893 became noted for her narrative poems with biblical and historical settings. In 1911, she wrote a book of poems on Ukrainian folklore *The Forest Setting*, which is considered to be her best work.

1918
Eugenia Bodoanova Bosh
(1879-1925)
Leader of the Secret Police, in 1918 she became People's Commissioner for Internal Affairs.

1953
Elena Kabashnaya (1953-)
She is president of DANA, a very active and influential women's organization in Ukraine. DANA focuses on achieving women's human rights, stopping the trafficking of Ukranian women in prostitution, improving women's health and all other issues affecting women.

1956
Larissa Latynina
She won the all-around title and three other gold medals, plus silver and bronze in gymnastics at the 1956 Melbourne Olympics. In 1960, she wins three gold, two silver and a bronze medal for gymnastics at the Rome Olympics <u>while three months pregnant</u>.

1964
Sonia Delannay (1885-1979)
She is one of the innovators of modern art in her use of shapes and strong colors for unusual shapes in her art. She painted murals and designed textiles and other soft material for the Paris Exposition of 1937. In 1964 she exhibited at the Louvre — only living woman to exhibit there.

1975
Dina I. Protsenka
From 1975-84, she was Chairman of the State Committee of the Protection of Nature.

1993
Yaryne Pastrytska
She was Deputy Chairman of the State Committee for Atomic Security from 1993-94.

1994
Syuzanna Ramanivna Stanik
Between 1994-96, she was Deputy Minister of Justice and became Minister of Justice in 1998.

1997
Yulia Voldyrovna Timoshenkno
From 1997-98, she was Chairman of the State Committee for Budget and in 2000 became Vice Premier Minister in charge of Energy Issues.

1998
Tetiana Kysiljova
She was Chairman of the State Committee for Standards and Metrology and Certification in the Council of Ministers from 1998-99.

UNITED KINGDOM

1342
Julian of Norwich
(1342-1412)
Known as the 1st English woman of letters, she is best known for her optimism and her repeated insistence of naming both God and Christ as "mother".

1406

Dame Juliana Berners

In 1406, she writes the first known essay on sports fishing "Treatise of Fishing with an Angle" in which she described how to make a rod and flies, when to fish and the many kinds of fishing.

1589

Jane Anger

She wrote *Her Protection for Women* in 1589, the first published English defense of women written by a woman.

1600

Bathsua Reginald Makin

(1600-1675)

Fluent in at least seven languages, she became tutor to Princess Elizabeth. In 1673 she wrote *An Essay to Revive the Ancient Education of Gentlewomen,* one of the earliest English polemics on the education of women.

1640

Aphra Behn (1640-1689)

She was the first professional woman writer in English and the most prolific dramatist of the Restoration. It is for her pioneering work in prose narrative that she achieved her place in literary history.

1666

Mary Astell (1666-1731)

In 1694, she published *A Serious Proposal to the Ladies for the Advancement of Their Time and Greatest Interest,* in which she suggests forming an academic community of women.

The treatise is the first published demand for women's higher education.

1731

Catharine Macaulay

(1731-1791)

The first noteworthy female English historian, she was best known for her 8-volumne scholarly history *The History of England from the accession of James I to that of the Brunswick line.* In 1790 she wrote *Letters on Education* in which she expresses her feminist ideals especially education for women.

1745

Hannah More (1745-1833)

Religious writer, her interests included female education, antislavery, and Christian life in general.

1764

Ann Radcliffe (1764 -?)

Author of tales of terror and suspense, she is considered the creator of the gothic tale.

1780

Elizabeth Fry (1780-1845)

Social reformer, she was one of the chief promoters of prison reform in Europe and worked to improve conditions in Newgate Prison where 300 women and their children are confined without adequate clothes or bedding. At Newgate, she started a school, taught needlework, instituted religious services and arranged for the hiring of prison matrons. She also helped to improve the British hospital system.

1792
Mary Wollstonecraft
In 1792 she published the feminist social study *A Vindication of the Rights of Woman* which was the first study to make women's rights into a cause. Her demand for "Justice for one-half of the human race" was too revolutionary but she succeeded in beginning the trend toward regarding women as an important social force.

1799
Mary Anning (1799-1847)
British paleontologist known as the "greatest fossilist the world ever knew", she discovered the first specimen of *Ichthyosaurs* acknowledged by the Geological Society in London. She also discovered the first nearly complete example of the *Plesiosaurus*; the first British *Pterodactylus macronyx*, a fossil flying reptile; the *Squaloraja* fossil fish, a transitional link between sharks and rays; and finally the *Plesiosaurus macrocephalus*.

1802
Harriet Martineau (1802 -?)
Best known for her writings on economics, she is also noted for her disabilities that ranged from deafness to heart disease.

1808
Caroline Norton (1808-1877)
Author and poet, she is better known now for her writing on the sorry treatment of married women under the laws of England. She wrote several pamphlets on child custody and worked for passage of the Infant Custody Bill in 1839. Later, she embarked on another legal campaign, one to protect the property and earnings of divorced or separated women.

1815
Julia Margaret Cameron
(1815 -?)
Pioneering photographer, she developed dramatic photographs through the use of close-ups and dramatic lighting in soft focus.

1827
Lydia Becker (1827 – 1890)
A keen writer and active member of Manchester's Ladies Literary Society, her book *Botany for Novices* was published in 1866. She established the Women's Suffrage Journal in 1870 and continued as editor throughout the 1870s and 1880s.

Frances Buss (1827 -?)
She established the North London Collegiate School for Girls in 1850, which soon developed a reputation for providing an excellent education for its students. In 1866, she joined the London Suffrage Committee and began organizing a petition-asking Parliament to grant women the

vote. She remained a strong supporter of universal suffrage.

1828
Margaret Oliphant
(1828-1897)
She published her first novel "*Margaret Maitland*" in 1849 and went on to have a prolific literary career. She wrote over 100 novels and 30 non-fiction books. During her last years she worked on a history of the Blackwood Publishing House, which is a rich source of 19th century literary gossip.

1831
Amelia Edwards (1831 -?)
An English traveler who traveled in Egypt, she published an account of her adventures, *A Thousand Miles Up the Nile* and become determined to halt the depredation of Egypt by treasure hunters.

1835
Emily Faithfull (1835-1895)
Publisher and feminist, she founded a printing house with women compositors in 1860 and was appointed printer and publisher-in-ordinary to Queen Victoria. She was inspired by her research on women printers in the 15th century. In 1863 she started the Victoria Magazine advocating the claims of women to remunerative employment.

Alicia Anne Spottiswoode
(1835-1900)
She is remembered as the composer of "*Annie Laurie*". She was a collector of traditional songs and wrote 69 of them often basing them on older pieces.

1836
Elizabeth Garrett Anderson
(1836-1917)
Physician and first English woman doctor, the University of Paris gave her degree of MD in 1870. She established a dispensary for women in London where she instituted medical courses for women. In 1908, she was elected mayor of Aldeburgh – the first woman mayor in England.

Isabella Mary Beeton
(1836-1865)
British writer on cookery, she became a household name after the publication of her Book of Household Management in a women's magazine covering cookery and other branches of domestic science.

1838
Octavia Hill (1838-1912)
Housing reformer and founder of the National Trust for Places of Historic Interest, she worked among the poor to improve the homes of people in the slums.

1848
Anne Bronte
In 1848, she publishes The Tenant of *Wildfell Hall*, in which she protests against the

social and legal confinement of women.

1851
Lady Isabella Caroline Somerset (1851 -?)
She started a treatment center for alcoholic women in 1895, the first of its kind in England and perhaps the world.

1854
Clementina Black
(1854–1922)
She helped form the Women's Trade Union Association in 1889 and wrote several books on the subject of low pay including *Sweated Industry and the Minimum Wage* and *A Case for Trade Boards*. One of the most successful of her books was *The Agitator*, a novel based on her experiences as a trade union leader.

Hertha Marks Aryton
(1854-1923)
A British physicist who worked in electricity, she wrote what became a standard textbook "*The Electric Arc*". She received the Hughes Medal for her original research into the electric arc and the sand ripples. She invented and patented an instrument for dividing a line into any number of equal parts as well as for enlarging and reducing figures, a sphygmograqph for monitoring human pulse and the Aryton Fan for dispersing mustard gas. In 1899 she was elected the first female member of the Institution of Electrical Engineers.

1855
Isabella Ford (1855-1924)
She helped form Machinists Society for tailoresses in 1885 to improve the pay and conditions of women working in the textile industry. She retained her interest in women's rights and in 1890 helped form the Leeds Women's Suffrage Society. Leeds was also an important writer of books on the struggle for equality. In 1893, she wrote a book called *Women's Wages*, which includes a section of sexual harassment in factories.

1862
Mary Henrietta Kingsley
(1862-1900)
She traveled to West and Central Africa to study African religion and law and was the first European to visit parts of Gabon. She wrote several books about her experiences in Africa and later was consulted by colonial administrators for her expertise and understanding of African culture.

1863
Margaret Murray (1863-1963)
A British scholar and specialist in Egyptian hieroglyphics, she obtained a degree in linguistics, which led to study of Egyptian hieroglyphics and Egyptology. She was an ardent feminist. In 1921, she published *The Witch Cult in Western Europe* in which she claimed that the

persecution of witches in Europe was an attack of patriarchal establishment on ancient, woman-centered religions. In 1931, she published a book on Egyptian archeology.

1864
Hilda Beatrice Hewlett
(1854-1943)
In 1911, she became the first British woman to obtain a pilot's license. In 1914 she co-founded a company to manufacture aeroplanes that supplied over 800 military aircraft during WW1.

1866
Barbara Bodichon
(1827-1891)
She was very critical of a legal system that failed to protect the property and earnings of married women and in 1857 wrote *Women and Work* where she argued that a married woman's dependence on her husband was degrading. In 1866, she formed the first ever **Women's Suffrage Committee,** which submitted a petition of 1500 names to the House of Commons.

Jessie Boucherett
English feminist, she founded the Englishwoman's Review in 1866, the principal feminist magazine in England until 1910.

1867
Louisa Starr Canziani
She became the first female gold medallist at the Royal Academy Schools in 1867. The painting "Undine" has been attributed to her.

Rosa Lewis (1867-1952)
She was a celebrated society caterer and owner of Cavadish Hotel in England.

1868
Gertrude Bell (1868 -?)
Because of her knowledge of the territory, the government appointed her a diplomat in Baghdad. She was the first European woman to travel in remote parts of the Middle East and wrote about her journeys and the excavations that she saw. During World War I, she acted as a British agent in Egypt.

Sarah Sewell
English antifeminist, she publishes *Women and the Times we Live In* arguing against women's higher education in 1868.

1871
Eleanor Fortescue-Brickdale
(1871-1945)
She pursued a dual career as a painter and illustrator of fine color-printed editions of literary texts. In 1902, she became the first female member of the Institute of Painters in Oils.

Lucy Walker
English mountaineer, in 1871 she became the first woman to climb the Matterhorn.

1872

Sophia Jex-Blake

A British physician, she founded the Edinburgh School of Medicine for Women in 1872. She establishes the London School of Medicine for Women in 1974 but does not received her license to practice medicine until 1877.

1873

Margaret Bondfield

(1873-1953)

In 1894, she was elected to the Shop Assistants Union District Council and began contributing articles to the union journal. In 1898, she created a storm when she described the ideal married couple as one in which both went out to work and shared the household tasks between them. She became known as Britain's leading expert on shop workers. In 1923, she became the first woman to be elected to the House of Commons. She became the first woman in history to gain a place in the British Cabinet when she was appointed Minister of Labor in 1929.

1879

Agnes Arber (1879-1960)

Botanist and philosopher, her works include *Herbals, Their Origins and Evolution* and *Water Plants*.

1880

May Arnold

In 1880, she patented an incubating and artifical hatching apparatus as well as a means for preventing the escape of poultry.

1882

Sylvia Pankhurst

(1882-1960)

Suffragist, she launched the British feminist movement (forerunner of the United State's version) and won women's voting rights in 1918.

1886

Rachel Kay Shuttleworld

(1886-1967)

British needlewoman, she devoted her life to the practice, teaching and appreciation of the art and craft of needlework. She became well known for her lace and embroidery.

1891

Lorna Mary Swain

(1891-1936)

An educator and mathematician, she was appointed Director of Studies at Newnham College in 1920. Her mathematical interests were in fluid dynamics and she worked on problem of vibration of propellers of aircraft. In 1929, she researched and published important work on the turbulent wake behind a body of revolution.

1892

Dorothy Annie Elizabeth Garrod

(1892-1968)

Archaeologist, she became an expert on the Palaeolithic or Old Stone Age and the first woman to hold a professorial chair at Cambridge in 1939.

From 1929-34, she led the joint American-English evacuation of Mount Carmel, Palestine where skeletal remains dating back 40,000 years were uncovered.

1895
Lilian Murray
In 1895, she becomes the first woman dentist in Britain.

1897
Baroness Wooton of Abinger
(1897-1988)
She was the first female life peer created in 1958 and was Deputy Speaker of the House of Lords from 1967-88.

1900
Dame Honor Briget B. Fell
(1900-)
A biologist, she became Director of Strangeways Research Laboratory in 1929. Her research focused upon the technique of organ culture and its employment to uncover differentiation and histo-genesis of bone, cartilage and associated tissues.

1902
Madge Sayers
She opened the door for women figure skaters when she entered the all-male 1902 world championships and places second. In 1905, she became the first woman world figure skating champion.

1903
Amy Johnson (1903-1941)
A British aviator, she was 1st woman to make solo airplane flight from London to Australia in 1930.

Barbara Hepworth
(1903-1975)
A sculptor, she designed large geometric shapes from wood and stone and introduced the "hole", painted hollows to abstract sculpture.

1906
Kathleen Mary Kenyon
(1906-1978)
She attended Somerville College in Oxford and later became the first female president of the Oxford Archeological Society. She contributed to the founding of the University of London Institute of Archeology. In 1951, she became honorary director of the British School of Archeology in Jerusalem and found evidence that pushed back the occupation at Jericho from the Bronze Age and Neolithic to the Natufian culture at the end of the Ice Age (10,000-9,000 BC).

1910
Cicely Corbett Fisher
(1885 - 1959)
In 1910, she joined the Women's Industrial Council, an organization that campaigned against low pay and bad working conditions. She was also an active member of the Anti-Sweating League, which was defined as (1) working long hours, (2) for low wages, (3) under unsanitary conditions. Most sweated labor took place in the homes of

workers and chief among its evils was the exploitation of child labor.

1911
Jo Cook (1911 -)
In 1952, she joined the Royal Naval Minewatching Service and became the first woman minewatching skipper in the world. RNMS was made up of volunteers to defend against mines laid by Soviet aircraft around British harbors at the height of the cold war. She later became the first woman to command an RNXS unit and finally commanded a 120-ton inshore minesweeper.

1913
Elizabeth David (1913-1992)
British writer of cookery books, she ran a kitchen shop in London from 1965 to 1973 which became a model for such shops throughout Britain and United States. Her books are credited with reviving current British interest in spices and exotic fruits.

Fanny Harwood
A British dentist, she is the first woman licensed as a dental surgeon by the Royal College of Surgeons in 1912.

1914
Margery Hunt (1914 -)
English businesswoman, she was founder of a successful Mayfair temporary employee agency and became one of the first women underwriters at Lloyd's.

1917
Constance M. Coltman
(1889-1969)
She was the first woman in England to be ordained a minister in the Congregational Church in 1917 and did much to help other women become ministers Her concern for peace led her to join the Fellowship of Reconciliation.

Viola Spencer
In 1917, she became the first British woman aviator to fly solo.

1919
Nancy Astor (1879-1964)
In 1919 she was the first woman member of Parliament. She devoted herself to causes of women and children, education, temperance and nursery schools.

1920
Bridget Biddy Martin Grundy
(1920 -)
She was the first woman to reach the rank of Air Commodore with the Women's Royal Air Force. Her service as a pioneer in the WAAF ranged from examining drains to commanding officer and her postings ranged from air bases in Ireland to intelligence.

Rosalind Elsie Franklin
(1920-1958)
British biophysicist who conducted X-ray diffraction studies on the structure of the DNA molecule. She discovered that the phosphate groups lie on the outside of

the molecule and that the structure was basically helical. This discovery played a vital role in the unraveling of the structure of DNA.

1924
Alexandra David-Neel
In 1924, she is the first European woman to travel to the forbidden city of Tibet.

Evelyn C. Pielou (1924 -)
She was a biologist who contributed significantly to the development of mathematical ecology. She wrote several books including "*Introduction to Mathematical Ecology*", "*Biogeography*", "*Population & Community Ecology*", "*Interpretation of Ecological Data*" and "*After the Ice Age*".

Dora Russell (1894-1986)
A lifelong advocate of birth control, women's rights and international peace, she founded the Workers' Birth Control Group in London in 1924.

1925
Margaret Thatcher (1925 -)
The first woman in European history to be elected Prime Minister, she became the first British Prime Minister in the 20th century to win three consecutive terms and the nation's longest serving Prime Minister since 1827. Upon entering office, she advocated measures that would limit government control, such as giving individuals greater

independence from the state, ending government interference in the economy, reducing public expenditures and return education, health care and housing to private control. In 1980, she helped Zimbabwe establish independence and oversaw the successful British seizure of the Falkland Islands in 1982.

1926
Lucia Welch
In 1926, she became the first woman sheriff in England.

1929
Brenda Colvin (1898-1981)
A pioneer landscape architect, she founded the Institute of Landscape Architects in 1919 and in 1951 The International Federation of Landscape Architects.

1930
Betty Boothroyd (1930 -)
As first woman speaker of the House of Commons, she deploys her formidable governess manner, teamed with lightning wit to keep the mainly male British MPs in order. She is often thought to become president of a republican UK should the country dispense with the monarchy.

Constance Spry (1886-1960)
An English flower arranger and cook, she was the first woman to open a School of Floristry. After World War II, she founded the Cordon Bleu Cooking School in London and

published 13 books on flowers and cooking.

Mary Quant (1934 -)
Fashion designer, she was responsible in the 1960s for the "Chelsea look" of England and the widespread popularity of the mini-skirt and "hot pants".

1938
Eileen Power (1889-1940)
An economic historian, she became the first woman to give the Lord Lectures at Oxford in 1938. Her special interests were the economic position of women in the 13th & 14th centuries, the life of the medieval peasant and the wool trade.

1939
Dorothy A. E. Garrod (1892-1969)
When elected Professor at Cambridge in 1939, she was the first woman to become a professor in any field at either Oxford or Cambridge. She was also the first woman to do research in Paleolithic archeology, promoted use of aerial photography in archeological excavations and made significant contributions on prehistoric migrations of man, prehistoric irrigation methods and hunting techniques and Paleolithic art.

Germaine Greer (1939 -)
Reformer, author and educator, she championed the sexual freedom of women in the "*The Female Eunuch*" published in

1970. However, critics called her book "*Sex and Destiny*" published in 1984 anti-feminist.

Erin Pizzey (1939 -)
In 1971, she founded Women's Aid; Britain's first battered women's shelter.

1945
Barbara Castle (1911 -)
An important force in British politics, she entered Parliament in 1945 as member of Labour for Blackburn. Castle attained cabinet rank as Minister of Overseas Development. As Minister of Transportation, she introduced 70mph speed limits and use of "breathalyzer" test for drunk drivers.

1946
Verena Holmes
Engineer and versatile inventor, she patented the safety paper cutter that was produced at the all-women firm of Holmes & Leather Ltd. founded in 1946 to give employment to women engineers. In 1958, she patented a stenciling apparatus intended for commercial use.

1948
Sylvia Crowe (1901 -)
She co-foundered the International Federation of Landscape Architects in England in 1948 and is known for designing new town landscapes.

Vicki Manolo Draves
At the summer Olympics in London, England in 1948, she became the first woman to win a gold medal in both diving events in the same Olympics.

1949
Carol Galley (1949 -)
As Vice-Chairman of Mercury Asset Management, she can make or break company chairmen and chief executives with her investment decisions. In making multi-million-pound investment decisions, she is looking after the retirement incomes of 2-million superannuation fund members.

1950
I. Violet Dawson
A dairy farmer, she invented a cooler that rapidly cools fresh milk to 40°F in 1950, which enabled her to sell the best milk in Sussex.

1961
Diana, Princess of Wales
(1961-1997)
She worked with AIDS organizations and charities for children. The current spotlight on the problem of land mines is due to the efforts of the late Princess Diana.

1965
Barbara Hepworth
(1903-1975)
She was an abstract sculptor whose work was characterized by highly simplified organic forms. Her abstractions are imbued with a dignified presence that has often been compared with the serene power of classical sculpture. In 1965, she became a Dame Commander of the British Empire and was lauded as a major figure in the international art world.

1967
Dame Cicely Saunders
(1918 -)
She was founder of the modern hospice movement and became founder, medical director and chairman of St. Christopher's Hospice. She promotes the principle of dying with dignity, maintaining that death is a natural process and can be eased by sensitive nursing and effective pain control.

1971
Erin P. Margaret Shapiro
(1939-)
British writer and campaigner for women's rights, she founded the first shelter for Battered Wives and their children in London in 1971. She also campaigned for legal protection and resources to help women and children to escape from violent men. Her book *Scream Quietly or the Neighbors Will Hear* encouraged national discussion of what had previously been a hidden problem.

Barbara Ward (1914-1981)
An English economist and writer educated at Oxford, she was the first woman to address the Vatican Council in Rome in

1971. She was appointed to the Vatican Commission for Justice and Peace in 1967. She also published 16 books on economics and politics.

1972
Mary Elizabeth Peters (1939 -)
She started competing in the pentathlon at age 17 and won the gold medal at the 1972 Olympics, setting a new world record. She also campaigned for more sports facilities in Northern Ireland and an athletics stadium in Belfast is now named after her.

1973
Margaret Burlidge
Astronomer, she became the first woman director of the Royal Greenwich Observatory in 1973 but she was denied the traditional title: astronomer royal.

1980
Sue Atkins
She often fought as "Sue Catkins" and pioneered women's boxing in Britain in the late 1980's. Amateur boxing for women is now sanctioned in Britain, but her efforts to legitimize the pro sport have been unsuccessful. Sue is now retired from the ring but founded the British Ladies' Boxing Association and still coaches semi-pro boxers in England.

1983
Mary Donaldson
In 1983, she becomes first woman Lord Mayor of London in

the 800 years of that office's existence.

1991
Helen P. Sharman (1963-)
She is Britain's first astronaut. In 1989 she was selected to be the British member of the Russian scientific space mission, Project Juno, spending eight days in space in 1991. She has since become a lecturer and broadcaster in science education.

1994
Pauline Green (1949 -)
She is leader of the Socialist group in the European Parliament. A former policewoman from Tottenham, she is a tough and down-to-earth Labourite who has bashed the Euro-Left into shape since she took over the parliament's biggest group in 1994.

1995
Rosalyn Higgins (1938-)
In 1995, Rosalyn Higgins made legal history by becoming the first woman to be elected as a judge of the International Court of Justice. Her most celebrated appearance came during the Lockerbie case, when as Britain's counsel, she won a court decision refusing Libya relief from United Nations sanctions aimed at securing the surrender of two Libyans wanted for the bombing attack.

Rachel Lomax (1946 -)
In 1995, she became vice-president of the World Bank in Washington. At the World Bank, her task is to promote economic and social progress in developing countries through loans, projects and advice to policy-makers.

1996
Anita Roddick (1943 -)
The chief executive and founder of the Body Shop, she publicly took on Shell about the plight of the Ogoni people in Nigeria in 1995 and in 1996 she launched a college to ensure that tomorrow's business leaders are more ethically aware.

1999
Countess Margaret of Mar
In 1999, she became Deputy Speaker of the House of Lords. She succeeded to the title in 1975 and in 1999 was one of the 92 Hereditary Lords elected to the Reformed House of Lords and the first Hereditary Peeress to hold any office in the Lords.

UZBEKISTAN

1935
Rano Kh. Abdullaeva (1935 -)
Between 1961-62, she was First Secretary of Samarkand. She became Deputy Premier Minister in 1971.

1953
Yanjamaa Nemendeyen Subaataryn
In 1953, she became the first non-royal woman to be acting head of state.

1967
Anna Brodova
Former Deputy Chief of Government of Tashkent, she was Minister of Public Service from 1967-89.

1974
Yadar Sadykovna Nasriddinova
Former Deputy Premier Minister of Construction Industry, she became Deputy Minister of Building Material in 1974.

1995
Dilbar Muhammadchonovna Gulomova
In 1995, she became Deputy Premier Minister and Chairman of the State Committee for Women's Affairs.

WALES

1480
Gwerful Mechain (1480 -?)
She is the only female poet of medieval Wales whose poetry survives. She is famous for her salacious verse and excels in her poems in defense of women.

1741
Hester Lynch Salsubury Thrale Piozzi (1741-1821)
An enthusiastic diarist, her diary called *Thraliana* which she began in 1776 contained a rich collection of anecdotes and conversations which provided insight into English society of her time.

1838
Lady Charlotte Guest
In 1838, she published the first of her translations from

the ancient collection of Welsh myths – the *Mahinogian*.

1925
Hilda Vaughan (1892 -?)
In 1925, she writes *Battle to the Weak*, set in Wales.

1935
Kate Roberts (1891-1985)
In 1935, she became director of a publishing house. She was a major force in developing the short story in Welsh writing. Using a mix of conventional language and dialect, she was able to convey the essence of mining village life.

1999
Edwina Hart
In 1999 she became Secretary of Finance with additional charge of Equal Opportunities and Anti-Poverty Policies added in 2000.

YUGOSLAVIA

1874
Ivan Brlic-Ma'uranic
(1874-1938)
One of Yugoslavia's outstanding writers of children's literature, she creates original stories and fables the characters and motifs of which are drawn extensively from Slavic folklore.

1958
Lidija Sentjurc (1911 -)
During World War II, she was a leading commander in the Resistance Army. From 1958-62, she was Federal Minister of

Social Policy and Communal Questions.

1963
Stana Tomasevic-Arnesen
(1922 -)
She was appointed Ambassador to Norway and Iceland from 1963-67, Chairperson of the Foreign Affairs Comminutes of the Federal Assembly and Ambassador to Denmark in 1974.

1979
Sena Sekulic
A professor of Architecture at the University of Zagreb, she was appointed Dean of the University of Zagreb in 1979.

1982
Mila Planinc (1925 -)
A Yugoslav politician, she became the first female Prime Minister of a Communist country when she was appointed in 1982.

1984
Franciska Herga
She was Member of Federal Executive Council from 1984-88 and Chairperson of the Council for the National Market from 1986-88.

1990
Bogdana Glumac-Levakov
From 1990-92, she was President of the Savezna Skupstina (Federal Assembly) and Vice President from 1989-90.

1993
Margit Savovic (1952 -)
Between 1993-94, she was
Federal Minister of Human
Rights and Minorities and
Minister without Portfolio in
charge of Human Rights and
Minorities from 1994-98 and in
1999.

1999
Borka Vucic (1927 -)
Former Head of Beogradska
Banka, she became Minister for
Relations with International
Financial Institutions in
1999.

North American Women

CANADA

1762
Marie-Henriette Ross
(1762-1860)
Known as "Granny Ross", she was an Acadian woman whose adventures and skills as a midwife and healer made her a part of Nova Scotia folk history.

1800
Shawnadithit (1800-1829)
Driven from the best fishing and hunting spots in Newfoundland and devastated by European diseases, the Beothuk was a dying race when she was born. As the last Beothuk, she lived with Europeans and explained her culture and language to Newfoundlanders who were concerned over the fate of the Beothuks.

1820
Emily Shaw Beavan
She wrote an informative book describing pioneer life in Canada. Her detailed account of life in the backwoods is fascinating.

1831
Emily Howard Stowe
(1831-1903)
Canadian feminist, physician and suffragist, she received a medical degree from New York College of Medicine and became 1st woman licensed to practice medicine in Canada

in 1880. She was founder and 1st president of Dominion Women's Enfranchisement Association in 1893.

1837
Agnes Maule Machar
(1837-1927)
An author and social critic, she addressed issues such as women's rights, compulsory education and workplace conditions. Her 1892 novel *Roland Graeme, Knight: A Novel of Our Time*, was one of the few in that period to deal with the negative aspects of industrialization.

1838
Frances Anne Hopkins
(1838-1919)
She traveled the fur trade routes and later produced large oil paintings of the huge, fur trade canoes and the colorful voyageurs who manned them. The "voyageur paintings" which provide a detailed record of a vanished way of life, are vaguely familiar to many Canadians, although few realize the artist was a woman.

1849
Henrietta Muir Edwards
(1849-1931)
In 1875, she published Canada's first women's magazine called "*Women's Work in Canada*". In 1893, she painted dishes for Canadian

Pavilion at Chicago World's Fair. She also published handbooks entitled *Legal Status of Women in Canada* and *Legal Status of Women in Alberta* in 1917.

1857

Adelaide Hoodless

(1857-1910)

When her baby son died from drinking contaminated milk, she dedicated her life to teaching girls and women the science of childcare and home management. Her idea of a practical, educational, self-help association for rural women became a reality in the form of the Women's Institutes.

1861

Victoria Belcourt Callihoo

(1861-1966)

The daughter of a Cree medicine woman, she was an expert teamster and freighted for the Hudson's Bay Company. Her vivid recollections, outlined in the *Alberta Historical Review*, are a remarkable window into 19th century Metis daily life.

1861

Emily Pauline Johnson

(1861-1913)

One of Canada's most well known poets, her first collection of poetry *The White Wampum* was published in 1895. *Legends of Vancouver* published in 1911 was a narrative and interpretation of stories she had been told by Chief Joe Capilano, a member of the Squamish tribe of British Columbia. Her novel, *The Moccasin Maker* focuses on the experiences of Canadian Indian and non-Indian women.

1862

Carrie Derick (1862-1941)

Geneticist who became internationally recognized for her work in heredity, she became the first female instructor at McGill University in 1891. Carrie eventually became the first woman ever appointed to a full professorship at a Canadian university. Her research on heredity was read by scientists around the world and paved the way for the future study of genetics.

1863

Robertine Barry (1863-1910)

A supporter of women's rights, education and literary culture, she raised the ire of Quebec's clerical elite. In 1895, she published her first book *Fleurs Champetres* that depicts with brutal honesty the harsh realities of the lives of women in rural Quebec including abuse and exploitation. Her most significant contribution was her bimonthly paper, *Le Journal de Francoise*.

1868

Louise McKinney (1868-1931)

An organizer and supporter of the Women's Christian Temperance Union, she became

the first woman elected
official in the British
Empire when she became Member
of the Legislative Assembly
in 1917 - the first election
in which women could vote or
run for office. In 1925, she
was one of 4 women to sign
the Basis of Union, which
formed the United Church of
Canada.

Emily Ferguson Murphy
(1868-1933)
A leader in the fight for
social reform, for women's
rights and in the votes for
women movement, she also led
the struggle to have women
recognized as "persons" in
the eyes of the law.

Irene Parlby (1868-1965)
An advocate for rural women
in Alberta, she organized and
became first President of
United Farm Women's
Association in 1916. In 1925,
she successfully sponsored
Minimum Wage for Women Act.
She became the first woman to
receive an Honorary Doctorate
of Law from University of
Alberta in 1935.

1869

Maude Abbott (1869-1940)
A physician and scientist,
she became a world authority
on congenital heart ailments.
Her book, *The Atlas of
Congenital Cardiac Disease*,
in which she described her
new classification system was
published in 1936 and was
praised as an important
addition to medical

knowledge. She also wrote a
history of nursing, which was
later used, in nursing
schools across the country.

1871

Emily Carr (1871-1944)
A painter of Indians and
landscapes of western Canada,
she was a preservationist of
native ways and traveled
extensively to Indian
villages to record the
vanishing tradiitons.

1872

Emelie Fortin Tremblay
(1872-?)
She was the first white woman
to cross Chilkoot Pass and
took part in the Klondike
Gold Rush. She was a lifetime
member of the Imperial Order
of the Daughters of the
Empire, a founding member of
the Ladies of the Golden
North and president of the
Yukon Women Pioneers. In
1913, she opened a woman's
clothing shop in Dawson City
and her shop is an historical
building today.

1873

Nellie Mooney McClung
(1873-1951)
A novelist, reformer,
journalist and suffragist she
led the fight to enfranchise
North American women in the
early 1910's. She went to
Geneva as a Canadian
representative to the League
of Nations in 1938.

1874

Elizabeth Rebecca Laird
(1874-?)
X-ray researcher, she studied the properties of "soft" x-rays, which occur in the area between known x-rays and the extreme ultraviolet rays.

1875

Edith Berkely (1875-1963)
She was an expert in the field of polychaete toxonomy (classification of marine worms). Dr. Berkely published 46 scientific papers and had several organisms named for her.

1876

Harriet Brooks Pitcher
(1876-1933)
Canada's first woman nuclear physicist, she made a number of discoveries about radiation which added important pieces to the jigsaw puzzle of modern nuclear science. She was among the early discoverers of radon and the first researcher to attempt to determine its atomic mass. She conducted research at Cambridge University and in Paris for the famous Marie Curie.

1879

Maude Menten (1879-1960)
She was one of the most versatile, innovative chemistry investigators in the early part of the century. She developed the Michaelis-Menton equation for enzyme kinetics, which gives an expression for the rate of an enzyme reaction and became key to the interpretation of how an enzyme reacts on its substrate. In histochemistry, her publication in 1944 of a new technique for the demonstration of enzyme alkaline phosphatase ushered in the new azo-dye method.

1880

Marie-Claire Duveluy
(1880-1968)
Librarian, historian and writer, she joined the Montreal Public Library and began writing her book, *Instructions pour la redaction des catalogues de bibliotheque*. In 1937, she played a leading role in the founding of the Ecole de Bibliothecaires at the Universite de Montreal.

1883

Augusta Stowe Gullen
(1857-1943)
In 1883, she was the first woman to study medicine and graduate from a Canadian university. She later became Professor of Pediatrics at the new Women's Medical College.

1887

Margaret Newton (1887-1971)
In 1922, she became the first Canadian woman to receive a doctorate in agricultural science. She became the best-known Canadian expert in stem rust, a fungus that destroys

wheat, and her work helped find ways to fight the disease. In 1969, the University of Saskatchewan made her an honorary Doctor of Laws.

1890
Agnes Macphail (1890-1954)
The first female Member of Parliament, she championed the rights of farmers and worked hard for social and prison reform.

1894
Mary Travers (1894-1941)
After she recorded La Cuistniere and La Servante, she became known and was universally referred to as "La Bolduc". Her songs were written in colloqual French and concerned mundane events of the common people during the 1930s. The evolution of the chanson in Quebec was greatly influenced by La Bolduc and her songs enjoy a special place in Quebec's musical legacy.

1895
Jean Dow
After earning her medical degree from the University of Toronto in 1895, she went to China where she did research into the organism, which causes Kala-azar, a wasting disease, which is prevalent in Africa, Asia and the Middle East. Her work paved the way for the development of treatment for this illness, which previously had a fatality rate of 70%.

1898
E. Cora Hind
She made her first crop prediction in 1898 and later became a world authority on crop predictions. Her predictions were used around the world and became the basis for determining the world price for Canadian wheat. As agricultural editor of the Winnipeg Free Press, she was the first journalist to write about agriculture as a business. She was also involved in the suffrage movement and in rural women's organizations.

1899
Helen Creighton (1899-1989)
She interviewed people who knew stories and song from pirate days while researching a journalistic project on pirates and realized that Nova Scotians were a rich source of folklore. Her collection of over 4,000 songs and many stories in English, French, Gaelic, Micman and German includes some from the 13th and 15th centuries as well as the now popular Farewell to Nova Scotia. Many of the songs have been commercially recorded and have become the basis of ballet, opera and symphony scores.

1902
Marie Tremaine (1902-1984)
Librarian and bibliographer, she compiled *A bibliography*

of Canadiana, which described pre-Confederation Canadiana held by the Toronto Public Library. She published *A bibliography of Canadian imprints, 1751-1800* in 1952. In 1947, She became director of the Arctic Bibliography Project of the Arctic Institute of North America and undertook the monumental task of editing the first 14 volumes of the *Arctic bibliography*.

1906
Jessie Mifflen (1906-1994)
She was instrumental in the establishment of regional libraries throughout Newfoundland. During World War II, she also served in the Royal Canadian Air Force.

1907
Marie Lacoste Gerin-Lajoie (1867-1945)
She founded the Federation Nationale Saint Jean Baptiste in 1907; an organization dedicated to the promotion of civil and political rights for women. She authored two treatises, *Traite de droit ussuel* in 1902 and *La femme et le code civil* in 1929, as part of her efforts to reform the civil code which attributed a married woman the inferior legal status of a minor. She struggled to amend laws that had changed little since the 16th century, working to achieve the right of married women to control their own income, the right to be guardians of minors,

and the right to limit the husband's freedom to give away family assets. She also supported efforts to obtain simpler and cheaper separation procedures, the rights of separated women to manage their own property and demands that a fixed proportion of a husband's estate go to the wife. In 1940, Quebec granted women the right to vote.

1910
Emily Murphy (1868-1933)
She was a prominent suffragist and reformer and in 1910 became the first woman Police Magistrate in the British Empire. In 1922, she wrote "*The Black Candle*" concerning the drug trade in Canada.

1908
Lucy Maud Montgomery (1874-1942)
An author, she published her first book, *Anne of Green Cables* in 1908.

1912
Carrie Derick
She was an inspiring teacher, adventurous scientist and a tireless advocate of women's rights. In 1912, she became the first woman promoted to a full professorship in a Canadian university.

1914
Alice Jamison
When appointed judge of the juvenile court in Calgary in 1914, she became the first

woman in Canada and in the British Empire appointed to a court.

1917
Louise McKinney
(1868-1933)
A leading member of the Nonpartisan League, she was elected as its candidate to the Alberta legislature in 1917, becoming the 1st female member of any legislative body in the British Empire. She dedicated her energies to temperance and feminist causes all her life.

Irene Ayako Uchida
(1917 -)
She is a cytogeneticist and world famous Down syndrome researcher. Interested in the effect of radiation on chromosome division as shown in Down syndrome, spontaneous abortions and other syndromes resulting from having the wrong number of chromosomes.

1918
Gladys Boyd
She received her medical degree from the University of Toronto in 1918. Dr. Boyd became one of the pioneers in the treatment of juvenile diabetes and one of first doctors to treat diabetic children with insulin. She was also an recognized expert on childhood nephritis (inflammation of the kidneys). In 1932, she was elected president of the Federation of Medical Women of Canada.

1920
Elsie Hall
In 1920, she became the first woman graduate of the College of Law, University of Saskatchewan.

1921
Ursula Franklin (1921 -)
She taught and researched extensively in the field of materials science and in the area of the social impact of technology. Much of her work has was done in conjunction with archaeologists on ancient materials, she pioneered the development of archaeometry, which applies the modern technique of materials analysis to archaeology.

Mary Ellen Smith
(1862-1933)
She was the first woman in the British Empire to achieve cabinet rank. She was appointed Minister without Portfolio in British Columbia in 1921, a post she held until 1922.

1922
Molly Reilly (1922 -)
One of the first recruits to join Royal Canadian Air Force (Women's Division) in 1941, she was hired by Southern Provincial Airlines as full-time charter pilot in 1957 and her later promotion to captain made her the first woman in Canada to hold this position. In 1965, she became first corporate pilot in

Canada when she was hired by Canadian Utilities as their chief pilot. She was inducted into the Canadian Aviation Hall of Fame in 1973.

1923
Cathleen Synge Morawetz
(1923-)
She became a mathematician and the first female director of the Courant Institute in New York. She has written numerous articles about applications of partial differential equations, especially transonic flow and scattering theory.

1924
Margaret Newton
One of the first two women in Canada to study agriculture at university, she discovered the "presence of physio-logical races in rust." By 1924, she was the leading Canadian authority on cereal rusts.

1930
Irene Parlby
Former Minister without Portfolio in the Province of Alberta, she was appointed Ambassador to the League of Nations in 1930, the first woman ambassador of the country.

1934
Helen Kinnear
In 1934, she became the first woman in Canada to be appointed King's Council and was later the first woman to argue a case before the Supreme Court. In 1943, she became the first woman in the British Commonwealth to be appointed a county court judge. In 1953, she was awarded a honorary Doctor of Laws.

Julia Levy (1934 -)
An immunologist and co-discoverer of photosensitizer anti-cancer drugs, she founded her own drug company, Quadra Logic. In 1993, the Canadian government approved photofrin for the treatment of bladder and other cancers. She started a fantastic new program to treat autoimmune diseases such as arthritis, psoriasis and multiple sclerosis with a second generation photodynamic drug called BPD.

1935
Joy Kogawa (1935 -)
A Canadian poet, novelist and children's writer, she published *Obasan* in 1981. The book focuses on Japanese Canadians and the many injustices they suffered during and after World War II. Her book won Books in Canada's First Nobel Award and the Canadian Authors Association's Book of the Year Award.

1937
Helen Marcelle Harrison
(1909-)
In 1937, she qualified for her instructor's, multi-engine and instrument ratings and was the first Canadian

woman to receive these licenses. She gave up flying in the late 1940s because she found it very difficult to find a job in aviation.

Elizabeth M. MacGill
(1905-1980)
She was first Canadian woman to graduate with a degree in electrical engineering from the University of Toronto. In 1937 she became the first woman to be admitted to corporate membership in the Engineering Institute of Canada. Three years after he death, she was inducted into Canada's Aviation Hall of Fame.

1940
Doreen Kimura (1940 -)
A behavioral psychologist, Doreen Kimura works on brain and hormonal mechanisms in human cognitive function, including sex and hand preference. She became a professor in Psychology at University of Western Ontario in 1967. Also, she is the founding president of a society for the maintenance of academic freedom and has a consulting business, which sells neuropsychological tests that she has developed.

1941
Emily Carr (1871-1945)
An important female Canadian painter, she is beloved for her paintings of Indian villages, totem poles and forests of West Coast. In 1941, she published tales of

Canadian life and won Governor's Award for non-fiction.

1943
Mary "Bonnie" Baker
(1918 -)
In the spring of 1943, she signed with the All-American Girls Professional Baseball League and played for the South Bend Blue Sox. In 1946, she stole 94 bases and batted .286. She inspired the composite character that Geena Davis portrayed in the movie *"A League of Their Own"*.

1944
Birute Galdikas (1944 -)
The world's foremost authority on orangutans, she believes that we must not turn our backs on our biological heritage. She is a Professor of Anthropology at Simon Fraser University.

1947
Kim Campbell (1947 -)
First woman Prime Minister of Canada, Minister of Justice and Attorney General of Canada (1990-1993), Minister of National Defence in 1993 and the first woman elected leader of Progressive Conservative Party.

1948
Jeannette Armstrong
(1948 -)
An Okanagan Indian, she is fluent in the Okanagan language and educates people about the truths of Okanagan

society and people. As an indigenous civil rights activist, she fights for the right of Native people to keep land that legally belongs to them. The first Native woman novelist from Canada, her books deal with such important issues as education and indigenous rights of Native people.

Barbra Ann Scott
In 1948, she wins the Olympic, World and European figure skating titles.

1949
Bobbie Rosenfield
She is named Canadian Woman Athlete of the Half Century in 1949. She excelled at most sports including ice hockey and softball and was a 1928 Olympic track and field gold medalist.

1950
Marion Anderson
She was the first female aboriginal band councilor in 1950 and an Elder Board Member for Northern Nishnawbe Education Council in 1980. She has shown leadership through her involvement in local politics, midwifery, and her continued efforts to improve working conditions for her people. She was awarded the Order of Ontario in 1998.

Beverly Hungry Wolf
(1950 -)
An author, she is a member of the Blood tribe of the

Blackfoot people. In 1980, she wrote *The Ways of My Grandmothers* which accounts for her tribe's unique domestic skills, tribal history and ancient ways. *Shadows of the Buffalo* published in 1983 discusses the constant thought process that is used to tell the difference between right and wrong and goes into great detail about Indian religion and beliefs in supreme being.

1951
Ethel Blondin-Andrew
(1951 -)
A Dene Indian from the artic region of Canada, she was the first native woman to sit in the Canadian House of Commons. She campaigned for the rights of aborigines and defending the trapping and fur industry.

Claire L'Heureux Dube
She graduated cum laude from Laval University's law school in 1951. In 1973, she was one of the first women in Quebec to be appointed judge of the Superior Court and in 1987 she became the second woman to be appointed to the Supreme Court of Canada. She is known on the bench for her desire to insure social justice.

1953
Mary Anne White (1953-)
A physical chemist, she researched adiabatic calorimetric measurement of heat capacities and

measurement of thermal conductivities of solids. She developed a new class of chemicals which absorb waste heat from industrial processes and which can be used to insulate homes.

1954
Deanna Brasseur (1954 -)
She enlisted in the Canadian Armed Forces in 1972. In 1979, Deanna earned her place in history when she was accepted at the Royal Military College for pilot training – one of the first four women to do so. Currently, she is Chief Executive Officer of the Canadian Precision Flight Team, an all-woman team that is scheduled to compete in the 1996 World Precision Flying Championship. This team will be the first and only all-female team to take part in this competition and will be Canada's only entry since the mid-1980s.

1958
Margaret Blance Meagher
From 1958-73, she served as Ambassador to Israel, Cyrpus, Austria, Kenya, Uganda and Sweden.

1964
Julie Payette (1964 -)
In 1992, she joined the Canadian Space Agency as an astronaut. As part of her training as an astronaut, she became a pilot and holds a multi-engine commercial license. In addition to her astronaut-training schedule, she participates in the development of the Mobile Servicing System for the International Space Station. She is a technical adviser for the design of its ground-control station, and she manages several projects designing advanced operator-machine interfaces for use in space.

1967
Ellen Binder
She operated the first formal library in the Mackenzie Delta and was present to officially open the library in Inuvik in 1967.

1973
Sigrun Bulow-Hube
(1913-1994)
Architect, her focus of work was interior architecture, furniture design and kitchen planning. She was elected to the Royal Canadian Academy of Arts in 1973 in recognition of her contribution to the development of modern interior architecture in Canada.

1975
Colleen McCrory
She has been crusading to protect the world's largest remaining temperate rainforest in British Columbia and advocating for the protection of endangered northern boreal forests throughout Canada and the world. In 1975, she founded the Valhalla Wilderness

Society and after extensive lobbying and campaigning, the Society succeeded in the establishment of the 49,600-hectare Valhalla Provincial Park. She founded Canada's Future Forest Alliance, an umbrella organization that represents one million Canadians, including native communities and labor unions, concerned about the future of the country's boreal forests.

1976
Helen Belyea
She was an award-winning geologist and the only female geologist allowed to work in the field by the Canadian Geological Survey until 1970. In 1976, she was made an Officer of the Order of Canada.

Janeane MacGillvray
She became the first woman underground miner in Canada at Whitehorse Copper Mine in 1976 and has held the first underground blasting permit issued to a woman in the Yukon.

1978
Judy Evans Cameron
(1953 -)
She graduated from Selkirk College's aviation program in 1975 with a certificate in Aviation Technology, the first woman in Canada to receive one. After working as a bush pilot for several companies, Judy Cameron became Air Canada's first female pilot flying Boeing

767 jet airlines in 1978 – the second woman in Canada to hold this type of position.

1980
Jeanne Sauve (1922-1993)
Former government minister, she was Speaker of the House of Commons from 1980-84 and Governor General of Canada from 1984-90.

1982
Bertha Wilson
She became the first woman appointed to the Supreme Court of Canada in 1982. As a member of the Supreme Court, she wrote many important decisions, including the controversial decision that overturned the section of the criminal code dealing with abortion.

1984
Jeanne Mathilde Benoit Sauve
(1922-1993)
First woman Governor General of Canada and Commander-in-Chief of Canada (1984-1990, Speaker of the House of Commons (1980-1984) and Member of Parliament from Quebec to be a Cabinet Minister in 1972. She had a national reputation as an outspoken advocate of women's rights.

1988
Sylvia Fedoruk
While chief medical physicist for the Saskatshewan Cancer Foundation, she was involved in the development of both the Cobalt 60 unit and one of

the first nuclear scanning machines. The YWCA named her Woman of the Year in 1986 and she was appointed Lieutenant Governor of Saskatchewan in 1988.

1991
Elizabeth Dowdeswell
(1948 -)
She played an important role in negotiation at the 1991 Earth Summit in Rio de Janeiro and the Montreal Protocol on ozone-depleting gases. She worked as home economics teacher, human rights ombudsman and Deputy Provincial Minister of Culture before becoming head of Canada's Atmospheric Environment Service and Assistant Deputy Environment Minister. As Executive Director of the United Nations Environment Program, Elizabeth Dowdeswell is reponsible for ushering in an era of "sustainable development" for a planet being ravaged by humans.

1992
Roberta Lynn Bondar
(1945 -)
She was the first Canadian woman astronaut in space and flew on the space shuttle Discovery as payload specialist on the First Microgravity Laboratory Mission in 1992. She received university degrees in zoology and biology and became a doctor specializing in neurology.

Manon Rheaume (1972 -)
In 1992, she made hockey history by being the first woman goalie to plan in a NHL exhibition game against St. Louis Blues. She was named on Olympic team and Canada won the bronze medal in ice hockey in 1997.

1995
Eva Turley
A biologist, she discovered the key role that hyaluronic acid plays in cell migration and mechanisms that start and stop cancer growth in 1995.

1998
Jeane Lassen
She is one of Canada's top female weightlifters. In 1998, she broke the Canadian Weightlifting Federation senior female record in the 75-kg class by half a kilo.

UNITED STATES
1595
Pocahontas (1595-1617)
She was the first Native-American woman for whom there is a written record and became known at age twelve for interceding with her father, Powhatan, chief of the Powhatan Confederacy, in 1607 to save Captain John Smith's life.

1647
Anne Broadstreet
First American woman poet, she wrote both meditative and lyrical poetry. Her first

book of poems was published in 1647.

1666
Sarah Kemble Knight
(1666-1727)

For a woman of her times, she was a businesswoman who lived an independent life profiting from land speculation and farming, and serving as a witness on over 100 legal documents. In 1704 she journeyed from Boston to New York, keeping a diary of her travels, which was published in 1825 as *The Journey of Madame Knight*. The book contains descriptions of early settlements, of inn life and of the customs and hardships of colonial travel. She founded a writing school in Boston in 1706 that Benjamin Franklin is supposed to have attended as a boy.

1670
Henrietta Johnson
(1670-1729)

One of the earliest painters in pastel, she was the first woman artist in America.

1677
Sybilla Righton Master
(1677-1720)

First female American inventor, she invented a method for cleaning and curing Indian corn. Other inventions include maize-stamping mill and a new way of working and staining in straw and palmetto leaf to produce women's bonnets.

1697
Susanna Wright (1697-1784)

She established a ferry along the Susquehanna River known as "the gateway to the West". Proficient in languages, she was a noted writer and was one of the first to express the idea that men and women should be considered equals.

1712
Sarah Wells

As an 18-year old, she moved alone to stake a claim in the New York State wilderness that became known as Land O'Goshen located due west of West Point. In the 20th century, she was commenorated in the area with the Sarah Wells Trail.

1720
Anne Catherine Green
(1720-1775)

She served as "Printer to the Province" from 1767 to 1775 and published the laws of the Maryland Assembly. She also printed the charter and by-laws of Annapolis and the *Maryland Gazette*, the only newspaper in Maryland until 1773.

1722
Eliza Lucas Pinckney
(1722-1793)

She went from managing her father's three South Carolina plantations when she was 16 to developing a hybrid indigo seed that became a mainstay crop of the new colony until the Revolutionary War cut off trade. Her studies of flax, hemp, and silk made her the nation's first prominent agriculturist and she also devised a method of preserving eggs in salt.

1724
Jane Colden Farquhar
(1724-1766)
An American botanist, who collected and classified many of the native plants of New York, she catalogued more than 300 plants and discovered and named the gardenia.

1728
Mercy Otis Warren
(1728-1814)
She was a playwright, political pundit and outspoken proponent of the American Revolution, who wrote one of the earliest histories of the war and its causes. Her plays, thick with political satire supported the revolutionary cause as early as 1772.

1729
Sr St. Stanislaus Hachard
She became the first nun to take her vows in New Orleans in the American colonies.

1738
Elizabeth Timothy
She became the first woman in America to edit a newspaper in 1738, the "South Carolina Gazette".

1742
Anne Hennis Bailey
(1742 – 1825)
A pioneer heroine, she was a skilled frontier scout, horsewoman, hunter, messenger and storyteller who wore buckskins and carried hatchet, knife and long rifle. In 1791, when Fort Lee was threatened with attack and low on ammunition, she rode alone through 100 miles of near wilderness to Fort Savannah at Lewisburg and returned with the needed powder to save the fort which today is Charleston, WV.

1755
Nancy "Nan'yehi" Ward
(1738-1824)
Cherokee tribal leader, she earned her title "Beloved Woman" in the Battle of Taliwa. She served as her people's sage, guide and attended General Council meetings. She was also a negotiator for the Cherokee at the 1785 signing of the Treaty of Hopewell, the first treaty the Cherokee made with the "new" United States.

1759
Martha Laurens Ramsey
(1759-1811)
She experimented with the growing of olives and invented the process of debittering and preserving olives.

1761

Deborah Norris Logan
(1761-1839)
A collector of historical records, she was a chronicler of provincial and early national history in the State of Pennsylvania.

1765

Barbara Heck (1734-1804)
Known as the "Mother of Methodism", she organized the first Methodist Church in the US in 1765.

1773

Queen Kaahumanu (1773-1832)
She was the Hawaiian ruler from 1819 to 1832. In 1824, she proclaimed what was Hawaii's first code of laws – forbade murder and theft and encouraged Sabbath observance and education.

1774

Elizabeth Ann Seton
(1774-1821)
She was the founder of the American Sisters of Charity and was the first American born saint of the Roman Catholic Church.

1775

Hannah Adams (1755-1831)
Compiler of historical data, she is remembered as the first American woman to support herself by writing. Her compilations include *Alphabetical Compendium of Various Sects*, *A Summary History of New England* and *History of the Jews*.

Mary K. Goddard (1738-1816)
Publisher, she printed the original Declaration of Independence. She became Postmaster of Baltimore in 1775, the first woman appointed in colonies and certainly the only to hold so important a post after the Declaration of Independence.

1776

Margaret Cochran Corbin
She was the first woman who manned a gun during the defense of Fort Washington in 1776 and also the first woman to receive a pension from the government as a disabled soldier.

Elizabeth Flanagan
A New York tavern keeper, she mixes rum and fruit juice, inventing the cocktail. The drink got its name from the rooster feathers she uses to adorn the glasses.

Sophia Germain (1776-1831)
An outstanding mathematician, she developed the modern theory of elasticity which is mathematical representation of stress and strain in materials such as steel beams. One of her textbooks containing a sentence describing how perturbations affected the stability of orbits led to the discovery of the planet Neptune.

1784
Elizabeth Clovis Lange
(1784-1882)
She was the founder and the initial Superior-General of the Oblate Sisters of Providence, the first black Roman Catholic order in the United States. Although she ran primarily an educational order, she became involved in many needy community outreach programs. More than 100 years after her death there are attempts to make her the first African-American female to be canonized by the Roman Catholic Church.

1788
Sarah Josepha Hale
(1788-1879)
Editor and writer, she was editor of Ladies' Magazine, the first successful US women's magazine, and Godey's Lady's Book. She vigorously promoted female education.

Sacajawea (1788-1812)
She was an Idaho-born Shoshone captive of the Hidatsa tribe, who was purchased by French-Canadian fur trader Toussaint Charbonneau in 1804. When Lewis and Clark hired Charbonneau as an interpreter for their expeditions, Sacajawea served the group as translator, emissary, and guide.

1792
Sarah Grimke (1792-1873)
With her sister Angelina, these daughters of a Southern slaveholder, were vehemently opposed to slavery and toured the nation writing and speaking out against "the institution" even though such public roles were unheard of for women.

Marie Laveau (1792-1897)
A famous herbalist, she became the most famous and powerful Voodoo Queen when she declared herself Pope of Voodoo African-American Voodoo Queen of New Orleans in the 1830's.

1793
Lucretia Mott (1793-1880)
She was a Quaker anti-slavery advocate, who together with her husband, opened their home as a stop on the Underground Railroad, helping runaway slaves escape to freedom, and later was equally committed to the causes of temperance, suffrage and universal peace.

Rolinda Sharples
(1793-1838)
America's first woman artist, she painted portraits as well as contemporary events. One of her larger works was *The Trial of Colonel Brereton* painted in 1834.

Mrs. Samuel Slater
In 1793, she was the first American woman to receive a patent – for cotton sewing thread.

1794
Susanna Rowson
An actress, novelist and playwright, she publishes the first American best seller *Charlotte Temple*, a tragic, sentimental novel about the fate of a girl seduced and abandoned.

1795
Fanny Wright (1795-1852)
She was one of the first American women to speak out against slavery and for the equality of women.

1796
Maria Martin (1796-1863)
One of the best nature artists of the 19th Century – she worked with John Audubon.

1797
Mary Lyon (1797-1849)
Women's education pioneer, she founded Mount Holyoke College and organized Wheaton College in Massachusetts. Her efforts were a major factor in the spread of higher education for women in the United States.

Sojourner Truth
(1797-1883)
She was born into slavery as Isabela Bomefree, but gained her freedom in 1827. She joined the anti-slavery crusade in 1843 and quickly became one of the most powerful anti-slavery spokespersons, touring the nation and speaking in defense of abolition and later black women's equality.

She delivered her powerful, "Ain't I A Woman" speech on behalf of black women's rights at the 1851 Women's Convention.

1798
Christiana Holmes Tillson
(1798-1872)
She wrote *A Woman's Story of Pioneer Illinois* to depict for her daughter the dramatic changes in society since her pioneer experiences. Her book is a significant historical document that reflects a microcosm of Illinois in 1822-27, which provides another dimension of frontier history from a woman's viewpoint.

1800
Gertrudis (Tules) Barcelo
(1800-1852)
In the 1840s, she became a prominent businesswoman in Santa Fe, New Mexico as owner of a gambling house and saloon where the growing populations of Europeans and Americans came together with Mexicans. She used some of her proceeds to aid the poor.

Catharine Beecher
(1800-1878)
Author and educator, she dedicated her entire life to the improvement of women's lot by acceptably feminine means. She co-founded a girl's school, wrote several books on "domestic science" to increase the respect commanded by housework and single-handedly changed

primary education from a male to a female profession in two generations. In 1856, she published *Physiology and Calisthenics for Schools and Families*, the first fitness manual for women.

1802
Dorothea Dix (1802-1887)
A New England teacher crusader for the rights of the mentally ill, she devoted her life to establishing psychiatric hospitals to provide care for those with mental and emotional problems. She compiled data that resulted in new treatments and acceptance of the concept that insanity was a disease of the mind and not a willfully perverse act by an individual.

1805
Harriot Kezia Hunt
(1805-1875)
Credited with being the first female physician in the US, she specialized in the treatment of women and children.

Mercy Otis Warren
She was first woman to write an American history book. It was a 3-volumne narrative history of the Revolutionary War published in 1805.

1808
Anna Pierce Hobbs Bigsby
(1808-1869)
A physician, she was confronted by an epidemic called milk sickness in 1828.

Although her analysis that the white snakeroot plants caused the disease, she received no official recognition for her discovery of the cause of milk sickness. In fact, the medical community did not recognize the plant as the cause of the disease until well into the 20th century.

1809
Mrs. Mary Kies
In 1809, she was first woman to receive a U.S. Patent for "a method to weave straw with silk and thread".

Laura Wright (1809-1886)
Missionary to the Seneca Indians, she devised a system of orthography for the Seneca language and printed readers and religious books in that language.

1810
Margaret Fuller (1810-1850)
She was the first female foreign correspondent and book review editor. In 1845, she published her book, *Woman in the Nineteenth Century*, which became a classic of feminist thought and helped bring about the Seneca Falls Convention three years later.

Abby Kelley Foster
(1810-1887)
An outspoken abolitionist and early suffragist, she spoke out against slavery and purchased Liberty Farm in Massachusetts with her husband in 1847 to house

slaves escaping north on the Underground Railroad. After the Civil War, she took up the cause of equal rights, lecturing in favor of women's suffrage to shocked crowds who had never heard a woman speak publicly before.

1812
Elizabeth F. L. Ellet
(1812-1877)
Author and historian, she was first American writer to emphasize the role of women in the development of this country.

Mary Rhodes (1782-1853)
A nun, she co-established the Sisters of Loretto at the Foot of the Cross in 1812, a teaching order of nuns and the first American sisterhood without European links.

1813
Margaret Haughery
(1813-1882)
From humble beginnings as a penniless Irish immigrant, she grew into an astute businesswoman entrepreneur and philanthropist who established four orphanages and several homes for the elderly.

Ann Preston (1813-1872)
Physician and opponent of bloodletting, advocate of medical ethics classes for physicians and expert on psychosomatic illness, she becomes the first woman dean of a medical college with her appointment in 1866 to that

post at the Female Medical College of Pennsylvania.

1814
Mary Ellen Pleasant
(1814-1904)
Born a slave in Augusta, Georgia, she was bought out of slavery when she was 9 by a sympathetic planter. She went on to devote her life to abolition, and some refer to her as "the Mother of Civil Rights." She amassed a small fortune estimated at $30 million as an entrepreneur. She participated in the Underground Railroad and other slave rescue missions. She later fled west and helped settle and shape San Francisco.

1818
Amelia Jenks Bloomer
(1818-1894)
Best remembered for her support of dress reform, she published the first women's rights newspaper and was a leader of the Iowa suffrage campaign. In 1849, she became the first woman to serve as Post Office Clerk.

Lucy Stone (1818-1893)
An abolitionist and women's rights leader who helped organize the American Woman's Suffrage Association and was its president from 1869 to 1872.

1819
Sarah Horton Cockrell
(1819-1892)
She turned a pile of debts left by her deceased husband into a small empire through shrewd investing and business acumen. She set up her own corporations, the Dallas Bridge Company and the S.H. Cockrell Co. She also built the first iron bridge over the Trinity River in Dallas in 1872 and the city's first three-story hotel. She was so successful in business that she went on to win most of what is now Dallas' central business district.

Julia Ward Howe (1819-1910)
An American social reformer, she is best known as the author of "The Battle Hymn of the Republic". In 1872, she proposed a national day honoring American mothers.

1820
Fanny Crosby (1820-1915)
Although blind, she taught at the New York Institute for the Blind for 23 years. After her marriage in 1858, she found her true vocation in writing hymns - writing as many as 6 or 7 hymns a day.

Florence Nightingale
(1820-1910)
Well-known for her nursing, she was also a talented mathematician. She was first person in the English-speaking world to apply statistics to the study of public health. She also invented the pie chart.

Harriet Tubman (1820-1913)
She escaped from slavery on a Maryland plantation where she was beaten and suffered a skull fracture. She used her freedom to become the principal conductor of the Underground Railroad. During the Civil War, she worked as a Union spy and scout, and later opened the Harriet Tubman Home for Indigent Aged Negroes.

1821
Elizabeth Blackwell
(1821-1910)
She was the first woman to receive a medical degree from Geneva College in New York in 1849. Her dismay over the social inequities of the time was one of the reasons she became a doctor.

1822
Elizabeth Cabot Agassiz
(1822-1907)
As co-founder of Radcliff College, she helped create a college for women, taught by the faculty of Harvard University.

1823
Mary Ann Shadd Cary
(1823-1893)
An educator and abolitionist, she was the first black woman to graduate from Howard University Law School and to vote in a federal election. Along with six other women, she founded the Colored

Women's Progressive Franchise Association in Washington DC, seeking equal rights for women in employment and voting.

1824
Ellen Curtis Demorest
(1824-1898)
Dress designer who co-invented the first mass-produced paper patterns, which allowed accurately, measured fashions to be made in the home. Through an uncharacteristic slip, she failed to patent the paper patterns, leaving the way open for Ebenezer Butterick to expand a business that continues today. In 1868, she founded Sorosis, the first women's professional club.

1825
Mary Brush
In 1825, she received an US patent for a corset. This was one of the earliest US patents awarded to a woman.

Caroline Merrick
(1825-1908)
She was one of the first pioneers in the Louisiana women's suffrage and temperance movements. In 1892, she organized the Portia Club, which was devoted to the study of the legal rights of women and children.

Hannah Lord Montague
In 1825, she made the first detachable shirt collar.

1826
Elizabeth H. Buckley
She received a patent in 1826 for the first sheet-iron shovel and the process of making shovels and other tools using sheet iron rather than forging each one individually.

Lydia Maria Child
An author of books on home management and childcare, she published the first magazine for children in America *"Juvenille Miscellany"* in 1826.

Martha J. Coston (1826 -?)
In 1859, she invented and patented a system of red, white and green "Pyrotechnic Night Signals". Her flares helped to win battles and to save the lives of countless shipwreck victims.

1827
Candace Thurber Wheeler
(1827-1923)
Pioneer in American textile design and interior decoration, she played a small but effective part in the development of Art Nouveau. Most important, she opened a new field for women in American design, in textile branches of applied art and in interior decoration.

Ellen G. White (1827-1915)
She was co-founder of the Seventh Day Adventist Church. She was a health reformer and educator.

1829
Marie Elizabeth Zakrzewska
(1829-1902)
She was one of the 19th Century's most influential female physicians and devoted her life to expanding women's opportunities in the field of medicine.

1830
Emily Pomona Edson Bridges
(1830 -?)
She wrote the Olivia Papers which chronicled politics in Washington, DC. The first woman reporter in the nation's capitol, she was a columist for the Washington Chronicle and the Philadelphia Press. She was the first president of the Women's National Press Association founded in 1882.

Emily Dickinson
(1830-1886)
This poet has often been referred to as "the greatest woman poet in the English language and perhaps the finest American poet".

Helen Hunt Jackson
(1830-1885)
She was a staunch and influential defender of Native American rights in the late 19th century. She published two widely read and devastating critiques of Federal Indian policy and White/Indian relations: A "*Century of Dishonor*" and the novel *Ramona*.

Belva Ann Lockwood
(1830-1917)
In 1879, she was first woman admitted to practice before the US Supreme Court. In 1884 and 1888, Lockwood was the candidate of the Equal Rights Party for the presidency of the US. In 1903, she was the author of the congressional enactment granting suffrage to women in Oklahoma, Arizona and New Mexico.

1831
Bernice Pauahi Bishop
(1831-1884)
Hawaiian high chieftess and philanthropist, she established a trust to create one of the state's leading educational institutions - Kamehmeha Schools where enrollment is limited to children of Hawaiian or part-Hawaiian ancestry.

Mary Mapes Dodge (1831 -?)
Author, she edited St. Nicholas Magazine, one of the first periodicals for children. She is best known for her classic novel *The Silver Skates* published in 1865.

Martha D. Maxwell
(1831-1881)
An accomplished hunter and taxidermist, she developed a method for preserving and stuffing animals in lifelike poses for display in natural habitat settings.

1832

Henrietta King (1832-1925)
She helped found the King Ranch in South Texas and ran the ranch for 40 years after her husband's death. She gave money and land to establish the city of Kingsville, and helped set up churches throughout South Texas with her generous land donations.

Mary E. Walker (1832-1919)
A physician in the Civil War, in 1865 she was awarded the Congressional Medal of Honor. She was a lifelong advocate of women's suffrage, dress reform and abolition of capital punishment.

1833

Lucy Hobbs Taylor
(1833-1910)
She was the first woman in America to graduate from the Ohio College of Dental Surgery with a degree in dentistry. She practiced in Lawrence, Kansas.

1835

Rebecca Latimer Felton
(1835-1930)
In 1922, she was sworn in as first woman Senate member, the oldest Senator at the time of swearing-in and, after resigning the next day, the distinction of being the Senator with the shortest term in service. She supported prohibition, woman's suffrage, and public education especially vocational training for girls.

1836

Harriet Maxwell Converse
(1836-1903)
She was the first white female to be made a Seneca sachem (chief). An author, folklorist and defender of Native American rights, she was committed to preserving Native American culture. In 1891, she intervened against a bill in the New York legislature that would have broken up reservations. As an honorary chief of the Six Nations, she was admitted to the secret Little Water Medicine Society.

Miriam Folline Leslie
(1836-1914)
Known as the "empress of journalism", she became editor of *Leslie's Lady's Magazine* in 1863. In 1871, she began editing *Frank Leslie's Lady's Journal*, turning it into a successful fashion publication.

1837

Sarah J.B. Hale (1788-1879)
Editor of Godey's Lady's Book which was one of the most influential periodicals of the 19th Century and arbiter of fashion and etiquette for the era. She was a strong spokesperson for property rights for married women, improved women's education and increased opportunities for women wage earners.

Mary Harris (Mother Jones)
(1837-1930)
She was considered "the most dangerous woman in America" by politicians of her time because she fueled the burgeoning labor movement. She took part in the rail strike of 1877 in Pittsburgh, organized the coalfields of Pennsylvania in 1899 and attended the convention of the International Workers of the World in 1905.

Hannah Farnham Lee
Her book, *Three Experiments in Living*, published in 1837 presents three scenarios of living under, with and beyond one's means. It goes through 30 editions showing that the public will accept money management advice from a woman.

Anne Elizabeth O'Hare McCormick (1880-1954)
The first woman to receive the Pulitzer Prize for foreign correspondence in 1937, she was a strong voice for the American ideal of freedom. She was one of the first journalists to recognize the danger posed by Italy's Benito Mussolini, whom she interviewed.

1838
Alice Cunningham Fletcher
(1838-1923)
Beginning with an interest in the archaeology of American Indians, from 1876 on she became active in working for better treatment of the living Indians of the west. An ethnologist, in 1887 she became an agent for the Department of the Interior and helps to implement the Dawes Act, which grants land and citizenship to Indians. She became the first and best-informed student of American Indian music. Although her major scholarly work was *The Omaha Tribe* in 1911, her most popular work was *Indian Story and Song from North American* in 1900.

Lydia Kamekeha Liliuokalani, Queen of the Hawaiian Islands
(1838-1917)
The first reigning queen of the islands, she ruled from 1891-1894 and the last native sovereign to rule. She organized institutions for the improvement of health, welfare and education of native Hawaiians. She was forced to abdictate in 1895 and wrote *Hawaii's Story by Hawaii's Queen*. Composer of the ever haunting Aloha Oe and more than 100 other songs.

1840
Helen Augusta Blanchard
(1840-1922)
She earned at least 28 patents - many of which were for improvements to sewing machines, including the first zigzag stitch machine. One of her machines (1873) is on display in the Smithsonian's Museum of American History. She also patented related items such as hat-sewing

machines and surgical
needles.

1841
Margaret G. LaForge
(1841-1880)
She was one of the earliest
woman business executives in
the US. In 1866, she was
promoted to Superintendent of
R H Macy in New York City.

1842
Ina Donna Coolbrith
(1842-1928)
She published three volumes
of distinctively simple
lyrical verse that earned her
selection as California's
first poet laureate in 1915.

Henriette Delille
(1813-1862)
She was an early feminist,
educator, social worker and
the co-founder of one of the
first orders of African
American Catholic nuns – the
Sisters of the Holy Family.

Ida Lewis (1842-1911)
She was a lighthouse keeper
on Lima Rock in Newport
Harbor and famous for her
many rescues. In 1879, the
federal government made her
keeper of the light she had
actually tended for more than
20 years.

Sarah Winnemucca
(1842-1891)
A Native-American Leader, she
dedicated her life to
ensuring that land taken by
the government was returned
to the tribes, especially her

own Paiute Tribe. Fluent in
five languages, she gave
speeches and lobbied
government officials for her
people's right to the land,
took her case to president
Rutherford B. Hayes, and
publicly condemned corrupt
Indian agents and Indian
Bureau officials.

1844
Mary Cassett (1844-1926)
In 1868, she had her first
painting accepted by the
Paris Salon, *A Mandolin
Player*. A series of ten color
aquatint prints in 1891 was
one of the major achievements
of her career as well as a
milestone in the history of
printmaking. She produced
over 220 prints and is
recognized as one of the
foremost American printmakers
of the 19th Century.

Harriet Russell Strong
(1844-1929)
An entrepreneur and engineer
specializing in irrigation
and water conservation, she
won several patents for dams
and water storage systems in
1887. Other patents include
window-related patents in
1884 and 1886 and hook and
eye in 19884. She spent her
life fighting for water
conservation and women's
rights.

1845
Mary Eliza Mahoney
(1845-1926)
She was the first African-
American registered nurse in

US who worked primarily as a private duty nurse. In 1976, fifty years after her death, she was inducted into the Nursing Hall of Fame.

Sarah Mather
An inventor, she received a patent for the submarine telescope and lamp in 1845.

Ella Flagg Young
(1845 - 1918)
In 1865, she became the first principal of the practice school of the Chicago Normal School. When appointed superintendent of the Chicago schools in 1909, she became the first woman in the US to head a metropolitan public school system.

1846
Sarah E. Bagley
In 1844, she organized the Lowell Female Labor Reform Association to combat deteriorating working conditions. Also she lead the petition drive that forced Massachusetts's legislators to investigate the conditions in the mills - the first governmental investigation into labor conditions. In 1946, she became the first female telegraph operator when she assumed the post at the newly opened Lowell, MA telegraph office.

Rebecca J. Cole (1846-1922)
She was the 2nd African American woman physician and the 1st black woman to graduate from Woman's Medical College in Pennsylvania. In 1873, she started a Women's Directory Center to provide medical and legal services to destitute women and children in Philadelphia.

Birute Galdikas (1946 -)
Anthropologist, primatologist and conservationist, she is the greatest authority on orangutans. She has directed the Orangutan Research and Conservation Project in Borneo's Tanjung Putting National Park since 1971.

Mary Seymour (1846-1893)
A businesswoman, she opens the first typewriting school for women in 1879. Over the next few decades, many women will learn to operate the new typewriting machines in order to enter the desirable, male-dominated field of clerical work. In 1889, she began printing Business Woman's Journal, which features ads for office supplies, articles for working women, recipes and fashion advice.

Sarah F. Whiting
(1846-1927)
The first professor of physics at Wellesley College, she introduced the teaching of astronomy at Wellesley. She was the first director of the Wellesley College Observatory after helping to establish it in 1900.

1847

Christine Ladd-Franklin
(1847-1930)
Mathematician, she wrote a dissertation in the area of symbolic logic while at John Hopkins on special status. She left in 1882 without the Ph.D. and continued to work in symbolic logic and physiological optics. In 1925, she was finally granted a doctorate from John Hopkins University - 44 years after the completion of her dissertation.

Sr Mary Meletia Foley
(1847-1917)
She was responsible for the establishment of the first Catholic women's college in America. Originally a boarding school, Notre Dame became a woman's college when the Maryland General Assembly granted its charter in 1896.

Maria Mitchel (1818-1889)
An astronomer, she discovered Comet Mitchel 1847V1 in 1847. She was the first woman professor of astronomy at Vasser College. In 1875, she was elected president of the American Association for the Advancement of Women.

Katherine Augusta Westcott Tingley (1847-1929)
In the early 1890s on New York City's East Side, she set up soup kitchens and emergency relief missions and established organizations for orphaned children, unwed mothers and destitute families. She also traveled worldwide establishing schools in several countries, emphasizing practical humanitarianism, education, prison reform and world peace. In 1900, she built the first open air Greek Theatre in America and formed youth and adult symphony orchestras.

1848

Elizabeth Lummis Ellet
In 1948, she published The Women of the American Revolution, which detailed the roles of more than 160 women in the nation's birth and is the first writer to recognize the breadth of women's contributions to America. She published Domestic History of the American Revolution in 1950 that contained more information.

Elizabeth C. Stanton
(1815-1902)
She dedicated her life to social activism, first anti-slavery and later women's rights. In 1848, she founded the women's movement and organized the first Women's Rights Convention in Seneca Falls, New York, where she was inspired to draft the Declaration of Rights and Sentiments, parodying the Declaration of Independence. With Susan B. Anthony, she organized the Women's Loyal National League to fight slavery (1863) and founded the National Woman Suffrage

Association (1869) of which Stanton served as president. She co-edited *The Revolution;* a weekly woman's suffrage paper published by Anthony, and wrote *The Woman's Bible* (1895), reinterpreting the more sexist passages of the Bible.

Caroline Ardelia Yale
(1848-1933)
Educator of the deaf, she helped formulate the "Northampton Vowel and Consonant Charts", a widely used teaching aid and helped gain national acceptance of the oral method of teaching in deaf schools.

1849
Elizabeth Bolt (1849-1932)
A textile manufacturer, she co-founded the firm of Winship, Boit & Co in 1888. Increasingly successful, she is a considerate employer, sending a streetcar for her workers on rainy days and instituting a profit-sharing plan.

Nellie Cashman
(1849-1925)
Known as the "Angel of Tombstone", she was an anti-violence peacemaker during the later half of the 19th Century. She ran a boarding house, raised orphans and campaigned against public hangings.

Eliza Nicholson (1849-1896)
Newspaper publisher, she inherited the New Orleans Picayune from her husband in 1875. In her 20 years of managing the paper, she opposes organized crime and champions animal rights, temperance and the interests of working women.

1850
Jennie Augusta Brownscombe
(1850-1936)
Sentimental genre painting was among the most popular type of art in America in the late 19th Century. She specialized in these genre works and paintings based on American history. Through her calendars, commercial prints and paintings, she reached thousands of Americans.

Kate Chopin (1850 -?)
She wrote vivid, realistic portrayals of Creole and Cajun life. Her books include *Bayou Folk* published in 1894 and *A Night in Acadie* published in 1897.

Isabel F. Hapgood
(1850-1928)
In 1886, she began a career as literary translator and is best known for her faithful translation of Russia's greatest writers.

Caroline Westcott Romney
(1850 -?)
At the Columbia Exposition, she exhibited an unpatented dairy invention – the iceless milk cooler and refrigerator.

1851

Alice Bennett (1851-1925)
An anatomist, she was the first woman to earn a Ph.D. from the University of Pennsylvania. She become the first female superintendent of a state mental hospital and soon abolishes the use of mechanical restraints such as straitjackets.

Ellen Amanda Hayes
(1851-1930)
Mathematician, teacher and author, she wrote several textbooks on algebra, calculus and trigonometry. In 1912, she was nominated for Secretary of State in MA and became the first woman to be a candidate for a state elective office in MA. She was an advocate of women's suffrage and actively connected with an experiment in adult education for working girls.

Martha Carey Thomas
(1851-1935)
As Dean and President of Bryn Mawr College, she helped build an institution dedicated to providing 19th Century women with an education equal to that available in the best men's college.

1852

Catherine E. Beecher
(1800-1878)
In 1852, she founded the American Women's Education Association to promote female education. She did not champion women's involvment in political affairs and opposed women's suffrage.

Mary Quaid Emery
In 1852, she had the distinction of being the 'Rock Island's first woman passenger'. The Rock Island and LaSalle Railroad was incorporated in 1817 by a special Act of the Illinois Legislature.

1854

Anna B. Comstock
(1854-1930)
Naturalist, scientific illustrator and wood engraver, her most lasting contribution was as leader in the nature study movement, which began in New York State in 1895.

Susette LaFlesche Tibbles
(1854 -1903)
Spokesperson for Indian rights, she contributed to the passage of the Dawes Severalty Act of 1887, which authorized the allotment of reservation land with citizen rights to individual Indians.

1855

Emeline Roberts Jones
She became nation's first woman dentist after serving an apprenticeship with her husband.

1856

Maria Louise Baldwin
(1856-1922)
She was appointed principal of the Agassiz School in

Cambridge in 1889, becoming the first African-American female principal in the Northeast to supervise a white faculty and a predominately white student body.

1857
Katharine Coman (1857-1915)
Economic historian and social reformer, she ardently advocated old age and unemployment insurance.

Fannie M. Farmer
(1857-1915)
Although she had polio at age 16, she became a teacher of cooking and food science. In 1896, she wrote *Boston Cooking School CookBook*, the first cookbook with clear instructions and precise measurements.

Kate Sessions (1857-1940)
She became a central figure in California and national horticultural circles with her landscaping, plant introductions and classes. In 1906 she co-founded the San Diego Floral Association. In 1939, she was the first woman awarded the prestigious Frank N. Meyer medal of the American Genetic Association for her work in plant introduction.

Mary Lemist Titcomb
(1857-1932)
Pioneer in the development of the public library, which was closely allied to the public school system. In 1904, she initiated the "Bookmobile" to allow people living on isolated farms or far back in the mountains to use library services.

1858
Elizabeth Knight Britton
(1858-1934)
Botanist who had 15 species of plants named for her and was the unofficial curator of mosses at Columbia College. She published 346 scientific papers and inspired the establishment of the New York Botanical Gardens. In her later years, she founded the Wild Flower Preservation Society of America and helped to push conservation measures through the New York Legislature.

Louise Caldwell Murdock
(1858-1915)
In 1907, she designed and built the first fireproof office building in Wichita and became a professional interior designer.

Hannah Greenbaum Solomon
(1858-1942)
She was a clubwoman and welfare worker who focused her efforts on child welfare. She organized nationwide Jewish women's congress as part of the 1890's World's Fair.

Beatrice Potter Webb
(1858-1943)
A social economist, she co-authored several books on labor, history and economics.

In 1883, she co-founded the Fabian Society and later founded London School of Economics.

1859
Katharine Lee Bates
(1858-1929)
Her most memorable work is her poem "American the Beautiful". The poem was put to music and is one of the nation's best known and best-loved songs.

Carrie Chapman Catt
(1859-1947)
A leader of the suffrage movement, she founded the Congressional Union in 1913 and was a founding member of the pacifist Women's Peace Party in 1915. Her program while at the helm of the National American Women Suffrage Association led to the "winning plan" that led to state-by-state enactment of suffrage and the final victory in a constitutional amendment in 1920.

Lydia Maria A. DeWitt
(1859-1928)
She was an experimental pathologist known for her pioneer studies in the chemotherapy of tuberculosis.

Madame Lefebre
By the 1920's, the process of converting nitrogen gas into fertilizer was widely used in the US, but Madame Lefebre patented the process as early as 1859 in England. It was overlooked and she was never given credit for this discovery.

Mabel Osgood Wright
(1859-1934)
Nature writer, she pioneered bird protection by planning and constructing Birdcraft Sanctuary on a tract of wasteland in Connecticut.

1860
Charlotte P. Gilman
(1860-1935)
An American social activist, writer and leading theorist of the women's movement at the turn of the century, she examined the role of women in society and put forth her social theories in "Women and Economics" published in 1898 and other nonfiction books. Many modern feminist nonfiction works reflect hers and it is being rediscovered that her ideas are relevant to contemporary problems.

Juliette Gordon Low
(1860-1927)
An American youth leader, she founded the Girl Scouts of America.

Annie Oakley (1860-1926)
She was the country's leading markswoman. A dead shot from early childhood, she used the money she earned hunting at age 14 to pay off her parents' mortgage. She even topped her husband, Frank Butler, a champion marksman, in a shooting match and later joined Buffalo Bill's Wild West Show.

1861
Frances Joseph-Gaudet
(1861-1934)
Of African-American and Native American heritage, she dedicated her life to social work and worked with the Prison Reform Association assisting prisoners unjustly accused. She was the first woman, black or white, to support juvenile prisoners in Louisiana and her efforts helped found Juvenile Court.

Kate Gordon (1861-1932)
She is best known for her work to secure the vote for women. In 1896, she founded the Equal Rights Association (ERA) to work for women's suffrage. The Club formed the Woman's League for Sewerage and Drainage to address the pressing matter of poor sewage and drainage, which was a major public health, hazard.

Dorothea Klumpke Roberts
(1861-1942)
Astronomer, measurer of nebulae and cataloguer of stars, she becomes director of the Paris Bureau of Measurements in 1891. In 1893, she won a prize from the Academie des Sciences.

Nettie Stephens (1861-1912)
She was the biologist who discovered that the X and Y-chromosomes determine the sex of humans, ending years of debate about whether sex was determined by heredity or other causes.

Sally Tompkins
In 1861, she was the only commissioned female officer in the Confederate Army.

1862
Ida B. Wells (1862-1931)
A founding member of the NAACP, she was a leader in the anti-lynching movement, who founded a newspaper in Memphis, *Free Speech*, dedicated to exposing and ending lynching. She later publishing a pamphlet entitled, "*A Red Record: Tabulated Statistics and Alleged Causes of Lynching in the United States, 1892-1894*." She was 1st president of the Negro Fellowship League in Chicago

Esther B. VanDema
(1862-1937)
First woman Roman archaeologist, her research forms the cornerstone of our understanding of Roman building. She laid the foundation for serious study of Roman architecture.

1862
Sherma M. B.King
(1862-1935)
She devoted herself to the preservation of outstanding scenic areas by lobbying strenuously and successfully for a National Park Service, which was established in 1916.

1863

Olympia Brown (1845-1926)
In 1863, she was the first woman college graduate of St. Lawrence University in Canton, New York. When she was ordained, it was the first time any denomination had formally ordained a woman as a preacher.

Mary Whiton Calkins
(1863-1930)
She was a female pioneer in psychology and was responsible for the creation of a method of memorization called the right associates method. She was the first female president of both the American Psychological Association and the American Philosophical Association.

Annie Jump Cannon
(1863-1941)
In 1921, she was first woman to receive a doctor of astronomy degree from Groningen University. She participated in the first x-ray experiment in this country and became the world's expert in classifying stars.

Elizabeth Brown Davis
(1863-1917)
She became a computer in the National Almanac Office and assisted in the preparation of Newcomb's Tables of the Sun and Planets. She also wrote magazine articles on mathematical subjects.

Sarah A. Collins Fernandis
(1863-1951)
She was the first black woman hired in Maryland as a social worker for a public welfare agency.

Rebecca Sherwood
She invented a method for reducing hemp, flax, straw and other fibrous substances for the manufacture of paper pulp in 1863.

Mary Harris Thompson
First surgeon, she received her MD in 1863 from the New England Medical College. In 1865, she founded the Mary Thompson Hospital in Chicago to care for widows and children of the poor, sustain free dispensary and to train nurses.

1864

Claribel Cone (1864-1929)
A doctor, she became the acknowledged authority on tuberculosis. All her study and work was devoted to prevention of the disease. She was appointed president of the Women's Medical College in Baltimore in 1905.

Rebecca Lee Crumpler
In 1864, she was first African-American woman to receive a "Doctor of Medicine" degree from the New England Female Medical College in Boston.

Georgia E. Washington
(1864-1900)
First African-American woman licensed physician and surgeon in the State of Tennessee and one of the first African-American medical missionaries in Africa.

1865
Evangeline Booth
(1865-1950)
She helped build the Salvation Army into the most charitable institutions in the United States. She organized training schools, old-age homes, missions and homeless shelters and gave the organization a modern fundraising system.

Kate Gleason (1865-1933)
She was first woman member of the American Society of Mechanical Engineers. In 1921, she developed a method of pouring cement and started selling low-cost concrete box houses, which became a model for many future suburban developments.

Jean Gordon (1865-1932)
She focused her life and energies on social service especially to better the labor conditions of working children. Her efforts were finally successful when the Louisiana Legislature passed the Child Labor Act of 1906. As president of the Milne Asylum for Destitute Orphan Girls, she established a model home/school for the

care and vocational education of the mentally handicapped.

Susan LaFlesche Picotte
(1865-1915)
First female Native American physician, she served her tribe "Omaha" as medical missionary and community leader for 25 years. She believed education, Christian principles and legal rights were key to her tribe's advancement.

Elizabeth C. Seaman
(1865-1922)
Under the pseudonym of Nellie Bly, she wrote articles exposing conditions in Pittsburgh factories and slums in the 1880's.

1866
Martha McChesney Berry
(1866-1942)
She developed an interest in the education of mountain children, giving them religious training and general education at several mountain communities not yet reached by public education. She dedicated her life's work to found and support Berry College, where students through a self-help program graduated with practical skills to augment their traditional arts and sciences education.

Mary P. Carpenter
A versatile, multiple inventor, she received the first patent for a mop wringer pail in 1866. It was

a galvanized bucket fitted with a device for wringing out string mops.

Sophonisba Preston Breckenridge (1866-1948)
Social worker and educator, in 1895 she became the first woman lawyer in Kentucky. Known for her studies exposing slum conditions, she was also instrumental in professionalizing social work and co-founded the Social Service Review in 1927.

Florence Prag Kahn
(1866-1948)
During her tenure in Congress (1925-37), she was instrumental in gaining congressional approval for the Bay Bridge connecting Oakland and San Francisco. Her support for the FBI was so great that she was referred to as the mother of the Bureau.

Annie Warburton Goodrich
(1866-1954)
Nursing educator, she was instigator of the first bachelor's degree in nursing while dean of the Yale University School of Nursing. Her drive and convictions led to the professionalization of nursing training in America.

1867
Emily Greene Balch
(1867-1961)
A social reformer and pacifist, she assisted in the establishment of the Women's International League for Peace and Freedom and was an indefatigable administrator, writer and promoter for peace. She shared the Nobel Peace Prize in 1946.

Mary Booth
A journalist, she becomes the first editor of Harper's Bazaar in 1867.

Elisabeth Luther Cary
(1867-1936)
In 1908, she became the full-time art critic for the New York Times.

Frances T. Densmore
(1867-1957)
She recorded several thousand Indian songs amount a vast range of tribes and her genuine interest in their culture enabled her to preserve ethnographic details as well. Also, she collected American Indian musical instruments, herbs, etc used in healing songs.

Linda Anne Eastman
(1867-1963)
Librarian, she edited an important annotated new book list and was an advocate for handicapped readers.

Madame Gardoni
A German immigrant, she became the first woman barber in Galveston, Texas and probably one of the first in the country.

Lucy M. Garrison

(1842-1877)

Musician and collector of slave songs, she published first and most complete collection of slave songs "Slave Songs of US" in 1867.

Maggie Lena Walker

(1867-1934)

A banker and entrepreneur, she established a bank in Richmond in 1903, the Saint Luke Penny Savings Bank. She remained its president until 1930. Other entrepreneurial ventures include a newspaper in 1902 and a department store in 1905. She also started scholarship programs for girls, founded the Richmond Council of Colored Women and was a founding member of the Negro Organization Society, a blanket association for African-American clubs and organizations.

Lillian Wald (1867-1940)

She was a nurse who organized the public health nursing service and the Henry Street Settlement in New York City to meet the needs of the urban poor.

1868

Isabel Hayes Barrows

(1845-1913)

A stenographer, she became first female employee of the US State Department in 1868.

Maud B. Booth (1868-1948)

Prison reformer and founder of the Volunteer Prison League, which believed that prisons should be a place for rehabilitation and reform, advocated prison educational programs, the parole system and the indeterminate sentence.

Henrietta Leavitt

(1868-1921)

She invented one of the most essential standards in the study of space, a rule that allows astronomers to measure distances from Earth to various stars. Her invention allows for the mapping of the universe and the discovery that it is expanding and has made her a legend in the history of astronomy.

Charlie Parkhurst

One of the earliest and best stagecoach drivers, it was discovered at his death that Charlie was a woman! When he cast a ballot in the 1868 elections, he became the first woman to vote – 52 years before that right was guaranteed to women by the 19th Amendment.

Martha Wollstein

(1868-1930)

Pathologist and medial researcher, she devoted herself to pediatric pathology. Her pathological studies helped sharpen the diagnostic acumen of generations of physicians.

1869
Alice Hamilton
(1869-1970)
She became the world's leading expert on industrial poisons and pioneered development of the new field of Industrial Medicine in US. She wrote *Industrial Poisons in the United States*, the first American textbook on industrial diseases, Her pioneering work in the field of industrial medicine contributed to the passage of early workmen's compensation laws. Included in her causes were child labor laws, protective legislation for women, suffrage and international relations. Her most important long-term legacies were adoption of the Federal Mine Safety & Health Act in 1969 and OSHA in 1970.

Harriet Irwin
In 1869, she was the first woman to patent a design for a house – a space-efficient hexagonal house that she built. Her objective was the economical use of space and building materials, to obtain economical heating medium through light and ventilation and facilitate inexpensive ornamentation.

Annie Turnbo Malone
(1869-1957)
As a businesswoman and philanthropist, she developed hair care products and built a factory and beauty-training school in St. Louis that was named Poro College.

Belle Babb Mansfield (1843-?)
She passed the Iowa State bar in 1869 and was officially recognized as first woman lawyer in U.S.

1870
Jessie Tarbox Beals
(1870-1942)
First woman news photographer in US, she photographed the 1904 St. Louis World's Fair.

Justina Laurena Carter Ford
(1871-1952)
In 1899 she graduated from Hering Medical College in Chicago and served a needy segment of society – the disadvantaged and under-privileged of all races. By 1950, she was still the only physician in Colorado to be both African American and female.

Margaret Knight (1838 -?)
She patented the brown paper bag machine in 1870 that has been updated over time but remains in use today. She also patented 26 other inventions such as window sashes, shoe-cutting devices, automotive valves, rotors and engines. In her time, she was known as the female Edison.

Esther McQuigg Morris
In 1870, she was named Justice of the Peace in South Pass City, Wyoming - a frontier-mining town, the first woman judge.

Louisa Swain

Since Wyoming was the first state to give women the vote, she became the first Wyoming woman to vote in 1970.

Maud Younger (1870 -?)

She dedicated her life to the labor movement and was a member of the women's suffrage movement. She was known as "the millionaire waitress" for unionizing waitresses and bar maids.

1871
Eleanor Clarke Slagle
(1871-1942)

Her work in the new field of occupational therapy dates the beginning of a planned program in occupational therapy for the mentally ill.

Edith Elmer Wood
(1871-1945)

As America's first woman housing economist, she struggled to arouse a widespread public interest in America's housing problems. She promoted not only housing reform, but also zoning and city and regional planning.

1872
Lettie Pate Evans
(1872-1953)

When appointed to the board of the Coca-Cola Company in 1934, she became the first woman director of a major American corporation.

Beatrix Jones Farrand
(1872-1959)

First American landscape architect, she popularized natural style of landscape design.

Julia Morgan (1872-1957)

She was a prolific and innovative architect, who paved the way for women in architecture. As owner of a firm in San Francisco, she rebuilt the Fairmont Hotel in 1906, which had been damaged during the San Francisco Earthquake. She also spent the next ten years building houses, stores, churches, and office buildings as well as the Hearst newspaper facilities in California and Mexico.

Mary Engle Pennington
(1872-1952)

The mother of modern refrigeration, she developed a system for refrigerating food products for shipment that used both insulation and ice beds to lock in coldness inside train cars. She was awarded a Notable Service Medal by President Hoover because of her work's importance during World War I, most notably a method of slaughtering poultry for food that is still in use today. She also invented an egg packing case that reduced breakage and in 1932 patented an air conditioning system for food storage.

Jane Wells

In 1872, she patented the baby jumper which has become a nursery standard. It has hardly been changed in more than a century.

1873

Sara Josephine Baker

(1873-1945)
She designed an entire new system of baby clothes inventing the obvious but previously unthought of system of making baby clothes all open down the front. McCalls Pattern Co copied her designs.

Amanda Theodosia Jones

With her patented "Jones Process" of canning, she opened the Women's Canning & Preserving Company. All officers and employees of her company were women. In the 1880's, she went to the oil fields of Pennsylvania and added a safety valve that controlled the amount of oil released from the pipe. The invention worked wonderfully and she won the praise of the US Navy for the great potential that her invention offered.

Edmondia Lewis

A sculptor whose work often depicts the struggles of blacks, Native Americans and women, she exhibits her work in San Francisco in 1873.

Ellen S. Richards

(1842-1911)
First woman to enter M.I.T as an accepted student and received her degree in chemistry in 1873. She was one of the founders of the Association of Collegiate Alumnae, which fought the myth that it was not healthy for young women to engage in serious study.

1874

Mary Katharine Layne Brandegee (1844-1920)

She was one of the most famous American botanists of the 19th Century. She earned a medical degree from the University of California and began studying plants with medicinal properties. Later, she became the curator of botany at the California Academy of Sciences. Two species of plants are named in her honor.

Zona Gale (1874-1938)

Writer, her best-known work, *Miss Lulu Brett*, was notable for depicting the harshness of midwestern life. She was a public advocate of women's suffrage and pacifism.

Mary Ewing Outerbridge

She introduced tennis to the US in 1874. The equipment is purchased in Bermuda and used to set up the first US tennis court at the Staten Island Cricket and Baseball Club.

Elsie Clews Parsons
(1874-1941)
An anthropologist, she was interested in the Pueblo Indian culture and culminated in the massive 2-volume of *Pueblo Indian Religion* published in 1939. These volumes contain a summary of practically all we know about Pueblo religion and are an indispensable source book for every student of Indian life.

Mary Heaton Vorse
(1874-1966)
Journalist and member of the suffrage women's group Heterodoxy in 1912, she was a political activist who covered labor demonstrations. She went on to write a proletarian novel called *Strike!* in 1930.

1875
Harriet Chalmers Adams
(1875-1937)
She was the organizer and the first president of the Society of Women Geographers, which she founded in 1925. The organization supported the aims and careers of professional female geographers by providing a forum for the exchange of information and news of job opportunities.

Kate Barnard (1875-1930)
She was the first woman elected to a statewide office. In 1907, she was elected commissioner of charities and corrections for the state of Oklahoma.

Eleanor Annie Lamson
(1875 - 1932)
Astronomer, she was never allowed to observe. In 1909 she was elected to the American Astronomical Society. When promoted to Supervisor of the Computing Bureau in 1921, she became the first female supervisor at the Naval Observatory.

Katherine Dexter McCormick
(1875-1967)
She was a co-founder of the League of Women Voters.

1876
Mary Ritter Beard
(1876-1958)
Historian and social reformer, she worked for women's suffrage, labor reforms and other progressive causes. She concentrated on her writing and lecturing by 1915to bring to light women's contributions to society across the centuries.

Gertrude Simmons Bonnin
[*Zitkala-Sa*] (1876-1938)
She was a Native American activist and writer, who worked to preserve her Sioux tribal heritage, while personally struggling with the conflict between tradition and assimilation, as well as the dignity of Indian religion. She took a strong stand in her editorials for the *American Indian Magazine* on enfranchisement of American Indians, Indian contributions to military service during WW

I, corruption in the Bureau of Indian Affairs, and allotment of tribal lands.

Eureka Frazer Bowne
(1858-?)
In 1876, she invented and patented the first successful street sweeping machine in New York City. She also received a patent for a non-refillable bottle in 1896.

Elizabeth Bragg
She received the first engineering degree awarded to an American woman from the University of California - Berkeley in 1876.

Eureka Frazer Bowne
In 1876, she invented and patented the first successful street sweeping machine in New York City. She also received a patent for a non-refillable bottle in 1896.

Emeline Hart
In 1876, she invented a commercial scale brick oven which featured revolving shelves to circulate heat, window for monitoring doneness, 4 separate compartments with a door for each and a temperature gauge. The oven could hold 60 pies or 70 loaves of bread.

Nellie Taylor Ross
(1876-1977)
In 1925 she became the first woman to serve as Governor of Wyoming. Later in 1933, she became the first woman to the position of director of the US Mint.

Nell Saunders
In 1876 she defeated Rose Harland in the first U.S. women's boxing match and received a silver butter dish as a prize.

Julia Evelina Smith
Julia E. Smith made the first Bible translation by a woman. It was published by American Publishing Company in 1876 and contained 1168 pages. The full title was *The Holy Bible containing the old and New Testament translated literally from the original tongues.*

Helen L. S. Woodbury
(1876-1933)
Labor historian, she wrote 12 volumes and many articles on labor history, labor problems and the labor of women and children.

1877
S. Brooks
In 1877, she was granted a patent for her improvement in the methods of producing lubricated molds in plaster, which allowed users to model ornamental designs out of butter.

Kate R. O. Cunninghham
(1877-1945)
She became a machinist apprentice and joined the International Order of Machinists in 1894. She inaugurated far-reaching

reform of the California prison system in 1939.

Isadora Duncan (1877-1927) Revolting against the strictures of ballet, she developed an expressive style of dancing that relied on spontaneity and freedom of movement. She became one of the founders of modern dance.

1878
Blanche Ames (1878-1969) Inventor and illustrator, she gained notoriety for her political cartoons depicting the struggle for women's suffrage. In 1939, she designed a hexagonal lumber cutter and received a patent for a water pollution device in 1969. During World War II, she designed, tested and patented a method for ensnaring enemy airplanes in wires hung from balloons.

Gertrude S. Bonnin (1878-1930) A Sioux Indian author and reformer, she worked for improving education, hospitals, health centers, resource conservation and preservation of Indian culture.

Hattie Wyatt Caraway (1878 – 1950) The first woman elected to the US Senate, she was particularly interested in farm relief and flood control. She also was a prohibitionist, a critic of lobbying groups, a friend of

veterans and co-sponsor of the proposed Equal Rights Amendment.

Lillian M. Gilbreth (1878-1972) An American engineering pioneer who laid the foundation for a new field of study called industrial engineering.

Emma Nutt In 1878, she became the first woman telephone operator. Women had been considered incapable of handling the sophisticated technology. She retired after 33 years as the Chief Operator.

1879
Nannie Burroughs (1879-1961) She was active in the Black women's church movement of the late 1800s and a prominent advocate of racial uplift as leader of the National Association of Colored Women. In 1909, she headed the new National Training School for Women and Girls, a church-supported boarding school in Washington DC, which emphasized domestic science and vocational trades such as barbering, shoe repair, and printing. In 1924 she helped found the National League of Republican Women.

Luisa Capetillo (1879-1922) She was a Puerto Rican labor leader who organized turn of the century workers in the island sugar industry. She was also a leader in the cigar factories of Tampa and New York. A feminist, she wrote and lectured extensively throughout Hispanic-American communities, Cuba and Puerto Rico.

Mary Fout Seymour
(1846-1893)
She opened the Union School of Stenography in New York City in 1879, the first secretarial school for women in America.

Mary Walton
In 1879, she developed a method for minimizing the environmental hazards of smoke from factories all over the country. Her system deflected the emissions into water tanks where the pollutants were retained and then flushed into the city sewage system. In 1891, she discovered sound-dampening apparatus for elevated trains.

1880
Charlotta Bass (1880-1969)
An African-American civil rights activist of the early 1900s, she became editor of *The Eagle*, the oldest West Coast newspaper for blacks. Under her leadership, the paper focused on social and political issues pertinent to blacks. She also wrote against policies such as harsh sentencing of black criminals, the intimidation and mistreatment of blacks and job discrimination.

Lulu M. Dryden (1880-1963)
She owned and operated her own iron and steel brokerage firm in Baltimore. In 1920, she became the first and only woman admitted to the National Association of Purchasing Agents.

Mary H. Myers
First woman balloon pilot, she flew balloon at Little Falls, NY in 1880. In 1886, she rose to an altitude of 4 miles - a world record in a balloon.

Jeanette Rankin
(1880-1973)
She was a pacifist, anti-war activist, and the first woman member of Congress when she was elected in 1916. While in Congress, she fought for women's suffrage, proposed a maternity and infant health bill that became law in 1921, and spoke out in vehement opposition to America's entry into WW I. At age 87, she participated in the anti-war demonstration in Washington in 1968.

1881
Clara Barton (1821-1912)
She served as a Union nurse during the Civil War. In 1881, she found the American Red Cross and was its president from 1882-1904. She also developed the first standardized "first aid" kit.

Clara Driscoll (1881-1945)
Deeply committed to Texas history, she made it her personal mission at the turn of the century to save the Alamo. When this important landmark fell into disrepair, and portions of it were about to be sold off to an eastern business that planned to build a hotel on the site, she used her own personal funds to buy the property. She then made an agreement with the Daughters of the Republic of Texas that they create a park about the Alamo's history.

Crystal Eastman (1881-1928)
A lawyer committed to feminism, peace and social reform, in 1909 she became the first female member of the New York State Employers' Liability Commission.

Hetty Goldman (1881 -?)
Archaeologist, her systematic excavations and recording of details at her excavation sites showd the relationship between Greece and the eastern Mediterranean. Her excavations of Tarsusin Turkey traced the city's development for more than 6,000 years.

Isabel Martin Lewis (1881-1955)
She published three books on astronomy: *Splendors of the Sky*, *Astronomy for Young Folks* and *A Handbook of Solar Eclipses*, which has remained a valuable resource even

today. While at the National Almanac Office, she developed a new method to calculate the northern and southern limits of visibility for an eclipse and developed formulae for computing solar eclipses. She favored women's suffrage and opposed the use of animals in scientific experiments.

Lelia Robinson
She was the first female to graduate from Boston University Law School in 1981 and the first woman to take the Bar in Massachusetts in 1982. Her first book "*Law Made Easy: A Book for the People*" reveals quite a bit about her early days in practice. In her second book *The Law of Husband and Wife* published in 1889 she hoped would educate women regarding the laws that especially concern women.

Edith Nourse Rogers (1881-1960)
She was the Massachusetts Congresswoman who introduced the "G.I. Bill of Rights" Act and the legislation that established the Women's Army Auxiliary Corp during World War II.

Eleanora Sears (1881 -?)
In 1918, she takes up squash after excelling at baseball, polo, golf, field hockey, swimming, tennis, yachting auto racing, and speedboat racing. She demonstrated that women could play men's games

and was a prime liberator of women in sports.

Florence Lois Weber
(1881-1939)
She was the first woman to successfully direct motion pictures in Hollywood. Many of her films, such as *Where Are My Children?*, dealt with controversial social issues, making pleas for birth control in some cases but condemning abortion.

Sophie Bell Wright
(1866-1919)
Despite a painful physical handicap, she furthered the education of women and the poor. In 1881, at age 15, she opened her "Day School for Girls" which has become one of New Orleans best private schools. In addition, she served on the Prison Reform Association and the Women's Christian Temperance Union.

1882
Belle Jennings Benchley
(1882-1973)
In 1927, she was promoted director of the San Diego Zoo – the only woman director of a zoo in the world. She also wrote books called *"My Animal Babies"* and *"My Life in a Man-Made Jungle"*.

Florence Aby Blanchfield
(1882-1971)
First woman to receive a regular commission in the US Army in 1947, she served as superintendent of Army Nurse Corps during World War II.

Her major interest and accomplishment was obtaining full military status for nurses and her efforts were successful with the passage of the Army-Navy Nurse Act of 1947.

Julia Anna Gardner (1882 -?)
Geologist and stratigraphic paleontologist, her work was of national and international importance to economic geology of the Western Hemisphere. During World War II, she was able to pinpoint the launch site of Japanese incendiary balloons because of her geological knowledge.

Susan Glaspell
(1882-1948)
Playwright and novelist, she won a Pulitzer Prize for *Alison's House* in 1930, a play about a spinster poet.

Janet Flanner (1882-1978)
A journalist, she was a correspondent for New Yorker for almost 50 years and was one of few women to be awarded the French Legion of Honor.

Emily Noether (1882-1935)
She was a mathematician in the first half of the 20th Century who developed the basis for group theory. Group theory is the mathematics behind the representation of all modern physics.

Frances Perkins

(1882-1965)

She was the first woman cabinet member, appointed Secretary of Labor in 1933 and retained the post until 1945. She drafted much of the New Deal legislation including the Social Security Act, the National Labor Relations Act, the Fair Labor Standards Act, and the National Industrial Recovery Act.

Rose Schneiderman

(1882-1972)

She established the Women's Trade Union League to address the concerns of working women.

Julia C. Smith

In 1882, she received a patent for her compound culinary tool - combination cake beater, dish cleaner and plateholder.

1883

Jessie Daniel Ames

(1883-1972)

She founded the Association of Southern Women for the Prevention of Lynching in the 1930s.

Charlotte Hawkins Brown

(1883-1961)

She founded Palmer Memorial Institute in North Carolina, a school for African-American women founded in 1902.

Dr. Susan Hayhurst

In 1883, she completed a course at the Philadelphia College of Pharmacy to become first woman pharmacist in the US.

Mary Francis Hoyt

She made the highest score of any person on the first civil service examination in 1883 and became a clerk that same year with a salary of $900.

Emma R. H. Jentzer

(1883-1972)

She was the first woman to serve as a special agent for the Bureau of Investigations, precursor of the Federal Bureau of Investigation. She became an agent in 1911 after her husband's death.

Margaret Morse Nice

(1883-1974)

In 1919, she embarked on a career studying nature and educating the public about the natural world. Her research on the song sparrow was one of the earliest documented long-term studies of an individual animal species. She published more than 250 papers on bird research and stressed the need for conservation efforts to preserve untouched areas for birds, animals, trees and flowers. She also protested the use of herbicides and certain logging practices.

Frances E. C. Williard

(1839-1898)

American educator and reformer, she founded the World's Women's Christian Temperance Union in 1883.

She was also identified with the movement for women's suffrage and the Prohibition Party, which she helped organize in 1882.

1884
Florence Ellinwood Allen
(1884-1966)
Jurist and women's suffrage activist, she served as legal counsel for the suffragist movement. In 1934, she was appointed to the Circuit Court of Appeals becoming the first woman named to a federal appellate chief judgeship.

May Hill Arbuthnot
(1884-1969)
Educator, she established the first nursery schools in Ohio. Her college textbook, Children and Books, published in 1947 became the most widely used textbook on children's literature.

Florence Ellinwood Allen
(1884-1966)
An active suffragist and peace activist, she broke barriers on numerous occasions. She became the first woman appointed to be assistant county prosecutor (1919), the first woman elected to be Judge (1920) and the first woman to preside over a murder trial (1921). In 1934 She became the first woman to sit on an Article III federal court and in 1959 she became the first woman to be chief judge of a federal circuit court.

Ethel Percy Andrus
(1884-1967)
A retired schoolteacher and farmer, she founded the American Association of Retired Persons, and was the first editor of Modern Maturity magazine.

Florence Nightingale Graham
(1884-1966)
In 1910, she founded Elizabeth Arden Inc and is considered one of the individuals responsible for the creation of the cosmetics industry. By pampering her clients and the skillful use of advertising, she made the cosmetic use respectable for the modern woman.

Harriet Quimby (1884-1912)
A pioneer pilot, she was the first American woman to receive a pilot's license and the first woman to fly the English Channel solo.

Eleanor Roosevelt (1884-1962)
An egalitarian and pacifist, she blazed new trails for the role of First Lady. She fought for women's right to vote and for protective labor laws for women and children, worked to promote racial equality and earned a reputation as a humanitarian. She sponsored an experiment in West Virginia, designed to bring small-scale manufacturing to impoverished coal miners in a self-sustaining community. As a US delegate to the United Nations from 1945 to 1953,

she chaired the commission that drafted the Universal Declaration of Human Rights.

1885

Edith Terry Bremer
(1885-1964)
Social reformer, she pioneered immigrant social service work. In 1910 she gained prominence as founder of the International Institute, which worked to improve the lives of female immigrants.

Ethel Harvey Browne
(1885-1965)
She is best known for her experimental work on the embryology of the sea urchin. Her book *The American Arbacia and Other Sea Urchins* deals not only with experimental work on sea urchin development but also to the distribution, behavior and general natural history of these organisms as studied in ancient as well as in modern times.

Louise Bryant (1885-1936)
An international correspondent, she published extensively on radical politics. She both witnessed and reported on Russian Revolution in 1917. She also was an advocate of women's suffrage, reproductive and sexual freedom and women's pursuit of professional careers.

Olive D. Wetzel Dennis
(1885 -?)
With an MA in mathematics and a civil engineering degree, she worked as service engineer with Baltimore and Ohio Railroad. She is responsible for such things as air conditioning, reclining seats and dressing rooms being installed on trains.

Mary Gartside
In 1885, she was the first person to have a successful appendectomy.

Amelia Laskey (1885-1973)
She banded thousands of birds and contributed valuable information to the U.S. Wildlife Service on migration of birds. She also published over 100 articles on birds and was a fellow of the American Ornithological Society.

Agnes B. Marshall
Owner of a cooking school, she patented an ice cream freezer and an "ice cave" or storage box for ice cream in 1885. She was also an author of several cookbooks, the first of which *Victorian Ices and Ice Creams* was published in 1885.

Ruth Bryan Owen
(1885-1954)
During her service in Congress (1929-33), she dedicated herself to the twin causes of domestic reform and international peace. Her

farsighted proposal included designation of the Florida Everglades as a national park.

Alice Paul (1885-1977)
A suffragist, she was the author of the Equal Rights Amendment in 1922 and an advocate of equal rights for women until her death. She was among the founders of the Congressional Union, later the National Women's Party, the activist group that fueled passage of the 19th amendment granting women the right to vote. In 1923, she organized a celebration in Seneca Falls, New York in honor of the First Women's Rights Convention. She was inducted into the National Women's Hall of Fame in Seneca Falls, New York in 1979.

Ruth Fanshaw Waldo
(1885-1975)
She was one of the 20th Century's first successful female advertising executive. Innovative and talented, she was especially good at promoting products that particularly appealed to women.

1886
Zoe Akins (1886-1958)
Playwright, she received the Pulitzer Prize for her dramatization of Edith Wharton's *The Old Maid* in 1935.

P. F. E. Albee
She became the first "Avon Lady" when she went to work for the California Perfume Company in 1886. The company became Avon Products Inc. in 1939.

Leonora Barry
Knights of Labor investigator who on an inspection of a corset factory in Newark, NJ, finds that the workers are fined a dime every time they eat, talk, laugh or sing.

Josephine Cochran
She invented and patents the first dishwashing machine in 1886, which she designed in a woodshed near her home. In 1893, her dishwasher won first prize at the Chicago World's Fair.

Carrie J. Everson
She invented the process of extracting precious metal from waste and patented the oil flotation process in 1886. These same separation fundamentals are used in mining today.

Edna Gladney (1886-1961)
Committed to child welfare, she devoted her 50-year career to finding homes for more than 10,000 Texas children. She launched educational programs for unwed mothers and helped find homes for their children As Superintendent of the Texas Children's Home and Aid Society in Fort Worth. She got laws passed that gave

adoptive children the same rights as biological children and convinced the legislature to eliminate the word "illegitimate" from birth certificates of babies born out of wedlock.

Isabella Selmes Greenway
(1886-1953)
In 1929, she established the Arizona Inn, a hotel resort, and a factory where disabled veterans made and sold furniture. She also owned and operated a cattle ranch and a Los Angeles based airline. While a member of Congress ((1933-37), she submitted measures to transfer Veterans Administration lands to the Interior Department for the benefit of the Yavapai Indians, protect land resources against soil erosion and improve public grazing lands.

Leta Stetter Hollingworth
(1886-1939)
Psychologist, educator and feminist, her test The Psychology of the Adolescent published in 1928 became the standard in the field for 20 years. She wrote the influential textbooks on giftedness, adolescence, mental retardation and special education. Her greatest contributions were in the study of the nurturance of giftedness.

Ida Rosenthal (1886-1973)
Inventor of the bra with cups, she co-founds Maiden Form Brassiere Company in 1923. She becomes the company president in 1958 and its CEO in 1959.

Clara Lemlich Shavelson
(1886-1982)
She was the labor union organizer who sparked the 1909 Shirtwaist Strike, which unionized the garment industry and helped shape the modern labor movement.

Catharine Waite
A lawyer, she founds the Chicago Law Times in 1886. This quarterly journal addressed many legal issues important to women including divorce and abortion. In 1888, she became president of the International Women's Bar Association.

1887
Ruth Benedict (1887-1948)
One of the first female anthropologists, she wrote of the differences between the cultures around the world and talked about different patterns related to culture and behavior. Her books serve as reference points of humanistic thought in the 20th century. She helped shape the discipline of anthropology not only in the US but also for the rest of the world.

Sarah Boone
An African-American, she invented and patented the ironing board in 1887.

Louise Arner Boyd
(1887-1972)
An American explorer of the Artic Ocean, she was the first woman to fly over the North Pole. During World War II, she served as an adviser on military strategy in the Artic. She also studied the effects of polar magnetic phenomena on radio communication.

Beulah Henry (1887-)
A descendant of Patrick Henry, she received her first patent in 1912 for a vacuum ice cream freezer. Her most successful invention was an umbrella with changeable, snap-on covers. She also created several educational inventions for children, including "Kiddie Klock" to teach time-telling and a board game "Cross Country" to learn about geography. For the office, she invented a photocopier in 1932 that made four typewritten copies of a document without carbon paper and in 1952, continuously attached envelopes for mass mailings. In all, Henry earned 49 patents, the last one in 1970.

Gertrude Muller (1887-1957)
She made a career of designing childcare products including the safety auto seat and the folding booster seat. In 1924, she created her own company to make the "Toidy Seat" a scaled down toilet that she had invented.

Ruth Thompson (1887-1970)
During her term in Congress (1951-57), she sponsored proposals to encourage development of public library services in rural areas and stimulate the growth of low-cost electric energy from a variety of power sources.

1888
Miriam E. Benjamin
In 1888, she received a patent for a gong and signal chair for motels.

Anna Bissell
Entrepreneur and co-founder of the Bissell Carpet Sweeper Company, she becomes its head after the death of her husband in 1888.

Ella Deloria (1888-1971)
A Dakota Indian, she devoted her life to the study of her people's language and culture.

Ellen Eglui
She invented the clothes wringer for washing machines in 1888 but sold the patent rights because if it were known that a Negro woman patented the invention, white ladies would not buy the wringer.

Lillian Janette Rice
(1888-1938)
After receiving her degree from University of California at Berkeley School of Architecture in 1910, she returned home with a set of architectural ideals, which

called for structures to be in harmony with their environment and the utilization of natural materials indigenous to the land.

1889

Emma Lucy Braun (1889-1971)
A dedicated pioneer ecologist of the first half of the 20th Century, she was instrumental in the development of plant ecology as a scientific discipline.

Bessie Hillman (1889-1970)
A labor leader, she founded the Almalgamated Clothing Workers of American in 1914.

Jennie Ward (1889-1918)
A member of the original Flying Wards flying return act, she was acknowledged to be one of the finest and most beautiful aerialists in the business. In 1906, she began performing for the great Ringling Brothers' Circus and established a standard of excellence, which carried over through future generations of trapeze artists.

1890

Dicksie Bradley Bandy
(1890-1971)
A telegraph operator during World War I, she was active in forming the first library board and creating the Dalton Regional Library System in Georgia.

Jenetta V. Bohannan
In 1890, she invented and patented two cigarette machines, which represented a new and/or improved technology for rolling tobacco in cigarette papers. Her third known invention was for a meat-slicing machine.

Marjory Stoneman Douglas
(1890-)
She has been a strident advocate for the restoration of Florida's wetlands, the Everglades. In 1947 she wrote *The Everglades: River of Grass*, which sounded an early warning of the environmental perils facing the Florida Everglades. In 1969, she co-founded Friends of the Everglades and is widely credited with helping to slow the destruction of the swamp ecosystem.

Amanda Jones
In 1872, she conceived a vacuum process of preserving foods and received 9 patents in the field. She founded the U.S. Women's Pure Food Vacuum Preserving Company in Chicago in 1890.

Lillian Russell (1890-1950)
She designed a costume dresser truck and had it patented in 1912. The dresser trunk was a series of drawers, lights, hooks, brackets, hinges and mirror that folded into themselves for easy shipping. In 1922, President Harding appointed

her special investigator on immigration problems.

Alice B. Sanger
In 1890, as a stenographer, she was the first woman to work at the White House.

Mathilde Schott
In 1890 she patented a surgical knife that had the distinguishing feature of a detachable blade.

Mabel K. Staupers
(1890-1989)
She was the woman responsible for the integration of the US Army's and Navy's corps of nurses during World War II.

Ada Van Pelt
In 1890, she invented the permutation lock with 3000 combinations. She patented a widely used house-door letter box in 1892 that signals the postal carrier when there is mail to be collected.

1891
Mary Anticharlook
(1891-1939)
Known as "The Reindeer Queen of Alaska," she pioneered reindeer herding in Alaska, bringing the first herds to the state and refining slaughtering and herding methods that saved the people from famine in 1898. The richest Eskimo woman of the time, she nonetheless became a foster mother to many children, and also opened her home as a way station for weary travelers on route to Nome.

Lizzie J. Darr
In 1891, she invented and patented a postage stamp vending machine.

Emma Sarah Edward
First woman to design a state seal, Idaho officially adopted it in 1891.

Lavinia Margaret Engle
(1892-1979)
In 1929, she was elected to the Maryland House of Delegates. During her tenure, she was a successful advocate and lobbyist for social insurance legislation including the passage of the first compulsory unemployment insurance compensation bill in Maryland.

Laura Gilpin (1891-1979)
Most important woman photographer of Southwest landscape and Native American culture especially Pueblo and Navajo Indians.

Zora Neale Hurston
(1891-1960)
Black American anthropologist and writer, she studied Black folklore and traveled around the country collecting material on African American culture.

Anna W. Keichline
(1890 -1943)
The first female registered architect of New York, she patented a number of kitchen

appliances and apparatus as well as furniture, children's toys, a wall-mounted folding bed and a compressed-air radiator/dryer.

Edith Hinkley Quimby
(1891 -)
Physicist, she created the new science of radiation physics. She also made accurate radiation dosage for patients possible, taught how to avoid radiation hazards and basic physics of radiation therapy to physicians.

1891
Beatrice Von Dressden
She makes her first parachute jump from a hot air balloon in 1891.

1893
Priscilla M. Burns
In 1893, she patented "Perfection Sifter" that not only measured flour but encased the sifting process to keep flour from flying about.

Irene Castle (1893-1969)
A famous ballroom dancer known for her elegant fashion, she popularized ballroom dancing in the early 20th Century. She was also an animal activist and fought for strong laws for the humane treatment of animals.

Bessie Coleman
(1893-1936)
She was the first woman to earn an International

Aviation License and the world's first licensed black aviator.

Crystal Dreda Bird Fauset
(1893 -)
A race relations specialist, she was the first black woman to be elected to the State Legislature of Pennsylvania in 1938. She helped create the Swarthmore College Institute of Race Relations in 1933.

Katherine Mahool Fowke
(1893 -)
She was first woman in Baltimore to start her own advertising firm and first woman elected to Board of Association of Advertising Clubs of Baltimore. She was the first "advertising woman of the year" in 1951 chosen by the Women's Advertising Club of Baltimore.

Lorena Hickok (1893-1968)
She was one of the first great female reporters and political analysts in American history.

Helen Elna Hokinson
(1893-1949)
She began her career in commercial design by selling fashion sketches to major department stores and became well known as creator of caricatures of plump, upper middle-class clubwoman that appeared regularly in the New Yorker magazine in 1925. Her satirical cartoons brought her fame and fortune as

readers chuckled at the antics depicted. In the late 1930s, she collected the best of her work in a series of books.

Margaret Leech (1893-1974)
In 1942, she was the first woman to receive the Nobel Prize in History for *Reveille in Washington*, a study of life in the nation's capital during the Civil War.

1894
Florence Bascom
(1862-1945)
She became the first woman fellow of the Geological Society of America in 1894.

Kathryn Elizabeth Granahan
(1894-1979)
She gained attention in Congress (1956-63) as the leader of an investigation of pornography and its effects on minors. In 1963, she became Treasurer of the United States and is known to many Americans from her signature on currency. She proposed the return of the two-dollar bill to circulation in 1964.

Cecil Murray Harden
(1894-1984)
She won five terms in the House of Representatives (1949-59) and promoted flood control for the Wabash Valley and secured funding for a dam and recreational facility. She also toured military supply installations to study ways of improving the procurement procedures.

Anna Williams
Physician and bacteriologist, she discovers Park-Williams #8, a type of diphtheria bacillus, in 1894. Within months an antitoxin is available resulting in a sharp decrease in diphtheria deaths throughout the US and in other countries as well.

1895
Elinore Morehouse Herrick
(1895-1964)
She became executive secretary of the New York Consumers' League in 1927 and produced perceptive reports on female workers in canneries, laundries and candy factories. During World War II, she became personnel director for Todd Shipyards and was responsible integrating women and minorities into the wartime work force.

Maude Elizabeth Kee
(1895-1975)
She was the author of "Washington Tidbits" a weekly column that was syndicated to West Virginia newspapers. The only woman representative from West Virginia (1951-65), she was ardently pro-labor, favored continuation of consumer and federal rent controls, economic aid to Europe, and higher Social Security benefits with extended coverage.

1896

May Edward Chinn

(1896-1980)

She was the first African-American woman to graduate from Bellevue Hospital Medical College, one of the first female African-American physicians in New York City and the first African-American woman to intern at Harlem Hospital. Her work in cancer research helped in the development of the Pap smear, a test for early detection of cervical cancer.

Virginia Kneeland Frantz

(1896-1967)

Surgical pathologist and medical educator, she publishes the monograph Armed Forces Atlas of Tumor Pathology in 1959, a standard reference work for many years.

Rose Knox

Co-founder of Knox Gelatine Company and a leader in the food industry, she was known especially for her forward-thinking management style that espoused paid sick leave, vacations and a 5-day workweek. In 1896, she compiled a booklet "Dainty Deserts" to advertise her product.

Mary Church Terrell

(1863-1954)

A teacher, lecturer, suffrage activist and leader in the black women's club movement, was president of the National Association of Colored Women in 1896. She was also a founding member of the NAACP and an active participant in the anti-lynching movement.

Lauretta Bender

(1897-1987)

Psychiatrist, her 4-volume *Bellevue Studies* was a major contribution on child psychology. She did important research in brain injury and childhood schizophrenia and devised the Bender Visual Motor Gestalt Test.

Dorothy Day (1897-1980)

She was a reformer and journalist who founded a newspaper at her kitchen table, *The Catholic Worker*, which advocated for labor unions, publicized Catholic social teaching and sought a more idealized and peaceful society. By 1936, she established 33 Catholic Worker houses across the country to house the homeless, and experimented with farming communes in Pennsylvania and New York. A suffragist and committed pacifist, she protested against the use of the atom bomb and the continued development of such weapons.

Edith Head (1897-1981)

She was the premier costume designer in Hollywood, whose fashions graced thousands of movies and influenced the nature of costume design for decades.

Florence Siebert
(1897-1991)
She was a scientist who made it possible to test for TB and pioneered safe intravenous therapy.

Margaret Chase Smith
(1897-1995)
During her service in both houses of Congress (1940-73), she earned a reputation for personal independence and integrity. She worked for passage of the 1948 Women's Armed Services Integration Act, which secured permanent regular status for women who served in the armed forces. In domestic affairs, she proposed legislation for the enlargement of the National Institute of Health and assistance to medical schools. She declared her candidacy for the Republican presidential nomination in 1964, but only received 27 first ballot votes at the Republican National Convention.

1898
Berenice Abbott
(1898-1991)
One of the earliest experts in the field of photography, she was best known for her portraits and documentary photographs of American life and society. She was also an inventor of photographic equipment, archivist, historian as well as a writer and teacher.

Katherine Blodgett
(1898-1979)
She received a patent for nonreflecting glass. In World War II, her glass was used in periscopes, range finders and aerial cameras. Since then, her coatings have found many diverse applications including making airplane wings ice-resistant and even artificial rainmaking.

Rachel Fuller Brown
(1898 -)
She was co-discoverer of Nystatin, the world's first successful fungus-fighting antibiotic. Nystatin has even been used to combat Dutch elm disease in trees and to restore artwork damaged by water and mold.

Ruth Leah Bunzel
(1898 -)
Cultural anthropologist, she undertook a study of Zuni Indian pottery and contributed important studies of Zuni ceremonialism.

Amelia Earhart (1898-1937)
An aviator, she was noted for her flights across the Atlantic and Pacific Oceans and her attempt to fly around the world.

Mary Elizabeth Pruett Farrington (1898-1984)
During the 1920s she founded a Washington-based newspaper syndicate that distributed news items from the capital to periodicals in the Midwest. She was sworn in as

a member of Congress in 1954 and submitted a bill for Hawaiian statehood in 1955.

Eleanor Touroff Glueck
(1898-1972)
Social worker and juvenile delinquency reformer, she was co-director of a long-term study on the causes, treatment and prevention of juvenile delinquency.

Lyda A. Newman
She received a patent for a hairbrush in 1898 that permitted easy cleaning by having a detachable unit, which carried the brush and bristles.

1899
Jane Addams (1860-1935)
A pacifist, suffrage activist, and social reformer, she founded Hull House in 1889, a settlement and recreation program for the poor and immigrants, which paved the way for modern social work. In 1915, she helped form the Women's Peace Party, and in 1931 as president of the Women's International League for Peace and Freedom, she was the first US woman to receive the Nobel Peace Prize.

Helen Elizabeth Brown (1899-)
She worked for women's rights and paved the way for women to run for public office and hold appointed positions in Maryland.

Emily Taft Douglas
(1899-1994)
During her term in Congress in 1945-47, she served on the Committee on Foreign Affairs and was widely recognized as a specialist in the field. She proposed legislation to put the United Nations in charge of international programs for arms control and the abolition of atomic weaponry. She also called for greater federal support for libraries particularly those in rural and low-income areas.

May Evans
She invented a moustache guard for attaching to spoons or cups when used in the act of eating soup or other liquid food or drinking coffee.

Mary Margaret McBride
(1899-1976)
She was the most popular woman radio broadcaster for two decades. Her program was the forerunner of the modern talk show.

1900
Dorothy Arzner
(1900-1979)
She made her directing debut in 1927 and became the Hollywood's only female director of the 1930s. During World War II, she made training films for the Women's Army Corps.

Josephine Perfect Bay
(1900 -)
She was the first woman to head a member firm of the New York Stock Exchange. If women were "active investment owners" and not "mere passive coupon clippers", she felt the US economy would be "more venturesome and more vibrant".

Helen Gahagan Douglas
(1900-1980)
She ran for Congress in 1944 and supported the United Nations and the independence of the Philippines. In domestic affairs, she supported organized labor and sought better housing. She was Chief House sponsor of the McMahan-Douglas Act that established civilian control of atomic energy.

Lillian M. Gilbreth
(1878-1972)
She was the first woman to speak at a University of California commencement when she obtained her BA in Literature in 1900. She pioneered industrial management techniques. Concerned with the human aspects of time management and she is the "Mother of modern management". She publisheed *The Home-Maker and Her Job* in 1927.

Estelle Griswold
(1900-1981)
Executive director of Planned Parenthood League of Connecticut, she led the legal battle for elimination of Connecticut's anti-birth control statute.

Helen Hayes (1900- 1993)
An actress, she worked with the Mary MacArthur Fund of the March of Dimes to care for children who were dying of polio. She helped parents through the ordeal and convinced Nyack Hospital in New York to set up a treatment and therapy department for the paralyzed children who survived. The Helen Hayes MacArthur Hospital was first hospital of its kind in the 1970s.

Alice Neel (1900-1984)
Her portraits offer a poignant record of the anxieties and ambitions found in modern American urban society during the middle decades of the 20th Century. She became a proponent of radical social and cultural reform, a commitment that strengthened her resolve to portray individuals from all walks of life and their personal struggles.

Olga A. Reifschneider
(1900-1978)
She attended Field School for Ranger Naturalists and obtained a BA in Botany in 1949. She lectured and wrote articles on wildflowers, the environment, desert biology, petroglyphs and Nevada history. In the field, she was an avid plant collector and photographer. One small

wildflower she collected in 1956 was identified as a new species.

Florence Woods
In 1900, she became the first American woman to get an automobile-driving permit.

1901
Dorothy Hansine Andersen
(1901-1963)
Pathologist and pediatrician, she discovered cystic fibrosis in 1938 and related diagnostic tests. She did work on congenital heart defects leading to break-throughs in open-heart surgery.

Alva J. Fisher
In 1901, she invented and devloped the first electric washing machine.

Harriet Boyd Hawes
(1871-1945
The first archeologist to discover and excavate a Minoan settlement at Gournia, dating to the Early Bronze Age, over 3000 years ago. She was the first woman to direct a major field project.

Sophia J. Kleegman
(1901-1971)
A pioneer in the study of infertility, she believed that gynecologists had a responsibility for helping and preventing conception. She advocated establishment of semen banks and artificial insemination.

Margaret Mead (1901-1978)
An anthropologist, she was widely known for her studies of primitive societies, most notably her research on child rearing in New Guinea, Samoa, and Bali. But she was also an avid commentator who analyzed problems in 20th century American society, especially those affecting young people, as well as women's roles and rights, and she didn't hesitate to share her views with the press.

Janet G. Travell (1901 -)
She was the first woman physician to hold the post of personal physician to the President of the United States (John F. Kennedy). A specialist in the study and treatment of musculoskeletal pain, she was a firm believer in rocking chairs as mild muscular exercisers.

1902
Ethelda Bleibtrey
(1902-)
She began swimming to overcome polio and went on to compete in the 1920 Olympics. Ethelda became first woman to win 3 gold medals and the only woman ever to win all the women's swimming events at any Olympic games.

Antonia Brico (1902-1989)
An internationally recognized conductor and first woman orchestra conductor in US. In 1935, she founded the Woman's Symphony Orchestra.

Vera Daerr Buchanan
(1902 -)
Sworn in as Congresswoman in 1951, she was an advocate of housing legislation and a proponent of the Turtle Creek Valley Control Flood and an ardent defender of unions and the rights of labors.

Felice Cohen (1884-1961)
In 1902, at age 18, she was admitted to the bar in Nevada - the youngest person to achieve that distinction. In 1911 she became involved in suffrage rights for women and founded the State Equal Franchise Society. Although a large portion of her law practices involved divorces, she also worked with child labor issues, foster homes, adoption and other legislative issues adversely affecting women and children.

Florence Dwyer (1902-1976)
As a representative for 16 years, she concentrated on issues of consumer protection, women's equality and procedural reform in the House of Representatives. She was chief sponsor of the act creating the Consumer Protection Agency and another act that sought to eliminate discriminatory lending practices.

Nita Martha Holder
In 1902, she was the first woman in the U.S. to have a hysterectory because she did not want to have children.

Xue Jinqin
A San Francisco Chinese women and feminist, in 1902 she spoke out in Chinatown for an end to restrictive customs like foot binding and educational opportunities for women.

Phoebe Fairgrave Omlie
(1902-1975)
One of the pioneers of aviation, she financed her early passion for flying by stunt flying for the Perils of Pauline motion pictures and demonstrated the nonmilitary value of airplanes by flying mercy missions during forest fire or flood emergencies and serving as fire spotters. Also, she was the first woman to receive an aircraft mechanic's license, operated the first airport in state of Tennessee and one of the nation's first flying schools. She successfully campaigned for taxation reform that would return aviation taxes for aviation use and for the establishment of state sponsored schools to train civilian pilots.

Leonor Kretzer Sullivan
(1902-1988)
The only woman representative from Missouri (1953-77), she was a defender of consumers and the author of the food stamps plan that distributed federally owned surplus food to the poor. She also sponsored legislation to protect consumers from

hazardous substances, harmful food color additives and cosmetics and tainted meat and poultry. Among her accomplishments was the passage of the 1976 Fishery and Conservation Management Act, which established a 200-mile fisheries conservation zone off the coasts of the United States.

1903

Mary Anderson
She was granted her first patent for a window-cleaning device in 1903. Her invention could clean snow, rain or sleet from a windshield by using a handle inside the car. By 1913, it was standard equipment on American cars.

Ella Baker (1903-1986)
She was the premier behind-the-scenes organizer and co-founder of the Southern Christian Leadership Conference (SCLC) headed by Martin Luther King, Jr.

Emily C. Duncan
In 1903, she patented a banking-related calculator that calculated interest on loans and in 1904, she patented another calculator that could quickly calculate the remaining term for loans of various amounts.

Gladys Anderson Emerson
(1903-)
She was a biochemist whose research increased our knowledge of vitamin

deficiencies on the human body.

Angela Gregory
(1903- 1990)
Sculptor and educator - she was one of the first female sculptors to carve stone and is credited with three public monuments. She has won a number of prizes for her bronze studies of African Americans.

Clare Booth Luce
(1903-1987)
A playwright, legislator, and diplomat, she began her career as a magazine writer in the 1930s with *Vogue* and *Vanity Fair*, and later wrote three plays that all became movies. She became a war correspondent during the early part of World War II, and from 1943-1947 she was elected to the US House of Representatives. In 1953 she became the first woman ambassador to a major country when appointed ambassador to Italy.

Maggie Lena Walker
First African-American woman bank president, she began the St. Luke Savings Bank in Richmond, Virginia in 1903. Her bank was so successful that after the stock market crash in 1929, it not only survived, it absorbed other local banks.

Edith S. Sampson
(1903-1979)
In 1927, she was the first woman to receive a graduate law degree from Loyola University School of Law. She went on to represent many firsts: the first African American to be appointed delegate to the United Nations, the first African American member of NATO and the first black woman to be elected as a judge in the US.

1904
Mary McLeod Bethune
(1875-1955)
A noted educator and social activist, she founded the Daytona Educational & Industrial Training School for Negro Girls - currently known as Bethune-Cookman College. In 1935, she founded the National Council of Negro Women.

Margaret Bourke-White
(1904-1971)
Pioneering news photographer who helped develop and define the field of photojournalism.

Mary S. Calderone (1904-)
A physician and public health educator, she was a crusader for birth control and sex education. She was a pioneer in establishing the field of human sexuality in the mid-1960s and edited the first extensive textbook on contraception.

Erna Gibbs (1904-1987)
She played a key role in using electroencephalograph (EEG) as diagnostic tool. Her application of the EEG was instrumental in understanding cause of epilepsy.

Lydia Scott Howell
She won three gold medals in archery, which was an unofficial Olympic sport at the 1904 St. Louis games.

Angelica E. Post
In 1904, she invented an electric pocket lamp - one of the earlier electric pocket lamps and the forerunner of the modern flashlight. She invented and patented the dry battery cell in 1906.

Georgia Dwelle Rooks
She received a medical degree from Meharry Medical College in 1904 and founded the first OB hospital for black women in Atlanta.

Mabel Hunt Slater
In 1904, she patented an ice-cooled refrigerator. She also invented a sleeping bag, which doubled as a garment that was used in the trenches in World War I.

1905
Catherine Krouse Bauer
(1905-1964)
Urban planner and housing expert, her book *Modern Housing* published in 1934 called for quality low-cost housing and led to her

appointment as executive secretary of the American Federation of Labor Housing Conference which brought about the first public housing legislation in the us.

Oveta Culp Hobby
(1905-1995)
As the first director of the Women's Army Corps, the first Secretary of the Department of Health, Education and Welfare, and the only woman to serve in Eisenhower's cabinet, she shaped the development of two major government institutions. She was also the first woman to rise to the rank of US Colonel. Because of her wartime service in Women's Auxiliary Army Corps, she helped pave the way for the promotion of women to a position of full equality in the military.

Claire McCardell
(1905-1958)
Fashion designer during World War II, she is known as "creator of women's sportswear" and is widely recognized as the woman who pioneered casual, comfortable American sportswear fashion for women. She was the first designer to use zippers, popularize leotards and put spaghetti straps on evening gowns. While other designers imitated Parisian fashions, she modified them for comfort and affordability and created fashions suitable for the active career woman. One of her most enduring ideas was the "separates" wardrobe that allowed women to "mix and match" outfits. Her fashions are on display in the Smithsonian Institute and the Fashion Institute of New York as examples of the American look in women's fashion. In 1956, she won the first American Sportswear Designer Award presented by Sports Illustrated magazine.

Sarah Breedlove M. Williams
(1867-1919)
Inventor and businesswoman, she developed a conditioning treatment for straightening hair in 1905. By 1919, she was a millionaire and one of the most successful business executives in the early half of the 20th century. She was a strong advocate and supporter of Black Women's economic independence, which she fostered by creating business opportunities for women.

1906
Midred Edie Brady
(1906-1965)
Consumer advocate, she became editorial director and senior editor of *Consumer Reports* in 1958.

Eleanor Lamson
She was the first woman astronomer employed by the United States Naval Observatory.

Edna Flannery Kelly

(1906 -)

The longest-serving Congresswoman from New York (1949-69), she proposed legislation to extend rent control and provide working mothers with tax relief. In 1951, she introduced a bill to provide equal pay for equal work for women and in 1955, she introduced amendments to the Social Security Act to lower the retirement age for beneficiaries of old age and survivors insurance benefits.

Maria Goeppert Mayer

(1906-1972)

She was the first American woman to win a Nobel Prize in Physics for her inspirational work in models of the nucleus of atoms.

Esther Peterson (1906 -)

She was a catalyst for change in the labor, women's and consumer movements. The instrumental force behind President Kennedy's creation of 1st Presidential Commission on Women in 1962, she was the head of the Women's Bureau in the Department of Labor. She also served as consumer affairs adviser and at the United Nations.

Irene Barnes Taeuber

(1906-1974)

Demographer and advocate of birth control, she became the first president of the Popoulation Association of America.

Mary A. Hallaren (1907 -)

Colonel Hallaren was one of the first women volunteers selected for Officer Candidate School in the Women's Army Auxillary Corps (WAAC) and appointed first Executive Officer. She was later Commanding Officer of the 1st WAAC Separate Battalion. A continuing champion for unlimited opportunities for military women, she lectures on her many travel experiences and has written several articles on the customs and traditions of the countries she has visited.

Julia Butler Hansen

(1907-1988)

In 1960, she was elected to Congress and served until 1974. During this time, she introduced joint resolutions calling for establishment of a national traffic safety agency and an independent Federal Maritime Administration. She also proposed the regulation of dairy imports and a joint congressional committee to investigate crime.

Luisa Morena (1907-1990)

She was a Guatemalan American woman labor activist and founding member of El Congreso de Pueblos de Habla Espanola. She led the first Mexican-American civil rights coalition in the US, and was a leader in organizing the UCAPAWA (the United Cannery,

Agricultural, Packing and Allied Workers Association).

Ruth Patrick (1907 -)
Her pioneering efforts in the field of limnology, the study of freshwater ecosystems, are responsible for the way that the environmental health of rivers and streams are evaluated. She invented the diatometer, a device that accurately determines the presence of pollution in fresh water.

Henriette Wyeth
(1907-1997)
Globally renowned as a portrait painter, many of her works are in the permanent collection of the National Portrait Gallery and other prestigious collections throughout the world.

1908
Sara Josephine Boke
She became director of the first Child Hygiene Bureau in New York City in 1908. The program included nutrition and health education, health checks of school children and licensing of midwives.

Lena King Lee (1908 -)
During her teaching career, she helped form the American Federation of Teachers. In 1969, she served as the first and only black woman lawyer when she became a Maryland General Assembly delegate. Her forte was social welfare and other legislation, which affected the removal of

archaic laws from the Code of Maryland.

Mary Emily Sinclair
(1878-1955)
She was the first woman to receive a Ph.D. in mathematics from the University of Chicago in 1908. Her work was primarily in the calculus of variations.

E. L. Todd
She was the first woman to invent an airplane. In 1908, she filed a patent for her invention – a collapsible airplane that folded up to a third of its size.

1909
Helen Eugenie Moore Anderson
(1909-1997)
In 1949, she was sworn in as US ambassador to Denmark, becoming the first female to serve as an official American ambassador. She helped coordinate Denmark's introduction into the NATO.

Mary Busch (1909 -)
Hired as a stenographer, she worked her way up an advertising company to become its Executive Vice-President. She earned the distinction of becoming the first woman elected to the Executive Committee of the Advertising Federation of America.

Annie Smith Peck
She became the first person to climb Mount Huascaran, the highest peak in Peru, in 1909

and plants a "Votes for Women" banner on top of Mt. Coropuna in Peru when she becomes the first woman to climb it in 1911. Her last climb was Mount Madison, NH at age 82.

1910
Jenny R. Bramley (1910-)
She invented the "microwave pumped high efficiency lamp", whose brightness in the "narrow spectral band…far exceed that of high power xenon arc lamps". IEEE has cited her "for achievement in spectroscopy, optics, mathematical techniques and their application for electron tubes, displays and light sources to engineering. She also invented techniques of coding and decoding pictorial information.

Jacqueline Cochran
(1910-1980)
A pioneer in women's aviation, she paved the way for female American pilots of the future. Her work as director of the Women's Airforce Service Pilots pushed the US military to accept women as part of its organization.

Millicent Hammond Fenwick
(1910-1992)
In 1948, she wrote *Vogue's Book of Etiquette*. In her 4 terms in Congress from 1975-83, she was a fiscal conservative and supported the Equal Rights Amendment, federal funding for abortions

and the food stamp programs. She also worked on the Helsinki Commission on human rights and worked to eliminate the tax provision that penalized working couples.

Edith Starrett Green
(1910-1987)
She left her mark on almost every education bill enacted during her tenure in Congress (1955-74) and was responsible for establishing the first federal program for undergraduate scholarships.

Annie Dodge Wauneka
(1910 -)
A Navajo health educator, she lead the implementation of Navajo health programs. She helped to educate her people about how to eradicate tuberculosis.

Alice Stebbins Wells
(1873-1957)
In 1910, her appointment as an officer of the Los Angeles Police Department marked women's formal entry into American law enforcement. She was instrumental in forming the International Association of Policewomen.

1911
Verna Aardema (1911 -)
She started writing children's stories in the 1950s and specializes in the modernization and adaptation of traditional African folktales. Most of her stories combine humor, magic

and adventure to recreate stories that have themes of heroism and morality.

Lucille Ball (1911-1989)
She was one of television's most popular comedic actresses. From 1962-1967, she was head of Desilu Production.

Helene Britton
In 1911, she became the first woman owner of a major league team, the St. Louis Cardinals.

Jovita Idar (1885-1946)
She was an organizer, writer and advocate for Mexican-American women's rights. In 1911 she founded the Liga Feminil Mexicanista to educate, instruct and support women and children in Laredo, Texas. The organization's first project was to provide free instruction to poor children. She founded a free kindergarten in 1917, and was active in the Democratic party.

Virginia Jackson (1911 -)
She has the distinction of being the only noted black woman portrait painter in the State of Maryland.

1912
Isabella Goodwin
She became first woman detective appointed by New York City Police Department in 1912. Since 1896 she had served as police matron.

Martha Wright Griffiths
(1912 -)
Best known for her promotion of the Equal Rights Amendment, she also was an advocate of tax, welfare and health care reform during her two decades in Congress (1955-74). She supported urban renewal, food stamp programs, increased federal aid for education and hospital construction, repeal of excise tax on automobiles, tax relief for single parents and reduction of social security taxes paid by low-income families.

Dorothy Height (1912-)
She began as a volunteer with the National Council of Negro Women. As its president and leader, she assisted the needy and sought to help build strong families.

Muriel Buck Humphrey
(1912 -)
Appointed to serve in her husband's seat in the Senate pending a special election, she used her brief term in office to speak on a number of issues. She urged ratification of the treaties turning over control of the Panama Canal to Panama and guaranteeing the canal's neutrality and sponsored an amendment to the Civil Service Act of 1978, which offered better job security to federal employees.

Barbara Tuchman (1912-1989)
Historian, she is the recipient of two Pulitzer Prizes in History for her historical books such as "*The Guns of August*. She is one of the most widely read American historians.

Chien-Shiung Wu (1912-1997)
A pioneering physicist, she radically altered modern physical theory. Her work disproved the "law of parity which stated that in reactions, like nuclear particles always acted symmetrically. In recognition of her contributions to atomic research and the understanding of the weak interactions and beta decay, she became the first woman to receive the Comstock Prize from the National Academy of Sciences. She was the first woman to receive an honorary doctorate of science from Princeton University, to be elected president of the American Physical Society and to receive the Wolf Prize from the State of Israel.

1913
Georgia Broadwich
In 1913, she was first woman to parachute jump from an airplane over Griffith Field in CA.

Bessie Olive Cole
(1883-1971)
In 1913, she was the first woman to graduate from University of Maryland's School of Pharmacy and receive the doctor of pharmacy degree. She became a registered pharmacist in Maryland and Washington D.C. and in 1915, a life-long active member of the American Pharmaceutical Association.

Florence Lawrence
A silent film actress, she was also an inventor of many mechanical devices for cars. In 1913, she invented a signaling arm, which was mounted on the back fender. The arm was raised and lowered by an electric button on the dash and told other drivers behind the car which way the car was turning. She also invented a braking indicator, which consisted of a flag on the back of the car that would rise whenever the brake was pressed.

Margaret Wentworth Owings
(1913-1999)
An artist and conservationist led efforts to save sea otters, sea lions, mountain lions and other wildlife and to protect the world's forests and oceans. Honored by the National Audubon Society in 1983 and listed in 1998 among the 100 people who had done the most to shape the environmental movement, she was also a folk artist who had one-woman exhibitions of her stitchery at galleries and museums.

Charlotte Thompson Reid
(1913 -)
During her tenure in Congress (1963-71), she supported the proposed Equal Rights Amendment to the Constitutio. She also endorsed improved safety standards for motor vehicles, the 1968 Omnibus Crime Control and Safe Streets Act, a measure to outlaw mail order and out-of-state sales of rifles, and a Truth in Lending law requiring disclosure of annual percentage costs of loans and installment plans.

Elizabeth Shull Russell
(1913 -)
A research scientist, she was elected to National Academy of Science in 1972. Her research interests include genetic effects of aging, action of deleterious genes, muscular dystrophy, and physiological genes.

1914
Georgia "Tiny" Broadwick
While demonstrating air-jumping techniques to the US Army in 1914, she pulled her release manually becoming the first person to make an intentional free-fall parachute jump from an airplane.

Katharine Bement Davis
In 1914, she was appointed New York City Correction Commissioner and became the country's highest-ranking female municipal agency executive. In 1915, she founded the Women's City Club of New York whose initial purpose was to prepare women to take an active, informed role in municipal government as voters once that franchise was won.

Hannah Marie Wormington
(1914-1994)
An archaeologist known for her study of Paleo-Indians in the Southwest, she contributed to the body of research of prehistoric cultures. Her most important publications were *Ancient Man in North America* and *Prehistoric Indians of the Southwest*. Both books are considered classics for synthesizing the incredible amount of data on the subject of Prehistoric Indians. In 1967, she became the first woman president of the Society for American Archaeology.

1915
Luisa Capetillo (1879-1922)
Puerto Rican feminist writer and activist, she is well known for being arrested in Cuba in 1915 for wearing pants in public.

Joan Dewind (1915-1997)
A noted amateur lepidopterist (butterfly expert), she was a founding member of the Xerces Society, the international organization that specializes in butterflies, moths and other such creatures. Her specialty was sphinx moths. As a conservationist, she

designed gardens that drew butterflies and was instrumental in the drive to preserve extensive farmlands in Connecticut for open spaces.

Frances Gabe (1915-)
Driven by her hatred of housecleaning, she developed and patented the most radical and yet practical invention – a Self-Cleaning House. She actually lives in her prototype house and after 40 years work and 68 devices; she is still fine-tuning her house. Dishes are cleaned, dried and stored inside a cupboard, which is also a dishwasher; clothes are cleaned, dried and stored while hanging in a closet, which is also a washing machine/dryer. The sinks, tubs and toilets in the house are self-cleaning and the bookshelves dust themselves.

Rosalie Jones
Pursuant to magazine article in 1915, suffragist, heiress, chauffeur and auto mechanic Rosalie Jones believed that everyone regardless of gender should work for a salary.

1916
Corinne Claiborne Boggs
(1916 -)
She became the first woman to preside over a national political convention when she served as chair of the Democratic National Convention in 1976. She worked to broaden interest in

and awareness of American history in addition to her legislative interest in housing policy, technological development, Mississippi River transportation and equal opportunities for women and minorities.

Ruth Colvin (1916 -)
Founder of the Literacy Volunteers of America, a group that began in her home in upstate New York and now has taught almost half a million people to read.

Kay Curtis
She introduced synchronized swimming as an integral part of the University of Wisconsin's physical education program in 1916.

Catherine East (1916 -)
In 1960's, she was key staffer on the first Presidential Commission on the Status of Women. She also was instrumental in the creation of the National Organization for Women to lead the drive advance women's rights and end gender discrimination.

Jeanette Rankin (1880-1973)
She was an American pacifist, politician and social activist from Montana. In 1916, she was elected to the US House of Representatives and was the first woman in the world to be elected to a major legislative body. She voted against US entry into both World Wars and led a

resistance movement against US involvement in Vietnam.

Margaret Sanger
A nurse, she opened the first birth control clinic in Brooklyn, New York in 1916. She later helped to found Planned Parenthood. An early advocate of birth control, she devoted her life to the struggle for contraceptive rights. She believed that reproductive freedom was a woman's fundamental right.

Emma Tenayuca (1916-)
She was a Mexican-American labor leader, who led 1,000 pecan shellers in San Antonio to strike over pay in the late 1930s.

1917
Charlotte Bridgwood
She was president of Bridgwood Manufacturing Company of New York, which came up with many practical inventions. In 1917, she patented her electric Storm Windshield Cleaner, which utilized rollers. She was unable to sell her invention and was not given credit for the idea. It was not until 1923 that the automatic windshield wiper became a standard feature on cars.

Gwendolyn Brooks (1917 -)
She was an African-American poet whose poems elevated image of African Americans to humble people with rich and complex culture. They further enhanced understanding among races in the early Civil Rights movement. She won the Pulitzer Prize for Poetry in 1950.

Alice Chatham (1917 -)
A sculptor, she was famous for designing oxygen masks.

Marion Donovan (1917-1998)
She helped revolutionize the infant care industry by inventing the prototype of the disposable diaper. Ten years later the creator of Pampers capitalized on her idea. Among her other inventions are a 30-garment compact hanger, a soap dish that drained into the sink and the Zippity-Do.

Mabel Edna Gillespie
(1877-1923)
In 1917, she organized and became the first president of the Stenographers' Union. She was also interested in the educational needs of women workers, and helped to establish the Boston Trade Union College in 1919.

Katharine Graham
(1917 -)
She is the only woman to serve as publisher of a major American newspaper during the 20th Century - The Washington Post. Its coverage of Watergate helped bring down President Nixon. She is an important symbol of American female entrepreneurship and business acumen.

Fannie Lou Hamer
(1917-1977)
One of the most eloquent speakers for civil rights movement in the south, she worked for political, social and economic equality for herself and all African Americans. She fought to integrate the national Democratic Party and became one of the first black delegates to a presidential convention.

Ruth Handler (1917 -)
Co-founder of Mattel Toy Corp., she created Barbie, the world's most famous doll. When she lost a breast to cancer in 1970, she founded Ruthon Corp and developed the "Nearly Me" prosthesis, which is more realistic than previous models.

Mary R. Rinehart
(1876-1958)
America's first woman war correspondent during WWI for the Saturday Evening Post, she wrote mystery novels and in 1921 was referred to as "America's Mistress of Mystery".

Hazel Hook Waltz
She invents the bobby pin in 1917 only to lose a fortune when a large manufacturer patents and markets a slightly different version.

1918
Annette Abbott Adams
When she served in the Northern California District in 1918, she became first woman District Attorney.

Patty Berg (1918 -)
She was the original organizer of the Ladies Professional Golf Association in 1949 and became the most decorated woman golfer in history.

Gertrude Belle Elion (1918-)
She spent her life developing drugs to combat leukemia, gout malaria, herpes and other autoimmune diseases. Her name appears on 45 patents. In 1988, she shared the Nobel Prize in Medicine for the invention of leukemia fighting drugs and drugs that facilitate kidney transplants.

Katherine G. Johnson
(1918 -)
As an Aerospace Technician at NASA, she has worked with the tracking teams of manned and unmanned orbital missions. Trained as physicist and mathematician, she has worked on challenging problems of interplanetary trajectories, space navigation and the orbits of spacecraft. She was the recipient of the Group Achievement Award for her pioneering work in the field of navigational problems,

Rosa Ponselle (1897-1981)
Her 1918 debut at the Metropolitan Opera launched a legendary career as one of America's most celebrated divas. In 1997, a US postage

stamp was issued in her
honor.

Gladys Noon Spellman
(1918-1988)
During her terms in Congress
(1975-81), she was a tireless
supporter of federal
employees. She resisted
restrictions on the hiring
and promotion of federal
workers and supported
adjusted cost-of-living
increases in the pay of
military retirees and a
measure requiring federal
employees to inform spouses
if they elected not to
provide survivors' benefits
payments.

1919
Margaret Burbidge (1919 -)
Astronomer and first woman
astronomer elected to the
National Academy of Science.
She has also been president
of the American Astronomical
Society and Director of the
Greenwich Royal Observatory.

Edith Clark (1883-1959)
In 1919, she was the first
woman to earn a Master of
Science degree from MIT and
the first woman to be elected
fellow of the American
Institute of Electrical
Engineers. She filed a patent
for a "graphical calculator"
in 1921 that is used in
solving electric power
transmission problems. In
1947, she became the first
woman to teach engineering at
the University of Texas -
Austin.

Sister Helen Margaret Feeney
(1919 -)
She was the first woman in
New England and one of the
first five nationwide to
serve as chancellor of an
archdiocese, the highest
position in the Roman
Catholic Church that can be
held by a woman.

Mary Grantz (1879-1970)
She staked her first mining
claims in Nevada in 1919.
She later made a fortune when
one of her mines produced
90,000 tons of magnesium and
tungsten during WWII. Still,
true to the gambling nature
of miners, she lost most of
her fortune through further
prospecting.

Agnes Fay Morgan
(1884-1968)
She organized a home
economics department at the
University of California in
1919. A founder of the
science of nutrition, her
research focused on the
analysis of nutrients in
foods, the stability of
vitamins and proteins during
food processing the
physiological effects of
vitamin deficiencies.
Especially noteworthy was her
discovery of the role of
pantothenic acid in adrenal
function and pigmentation.

Nancy Harkness Love
(1914-1976)
She and her husband built a
successful aviation company
for which she was a pilot.

While flying for the Bureau of Air commerce, she tested three-wheeled landing gear, which subsequently became standard on most planes. In 1942, she became director of the Women's Auxiliary Ferry Squadron (WAFS) which helped transport planes from factories to bases.

Alice H. Parker
In 1919, she was issued a patent for a heating furnace. This invention provided a mechanism for regulating heat to be carried to various rooms of a building.

1920
Bella Abzug (1920 -)
One of the most colorful and well-known members of Congress in the 1970's, she has been an aggressive spokesperson for women's rights throughout her life. In her first term, she challenged the seniority system and the method of committee assignment while seeking to influence the most important issues of public policy.

Susan B. Anthony
(1820-1906)
A teacher, abolitionist and avid temperance crusader, she founded the Daughters of Temperance in 1849 as one of her earliest political activities. In 1851, she began a life-long campaign for women's rights, helping to pass the Married Women's Property Acts in New York in 1860. Through her work, many professional fields became open to women by the end of the 19th century. Best known for her suffrage work, she co-founded the National American Woman Suffrage Association and wrote a history of the battle for women's rights and a newspaper called *The Woman's Journal*. At the time of her death, only 4 states – Wyoming, Colorado, Idaho and Utah - had granted suffrage to women.

Theresa Weld Blanchard
In 1920, she wins the first US medal in the winter Olympics – a bronze medal for figure skating. She is scolded for putting a salchow jump in her program.

Lilly Dache (1892-1989)
She owned the House of Dache in New York from 1920-1968 where thousands of designs identified her indelibly with hats, particularly her signature turbans, half-hats and snoods.

Elaine Fried deKooning
(1920-1989)
A painter and art critic, she became one of the most important and outspoken members of the 2nd generation of American Abstract Expressionists.

Helen H. Gardener
(1853-1925)
In 1920, she was appointed Commissioner of the US Civil

Service Commission and was the first woman to occupy so high a federal position.

Marguerite Hall Higgins
(1920-1966)
Pulitzer-Prize winning journalist, she was the only woman news correspondent during the Korean War. She also reported from the battlefields of WWII where she witnessed the liberation of Dachau and covered the Nuremburg Trials.

Marjorie Sewell Holt
(1920 -)
During her time in Congress (1973-87), she focused on issues of national defense and the armed services. She was a persistent advocate of increased defense spending and improved benefits for armed services personnel.

Anna W. Keichline (1890 -)
The first female registered architect of New York State, she also focused her ingenuity on items for use in the home. She patented a number of kitchen appliances and apparatus, children's toys, a wall-mounted folding bed and a compressed-air radiator/dryer in the 1920's.

Katherine Siva Saubel
(1920 -)
Born on a reservation in great poverty, she was determined to preserve her tribe's culture and language. She became a learned ethnoanthropologist and founded the Malki Museum on the Morongo Reservation in California. This is the first museum founded and run by Native Americans.

Hilda W. Smith (1888-1984)
She was a pioneer in the workers' education movement of the 1920s and 1930s. The movement was dedicated to offering educational opportunities uniquely relevant to the lives of industrial workers. Her particular interest was in the education of women workers, an area to which she made important contributions for many years.

Edith Wharton (1862-1937)
She was a writer who received the Pulitzer Prize for her most famous novel "The Age of Innocence" in 1920.

1921
Betty Friedan (1921 -)
American social reformer and feminist, she began the late 20th Century women's rights movement in the United States. In 1966, she founded the National Organization for Women (NOW). It concentrated on enacting Title VII of the Civil Rights Act of 1964.

Maud Griffin (1880-1971)
In 1921, she became the first licensed female boat pilot in the State of Texas. Employed as Captain of the New Brunswick, her nickname was "Tugboat Annie".

Beatrice Mintz (1921 -)
A biologist, she has published over 150 papers on a wide range of experimental approaches in the field of developmental biology helping to establish the role of genes in differentiation and certain kinds of cancer such as melanoma.

Emily Post (1872-1960)
She published her first etiquette manual in 1921, which sold over 666,000 copies. Through her columns in *McCall's* and over 100 newspapers, a weekly radio show, and the Emily Post Institute (founded 1946), she established herself as the leading authority on good manners.

Yoshiko Uchida (1921-1992)
An acclaimed writer of fiction, she is best known for her representations of the experiences of Japanese-Americans in internment camps during World War II.

Barbara F. Vucanovich (1921 -)
As a member of Congress (1983 to date), she has focused on a variety of issues including federal wilderness and national park policy, public land use and nuclear waste disposal.

1922
Marie Luhring
With a Master of Engineering degree from New York's Cooper Union in 1922, she was the first woman automotive engineer and the first woman voted as associate member of the Society of Automotive Engineers.

Madeline Houston McWhinnery (1922 -)
She was founder of the First Women's Bank in New York City, the first full-service US commercial bank to be predominantly owned and operated by women.

Nina Otero-Warren (1881-1965)
She was an educator, suffrage worker, author and businesswoman of New Mexico. She served as Superintendent of Sante Fe County schools from 1917-1929. She engaged in efforts to preserve traditional arts and crafts of northern New Mexico and supervised adult education programs in New Mexico. She was the first woman to run for Congress in New Mexico in 1922.

1923
Helen Delich Bentley (1923 -)
She was elected to House of Representatives in 1984. Her central legislative achievements was to obtain federal support for the dredging and improvement of Baltimore harbor and was interested in legislation that protects American jobs and industry against foreign competition.

Willa Cather (1873-1947)
In 1923 she won the Pulitzer Prize for her novel "*One of Ours*". She was also the first woman to receive an honorary degree from Princeton.
Later, the National Institute of Arts and Letters awarded her its gold medal.

Helen Murray Free (1923 -)
A distinguished chemist and promoter of science, she invented a number of tests that revolutionized certain types of analysis in the laboratory and diagnosis at home. The most important of these was a 'dip-and-read' test that allowed diabetics to monitor their blood glucose level instantly and at home. In 1975, she co-authored the book *Urinalysis in Laboratory Practice*, which is still a standard work in the field.

Mabel Gillmore Reinecke
Appointed by President Harding in 1923, she was first woman Internal Revenue collector for the federal government.

Edna Jo Hunter (1923 -)
An expert on military families and prisoners of war, she served on the faculty of the US Military Academy at West Point. She was the first woman named as distinguished military psychologist of the American Psychological Association.

Betty Mae Tiger Jumper (1923-)
A woman of first - first Seminole woman to graduate from High School, the first Seminole woman to become a nurse, the first woman elected to Seminole Tribal Council and the first woman to lead a tribal council.

Edna Vincent Millay (1892-1950)
She published her first work when she was 14 years old. In 1923, she received the Pulitzer Prize for Poetry for the "*Ballad of the Harp Weaver*".

Beate Sirota (1923-)
She joined General Douglas MacArthur's team after World War II, and was the only woman who helped author the new Japanese Constitution. She successfully fought to include two paragraphs dealing specifically with the rights of women, and as a result she has become a heroine in Japan.

Louise Stanley (1883-1954)
She earned a Ph.D. in Biochemistry from Yale in 1911. In 1923, she was appointed chief of the US Department of Agriculture's Bureau of Home Economics. As bureau chief, she developed important research and education programs in Nutrition during the Depression and World War II. A strong consumer advocate, she was the first woman to be

appointed to the American Standards Association.

1924

Margaret K. Butler (1924-)
A pioneer in computer hardware, she helped develop one of the world's first digital computers for science in the 1950s.

Shirley Chisholm (1924-)
She was the first black woman elected to the US Congress. A long-time advocate for the needs of minorities, women and children, she supported employment and education programs, expansion of day care, and other programs to improve inner city life and opportunity, along with the end of the military draft and reduced defense spending.

Bette Nesmith Graham
(1924-1980)
Inventor of Liquid Paper, she applied for a patent and trademark in the 1950s. By 1975, the company employed 200 people, made 25 million bottles of Liquid Paper and distributed the product to 31 countries.

Evelyn Boyd Granville
(1924 -)
In 1949, she was one of the first black women to obtain a Ph.D. in Mathematics from Yale. She worked at Space Technology Laboratories as mathematical analyst studying rocket trajectories. Her contributions to the US Space Program included the development of computer programs that were used for trajectory analysis in the Mercury and Apollo Projects.

Catherine Small Long
(1924 -)
During her brief tenure in Congress (1985-87), she sought to preserve price supports to sugar and was co-sponsor of the Economic Equality Act of 1985 which secured pension and health benefits for women and sought to restrict racial and sex discrimination in insurance practices.

Dorothy V. McClendon
(1924 -)
She received BS in Biology in 1948 from Tennessee State University and has been a professional microbiologist for 24 years. Currently, she coordinates microbial research for the U.S. Army Tank Automotive Command (TACOM) in Warren, MI.

Alma Thomas (1891-1978)
She became the first graduate of Howard University's Fine Arts Department in 1924. She was the first African-American woman to have a solo exhibition at the Whitney Museum of American Art.

Hazel Wightman (1886-1974)
She won two gold medals in the 1924 Paris Summer Olympic games and is credited with doing more to build American and International women's tennis than any other player.

1925

Evelyn Berezin (1925 -)
A computer designer, she designed a digital on-line racetrack betting system and one of the world's first word processors.

Sala Burton (1925-1987)
She was elected to the House of Representatives in 1983 and served as an advocate for social welfare programs, child nutrition assistance, bilingual education and the Equal Rights Amendment.

Joan Miller Platt
(1925-1998)
When few women were working and when surgery was done exclusively by men, she graduated from medical school, entered private practice and helped to develop reconstructive surgery techniques for burn victims and infants with cleft palates.

Felice N. Schwartz
(1925-1996)
She founded Catalyst in 1962, the premier organization working with corporations to foster women's leadership.

Maria Tallchief (1925 -)
First Native American (Osage) prima ballerina, she has been with the New York City Ballet for 15 years. In 1967, she received the Indian Council of Fire Achievement Award.

1926

Violette Neatly Anderson
She was first African-American woman from Chicago to practice law before the US Supreme Court in 1926.

Carolyn Heilbrun (1926 -)
Writer and educator, she is noted for mysteries and books on feminist issues including best-seller "*Writing, a Women's Life*" published in 1988.

Jeane Kirkpatrick (1926 -)
She was the first woman to serve as American Ambassador to the United Nations from 1981-85.

Clara Senecal
In 1926, she became the first woman sheriff in New York State.

1927

Mary Ritter Beard
Historian, she co-authored *Rise of American Civilization* in 1927.

Theo Colborn (1927 -)
Zoologist, she co-authored *Our Stolen Future* in 1996. This book provides research evidence that PCBs and dioxins, manmade chemicals in the environment, are disrupting the endocrine systems of animals, and most likely those of humans, to cause severe reproductive problems.

Rebecca Ann L. Felton
(1835-1930)
She was the first woman to serve in the US Senate. She was a supporter of education for women, women's suffrage and prison reform and a member of the Woman's Christian Temperance Union. In addition, she was an outspoken critic of Catholics, Jews, Negroes, evolution and child labor laws.

Elizabeth Graham
A female goalie from Queens University, in 1927 she wore the first goalie face mask – a wire fencing mask to protect her face during collegiate hockey games.

Paula Fickes Hawkins (1927-)
During her term as Senator (1981-87), she focused on the problem of missing children. One result was the Missing Children's Act of 1982, which provided for a central information center for missing children. She sponsored other legislation to facilitate the search for children and to provide federal guidelines for the prevention of child abuse in child-care centers and institutions.

Frances Kellor
While chief executor of the American Arbitration Association, she wrote an ethical code for arbitration in 1927 and educated the public on the use of formal arbitration as a settlement procedure for disputes ranging from labor/management level to wars between nations.

Blanche Wilbur Hill
Aviation pioneer, she co-founded Avion Corporation in 1927, the company that built the first metal airplane. She also started a business to train aviation-industry workers.

Coretta Scott King (1929-)
She is a Civil Rights activist who picked up the torch for African-American equality when her husband was assassinated. She maintains the Martin Luther King Center in Atlanta and continues to speak for racial equality.

Alice S. Marriot
In 1927, she co-founded a Washington DC restaurant that will grow into a billion-dollar hotel and food service corporation.

Patsy Takemoto Mink
(1927-)
In the Hawaii State legislature, she concentrated on education issues and equal pay for equal work while continuing her work in the statehood movement. During her tenure in Congress (1965-77 and 1990 to date), she introduced or sponsored were the first childcare bill and legislation establishing bilingual education, student loans, special education and

head start. She continues to defend equal rights for women and co-sponsored Title IX of the Civil Rights Act, which bars discrimination in education, including athletics and financial aid.

Ruth Nichols (1901-1960)
Aviator, she was the first woman in the world to earn a hydroplane license. In 1927, she became one of two women to get a Department of Commerce transport license.

1928
Patricia Billings (1928-)
She invented Geobond - one of the most revolutionary substances in the history of modern construction industry. This material is non-toxic as well as indestructible and fireproof; it is also the world's first workable replacement for asbestos. Billings has won two patents for her work.

Mary Breckinridge
(1881-1965)
A pioneer in American midwifery, she founded the Frontier Nursing Service in 1928.

Marjorie Joyner (1896 -)
In 1928, she invented a permanent wave machine – a dome-shaped device that applied electrical current to pressed and clamped one-inch sections of hair creating a hairdo that lasted a considerable time. In 1945, she co-founded the United

Beauty School Owners & Teachers Association.

Norma Merrick Sklarek (1928-)
She was the first African-American woman to become a licensed architect in New York in 1954.

Nellie Zabel Willhite
She became South Dakota's first licensed woman pilot in 1928 and probably the first pilot who was almost completely deaf.

1929
Toshiko Akiyoshi
A composer and pianist, she has significantly enriched jazz through a blend of Eastern and Western instruments and techniques.

Florence L. Barnes
(1901-1975)
An adventurous pioneer aviator, she became the first woman, motion picture stunt pilot when she flew in Hell's Angels in 1929.

Shirley Temple Black (1929 -)
A juvenile star of international renown, she devoted her adult years to diplomacy. She worked for the US Department of State and served as Ambassador to Ghana and Czechoslovakia.

Elaine Schwartzenburg Edwards
(1929 -)
She was appointed to the Senate in 1972 and co-sponsored an amendment to increase the permissible

amount of outside income for Social Security recipients.

Dorothy Leib H. W. Eustis
(1886-1946)
In 1929, she founded "The Seeing Eye", a guide dog training school for the blind.

Edith M. Flanigen (1929-)
One of the inventive chemists of all time, she has earned 102 US patents for her innovations in the fields of petroleum research and product development. Her innovations have made the production of gasoline in the US and around the world greater, cleaner and safer. Her "molecular sieves" are used in other processes such as water purification and environmental cleanup. She is also co-inventor of a synthetic emerald produced and marketed by Union Carbide.

Rose Kushner (1929-1990)
Most widely recognized as the woman who helped end radical mastectomy as the only choice for women with breast cancer. She influenced the introduction of successful congressional bill for Medicare coverage for screening mammograms. She also wrote seven books, the best known of which is *Alternatives: New Developments in the War on Breast Cancer*.

Ida Stephens Owens
(1929 -)
She received a Ph.D. in Biology -Physiology from Duke University in 1967. She conducted studies in the genetics of detoxification enzymes, research that is aimed at shedding light on how the human body defends itself against poison.

Betty C. Tianti (1929-1994)
She was Connecticut's first woman Commissioner of Labor - her final step in a 30-year career of assuming positions never before held by women.

1930
Helen Blair Bartlett
She developed new insulation for spark plugs. A geologist by training, her knowledge of petrology and mineralogy was critical in the development of innovative uses of alumina ceramics.

Ellen Church
A nurse from Iowa, she became the first airline flight attendant in 1930. Her first flight was on Boeing Air Transport at a monthly salary of $125.

Alice Catherine Evans
(1881-1975)
She was the first woman scientist to have a permanent appointment in the US Dairy Division of the Bureau of Animal Husbandry. She worked in the field of bacteriology of milk and cheese and demonstrated that raw milk

could transmit bacteria. She advocated pasteurization of milk to effectively kill bacteria. Her recommendations and findings were not taken seriously partly because she was a woman and had no Ph.D. degree. In time she succeeded and pasteurization of milk became mandatory in the US dairy industry in the 1930's.

Dolores Huerta (1930 -)
American labor leader and social activist, she is the co-founder of the United Farm Worker's union. For more than 30 years, she dedicated her life to the struggle for justice and dignity for migrant farm workers and as a role model for Mexican-American women.

Alice L. Marston
Working at an airport in Concord, New Hampshire in the 1930's, she was likely the first woman dispatcher.

Maria Telkes
A pioneer in the use of solar energy, she designed and built a solar house in the 1930's.

Dorothy Thompson
(1893-1961)
A noted and influential journalist, she interviewed Adolf Hitler for *Cosmopolitan* magazine in 1931, and was the first to recognize Hitler's threat in the world arena. Her writings on the subject caused her to be expelled from Germany in 1934. Her

influential newspaper column, "On the Record," ran for over two decades and offered advice on world affairs that was devoured by leaders around the world.

1931
Jane Adams (1860-1935)
She was the first woman to be awarded the Nobel Prize for her work as a social worker for the immigrant poor in Chicago. She is the founder of Hull House, a social welfare center in Chicago.

Gloria Hollister Anable
She set a new depth record for a woman in 1931, when she descended 1,208 feet below the ocean in a bathysphere.

Pearl Buck (1892-1973)
She was awarded the Pulitzer Prize in 1931 for her novel "*The Good Earth*" and the Nobel Prize for Literature in 1938.

Cardiss Collins (1931 -)
After winning the special election in 1973, she has become the longest serving African-American in the history of Congress. In 1979, she became the first African-American and first woman to serve as Democratic whip-at-large. She has been at the forefront of congressional efforts to increase airport security and air safety.

Maxine Dunlap
She received the first glider license awarded to a woman by

the National Aeronautic Association in 1931. The requirements were a flight of 1-minute duration with 2 s-curves and a normal landing.

Audrey Flack (1931 -)
A graduate of Yale University's School of Art & Architecture, she is identified as one of the leading artists of photo-realism. By the early 1960's she began working from photographs, often representing strong socio-political events as civil rights marches and anti-war protests.

Margaret M. Heckler
(1931 -)
During her tenure in Congress (1967-83), she was an advocate of child care for working parents, supported the proposed Equal Rights Amendment, opposed the use of federal funds for abortion and endorsed tuition tax credits. In 1983, she was appointed Secretary of the Department of Health & Human Services and managed the establishment of new guidelines for Social Security disability program. She also led a campaign to increase federal funding for research and care for patients with Alzheimer's Disease and AIDS.

Virne Beatrice Mitchell
She was first woman baseball pitcher for the Chattanooga Baseball Club. In a 1931

exhibition game, she struck out Babe Ruth and Lou Gehrig, back to back. It was said she could throw a baseball 100 mph.

Constance A. Morella
(1931 -)
During her service in Congress (1987 to date), she emphasized issues such as federal pay, parental leave and health care.

1932
Yvonne Brathwaite Burke
(1932 -)
She was the first African-American woman in the California legislature in 1967. In her first term in Congress, she sought funding for resettlement of Vietnamese refuges and secured a human rights amendment to the foreign aid bill. In 1977, she introduced the Displaced Homemakers Act, which authorized job-training centers for women entering the labor market.

Ella Cara Deloria
(1889-1971)
Author of several books, she is concerned with traditional and contemporary Dakota language and cultural life. Her first book, *Dakota Texts*, published in 1932 is a collection of traditional stories that stands today as the starting place for any study of Sioux dialects, mythology or folklore.

Dian Fossey (1932-1985)
She was an American zoologist, whose studies of wild gorillas in the mountains of Rwanda and Zaire dispelled many myths about the violent and aggressive nature of gorillas.

Helene Madison (1913-1970)
She won 3 gold medals at the 1932 Los Angeles Summer Olympic games. That same year she held all 16 women's world freestyle swimming records and 56 American records.

Frances Perkins (1880-1965)
She became the first woman member of a presidential Cabinet, when President Franklin D. Roosevelt appointed her Secretary of Labor in 1932.

Laurette Schimmoler
First airport manager, in 1932 she was appointed at Port Bucyrus, OH at an annual salary of $510.

1933
Tillie Lewis
Entrepreneur, she introduced the Italian tomato industry to the US in 1934.

Dianne Feinstein (1933-)
In 1992, she became the first woman Senator and first Jewish Senator from California.

Ruth Ella Moore (1903 -)
In 1933, she was first black female to earn Ph.D. in Bacteriology from Ohio State University. Her research focused on blood grouping and enteriobacteriaceae.

Nellie Taylor Ross
In 1933, she was first woman to serve as director of the Philadelphia Mint. She oversaw the construction of the Fort Knox gold vault and dealth with serious paper shortages during the war.

Ruth Wakefield
Restaurateur and owner of the Toll House Inn in MA, she created the chocolate chip cookie in 1933.

1934
Ana Isabel Campana (1934-)
A senior architect for General Electric Company since 1974, she specializes in the design of power plant facilities.

Maureen Connolly
(1934-1969)
She was one of the most powerful and effective women's tennis players in modern history. In 1953, she was first women's tennis player to achieve the Grand Slam.

Mary Hirsch
In 1934, she became the first woman to be a licensed trainer of thoroughbreds.

Audre Lorde (1934-1992)
She was an African-American poet, autobiographer, essayist, and fiction writer who used her writings to

combat racial and sexual injustice. She was a visible and outspoken feminist, a gay rights advocate and an award-winning poet whose work appealed to mainstream audiences.

Phoebe Omlie

In 1934, she founded the National Air Marking Program, the first federal program directed by a woman with an all-woman senior staff. These pilots organized the writing of names of towns and cities on barns and buildings thereby creating navigational aids.

Gloria Steinem (1934 -)

She is one of the most visible and prolific feminist leaders, writers and social activists of our time. She not only co-founded *Ms.* magazine in 1972, but she recently organized the investors' group that re-purchased the magazine in an effort to extend its outreach and become profitable. She also helped found the National Women's Political Caucus and the Women's Action Alliance; both organizations were formed to promote women's rights and fight discrimination.

Cora Sterling

A commercial transport pilot with the Seattle police force, she became the first aerial police officer in 1934.

1935

Ada Deer (1935-)

A Menominee, she was the first woman to head the Bureau of Indian Affairs. In 1973, she establishes the National Committee to Save the Menominee People and Forests, which manages to return the Menominee land to reservation status after its nearly disastrous conversion to an ordinary Wisconsin county.

Zoe Akins (1886-1958)

Playwright, she received the Pulitzer Prize in 1935 for her dramatization of Edith Wharton's *The Old Maid*.

Mary Haas (1910-1996)

In 1935, she earned a Ph.D. at Yale specializing in linguistic prehistory and in Thai and American Indian languages. She is the author of *Spoken Thai* and *Prehistory of Languages*.

Judith Margaret Devlin Hashman (1935 -)

Known as the "Babe Ruth of badminton", she dominated the sport in local, national and international competitions.

Vera C. Hodges

She patented a starter for engines in 1935 that was assigned to Eclipse Aviation Corporation where it was manufactured and used.

Carmen Delgado Votaw

National and international leader, she worked for civil

rights particularly for Hispanics and women. In 1978 she was elected president of the Intro-American Commission of Women and significantly influenced the status of women.

1936
Elizabeth Dole
A dedicated government official, she served as Secretary of Transportation (1983-1987) and Secretary of Labor (1989-1990). She started a glass ceiling initiative to move qualified women and minorities beyond mid-management levels.

Carol Gilligan (1936 -) Psychologist, she is best known for investigations of how women develop their self-identities and values in societies dominated by patriarchal values.

Barbara Jordan (1936-1996) She was the first African-American to serve in the Texas Senate since Reconstruction, the first black woman elected to Congress from the South, and the first black to be keynote speaker at a national political convention - the 1976 Democratic National Convention. During her three terms in Congress, she earned recognition as a defender of constitutional rights and sponsored legislation broadening the provisions of the Voting Rights Act of 1965 to include Hispanic

Americans, Native Americans and Asian Americans.

Barbara B. Kennelly (1936-) She was first woman in American History to serve as Deputy Majority Whip and to serve on the House Intelligence Committee.

Barbara Ann Mikulski (1936 -) During her House career (1977-87), she proposed or supported legislation dealing with childcare, women's rights, national health insurance and consumer protection. She worked on legislation affecting the Port of Baltimore, one of the state's largest employers, as a member of the Merchant Marine & Fisheries Committee. In 1987 she was elected Senator and continues her legislative work on social issues.

Eve Rabin Queler (1936 -) One of the few women orchestra conductors, she organized the Opera Orchestra of New York in 1967, in part to give herself experience in conducting at public performances and to give opportunities to singers and instrumentalists. She has also served as conductor or guest conductor for many orchestras in the US, Canada and Europe.

Helen Stephens

(1918-1993)

She set a world record and won 2 gold medals in track and field at the 1936 Olympics. As an amateur, she set Olympic, American and Canadian records in running, broad jump and discus. A lifetime sports advocate, she also became first woman owner/manager of women's semiprofessional ball team.

1937

Mae Bainton

In 1937, she became the first woman to be appointed Deputy US Marshall.

Jean Broadhurst (1883 -?)

A woman bacteriologist at Columbia University, she succeeded in identifying the virus bodies of measles - the first step in new measles diagnosis.

Margaret Rudkin

She began baking and selling bread from her home and in 1937 founded Pepperidge Farm.

Violet Hill Whyte (1898 -)

In 1937, she was became the first black woman law enforcement officer in Baltimore. She received a special citation from the federal government for her role in the arrest and conviction of major narcotics gang in Baltimore.

1938

Katherine Blodgett

(1898-1979)

She was first female scientist to be hired by General Electric in 1917 and first woman to earn Ph.D. in Physics from Cambridge University in 1926. In 1938, she received a patent for "Film Structure and Method of Preparation" that gave the world invisible glass. Her coatings have found many diverse applications including making airplane wings ice-resistant and even artificial rainmaking.

Rosario Ferre (1938 -)

A professor at the University of Puerto Rico and contributing editor for the San Juan Star, she has written poetry, criticism and biography in addition to the fiction for which she is best known. She began her writing career as editor and publisher of the Zona de Carga y Descarga, an important journal devoted to new Puerto Rican literature.

Katie Beatrice Hall

(1938 -)

During her only full term in the House of Representatives (1982-85), she introduced the bill to make the birthday of Martin Luther King a federal holiday in 1983. She also supported bills for full employment, measures to prevent child abuse and family violence and endorsed the Equal Rights Amendment to the Constitution.

Joyce Sachiko Tsunoda (1938-) She was a pioneer in higher education in the state of Hawaii as well as the nation. As the first woman to become chancellor of community colleges in the University of Hawaii System, she is now the highest-ranking Asian-American woman administrator in an institution of higher learning in the United States.

1939
Paula Gunn Allen (1939 -) Laguna and Sioux scholar and writer, she is a poet and novelist who incorporated feminist issues in writing of Indian culture. Her poetry collections include "*The Blind Lion*" and "*Skins and Bones*" and her books include *The Woman Who Owned the Shadows* and *The Sacred Hoop*.

Marian Wright Edelman (1939 -) An attorney and civil rights advocate who founded the Children's Defense Fund - the nation's strongest advocate group for children. The group is now working on health care and help for homeless children.

Sandra Feldman (1939 -) Union leader, she became president of the United Federation of Teachers in 1986 - the first woman to head this union. She became known as a tough and dedicated advocate of the labor union movement and the cause of public education.

Winifred Goldring (1888-1971) In 1939, she became first woman "state paleontologist" in New York and the first woman President of the Palentological Society in 1949.

Dorothy Ray Healey A veteran labor organizer, she mobilized Mexican cannery and African-American tobacco workers in a successful strike at the California Sanitary Canning Company in 1939.

Hattie McDaniel In 1939, she was first African-American woman to win an Academy Award for best supporting actress for her role in "Gone with the Wind".

Margaret Mitchell (1900-1949) Her book "*Gone with the Wind*" became a publishing phenomenon and in 1939, she received the Pulitzer Prize for fiction.

Barbara Walters (1939 -) First woman to co-host the network evening news and now has the power to interview just about anybody. She continues to co-host 20/20 and to presents specials. Celebrities whom she has interviewed include Princess

Grace of Monaco, Egyptian President Anwar Sadat, Israel Prime Minister Menachem Begin, Ronald Reagan and Duchess of York.

Ellen Taffe Zwilich
(1939 -)
She is one of America's foremost composers of art music and the first woman to win Pulitzer Prize in Music. In 1975, she received the first Julliard doctorate awarded to a woman and has had an active career of composing modernistic but communicative music.

1940
Olive Ann Beech
She co-founded Beech Aircraft with her husband in the 1930s. She became President and CEO after his death and transformed the company into a multimillion-dollar, international aerospace corporation.

Barbara Boxer (1940 -)
Congresswoman in 1983 and Senator in 1993, she played a leading role in the exposure of Pentagon procurement scandals and has worked to ensure greater accountability from the military. Other legislative priorities include health care, especially federal funding of the fight against AIDS and the fight for a woman'' right to choose.

Gladys Hobby
A microbiologist, she was a member of the team that purified penicillin in 1940 to treat patients with infections. She later developed another antibiotic known as Terramycin.

Nannerl O. Keohane (1940 -)
She was the first woman to head both a major woman's college (Wellsley) and a research university (Duke). Her efforts have increased minority student enrollment and improved faculty diversity.

Maxine Hong Kingston (1940-)
She is a highly acclaimed writer of both fiction and nonfiction and was one of the first Asian Americans to make it to the top of the literary world in America. Her first book *The Woman Warrior: Memoirs of a Girlhood Among Ghosts*, published in 1976, was about the conflicting cultural messages she received as the daughter of Chinese immigrants growing up in American in the 1950's.

Bernice M. McPherson
(1901-1971)
In 1940, she won the US Navy Award for developing a welding process for weapons that greatly reduces production costs. She later became the first woman member of the American Welding Society.

Ann Moore (1940 -)
She designed and patented "Snugli" in 1969, a rugged, adjustable, pouch-like infant carrier.

Cynthia Moss (1940 -)
Wildlife biologist who was primarily an elephant researcher, she proved that elephants are led by the oldest and wisest cow and that the males are inveterate bachelors.

Shirley Muldowney
First woman licensed to drive professionally for National Hot Rod Association.

Mary Rose Oakar (1940 -)
In eight terms in Congress (1977-1993), she pursued such issues as economic redevelopment of older industrial areas, equal and comparable pay for women in the workforce and benefits for congressional employees.

Mary Brook Picken
The first dictionary compiled by a woman was *Language of Fashion* by Mary Brook Picken. It was published in 1940 in New York City and contained 8000 terms and 600 illustrations relating to clothing.

Patricia Schroeder (1940-)
As Senator (1973-95), she focussed her legislative efforts on issues ranging from arms control to welfare reform to benefits for federal workers. She has worked to establish a national pro-family policy, promoting issues such as parental leave, childcare and family planning. One of her achievements has been the Family and Medical Leave Act. She also co-founded the Congressional Caucus for Women's Issues.

Jaune Quick-to-See Smith (1940 -)
Her art presents a cross-cultural dialogue between the values and experiences of the late 20th Century and the artist's Salish, French, Cree and Shoshone heritage. She works in paint, collage and mixed media using a mixture of representational and abstract images to confront such subjects as the destruction of the environment, governmental oppression of Native American culture and the pervasive myths of American cultural identity.

Mary Spaeth (1940 -)
She invented the tunable dye laser, which can be manipulated to produce light of different wavelengths and different colors. Her resonant reflector is an integral part of laser devices used to scan bar codes at cash registers.

Pearl Young
In 1940, she became NACA's first female physicist paving the way for women to work in laboratories and making her

one of the most prominent women in the Agency. She also pioneered a process for aeronautical engineers to communicate their ideas and technical information to disseminate to industry, academia and other government labs.

Roger Arliner Young
(1889-1964)

She was the first black woman to conduct and publish research in the field of zoology and the first black woman to receive a Ph.D. in zoology from University of Pennsylvania in 1940. In 1928, she published several notable studies on the effects of direct and indirect radiation on se urchin eggs.

1941
Elda E. Anderson
(1899-1961)

She earned her Ph.D. in Chemistry at the University of Wisconsin in 1941 and went to work at Los Alamos Project as part of the Manhattan Project. She had a vital role in the making of the atomic bomb and witnessed the first atomic explosion at the Trinity site. She published articles on the peaceful applications of nuclear power and was a founding member of the Health Physics Society.

Joan Baez
After achieving great success as folksinger, she used her influence to support causes ranging from civil rights, global peace and protest against ware in Vietnam.

Linda Darnell
Motion picture actress, she was the first woman to sell securities on the floor of the New York Curb Exchange in 1941.

Barbara Ehrenreich (1941 -)
An independent writer, she became known for her outspoken feminist-socialist analyses of contemporary issues, particularly health and the politics of gender and class.

Margaret J. Hagood
(1907-1963)

In the late 20th century, she was a pioneer in two fields, statistics and demography that was central to the study of sociology. She made significant contributions to the application of statistics to sociological research. Her landmark book, *Statistics for Sociologists*, published in 1941, influenced the social sciences to become more quantitative and to embrace statistical methodologies.

Alma Heflin
First woman test pilot, her first production test flight was in 1941 for Piper Aircraft Corp in PA.

Elizabeth Holtzman (1941 -)
A member of Congress (1973-81), she contributed to the development of new rules for the presentation of evidence in federal courts and worked to revise immigration laws. She also helped secure sex discrimination prohibition in federal programs.

Linda Schele (1942-1998)
A visit to the ruins of the ancient Mayan City of Palenque was a revelation and led her to focus the rest of her life on the study of the Maya and their culture. Later, her academic interest expanded to include the culture of contemporary Maya and she organized workshops on hieroglyphic writing to Maya speaking peoples of Guatemala and Mexico. The goal of these workshops was the reintroduction of hieroglyphic writing and the stimulation of interest in ancient Maya history among the modern Maya.

1942
Gloria Anzaldua (1942-)
She is a Mexican-American writer, feminist and social activist who was among the first to articulate the concept of the borderlands from a Chicana perspective.

Teresa James
This pioneer pilot earned her commercial license in 1940. In 1942, she part of select group of women pilots who ferried military planes between manufacturer and military bases. In 1950, she accepted a commission in the Air Force Reserve and retired 27 years later at the rank of Major.

Marguerite T. Williams (1895 -)
When she earned her Ph.D. in Geology from Catholic University of America in 1942, she became the first African American to earn a doctorate in geology in the United States.

Gloria Yerkovich (1942 -)
After her own daughter was abducted, she founded Child Find, a national organization the helps to locate missing children. Her concept is the prototype for the National Center for Missing and Exploited Children.

1943
Ruth Leach Amonette
When the IBM Board of Directors elected her to the position of IBM Vice President, she became the first woman to hold a corporate position at IBM and one of the few women at that time to hold an executive position in any large company in the US. She devoted herself to the advancement of women in business and industry.

Henrietta Mahim Bradberry
In 1943, she patented a bed rack, which was an attachment to the bed that permitted air

to pass through and refreshed worn clothes. The device was operated pneumatically and in 1945 was adapted to discharge torpedoes under the water surface.

Esther Fordes (1891-1967)
She won 1943 Pulitzer Prize for her biography of Paul Revere called "*World He Lived In*".

Faye Wattleton (1943-)
An African-American nurse, she became the first black president of Planned Parenthood, and the first woman to hold the post since founder Margaret Sanger. She developed a major nationwide grassroots organization that has become a powerful political force to block efforts to restrict or eliminate the right to birth control and abortion.

1944
Angela Yvonne Davis (1944-)
She was an African-American activist, writer and scholar. She taught at UCLA in 1969 even while administrators tried to oust her for being a Communist. She went on to become the vice-presidential candidate of the Communist party in 1980.

Mitsuye Endo
She bravely became the test case for Japanese Americans who were detained against their will at interment camps during World War II. Her petition for freedom from the camps prompts the 1944 Supreme Court ruling declaring such detention as illegal and granting an "unconditional release."

Helen Brooke Taussig (1896-1986)
In 1944, she developed the pioneering operation, which solved the often-fatal "blue baby" (heart defect) syndrome.

1945
Anna Mae Aquash (1945-1976)
She is an active member of American Indian Movement (AIM). In 1968, she became a symbol of the movement for Indian rights when Native Americans were calling for equal rights, cultural recognition and fulfillment of promises made in treaties.

Florence Chadwick
In 1950, she became the first woman to swim the English Channel both ways. She appeared in the movie "*Bathing Beauty*" with Esther Williams.

Dorothy Rodgers
In 1945, she invented a tool for cleaning toilet bowls called "The Jonny Mop" that had a plastic handle and flushable cleaning head. She also invented Try-On Dress Patterns and an educational game for children called the Turn & Learn Books.

Esther Rome (1945 -)
Women's health advocate, she was the guiding force behind the ground-breaking Our Bodies, Ourselves, the first medical book that treated women as individuals. It was the most honest and practical medical book ever written about women's bodies in the history of the world.

Diane Sawyer (1945 -)
A broadcast journalist, she was the first female correspondent on TV's "60 Minutes". She was also host of "Prime Time Live" and co-anchor of "Day One" and "Turning Point".

Dorothy Shaver
A business executive, she becomes president of Lord & Taylor Department Store in 1945 at a salary of $110,000 per year – the highest salary on record for any woman in the United States.

1946
Emily Greene Balch
(1867-1961)
A scholar, anti-war activist, social reformer and a woman's rights advocate. She won the Nobel Prize for Peace in 1946 for her lifelong efforts to promote alternatives to war.

Adele Goldstine
She made an indelible contribution to the ENIAC project by authoring the "Manual for the ENIAC" in 1946. This original technical description of the ENIAC detailed the machine right down to its resistors.

Mary G. Hodge (1946-1996)
The leading authorities on Aztec archaeology and ethno history, she studied Aztec city-states and the Aztec Empire. She also worked to perfect the ceramic sequence associated with the emergence and expansion of the Aztec Empire.

Marcy Kaptur (1946 -)
During her service in Congress (1983 to date), she has concentrated on issues of home ownership and the protection of individuals' bank deposits.

Ann Petry (1908 -)
She was first Black female author to address the problems African-American women face as they struggle to cope with life in the inner city. Her novel, *The Street*, published in 1946 was the first book by an African-American woman to sell over a million copies.

Jessie T. Pope
She invented the thermostatically controlled curling iron, patented it in 1946 and founded a company to manufacture it in 1958.

1947
Hillary Rodham Clinton
(1947-)
The first career woman to become First Lady, she has used her position to continue

to aid and improve the lives of children. She was a staff attorney for the Children's Defense Fund in 1973. During her tenure as First Lady, she wrote the best-selling book, *It Takes a Village*.

Margaret Joan Geller
(1947 -)
Senior scientist at the Smithsonian Astrophysical Observatory and Astronomy professor at Harvard University, she helped discover a "Great Wall" of galaxies - space stretching at least 500 million light years. The existence of this structure presents an intricate and difficult problem for theorists who study the universe.

Gerty Theresa Gori
(1896-1957)
Biochemist, her research led to understanding of metabolic process in enzymatic synthesis of glycogen and its subsequent cleavage into glucose. She was awarded Nobel Prize in Physiology in 1947.

Lillie Rosa Minoka-Hill
A Mohawk Indian physician, she is outstanding Indian of the Year in 1947 and made an honorary member of the Oneida tribe for her contribution to its collective health.

Sandra Kurtzig (1947-)
She invented monitoring and information-sharing software for businesses. In 1972, she founded ASK Computer and is called one of the "heroes of Silicon Valley".

Sherry Lansing (1947 -)
As head of Paramount Pictures, she produced "The China Syndrome" and "Kramer vs. Kramer". By backing "Forest Gump" her status as Hollywood's only female mogul was confirmed.

Claudia Jean Kennedy
(1947 -)
Lt Gen Kennedy is the Army's senior intelligence official and its first female three-star general.

Claudine Schneider
(1947 -)
As a member of congress (1975-91), she focused on environmental issues. She played a central role in the decision to halt construction of the Clinch River nuclear reactor and helped lead the effort to ban ocean dumping of sludge and medical waste.

1948
Alice Coachman
She is the first African-American woman to win a gold medal in the 1948 London Summer Olympic games.

Marie Maynard Daly
(1921 -)
In 1948, she was the first black female to earn a Ph.D. in chemistry from Columbia University. Her area of research focuses on nucleic acids.

Gladys Ward Dunn
(1907-1980)
After becoming licensed in psychiatry, she became the clinical director of the New Hampshire State Hospital in 1948, a position she held for 25 years. She was responsible for the development of a treatment program for alcoholics, which relied heavily on Alcoholics Anonymous and for the establishment of outpatient clinics throughout New Hampshire.

1950
Gwendolyn Brooks (1917 -)
She is the first African-American woman to win the Pulitzer Prize for Poetry for her collection "*Annie Allen*".

Marion Donovan
She developed the disposable diaper in 1950 in New York from a shower curtain and absorbent padding. She also invented a skirt hanger and an elastic zipper pull.

1951
Bessie Blount (1914 -)
A practicing physical therapist and teacher at Bronx Hospital, she conceived of an electrical apparatus, which allows people without arms to feed themselves, and received a patent in 1951.

Alexa Canady (1951 -)
She was the first African American woman to become a neurosurgeon. According to her, one major problem for African Americans stems from the dearth of research targeting their specific health concerns.

Marguerite Higgins
(1920-1966)
While covering the Korean War, she became the first woman to win Pulitzer Prize for International Reporting in 1951.

Elizabeth Kee (1899-1975)
In 1951, she was the first and only woman to be elected to the United States Congress from West Virginia. She focused on the growing unemployment in southern West Virginia and brought attention to the effect of unemployment on women and families. One outgrowth of her efforts was the development of New River Gorge, which later sparked a boom in the state's tourism industry.

Marianne Moore (1887-1972)
An American poet, she won the Pulitzer Prize and National Book Award in 1951 for her "*Collected Poems*". She was awarded the National Medal for Literature in 1968 - America's highest literary honor.

1952
Virginia Apgar (1909-1974)
In 1952, she developed a method, known now as the Apgar score, for quickly determining a newborn baby's health and if any medical

emergency exists. The test, which assesses color, heart rate, reflexes, muscle tone and breathing, and is standard for all births.

Ileana Ros-Lehtinen
(1952 -)
During her service in the Florida State legislature, she played a large role in the passage of legislation dealing with victims' rights, drug-free workplaces and tuition assistance for Florida college students. In 1989 she was elected to House of Representatives and became the first Cuban-American elected to Congress.

Patricia McCormick
She was first American woman bullfighter to fight professionally. Her debut in 1952 was in Ciudad Juarez, Mexico when she killed two bulls.

1954
Jody R. Cohen (1954 -)
She was first woman in Connecticut to serve a synagogue as Associate Rabbi and first to have an extended tenure as rabbi of her own congregation.

Louise Erdrich (1954 -)
She is known for her moving and often humorous portrayals of Chippewa life in North Dakota. She draws on her Chippewa heritage and her years in North Dakota to celebrate the great endurance of women and Native Americans

in 20th Century America. Based on her personal knowledge of the American Indian oral tradition, she explores Native American themes in her books with major characters representing both sides of her heritage.

Erna Schneider Hoover
In 1954, she began her research career at Bell Laboratories where she invented computerized switching system for telephone traffic and earned one of the first software patents ever issued. Her system earned her a position as the first female supervisor of a technical department at Bell Labs in 1971.

Norma Merrick Sklarek (1928-)
In 1954, she became first African American woman to be licensed as an architect in the US. Later, she became first African American women to form her own architectural firm in 1985.

1955
Marian Anderson
She was the first African-American singer to perform on the stage of the New York Metropolitan Opera House in 1955.

Lois M. Haibt
Programmer, she becomes one of the developers of the early computer language FORTRAN in 1955.

Emma Sadler Moss
When elected president of the American Society of Clinical Pathologists in 1955, she became the first woman to head a major medical society.

1956
Angela Bamface (1898-1975)
Known as Maryland's 1st Lady of the Labor Movement, she was a strong advocate of political participation by the union as a means of achieving its goals. In 1956, she became the first woman elected to the Vice-President of the ILGWU.

1957
Jackie Jackson (1957)
She has 2 patents (1975 & 1978) for an all purpose household lighter which replaces matches for lighting barbecues, fireplaces, candles and ovens. The lighters are long wands using disposable butane cartridges.

Grace Elizabeth "Libby" Mitchell
She joins the FORTRAN project in 1957 and designs the IBM 704 operating system, the ancestor of all computer operating systems.

Chien Shiung Wo
(1912-1997)
A physicist who disproved the law of conservation parity (which had been one of the basic assumptions in physics) is 1957 while at Columbia University.

1958
Susan Molinari (1958 -)
A member of Congress (1990 to date), she emphasized environmental issues such as water pollution, ocean dumping and protection of wetlands. She is also an advocate of reasonable defense spending.

Mary Velasquez Riley
(1908-1987)
An Apache raised on a reservation, in 1958 she became the first woman elected to the tribal council, where she spent two decades fighting for her tribe's right to control its own resources and promote economic development. It was her business acumen and lobbying skills that facilitated the development of the Sunrise Ski Resort and the Fort Apache Timber Company, two multi-million dollar enterprises owned by the tribe.

Mabel M. Rockwell
In 1958, she received the Society of Women Engineers of American's Achievement Award for her work on electrical control systems.

Ruth Carol Taylor
In 1958, she was the first African American hired as a flight attendant. She made her first flight on Mohawk Airlines.

Anita Rose Williams
(1891 -)
She was the first black social worker in the US employed by the Association of Catholic Charities. In 1958, she received the Papal Cross for her services in the role of social worker.

1959
Evelyn Berezin
In 1959, she received a patent for "Data Processing System". She is credited with designing the first office computer.

Florence Griffith Joyner
(1959-1998)
A track athlete, she won the silver medal in the 200-meter dash in the 1984 Olympics. Her prowess, glamour and style made "Flojo" a media sensation and one of the highest-paid sports figures in the world. In 1988, at the Olympic Games in Seoul, she won gold medals in the 100- and 200-meter races and in the 400-meter relay and a silver medal in the 1600-meter relay.

Mary Beatrice D. Kenner
In 1959, she received a patent for sanitary belt with moisture-proof napkin pocket.

Margaret Leech
Historian, she wins the Pulitzer Prize for In the Days of McKinley in 1959, which is lauded as a first rate study of a second-rate President.

Ruth Orkin (1921-1985)
She was named one of "The Ten Top Women Photographers in the US" by the Professional Photographers of America in 1959.

1960
Florence Beebe Anderson
In 1960, she received a patent for semi-automatic ice cube maker. She is also credited with the parking meter, a host of household gadgets and appliances including a toaster.

Nina Starr Braunwald
In 1960, she was the first woman in the US to perform open-heart surgery.

Jessica Govea
During the 1960's and 1970's, she was an organizer for the United Farm Workers planning and directing boycotts in the US and Canada. She currently teaches in the Labor Studies Department at Rutgers University in New Jersey and works with the Union Leadership Academy - an organization that provides continuing education for farm workers.

June Wayne
By establishing Tamarine Lithography Workshop in 1960, she helped elevate the craft of lithography and was responsible for establishing the legitimacy of all print media. In addition to being a master lithographer, she is an actress, award-winning

filmmaker, teacher, lecturer, critic, author, illustrator, and an advocate and activist for artists everywhere.

1961
Rachel Carson (1907-1964)
She was an exacting scientist who entranced the public with the exciting literary style she used to present basic scientific information. Her 1961 book "*Silent Spring*" shocked the world and touched off a major international public controversy over the effects of pesticides.

Jane Jacobs (1916 -)
An Urban theorist and Associate Editor of Architectural Forum from 1952-68, she gained a reputation for attacking urban planners who destroy diverse older districts with expressways and housing projects. Her most influential work was *The Death and Life of Great American Cities* published in 1961.

1962
Felice N. Schwartz (1925-1996)
In 1962, Schwartz founded Catalyst, a national organization dedicated to helping women re-enter the work force after years at home. Her efforts at Catalyst and her pioneering research on job-sharing; dual-career couples, parental leave and other work/family issues have significantly impacted corporate America.

1963
Betty Friedan (1921-)
Author and feminist, in 1963 she published *The Feminine Mystique*, which identifies and condemns the means by which women are conditioned to accept domesticity as their only role. The book rejuvenates the US feminist movement and she begins the late-20th century women's rights movement in the US. In 1966, she founded the National Organization for Women (NOW) and continues to work for human rights and equality of the sexes.

Marie Goepperet-Mayer (1906-1972)
In 1963, she won the Nobel Prize in Physics for discoveries concerning nuclear shell structure.

Julie Krone (1963 -)
As one of the top jockeys in the United States, she has spent her entire career proving that woman can be successful in this field. In 1993, she became the first woman to win one of the Triple Crown races - riding Colonial Affair in the Belmont Stakes.

Misha Mahowald (1963 -)
In 1992, she obtained her doctorate from the California Institute of Technology in computational neuroscience. During her research, she made pioneering contributions to the emerging field of neuromorphic engineering -

the application of analog CMOS VLSI technology to the fabrication of analog electronic circuits that emulate real neural systems. In 1991, she developed a "Silicon Neuron" which had electrical properties very similar to biological neurons and which could be used for building large biologically realistic neural networks.

Jean Nidetch (1923 -)
A compulsive eater from Brooklyn, she founded Weight Watchers International in 1963, the world's most successful diet plan corporation.

1964
Dorothy Crowfoot Hodgkin (1910-1994)
In 1964 she won the Nobel Prize in Chemistry for her determination by x-ray techniques of the structure of biologically important molecules.

1965
Donna DeVarona
In 1965 she becomes the first woman sports broadcaster on national TV for ABC. She is also founder of the Women's Sports Foundation.

Patricia Harris
Lawyer and political official, she becomes ambassador to Luxembourg in 1965, the first black U.S. ambassador. In 1966, she becomes a delegate to the United Nations.

Marguerite Higgins
Journalist and well-known war correspondent in Korea, she publishes *Our Vietnam Nightmare* in 1965.

Stephanie Kwolek
She is an inventor who discovered the technology that became the foundation of Kevlar fiber in 1965. This fiber is used in bulletproof vests, brakes, fire protection clothing and aircraft and space vehicle construction. She is the sole holder of 7 patents and is a member of the American Chemical Society.

Marlee Mattin (1965 -)
She is the only hearing-impaired person to ever win an Academy Award for best actress in Children of a Lesser God. She has dedicated herself to fighting for the needs and rights of other hearing impaired people. She is also an advocate for children with AIDS, the elderly and the rain forest.

1967
Muriel Siebert (1932 -)
In 1967, she was first woman to own a seat on the New York Stock Exchange. She was also the nation's first discount broker and the first woman to serve as Superintendent of Banks for the State of New York.

1968

Catherine Filene Shouse

She was the first woman to receive a M.Ed degree from Harvard University and the first woman appointed Chairman of a Federal Women's Prison for the Rehabilitation and Education of Women. In 1968, she established Wolf Trap Foundation where "young people with talent could be heard, seen and taught the demands of a professional career in the arts".

Eunice Mary Kennedy Shriver
(1921-)

She has worked to provide persons with mental retardation the chance to become useful and productive citizens who are accepted and respected in their communities. In 1968, she established the world-renowned Special Olympics as the first systematic effort to provide sports training and athletic competition for individuals with mental retardation.

1969

Marie Van Brittain Brown

She patented a home security system in 1969 that had both video and audio components. It allowed the occupant of the house to scan a would-be visitor outside the front door, to talk with the caller and even to release the door lock without getting out of bed.

Joan Ganz Cooney (1929-)

After studying the use of television for preschool education, Cooney founded the Children's Television Workshop and created Sesame Street, which debuted in 1969. Her research on children's inquisitive nature and on education of the impoverished together with her creativity has led to a television program of unequaled success.

Diane Crump

First female jockey to ride in a pari-mutuel horserace against men in Florida in 1969.

Pansy Ellen Essman

In 1969, she invents and patents a sponge pillow to hold babies safely still while they are bathed.

Nancy Wexler

In 1969, Nancy Wexler became president of the Hereditary Disease Foundation, a clinic founded by her father to research the causes and cures for Huntington's Disease. She was instrumental in discovering the complex chromosomal test, which can tell patients if they will develop the disease.

1970

Maggie Kuhn (1905-1995)

After a forced retirement, Kuhn formed the Gray Panthers in 1970, an organization that has addressed pension rights and age discrimination, as well as larger public issues, including nursing home reform, forced retirement and fraud against the elderly.

Pat Palinkas
She is the first woman to play in a professional football game in 1970. She held the ball for the place kickers on the Orlando Panther's team.

Phyllis F. Shantz
In 1970, she became the first woman member of the Secret Service auxiliary that guards the president and his family while they are in Washington.

1971
Florence Wald (1916 -)
She received her nursing degree from Yale University in 1941 and has devoted her life to caring for others. Her most lasting impact has come from her work in bring the Hospice movement to the US in 1971.

1972
Juanita Morris Keys
She was first woman to serve as director of the New York Stock Exchange in 1972. She was professor of economics and dean of the Women's College at Duke University, NC.

Sally Jane Priesand
(1946-)
She was ordained a Reform rabbi in 1972, the first woman to be so ordained in this country.

Arlene Anderson Swidler
Theologian and co-founder of the *Journal of Ecumenical Studies*, she publishes the book *Woman in a Man's Church* in 1972.

Jean Wilkowski (1919 -)
She is sworn in as US Ambassador to the Republic of Zambia in 1972, the first woman ambassador to Africa.

1973
Leslie Arp
In 1973, she becomes the first woman chef at New York's Waldorf Astoria Hotel.

Joni E. Barnett
In 1973, she became the first female athletic director of a major university when placed in charge of physical education at Yale University.

Vivian S. Crea
Commissioned in 1973, Captain Vivian S. Crea was the first female aircraft commander in the Coast Guard and the first female Commanding Officer of the Coast Guard Air Station Clearwater, the largest air station in the Coast Guard.

Emily H. Warner
In 1973, she became the first pilot on a regularly scheduled major airline when Frontier Airlines hired her as co-pilot on Boeing 737.

Patricia Wiener
Inventor and computer entrepreneur, she patented one of the first memory

systems to be contained on a single silicon computer chip in 1973.

1974
Susan Chandler
She received a patent in 1974 for a pill tray which has a rectangular base with a depressed trough formed on one side and a retaining wall formed on the other sides. This is what pharmacists use to count out pills when filling prescriptions.

Libby Howie
In 1974, she became the first female art auctioneer for Sothebys in London. After two years, she took charge of the 19th and 20th Century prints.

Barbara A. Rainey
(1948-1982)
First woman pilot in the history of the US Navy, she earned her gold wings in 1974. She was killed while training another pilot in an air accident in Florida.

Betty Bone Schiess (1923-)
She led the successful effort to have women ordained as priests in the Episcopal Church in America in 1974, elevating the position of women in the Church at all levels.

1975
Virgie M. Ammons
In 1975, she received a patent for a fireplace damper actuating tool. The tool opens and closes a fireplace damper and is also intended to operate as a securing means to prevent fluttering of the damper due to wind.

Anne Dillard (1945 -)
Author of essays and poetry, she is best known for her 1975 Pulitzer Prize winning book Pilgrim at Tinker Creek.

Anna M. Fillspki
In 1975, she co-invented an anti-theft device designed to spring out and startle a thief causing him/her to drop the stolen items.

1976
Bonita Bergin
A teacher, she founds Canine Companions for Independence in 1976 - an organization that teaches dogs to help disabled people be independent.

Sarah Caldwell
A major force in producing, stage directing and promoting opera, she has broken new ground for women in the arts. She was the first woman to conduct at the Metropolitan Opera House in New York City. Opera star, Barbara Sills, refused to sing unless Caldwell conducted.

Shirley Cross
She received a patent in 1976 for an orange peeler tool that she invented. The tool has a handle to which is attached a curved blade which is basically spoon-shaped and having a sharp corner edge

making it possible to cut a slit in the orange peel the depth of the peel.

Susan Huhn Eustis (1940-)
In 1976, she invents and patents an electronic voting machine that represents a major advance in the field. As of 1982, she had applied for patents on two major inventions in the computer field – a new CPU for computers and a chip for scrambling or encrypting data and programs.

Pauline Frederick
Pioneer for women reporters on radio and television, she was first woman to report serious television news. In 1976, she was the first woman to moderate televised presidential-election debate.

Roberta A. Kankus
A nuclear engineer, she became the first woman and youngest person to be licensed as a nuclear power plant operator in 1976.

Junko Tabei (1939 -)
In 1976, she becomes the first woman to reach the top of Mt. Everest.

1977
Mari-Luci Jaramillo
(1928-)
An early proponent of bilingual and bicultural education, she is known for promoting quality education for Latinos. She was appointed US ambassador to Honduras from 1977-81.

Marie Ledbetter
She became the first woman to win the World Accuracy Title for parachuting in 1977.

Ronnie Sandler
She is a carpenter and first woman to join United Brotherhood of Carpenters and Joiner of America in Michigan in 1977.

Josephine Figliolia Straino
In New York City, she was issued the first Master Plumber's license given to a woman in 1977.

Cherry Sue Summers
In 1977, she received a patent for a baby walker enclosure that could be attached to a baby walker mounted on casters and having a frame with a seat for the child. The enclosure extends over and surrounds the child to prevent the child from reaching objects.

Dr. Rosalyn S. Yalow
(1921 -)
A nuclear physicist, she won half of the 1977 Nobel Prize in Medicine for the development of radioimmunoassays of peptide hormones.

1978
Lois Gibbs
She has been at the forefront of the environmental movement in the US. She became concerned about reports of

chemical waste in her neighborhood in 1978 – the now infamous Love Canal. Her efforts also led the creation of the US Environmental Protection Agency's "Superfund" which is used to locate and clean up toxic sites throughout the US.

1979
June Bacon-Bercey (1934-)
A scientist and international expert on weather and aviation, in 1979 she became Chief Administrator of television activities for National Organization of Atmospheric Agency (NOAA).

Molly DeGezelle (1979-)
In 1991, she invented a building material composed of recycled paper and glue.

Sylvia Earle
In 1979, she became the first person in the world to dive to a depth of 1,250 feet. She led an all-woman team of scientists in an experiment in undersea living, staying for two weeks in a submerged capsule in the Caribbean Sea.

Deirdre Hickey
The Long Island Rail Road placed the first train operated exclusively by women in service in 1979. Its conductor, Deirdre Hickey was the first woman to qualify in land, freight and passenger service.

Shannon W. Lucid (1943-)
In 1979, she became a member of the first astronaut class to admit women. She holds the international record for the most flight hours in orbit for any non-Russian and the most flight hours for any woman in the world. The science experiment she performed during her flights broke ground in spacecraft deployment, earth science studies, space materials processing, biomedical experimentation and atmospheric ozone research. She was the astronaut who set the record for the longest space flight by an American in 1996 and her work was recognized when she became the 9th person and the 1st woman to receive the Congressional Space Medal of Honor.

Mary Ann Moore
In 1979, she received a patent for pain relief composition and method of preparing it.

1980
Jeanette W. Barron
In 1980, she received a patent for a patient's hospital gown. The gown has two flaps; one is adapted to overlap the other and to be wrapped around the body of the patient for attachment to the other flap by straps or release fasteners.

Florence Borkan

She invented and patented a child resistant container and safety closure therefor in 1980 that are commonly used in prescriptions and other medicines.

Graciela Casillas

A pioneer of women's boxing in the early 1980's and held the World Women's Boxing Association bantamweight title. Her first love was TaeKwonDo but she also became a dominant force in sport karate and held the World Karate Association world bantamweight title.

Candy Lightner

In 1980, she founded Mothers Against Drunk Driving (MADD) after a drunk driver killed her daughter. The goals of MADD are to educate, prevent, deter and punish drunk driving and have caused judicial reforms throughout the United States. She has received the President's Volunteer Action Award and has received an Honorary Doctorate in humanities and public service.

Nancy Perkins

In 1980, she patented better vacuum cleaners and even a car battery.

Mildred Austin Smith

In 1980, she received a patent for a card game that explores genealogical family relationships. The game is also available in braille.

1981

Nancy Buron (1948-)

In 1981, she received a patent for a computerized machine that would use a photograph of a person to create an image of the way the face would look 10 or 20 years later. It can also be used in reverse to create a younger image and can create composite faces. It is used in medicine, film and most importantly in law enforcement.

Judith Esser-Mittog

She designed the O.B.® tampon for Johnson & Johnson in 1981 that consisted of rolled fiber pad layers and comes in three sizes and absorbencies.

Sandra Day O'Connor

(1930 -)

In 1952, she graduated from Stanford University Law School. She served as assistant Attorney General in Arizona, an Arizona State Senator and on the Arizona Court of Appeals. In 1981, she was appointed the first woman Supreme Court Justice.

1982

Sally Fox

She received a patent and three Plant Variety Protection Certificates for her naturally colored cottons in 1982, which are grown in brown, red and green. Two of the numerous advantages of naturally colored cotton are they eliminate the need for dying and finishing steps which are detrimental to the environment and they are innately more fire-resistant than white cotton. The popularity of her invention has sprouted two successful companies --Vresesis Ltd and Natural Cotton Colours.

Lisa Hensen

During her senior year at Harvard University in 1982, she became the first woman to service as president of The Harvard Lampoon, the university's comic review. She majored in ancient Greek and folklore mythology and went on to become president of Columbia Pictures in 1994.

Sally Ride (1951 -)

An American astronaut, who was a crewmember on the space shuttle Challenger, she was the first American woman to fly in space. She continues to be a spokesperson for US space efforts.

Lisa Thorson

A jazz singer, songwriter and actress, she is physically challenged. In 1982, she created Spokesong, a musical production designed to educate the public about disability issues in the form of a delightful performance. For five years, she was the Access Education Coordinator at Boston's Adaptive Environments Center where she designed and presented training programs to help integrate the physically challenged into culture and the arts. Her current project is making beaches accessible to those in wheelchairs.

Janine Pease-Windy Boy
(1949-)

She is one of the most active living American Indian educators. Since 1982, she has been the 1st and only President of Little Big Horn College, one of the United States 27 tribally controlled community colleges. In 1990 under her leadership, Little Big Horn College earned full regional accreditation.

1983
Ann Armstrong Daily

She founded Children's Hospice International in 1983, which provides emotional shelter for dying children and their families. She has been instrumental in helping health care professionals provide better understanding and care of terminally ill children.

Barbara McClintock
(1902-1992)

In 1983 she received the Nobel Prize in Medicine for her discovery of mobile genetic elements. She also traced the evolutionary history of domesticated maize to determine the genetic ancestor of the grass we now call corn.

Alice Walker

In 1983, she was first African-American woman to win

the Pulitzer Prize for fiction for her book "*The Color Purple*".

Fran Ulmer
In 1983, Fran was elected Mayor of Juneau and was subsequently elected the first chair of the US Conference of Women Mayors. She later served in the House of Representatives where she successfully sponsored dozens of bills on victim rights, criminal penalties, criminal justice, recycling, health, education and children's well being. In 1994 she was elected to the office of Lt. Governor, the first woman in Alaska history to hold a statewide office.

1984
Geraldine Ferraro (1935 -)
While in Congress (1979-85), she fought for increased federal funds for urban mass transit systems, issues of wage, pension and retirement equity for women and was co-sponsor of the 1982 Economic Equity Act. In 1984, she became first woman to be nominated for Vice President of the US by a major political party.

Helen G. Gonet
An inventor, she patented an electronic Bible in 1984.

Kathyrn Sullivan
In 1984, she became the first U.S. female astronaut to "walk" in space when exited the space shuttle Challenger

and worked in space for 3½ hours attached only by a narrow life-support tether.

Beatrice Wood
Potter, ceramist, artist and photographer, this artist was declared a California Treasure in 1984. She was renowned for her rare and beautiful luster glazes and her often blithe and humorous depiction of women and men in varied situations. Her ceramics are in the Smithsonian Metropolitan Museum in New York and other international museums.

1985
Amy Eilberg (1954-)
In 1985, she was first woman to be ordained as Rabbi in the Conservative branch of Judaism.

Penny Harrington
In 1985, she became first woman Chief of Police Department in Portland, OR.

Elaine K. Harris
After being diagnosed with Sjogren's syndrome in 1985, she started the Sjogren's Syndrome Foundation. She is recognized as the leading source of public information and patient service education on Sjogren's syndrome. In 1989, she was elected to the Hall of Fame of Hunter College in recognition of her work on behalf of Sjogren's syndrome patients.

Libby Riddles
In 1985, she became the first woman to ever win the Iditarod dog sled races in Alaska.

Leola E. White (US)
She invented a seam ripper in 1985 that is comprised of a holder and a blade with a guide portion in the holder. The guide portion has an upper and lower surface, which forms a wedge for separating the cloth from the seam so that only the stitching in the seam is engaged by the blade.

Lynnette Woodard
A basketball player, in 1985 she became the first woman member of the Harlem Globetrotters.

1986
Diane Chase
Archaeologist, she discovered the tomb of 7th century Mayan woman in Belize. The height of the pyramid and elaborate nature of the burial chamber indicate that the woman's stature in Mayan society was very high. The discovery led some archaeologists to reconsider the assumption that women were held in low esteem among Mayans.

Anita DeFrantz
In 1986, the International Olympic Committee appointed her to lifetime membership. She is both the first African-American and the first American woman to serve.

Maria Fisher
She had a long and illustrious career as a film actress appearing in over 60 films and a successful singing career. In 1963, she founded the American Opera School and developed educational programs and provided scholarships for young opera singers. In 1974, she founded the Beethoven Society of America through which she offered major concerts at nominal or no charge to the public. In 1986, she acted on her belief that "*JAZZ is America's classical music*" and founded the Thelonious Monk Institute of Jazz.

Jackie Joyner-Kersee
In 1986, she became the first woman to break the 7,000 mark in the Olympic heptathlon, winning the first of two gold medals. She also became the first woman athlete to be featured on the cover of Sports Illustrated (aside from the swimsuit edition) in 1987.

Christa McAuliffe
(1948-1986)
In 1986, she stepped from the classroom into history when she was selected to be the first civilian in space as part of NASA's radical new teacher in space program. The mission ended tragically when

the shuttle exploded within seconds of blast-off.

Muriel Ross

In 1986, she became founder and senior scientist of the Biocomputation Center at NASA's Ames Research Center. Her computer-based research has allowed surgeons to plan complex surgical procedures and visualize the results of reconstructive surgery in a virtual environment simulator.

Debi Thomas

In 1986, she became the first black woman to win the US figure skating singles championship.

1987
Johnnetta B. Cole (1936 -)
In 1987, she became the first black woman president of Spelman College in Atlanta, GA. Spelman is the oldest, largest and most high respected historically black liberal arts colleges for women in the United States.

Le Ly Hayslip (1949 -)
In 1987, she created the East Meets West Foundation to build clinics, schools and rehabilitation centers in Vietnam.

Wilma Mankiller (1945 -)
In 1987, she was the first woman to be elected Chief of the Cherokee Nation in Oklahoma and a politically powerful leader working for the betterment of Native

American people. In 1994, she was entered into the Women's Hall of Fame in New York City.

Sandra McBrayer

In 1987, she founded and developed the first successful school in the United States for homeless and unattended youth. She is the executive director of the Children's Initiative, an organization dedicated to strengthening children and families by working for integrated services that promote the values of collaboration, prevention and measurable outcomes in the fields of health, education, safety and economic security. She advocates and testifies on public policy issues that affect children, youth and families.

1988
Patricia E. Bath
A renowned ophthalmologist, she invented and patented an apparatus that efficient removes cataracts in 1988.

Roberta L. Hazard

She was selected for promotion to Rear Admiral Upper Half in 1988 and is the highest-ranking woman in the US military. Since 1988, she is Director, Human Resources Management, Office of Chief of Naval Operations. In this position she is responsible for developing policy and career opportunities for

women officers and enlisted
personnel.

1989
Temple Grandin
She earned a Ph.D. in Animal
Science from the University
of Illinois in 1989. Her area
of expertise is the care and
handling of livestock
including their processing in
meat plants. She designed a
number of systems that use
behavioral principles instead
of brute force or fear to
handle livestock.

Barbara Harris
An American clergywoman, she
broke a 2000-year tradition
when she was ordained as a
bishop in the US Episcopal
Church in 1989.

Krisztina Holly
In 1989, she helped develop
the world's first computer-
generated, full-color
reflection hologram. She
invented and patented "The
Stylus" in 1992, software
which operated basically as a
consumer's personal
interpreter and mediator in
the languages of bar code and
touch-tone. In 1993, she co-
invented Visual Voice, a tool
that allowed even a modest
software developer to create
and coordinate complex
telephony systems.

1990
Lori Cupp
Upon graduating from Stanford
University Medical School in
1990, she became the first

female Navaho Indian to
become a surgeon. She
believes that Navaho culture,
which is matriarchal; give
women a sense of power and
independence.

Sylvia A. Earle
Environmentalist and marine
biologist, she was first
female chief scientist of the
National Oceanographic &
Atmospheric Association
(NOAA) in 1991. She made the
world's deepest untethered
dive in 1979 when she walked
along the ocean floor off
Oahu, HI at depth of 1250
feet.

Marcelite Jordan Harris
First and only African-
American female US Air Force
General, she was promoted in
1990.

Bernadine Healy (1944 -)
In 1991, she became the first
woman to head the National
Institute of Health. She has
been particularly effective
in addressing medical policy
and research pertaining to
women.

Antonia Novello
A Puerto Rican pediatric
physician, she was the first
woman and first Hispanic to
be appointed Surgeon General
of the United States Public
Health Service. She directed
the nation's attention to
AIDS-infected children, the
perils of smoking and teenage
drinking and women's health
issues.

Ellen Ochoa (1959 -)
In 1990, she was first Hispanic female astronaut selected by NASA and made her first flight on the space shuttle Discovery in 1993. She co-invented and received patents for three optical devices: a system that inspects objects; a system that identifies and can "recognize" objects and a system that minimizes distortion in the images taken of an object. In 1994, she received Women in Science & Engineering (WISE) Engineering Achievement Award. Her dream is to build a Space Station, which she says is "critical to human exploration in space, a transportation mode to new frontier".

Elizabeth M. Watson
In 1990, she became the first woman to head the police force of a major city. She wore maternity "uniforms" and became the first police chief to give birth while on active duty.

1991
Molly DeGezelle
In 1991, she invented a building material composed of recycled paper and glue.

1992
Mae Jamison
Astronaut, physician and chemical engineer, she was the first African-American woman in space on the shuttle Endeavor.

Jeanie Low
Best known for her "The Kiddie Stool invention for which she received a patent" at age 7 in 1992. Since then, she designed and built a bathtub alarm that gives warning when the tub starts to overflow or when a small child is in danger of drowning. She has also invented a doormat with automatic brushes and easy-grip doorknobs for people with arthritis.

Carol A Mutter
Lt. Gen Mutter is first Marine woman to wear three stars and also was first woman to command a major tactical deploying unit in Okinawa in 1992.

Naomi Nakao
A gastroenterologist, she invented a warning system for IV lines to prevent air bubbles from entering a patient's vein in 1992. She has also invented several other devices to increase the safety and comfort of patients.

Nydia Velaquez
In 1992 she became the first Puerto Rican woman to be elected to the US House of Representatives and is lead sponsor of the Family Violence and Prevention Act, which established family prevention services and educational programs. In her role in Congress, she is particularly concerned with

speaking out for the rights of disenfranchised people, especially minorities, and women and children.

1993
Ann Bancroft (1955 -)
She was the first woman to travel across the ice to the North Pole. She was also first woman to travel across Greenland on skis and in 1993 was leader of the American Women's Expedition, a group of 4 who skied more than 600 miles to the South Pole.

Ruth Bader Ginsburg
(1933 -)
In 1972, she was the first female faculty to achieve tenure at Columbia University. In 1993, she was sworn in as the second Supreme Court Justice of the United States. Some consider her as "the legal architect of the modern women's movement".

Toni Morrison (1931 -)
Black woman novelist, she was first black American woman to be awarded 1992 Nobel Prize for Literature for the visionary force and poetic import of her novels which richly express depictions of black America.

Janet Reno
In 1993, she became the first woman to be appointed US Attorney General.

Betty M. Rozier
In 1993, she received a patent for a simple device that makes it safer and easier for hospitals to provide patients with IVs, which she co-invented

Christine T. Whitman
(1949 -)
Elected first female governor of New Jersey in 1993 on promise to cut taxes. Succeeded in slashing New Jersey's tax rates by 15% in her first year in office. She is the most imitated Republican Party politician in America and was chosen to deliver the party's response to last year's State of the Union address by President Clinton.

Sheila E. Widnall
Internationally known for her work in fluid dynamics, she worked specifically in the areas of aircraft turbulence and the spiraling airflows. She was appointed Secretary of the Air Force in 1993, and is responsible for the current and future readiness of the Air Force to accomplish its missions. During her tenure she concentrated on quality of life issues, modernization, acquisition reform and scientific and technological development.

1994

Kara Hultgreen

She is the first woman to qualify in combat ready F-14 Tomcat.

Chelsea Lanmon

In 1994, she received a patent for a "Pocket Diaper". Each diaper has a disposable pocket, which holds a disposable baby wipe and a baby-powder "puff".

Mary D. Lin

She invented and patented in 1994 disposable dust mop and broom covers made of soft, non-abrasive material to insure that surface being cleaned is not harmed. The covers can be used several times before disposing of it and avoid the need to launder dirty dust mop heads.

Olympia J. Snowe (1947 -)

She was elected to the US Senate in 1994 representing the State of Maine – the first Greek-American woman elected in the Senate. Senator Snowe is known nationally for her work on budget deficiet reduction, fiscal issues, health care, women's issues and foreign affairs.

1995

LTC Eileen Collins

(1956 -)

She is a pilot instructor at the US Air Force Academy and the first woman to pilot the space shuttle Discovery. She has an MS from Stanford University in Operations Research and an MA from Webster University in Space Systems Management.

Doris Kearns Goodwin

(1943 -)

In 1995, she was awarded a Pulitzer Prize for her biography of Franklin and Eleanor Roosevelt, *No Ordinary Time.*

Rebecca Marier

In 1995, she became the first woman West Point Cadet to graduate at the top of her class.

Annie Proulx

In 1995, she won Pulitzer Prize for Literature for her book *The Shipping News.*

Amy Smith

She earned a Master's in Mechanical Engineering from MIT in 1995. Her inventions include a laboratory incubator that does not require electricity and a microscope slide warmer to prepare slides for rapid tuberculosis diagnosis.

1996

Dale Emeagwali

In 1996, she received the National Technical Association's Scientist of the Year award in the field of cancer research. She continues her research in the fields of microbiology, fermentation, enzymology, virology, molecular biology, biochemistry and protein structure and function.

Arcela Keh (1933 -)

She had a child in 1996 at age 63 and is the oldest woman in history known to have given birth.

Carol A. Mutter

Upon advancement to Lieutenant General in 1996, she is the most senior woman officer and the first woman to receive the rank of Lieutenant General in the United States Marine Corps. Her achievements include development of new Marine Corps automated pay and personnel systems for active duty, retired and reserve Marines.

Ruth Patrick

A pioneer in the field of limnology, she is a world-renowned scientist who has studied the waterways of South Carolina for more than fifty years. She was the first scientist to diagnose the health of a river or stream by plant life and animal species. Her early studies contributed significantly to the developing field of ecology and established a set of aquatic indices that describe the health of water and impact of industrialization. In 1996, she was inducted into the South Carolina Hall of Science and Technology.

Alice Mitchell Rivlin

(1931 -)

In 1996, she was appointed vice-chairman of the US Federal Reserve Board, giving her a key voice in setting US interest rates, which help determine the fate of the world economy.

1997
Madeline Albright

(1937-)

She was the first woman Secretary of State and the highest-ranking woman in the US government when she was appointed in 1997. Prior to that post, in 1992, she was named the US permanent representative to the United Nations and head of the US delegation to that body.

Ruane Sharon Jeter

In 1997, she received a patent for a hand-held, multi-functional all-in-one device including a stapler, stapler remover, pencil sharpener, hole punch, calculator, tape measure, architectural and engineering scale.

Claudia J. Kennedy

She is the first and only woman to ever receive the flag rank of Lieutenant General in the United States Army. The Senate confirmed her in 1997 and assigned to the position of Deputy Chief of Staff for intelligence.

Gabrielle K. McDonald
She was President of the
United Nations International
Criminal Tribunal from 1997-
99.

Jody Williams
She received the 1997 Nobel
Peace Prize for her work for
the banning and clearing of
anti-personnel mines.

Janet L. Yellen (1946 -)
In 1997, she was appointed
Chair of the Council of
Economic Advisor of the
Federal Reserve System. She
had previously served as an
economist with the Federal
Reserve's Board of Governors
specializing on issues of
international trade and
finance. While focusing on
the causes, mechanisms and
implications of unemployment,
she has written on a wide
variety of macroeconomic
issues. A recognized scholar
in international economics,
she is also recently focusing
on the determination of trade
balance as well as the course
of economic reform in Eastern
Europe.

1999
Carleton Sneed Fiorina
(1954 -)
In 1999, she became
President/CEO of Hewlett-
Packard Co., the first woman
to head any major US high-
technology company.

Shirley Ann Jackson
(1946 -)
In 1999, she was the first
African-American woman to
receive a doctorate from MIT
in Theoretical Solid State
Physics and was named
President of Rensselaer
Polytechnic Institute. A
theoretical physicist, her
interests include the
electronic, optical, magnetic
and transport properties of
novel semiconductor systems.

2000
Christina M. Lennox
In 2000, she co-invented and
patented a pickup truck
tailgate monitor which
include a control panel
mounted adjacent to an
operation station in the cab
of the truck. The monitor
warns the driver if the
tailgate is left open or
opens while the truck is
moving.

Oceania Women

1964

Mere Mariota Tuiasosopo Beetham

Former primary school teacher, she was a Delegate to UNESCO in 1964 and Secretary of Education from 1972-76. She became Judge at the High Court of American Samoa in 1991, the first woman judge.

1980

Aviata Fano Faalevao

From 1980-84 and 1989-93, she was Attorney General. In 1996, she became Chairperson of the Republican Party of American Samoa.

AUSTRALIA

1825

Catherine Helen Spence

(1825-1910)
In 1854, her novel Clara Morison was published - the first novel written about Australia by a woman. She founded the Boarding Out Society in 1872 and became very involved in helping destitute women and children. An ardent supporter of women's advancement, she urged education for women which resulted in the establishment of kindergartens and the Advanced School for Girls, the first government secondary school for girls in Australia.

1848

Louisa Lawson (1848-1920)

A feminist and fighter for women's rights, she was referred to as "The mother of womanhood suffrage". In 1888, she launched "The Dawn" a journal for women, written, edited and printed by women - the first of its kind. The Dawn advised on women's issues, discussed divorce, the age of consent and women's right to vote.

Marian Ellis Rowan

(1848-1922)
While best known for her Australian wild flower paintings, she searched to find and record every species of wildflower on the continent of Australia. In 1898, she wrote "*Flower Hunter in Queensland and New Zealand*".

1855

Katherine Langloh Parker

(1855-1940)
She is a collector of Australian Aboriginal Legends. Her book Australian Legendary Tales written in 1896 has become a classic in Australian literature.

1857

Ethel Clifton (1857-1933)

She became acquainted with an Aboriginal tribe living nearby and made notes on the native way of life, their habits, laws and customs and legends told her by the women of the tribe. Her manuscript was completed in the early 1900's.

1863
Daisy May Bates (1863-1951)
A welfare worker among the Aboriginal tribes of Western Australia, she built up extensive anthropological knowledge of Aboriginal cultures, which she recorded in numerous articles and her autobiography. Her place in Australian folklore has been formalized by the opera *The Young Kabbarlie*.

1865
Ida Louise Marriott
(1865-1943)
She approached geography from a historic prospective and reconstructed the exploration of Australia by the British through the study of logbooks, journals and lost charts found in the British Admiralty.

1870
Jane Ada Fletcher
(1870-1956)
She published a number of books on nature and nature study as well as books and articles on Tasmanian history and Aborigines and ornithology. Her final book was *Tasmania's Own Birds*.

1872
Evelyn Mary Clowes
(1872-1942)
She published her first novel was in 1901 and later wrote more than 30 novels and books of short stores. She wrote extensively of her travels in Australia and her impressions of Victoria.

Roberta Henrietta Margaritta Jull (1872-1961)
A physician, she became active in social welfare, public health and politics. She became the first Medical Officer of Schools in Western Australia's Public Health Department in 1918, and played a leading role in the infant health movement.

1875
Georgina Sweet (1875-1946)
A zoologist, her research included the zoology of Australian native animals and the parasites infesting Australian stock and native fauna.

1876
Bertha Southey Adams
(1876-1957)
A writer of children's radios programs, she also wrote novels and short stories for adults which was published in the *Launceston Examiner*.

1878
Mary Grant Bruce
(1878-1958)
She is mainly remembered for the Billabong Series books, which made her one of the leading Australian writers of her era. The characters in the books still intrigue readers with the "legend" of the Australian bush, its "mateship" and its supportive family life.

1883
Dorothea Mackellar
(1883-1960)
She is known nationally for her poem "My Country" which is probably the best known of all Australian poems. The poem contrasts Australia with England.

Katherine Susannah Prichard
(1883-1969)
Her first novel, *The Pioneers*, won the Hodder & Stroughton Colonial section prize and was made into an Australian film. In 1920 she was a founding member of the Communist Party in Australia. She was elected federal president of the Australian Writers' League in 1935 and established the Modern Women's Club in 1938.

1891
Ethel Irene McLennan
(1891-1983)
An Associate Professor of Botany, she joined the staff of the University of Melbourne in 1915. Her specialty was mycology and plant pathology. In 1927 she was awarded the Syme Prize and in 1934 she was president of the Australian Federation of University Women.

1897
Marjorie Faith Barnard
(1897-1987)
Novelist, historian and biographer, she was commissioned to write a history of radar, which she completed in 1946.

1902
Ella Simon (1902-1981)
In 1962 she became the first Aboriginal woman to be appointed a justice of the peace. In her autobiography *Through My Eyes*, she imparts the obstacles and mistreatment encountered by the Aboriginal community of her era.

1906
Jean Galbraith (1906 -)
A prominent naturalist, she joined the Field Naturalists' Club of Victoria in 1923 and was awarded their Australian Natural History Medallion in 1970. In 1950 She published "Wildflowers of Victoria".

1907
Dorothy Hill (1907-1997)
Research Professor of Geology at University of Queensland. She has published widely on paleontology, stratigraphy and geology. In 1965, she was first Australian woman elected to the Royal Society and in 1970 the first female President of the Australian Academy of Science.

Annette Kellerman
In 1907, she is the first underwater ballerina at the New York Hippodrome. She was arrested for swimming in an 'indecent' one-piece swimsuit Boston Harbor that exposed her legs.

1908
Annabella Rankin (1908-1986)
She was Senator from 1941-71 and Minister of Housing from 1966-71. In 1971 she became High Commissioner to New Zealand, the first female Ambassador.

Ethel Roberts (1870-1946)
A novelist, she publishes her first novel *Maurice Guest* in 1908, a landmark in the treatment of homosexuality in English fiction.

1909
Isobel Ida Bennett (1909 -)
A marine scientist, she took part in a complete ecological survey of the Great Barrier Reef in 1953 and wrote "*The Great Barrier Reef*" in 1971 – the first book to give a general picture of the whole of the Great Barrier Reef. One genus, five species of marine animals and a coral reef have been named after her.

1911
Dorothy Margaret Tangney (1911-)
Labor politician, she became the first woman member of the Australian Senate in 1943.

1912
Stella Grace Maisie Carr (1912-1988)
She was an ecologist best remembered for her work on the Bogong High Plains during the 1940s and also spent many years studying Eucalyptus. She edited *People and Plants in Australia* and *Plants and Man in Australia*.

1918
Faith Bandler (1918 -)
A forceful power within the Advancement of Aboriginals and Torres Strait Islanders cause, she was director of the New South Wales referendum campaign in 1967, which was instrumental in gaining equal citizenship for Aborigines under the Australian Constitution. She wrote *The Time was Ripe: A History of the Aboriginal People in Australia in 1984*.

1920
Oodgeroo Noonuccal (1920-1993)
A poet and writer, her books include Australian Legends and Landscapes in 1990 and Australia's Unwritten History: more legends of our land in 1992.

1921
Edith Cowan
In 1921, she was elected to Legislative Assembly, the first woman elected to any Australian Parliament.

1922
Nancy Fannie Millis (1922 -)
Professor of Microbiology at the University of Melbourne, she is a pioneer of the study of fermentation technology in Australian. In 1981, she was chairman of the Commonwealth Government Recombinant DNA Monitoring Committee.

1923
Elizabeth Jolley(1923 -)
One of Australia's most acclaimed authors; she has been awarded an honorary doctorate from the Western Australia Institute of Technology (now Curtin University) and an Order of Australia Medal.

Eva Klein Nelson (1923 -)
An applied chemist, she worked in the research laboratories of Kodak (Australia) and developed a new method of purifying one of Kodak's used solvents.

1924
Monica Clare (1924-1973)
She became an activist in the Aboriginal cause, secretary of the South Coast Illawarra tribe and delegate to several conferences of the Federal Council for the advancement of Aborigines and Torres Strait Islanders. In 1978, she wrote a fictionalized account of her childhood, possible the first novel by an Aboriginal woman.

1925
Dame Leonie Kramer (1925 -)
A one-time ABC chairwoman and formerly one of the country's most prominent businesswomen, in 1968 she became the first female professor at Sydney University upon her appointment as head the Australian literature department. In 1991, she became Chancellor of the University of Sydney, Australia's oldest university.

1926
Patsy Adam-Smith 1926 -)
During the Second World War, she enlisted as a VAD and was the first woman to gain her articles as a radio officer and worked on an Australian merchant ship. Her main interest is the Australian railways on which she has written widely. In 1993, she received the triennially awarded National Book Council Order of Australia Book Prize.

1930
Pamela Elizabeth de Silva (1930-1997)
She was a scientific officer and head scientist of the Industrial Hygiene Division of the Victorian Health Department. Her particular area of expertise was lead poisoning. She published a paper arguing that it is not high levels of lead in children's blood that causes lower intelligence but rather that young children with lower intelligence may eat more soil or paint containing lead and thereby have higher blood lead levels. She became first Australian president of International Occupational Hygiene Association in 1989.

1931
Eve Laron (1931 -)
Founder of Constructive Women (The Association of Women Architects) and is fellow of Royal Australian Institute of Architects. The focus of her work is residential although she is also interested in

solar and environmental design and feminism.

1933
Elizabeth Kenny (1880-1952)
An Australian nurse, she founded a clinic in Australia in 1933 where practices a new technique for the treatment of poliomyelitis which involved muscle therapy. She went on to found clinics in Britain in 1937 and Minnesota in 1920.

1934
Inga Clendinnen (1934-)
She spent her career as historian, an archeologist, and anthropologist. She studied the lives of the Aztec Indians, the Mayans and other Latin American civilizations and theorizes about their lives. The topics of the many books she has written range from histories of societies to the faith and beliefs of societies.

Beverley Raphael (1934 -)
Professor of Psychiatry at University of Queensland since 1987, much of her research has been based on exploring psychiatric vulnerability and preventive psychiatry.

1937
Nugi Garimara (1937 -)
She studied journalism at Curtin University and later worked in film and video production. Her manuscript *Caprice: A Stockman's Daughter* won the 1990 David Unaipon Award for unpublished Aboriginal and Torres Strait Island writers and was published in 1991.

1938
Ann Kirsten Carr-Boyd (1938 -)
Composer, teacher and music historian, she is a leading authority on Aboriginal and early Australian music. Her musical output is well established in the repertoire of Australian music and she is fascinated with composing for unusual combinations of instruments. Complementing her work as a composer, she continues her pioneering work in documenting the history of European music in Australia.

1939
Daisey Bates (1861-1950)
Social worker, she published *The Passing of the Aborigines* in 1939.

1946
Anne Infante (1946 -)
A member of Crime Writers of Queensland, she has written five crime novels, is a freelance editor and conducts crime-writing workshops. Her first mainstream novel *Escape from the Past* was published in Australia in 1997. It is set on Queensland's notorious colonial prison island – St. Helena.

Fiona Juliet Stanley (1946 -)
A pediatrician, she has been founding director of TVW Telethon Institute for Child Health Research since 1989. Her research has helped to reduce the incidence of spina

bifida and cerebral palsy in children.

1948
Jennie George (1948 -)
The first woman president of ACTU and a former head of the NSW Teachers' Federation, she has long championed the rights of working women. Part of her mission is to modernize working conditions so they better meet the needs of families.

1950
Louise Hanson-Dyer
(1884-1952)
She established a music-publishing house that helped to revive early music. In 1950, her publishing house issued long-playing records of 18th Century music. She was the first Australian woman to be cited in Harvard Dictionary of Music.

Louise St. John Kennedy
(1950 -)
She was the first woman architect appointed to the Architect's Board of Western Australia. The focus of her work is residential.

1954
B. Byer
In 1954, she catches a 1,052-lb white shark – the largest white shark ever caught by a woman.

Mary Josephine O'Kane (1954 -)
She was appointed vice-chancellor at the University of Adelaide in 1996. She is a computer expert whose specialty is computer voice recognition.

1958
Debra Adelaide (1958 -)
A university teacher and researcher, she has written eight books. Her books include *Australian Women Writers*, a bibliographic guide, *A Bright and Fiery Troop*, *Australian Women Writers of the 19th Century* and *Bibliography of Australian Women's Literature 1795-1990*.

1959
Roberta Anne Vaile
(1959-1996)
An astrophysicist, she was instrumental in forming SETI (Search for Extraterrestrial Intelligence) Australia Centre in 1995 and received the Australian Science Communicator Unsung Hero Award.

1960
Judith Anderson
(1918 -)
Actress Dame Judith Anderson has astounded audiences everywhere. In 1940, her stunning performance in *Rebecca* won her an Academy Award nomination. Her portrayal of *Macbeth* won her an Emmy. Queen Elizabeth at Buckingham Palace knighted her in 1960. Throughout her career, Dame Judith has generously contributed her time and talent in coaching young actors and actresses,

helping them to achieve their dreams.

1963
Josephine Flood (1963 -)
Dr. Flood has participated in archaeological fieldwork in most states and territories in Australia – her most recent research being on the rock art in the Northern Territory.
She has been instrumental in listing some 5,000 Aboriginal sites in the Register of the National estate during her years as Director of the Aboriginal Section with the Australian Heritage Commission.

1965
Roma Mitchell
She was Judge of the Supreme Court of Australia from 1965-83.

1966
Dame Annabelle Rankin
(1908-1986)
She became Australian housing minister in 1966 and was 1st woman to head an Australian cabinet department; she became Australian high commissioner to New Zealand in 1971 and was the 1st female Australian ambassador.

1970
Germaine Greer
Her best seller "*The Female Eunuch*" published in 1970 portrayed marriage as a form of legalised slavery for women. She is now an advocate of radical celibacy in middle age and a passionate opponent

of hormone replacement therapy.

1973
Catherine Astrid Salome Freeman (1973 -)
An Australian track athlete, she was the 1st aboriginal athlete ever to compete on Australian Olympic Team in 1992. She became 1st Australian aboriginal to win a world track record in 1997.

1974
Ruth Dobson (1918-)
Australia's first female career diplomat, she was appointed to serve her country as ambassador to Denmark in 1974.

1983
Susan Ryan
In 1983, she became the first Labor woman federal minister. As the Minister Assisting the Prime Minister for the Status of Women, she introduced the *Sex Discrimination Act 1984*.

1987
Mary Gaudron (1943 -)
In 1974, she became the youngest federal judge when appointed deputy-president of the Arbitration Commission and in 1981 was the youngest solicitor general. In 1987, she became the first woman to be appointed to the High Court of Australia.

1993
Cheryl Kernot (1949 -)
In 1993, she became leader of the party and is credited with

saving the Democrats from political extinction. In 1990, she entered parliament as a senator for Queensland and has become the best-known and most successful female politician in the country.

1994
Susan Wyber Serjeantson
(1946 -)
In 1994, she became director of Institute of Advanced Studies and Deputy Vice-Chancellor of Australian National University. Her research is in the areas of inherited diseases and transplantation antigens especially in Pacific peoples.

1996
Joyce Stevens
She helped produce the first women's liberation newspaper in Australia *Mejane* and Australia's first socialist-feminist magazine, *Scarlet Woman*. Also, she helped set up the Control Abortion Referral Service, which established the first two women's health centers in Sydney. She worked for the Women's Employment Action Centre on its register of women in non-traditional jobs and their attempts to establish a comparable worth case between pay rates in traditional female and male occupations. In 1996, she received an Order of Australia for service to social justice for women as an activist and writer.

1999
Aleysha Healey
In 1999, she rides Eunuch to victory in the 3rd Annual Desert Sands 2000 camel race in Queensland where some of Australia's finest outback camels show their paces.

COOK ISLANDS

1965
Margurite Eikura Kitimira Stoery (1921 -)
From 1965-79 and 1983, she was President of the Legislature.

1978
Margaret Ariki (1919 -)
She was President of the House of Ariki from 1978-80 and 1990-94. She had the title of Makea Karika Takau since 1935 ans was the Highest Ranking Chief in the House of Ariki.

1980
Lady Davies (1923-1990)
She inherited the title of Pa Tapaeru in 1932, the highest ranking traditional leader in the Cook Islands. In 1980, she became President of the House of Arikis.

1983
Fanaura Kingstone
In 1983, she became Minister of Internal Affairs and Postmistress General, the first female MP.

1995
Tiramate Ngatokaorua
She became Assistant Minister for Internal Affairs and responsible for women in 1995.

1999
Ngamau Munokoa
In 1999, she became Minister of Internal Affairs and of Works, Energy and Physical Planning with responsibility for Water Supply, Building Control, Civil Engineering, Punanga Nui, Religious Affairs, Women, Youth and Children.

Angelina Tuara
Former Head of the Probation Unit in the Ministry of Justice, she became Minister of Internal Affairs in 1999.

FIJI
1960
Adi Losalini Dovi
A Fijian politician who began her career as a civil service stenographer In 1966, she became a member of the Legislative Council - the first female member of the Legislative Assembly. In 1976, she became Assistant Minister for Urban Development, Housing and Social Welfare – the first female minister in Fiji.

1976
Irene Jai Narrayen
She was President of the National Federation Party (1976-79)and Minister of Indian Affairs (1987-92). In 1995, she co-founded and was co-leader of Fiji Indian Congress.

1980
Taufa Vakatale
From 1980-92, she was Deputy Ambassador to United Kingdom, in 1993-95 Minister of Education Science and Technology, Women and Culture and in 1997-99 Deputy Prime Minister and Minister of Education and Technology.

1999
Adi Kuini Teimumu Vuikaba Speed, *the Tui Nokoro and Paramount Chief of Navosa*
She succeeded her father, the Tui Nokoro and in 1999 became Deputy Prime Minister and Minister of Fijian Affairs. In 2000, she and the rest of the government was deposed in a coup d'etat.

Adi Samamunu Cakobau Tolakuli
A High Chiefess, she was Chairperson of the Great Council of Chiefs from 1994-95. In 1999, she was appointed ambassador to Malaysia, Thailand and the Social Commission for Asia and Pacific.

2000
Marieta Rigamoto
She became Assistant Minister of Agriculture, Fisheries and Forests in 2000, assisting the Prime Minister with the responsibility for the Rotuma Agreement.

FRENCH POLYNESIE
1990
Ioanne Temasuri
From 1990-94, she was Minister of Family and Relations with the Assamblee Territoriale and with the Council for Economic and Social Development,

Minister of Archipelago
Development and Property.

1994
Haammoetin Legarde
In 1994-97, she was Minister
of Agriculture and Women's
Affairs with responsibility
for the Relations with the
Assamblee Territoriale and the
Economic and Social Assembles.
Since 1999, she was vice-
president of the Permanent
Commission of the Assembly.

1997
Lucette Taero
She became Minister for
Employment, Professional
Training and responsible for
Social Dialogue and Women's
Affairs.

1999
Louise Peltzer
Former Minister of Culture and
Higher Education, in 1999 she
became Minister in charge of
Promotion of Polynesian
Languages.

MAORI
1835
Marie Henriette Suzanne Aubert
(1835-1926)
A Catholic nun, who did
missionary work among mainly
rural Maori people, she
undertook commercial
production of Maori herbal
remedies and published books
in the Maori language.

1893
Meri Te Tai Mangakahia
(1868-1920)
In 1893 she addressed the
Kotahitanga Parliament and was
the first woman to do so. She
requested that Maori women be
given the vote and be eligible
to sit in the Maori parliament
and argued that many Maori
women owned and administered
their own lands.

1920
Te Puea (1884-1952)
A Maori princess, she was the
first woman to inspire the
revival of the traditional way
of life among her people in
1920. She encouraged the
return to traditional
agriculture and to revive
native crafts and long-
forgotten arts.

1931
Te Arikinui Dame Te Atairangikaahu Ariki
As Queen/Kuini of the Maori
and Paramount Chief of the
other Maori groups, she
succeeded her father as the 6th
Maori Regent in 1966.

1939
Mabel Te Aowhaitini Mangakahia
A registered nurse and
midwife, she became the first
Maori to receive a
postgraduate diploma in Public
Health Nursing in 1939.

1943
Georgina Te Heuheu (1943 -)
She became Minister for Courts
and Women's Affairs, Associate
Minister in charge of Treaty

of Waitangi Negotiations and Associate Minister of Health in 1998. The Treaty of Waitangi set up the relations with the Maori population in the late 1900 century.

1952
Sandra Rose Te Hakamatua Lee
(1952 -)
She became Minister of Conservation and Minister of Local Government, Associate Minister of Maori Affairs and Associate Minister for Biodiversity Strategy in 1999. She has been active in Poutin Ngai Tahu tribal affairs.

1972
Tini Whetu Marama Tirikatene-Sullivan, Te Hiwi Marama
(1932 -)
She became Associate Minister of Social Affairs in 1972. Te Hiwi Marama is a maori nobility title. She was MP for the South Maori Constituency from 1967-96.

MARSHALL ISLANDS
1992
Carmen Bigler
She was Secretary of Internal and Outer Island Affairs from 1992-97.

Marie Maddison
From 1992-94, she was Secretary of Education and Foreign Secretary from 1994-99. As Foreign Secretary, she was Deputy Minister of Foreign Affairs.

1993
Evelyn Konou
Between 1993-94, she was Minister of Health Services and Environment and from 1994-97 Minister of Education.

NAURU
1986
Ruby Sedjna Dediya
She was Minister of Finance from 1986-89.

1991
Nimes Ekewona
From 1991-93, she was Minister of Education.

1996
Millicent Aroi
In 1996, she was appointed Ambassador to Fiji, the first woman ambassador of her country.

NEW ZEALAND
1820
Mary Ann Muller (1820-1901)
Feminist and suffragist, in 1869 she wrote the first pamphlet on the women's vote published in New Zealand, An Appeal to the Men of New Zealand. The pamphlet argued that women should not be discriminated against in law or politics on ground of their sex, that they had a just claim to the vote as men and that without political rights they could not make their full contribution to the progress of the nation.

1829

Catherine Henrietta Elliot

(1829-1919)

Diarist and advocate of women's suffrage, her diaries reveal the trials and successes of pioneering life. In 1885, she founded the local branch of the Women's Christian Temperance Union and was its first president.

1837

Lady Jane Franklin

In 1837, she became the first woman to climb Mount Wellington in New Zealand.

1857

Kate Millington Edger

(1857-1935)

She became the first woman university graduate in New Zealand in 1877 and the first woman in the British Empire to earn a BA.

1858

Anna Paterson Stout

(1858-1931)

A feminist whose philosophy was that women should have equal rights with men and be free to develop their intellectual ability to its highest capacity. She founded the Southern Cross Society, which aimed at educating women politically, promoting their independence and equality and improving the living conditions of women who worked for wages.

1863

Ada Wells (1863-1933)

An advocate for women's equality and economic independence, she argued for free kindergartens, access to secondary education, reform of local government and prisons.

1864

Rosaline Margaret Frank

(1864-1954)

She was New Zealand's first professional woman photographer. Her legacy was her collection of about 200,000 glass-plate negatives dating from the early days of the settlement. These are now held in the Nelson Provincial Museum and form the basis of one of the largest photographic collections in New Zealand. Its importance lies in its portrayal of the development of the Nelson region.

1875

Ethel Rebecca Benjamin

(1875-1943)

New Zealand's first woman lawyer, she was the first woman admitted to the law school at the University of Atago in 1893 which was the first university in Australia to permit women to take a law degree.

1877

Ettie Annie Rout

(1877-1936)

Journalist, businesswoman, sex hygiene campaigner and writer, she gained a public profile as a cyclist, vegetarian and physical culturist. In 1902, she became one of the first government appointed shorthand writers working in the Supreme Court. In 1910, she set up the *Maoriland Worker* with the New Zealand Shearers' Union of which she was editor.

1879
Learmonth White Dalrymple
An educator, feminist and temperance advocator, she published *The Kindergarten* in 1879.

1889
Harriet Morison (1862-1925)
She was a suffragist and advocate for working women. In 1889, she became first vice president of the Tailoresses' Union of New Zealand – the first organization to represent women workers in New Zealand. In 1892, she founded the Women's Franchise League, the first in New Zealand.

1893
Grace Neill
In 1893, she becomes New Zealand's first female factory inspector.

1898
Muriel Emma Bell
(1898-1974)
In 1926 she became the first woman to be awarded a MD by the University of Otago. She was appointed the first nutrition officer in the Department of Health in 1940. Active in numerous campaigns to improve people's health, she contributed the the

introduction of iodized salt, worked to advertise the benefits of drinking milk, fought for fluoridation in New Zealand and conducted research into cholesterol and heat disease.

1905
Sylvia Ashton-Warner
(1905-1985)
An innovative educator who developed a method of teaching that effectively helped children learn. In 1982 was made a member of the Order of the British Empire, the first official recognition of her position as one of the world's most influential educators.

1928
Anita Brookner (1928 -)
Writer and art historian, she is an authority on 18th Century painting. She published many novels and won the Booker Prize in 1984 with *Hotel du Lac*.

1934
Fleur Adcock (1934 -)
Her poetry is notable for its unsentimental treatment of personal and family relationships, its interest in classical themes and its psychological insights. She has also edited *The Oxford Book of New Zealand Verse* and *The Faber Book of 20th Century Women's Poetry*.

1944
Margaret Ann Hercys (1944 -)
In 1988 she was appointed
Ambassador to the United
States and to the UN in 1989.

1947
Marion Hobbs
In 1999, she became Minister
of Broadcasting, Minister of
the Environment & Biosecurity,
Minister responsible for the
National Library and National
Archives and Associate
Minister of Communications.

1949
Cynthia Mackenzie
In 1949, she was appointed
Ambassador to France.

1952
Jennifer Mary Shipley (1952 -)
She held various National
Party positions at branch,
electorate and divisional
levels. In 1996, she became
Minister of Transport, State-
Services and State-Owned
Enterprises and Accident
Rehabilitation & Compensation
Insurance. She became Minister
in charge of New Zealand
Security Intelligence Service
in 1997.

1954
Jane Campion (1954 -)
Film director, whose film *Peel*
won the 1986 Cannes Palme d'Or
for best short film. She
earned The Academy Award for
Best Original Screenplay for
*The Piano in 1993, which s*he
wrote as well as directed. T*he
film which was* a love story
set in colonial New Zealand

also shared the Palme d'Or at
the 1993 Cannes Film Festival
-- the first such award for an
New Zealand production and the
first for a woman director.

1968
Helen Hampton
In 1968, she was appointed
Ambassador to the UN in
Geneva.

1989
Frances Wilden
In 1989, she became Minister
of Disarmament, Weapon-Control
and Tourism. She became Mayor
of Wellington in 1992.

1993
Helen Clark (1950 -)
In 1993, she became the first
woman leader of a major
political party in New
Zealand's history. She has
presided over a crucial but
difficult period of reform
within her party.

1996
Christine Fletcher
In 1996, she became Minister
of Cultural Affairs and Local
Government and Associate
Minister of Women's Affairs.
She became Mayor of Auckland
in 1998.

1999
Sian Seerpoohi Elias
She became Administrator of
the Government (Deputy
Governor-General) in 1999. As
Chief Justice of New Zealand,
she is the first deputy of the
Governor General and acts in

his place when he is abroad or otherwise incapacitated.

Margaret Wilson
In 1999, she became Attorney General, Minister of Labor, Minister in charge of Treaty of Waitangi Negotiations, Associate Minister of Justice and Associate Minister of Social Justice.

2001
Silvia Cartwright (1943 -)
In 1989, she became the first female Chief Justice of a District Court and in 1993 the first woman in the Supreme Court. She will be inaugurated as Governor General of New Zealand in 2001.

NIUE
1993
O'Love Tauveve Jacobsen
From 1993-99, she was Minister of Environment, Education, Cultural and Etnic Arts, Religion, Sports and Youth Affairs. She was candidate for post of Premier in 1999.

NORFOLK ISLANDS
1989
Gaye Ewans
From 1989-92, she was Deputy Premier and Deputy President of the Legislature.

1994
Monica Anderson
Between 1994-97, she was Member of the Executive Council and Deputy President of the Legislative Assembly.

NOUVELLE CALEDONIE
1979
Yvonne Hnada
In 1979, she became Member of the Council of Government.

1997
Marie-Noelle Tenemerau
From 1997-99, she was Member of the Commission Permanente du Congress de la Territorie and in 1999 became 1st Vice President of the Brueau du Congress.

1999
Annie Beustes
She became Minister of Economic Affairs and Relations with the Economic and Social Council in 1999.

REPUBLIC OF PALAU
1989
Sandra Sumane-Pierantozzi
From 1989-97, she was Minister of Administration and Budget and a 1997 candidate for vice president. She is currently senator in one of the states.

1990
Dilmei L. Olkeriil
She was Minister of Culture and Community Development from 1990-93.

1998
Katheleen M. Salii
The first woman appointed Judge in the Supreme Court, she became Acting Attorney General in 1998.

PAPUA NEW GUINEA

1972
Josephine Abayah
In 1972, she became the first woman member of Parliament in Papua New Guinea.

1977
Nahau Roohey
In 1977, she became Minister of Justice, Corrective Institutions and Liquor Licensing and in 1985, Minister of Culture, Tourism and Civil Aviation.

1988
Margaret M. Taylor
She was appointed ambassador to United States in 1988, Canada in 1989 and Mexico in 1991.

1989
Alphmelody Joel
In 1989, she became Deputy Minister of Labour and Employment.

1994
Flora Carruthers
In 1994, she became Chief Manager of the Bank of Paua New Guinea.

PHILIPPINES

1894
Josepha Abiertas
(1894-1921)
Lawyer and feminist, she was the first woman to graduate from the Philippine Law School.

1912
Maria Paz Mendoza-Guazon
Already the first Filipina to graduate from high school, in 1912 she becomes the first Filipina doctor. Later she will become the first president of the Philippine Women's Medical Association.

1914
Natividad Lopez
She becomes the first woman lawyer in the Philippines in 1914. Later she will become the first Filipina judge.

1922
Sister M. Rosalina Abejo
(1922 -)
She composed more than 400 works and became the first nun in the world to direct and conduct a symphonic orchestra, Cagayan de Oro in 1957.

1941
Elisa Ochoa
In 1941, she became the first female member of the Parliament in the Philippines.

1947
Miriam Defensor Santiago
(1947 -)
A former judge, she was appointed head of the Commision on Immigration and Deportation in 1988 under Corazon Aquino's government. She declared war on powerful crime syndicates dealing in guns, prostitution and drugs, and on corrupt politicians and police who protect them. In the 1992 and 1998 presidential elections she was a close

second and should not be ruled
out as a future president.

1949
Asuncion Arnola Perez
Between 1941-44, she was Lt.
COL in the resistance movement
in the Pacific War. In 1949,
she became Cabinet Minister.

1962
Trinidad Fernandez Legarde
In 1962, she was appointed
ambassador to The Republic of
South Vietnam. She became
ambassador to Vietnam, Laos
and Cambodia in the 1980's.

1975
Leticita Ramos-Shahani
Between 1975-78, she was
appointed ambassador to
Romania, Hungary and German
Democratic Repubic, and from
1978-80 to Australia. She was
Assistant Secretary General to
the UN for Social Development
and Humantarian Affairs in
1981-86. From 1997-99, she was
President Pro-Tempore of the
Senate.

1978
Imelda Ramualdez Marcos
In 1978, she became Secretary
of Ecology. Between 1975-86,
she was Governor of Manila and
has been presidential
candidate in 1992 and 1998.

1981
Rosario G. Manago
She was Ambassador to the
European Communities between
1981-87, to France 1990-95 and
to Finland, Sweden, Norway and
Denmark 1995-97.

1986
Corazon Aquino (1933 -)
Became first female President
of the Philippines in 1986.
Supported by the United States
and the Roman Catholic Church,
Aquino's government faced
innumerable obstacles; severe
factionalism and social
problems made success almost
impossible.

1987
Luz Culta R. Bakunawa
In 1987, she became Executive
Secretary to President. This
is the highest-ranking
secretary, the office is
placed in the Office of the
President.

1989
Ejercito Estrada
She founded the "Erap Para sa
Mahirap" Foundation in 1989,
which provides scholarship for
the underprivileged but
deserving students. As First
Lady, she intends to support
through private and non-
governmental initiative
projects in advancing the
development of the Philippines
and attending to the basic
development needs of the
citizenry, particularly the
poor masses.

1990
Lourdes Quisumbung
Between 1990-92, she was
Ambassador and Secretary
General of UNESCO National
Commission in the Philipines
and Member of the Executive
Board in Paris.

1997
Erlinda F. Basilo

Former Assistant Secretary of Foreign Affairs, she has been ambassador to Sweden, Denmark, Norway, Estonia, Latvia and Lithuania since 1997.

1998
Henrietta Demetrieou

In 1998, she became Member of the Cabinet and Chief of Presidential Legal Council.

2000
Lilia R. Bautista

In 2000, she became Senior Undersecretary of Trade and Industry.

SAMOA
1988
Ietuao Toa Alama

Obstetrician and gynecologist, she became Clerk of the Legislative Assembly in 1988, Chief Electoral Officer from 1998-90 and Registrar of Elections in 1990.

1991
Matai Fiame Naomi Mulinu'u MATA'AFA

She became Minister of Culture, Youth and Sports in 1991. (Matai means chief.)

1994
Polataivao Fosi

In 1994, she became Minister of Internal and Women's Affairs.

1998
Brenda Heather

In 1998, she became Attorney General.

1999
La'ulu Fetavimalemau Mafe'afa

She had been Consul General since 1989 and was appointed Ambassador to New Zealand in 1999.

TONGA
1996
Alkosita Finenganofo

Former Director in the Ministry of Foreign Affairs, she was appointed Ambassador to United Kingdom, Belgium, The Netherlands and Luxembourg, European Union, Germany, Denmark, Sweden, Finland, Iceland and United States in 1996.

TUVALU
1989
Naama Sopeta Maheu Laatasi

From 1989-93, she was Minister of Local Government, Education and Health, the first and only female MP. She was member of Nanumea Island Parliament and responsible for Education, Culture, Women's Affairs, Youth, Sport, Community Affairs, Non-Governmental Organizations, Museums, Libraries and Archives from 1989-99.

South American Women

ARGENTINA

1890
Victoria Ocampo (1890-1974)
Advocate of women's rights, she was the most influential woman of letters and cultural promotion in 20th century Argentina. In 1931, she founded the periodical Sur that has been the center for intellectual life in Argentina for 40 years.

1889
Cecilia Grierson
She became Argentina's first licensed woman physician in 1889.

1916
Alfonsina Storni
(1892-1938)
Poet, she published her first volume of verse La *Inquietud del Rosal* in 1916. She is considered the first writer in her country to write from the women's point of view.

1919
Elvira Rawson de Dellipiani
Feminist, doctor and teacher, she founded the Women's Rights Association in 1919, which was dedicated to political equality, access to prestigious jobs and protective labor legislation for women.

1921
Lydia Gueiler Tejada (1921 -)
In 1952, she was Commander in the National Revolutionary Force and the only female head of a battalion. She was appointed Ambassador in Embassy to West Germany in 1982 and to Venezuela in 1983.

1928
Griselda Gambara (1928-)
Although she began her career as a fiction writer, she is best known as a playwright. Her political plays show a fusion of sociopolitical commitment with verbal and non-verbal expressions of violence.

1941
Martha Argerich (1941 -)
Her ability to play the piano is described as a true gift. Her orchestral debut was in Buenos Aires in 1949 playing concertos by Mozart and Beethoven. In 1965, she took first prize at the Warsaw Chopin Competition.

1945
Cora Ratto de Sadosky
(1912-1981)
She was a mathematician who devoted her life to fighting discrimination, oppression, and racism. In 1945, she created "The Victory Union" which was the first women's mass organization of its size in Latin American and was significant for its solidarity against the Nazis. Also she was the co-author of "Introduction to Linear

Algebra", a remarkably modern and rigorous text and the first of its kind in Spanish.

1946

Olga Orozco (1920 -)

Poet, she was first published in 1946. Among Argentine poets, her style is unique as her poetry elusively and delicately treads between the harshness of life and the dreams of idealism.

Eva Peron (1919-1952)

Argentine political leader, she was the second wife of Argentine president Juan Peron and co-governed during his first term as president in 1946.

1960

Elsa Tabernig de Pucciarelli

Educator, she became head of the Institute of Foreign Languages at La Plata in 1960.

1982

Leonore Calvera

Poet, translator and feminist, she published *El Genero Mujer* in 1982. It is an analysis of women's history from Paleolithic period to present.

1986

Lucia Garcia de Solar

In 1986, she was appointed Ambassador to Washington, DC.

BOLIVIA

1809

Juana Azurduy (1781-1862)

The first woman to lead a revolt against Spanish rule in her country, she was a military leader of both women and men in the guerilla wars for independence in Bolivia.

1926

Amelia Villa (1942-)

She earned her degree in 1926 and became the first female physician in Bolivia. At the end of her career she was honored by the government for her work in pediatrics. A children's ward at Oruro Hospital bears her name.

1969

A. Espinoza

In 1969, she became Bolivia's Labor Minister, the first woman in the cabinet.

1979

Lydia Guelar Tejada

In 1979, she became Prime Minister of Bolivia - the 2nd Western Hemisphere nation to have a woman head of state. She was Ambassador in Embassy to West Germany (1982-83) and to Venezuela (1983-86) and (1993).

BRAZIL

1834

Marie Durocher (1809-1893)

In 1834, she was the first individual to earn a degree at the medical school in Rio de Janeiro and was among the first women physicians in Brazil.

1847

Chiquinha Gonzaga (1847 -?)
One of Brazil's most popular composers, she wrote more than 2,000 works. She was also active in the anti-slave movement.

1887

Rita Lobato de Freitus Velho Lopez
In 1887, she became the first licensed female physician in Brazil.

1897

Virginia Salgado Fiuza (1897 -?)
Teacher and composer, she became deputy director of the Brazilian Conservatory of Music in 1948.

1905

Dinor de Carvalho (1905 -)
A pianist, composer and conductor, she was elected the first woman member of the Brazilian Academy of Music. In 1939, she founded and directed the Feminine Orchestra of Sao Paulo.

1920

Clarice Lispector (1920-1977)
Considered one of the major writers in Portugese, her masterpiece *A hora da estela* published in 1977 was her most socially committed work. A film based on this novel received the first prize at the Havana Film Festival in 1986.

1922

Bertha Lutz (1899-1976)
She organized the Brazilian Association for the Advancement of Women in 1922, a group dedicated to child welfare and to women's suffrage and education. She joined the staff of the National Museum in Rio de Janeiro in the 1920s, thus becoming the first woman in Brazilian government service. Lutz organized and was instrumental in achieving the franchise for women in 1932. In 1936, she served in Brazil's Parliament.

1933

Carlotta Pereira de Queiroz
She became Brazil's first woman deputy when she was elected to the National Assembly in 1933.

1955

Dorothea Fonesca Furquim Werneck
In 1990, she became Secretary of Economy in Ministry of Economy, Finance and Planning and Minister of Industry, Commerce and Tourism in 1995.

1959

Beata Vettori
She was the first female Ambassador from Brazil to the European Economic Community in Strasbourg, France from 1959-60 and Ambassador to Ecuador and Senegal from 1966-69.

1960
Carolina Maria de Jesus

In 1960, she publishes her diary, which is a detailed and sensitive account of favela life. It becomes a best seller and allows her to escape her life of poverty.

1961
Frida Baranek (1961 -)

Representative of the new generation of sculptors, she is best known for her large scale, non-objective sculptures using industrial debris. Her pieces, which appear to be ruins, constantly threaten viewers with the imminence of their collapse.

1962
Sandra Martins Cavalranti

In 1962, she became Secretary of Social Service.

1965
Dora Vasconcelos

She became Ambassador to Canada, Trinidad and Tobago in 1965.

1976
Marcia Haydee (1939 -)

Dancer and director, she was appointed artistic director of Stuttgart Ballet in 1976.

1977
Maria Pia Esmerada Matarazzo (1942 -)

In 1977, she became the only female executive of a major enterprise – Remundas F. Matarazz, Brazil's 10th largest private company.

1998
Iara Gloria Areias Prado

In 1998, she became Secretary of Fundamental Education in Ministry of Education and Sport.

CHILE

1872
Isabel Pinochet

In 1872, she founded an all-female high school. Through her efforts, a formal decision known as the Amunatequi Decree fully opened educational doors to women in 1876.

1887
Eloisa Inunza Diaz

In 1887, she became the first licensed female physician in Chile.

1898
Marea Teresa del Canto Molina (1898-?)

Former Professor of English at the University of Santiago de Chile, she became Minister of Health from 1952-53.

1910
Maria Luisa Bombal (1910-1980)

Her novels *La ultima niebla* and *La Amortajada* clearly indicate her innovative preoccupation with feminist themes and her desire to subvert traditional narrative techniques.

1917

Amanda Labarca

(1917-1975)

Educator, she was concerned with upgrading education for all Chileans but primarily with improvement of status of women.

1919

Myriam Waisberg (1919 -)

She is an architect and professor of architecture at the University of Chile since 1951.

1922

Conchita Cintron

(1922 -)

She begins fighting bulls in 1937 and is recognized as the first woman to compete at a high professional level as a bullfighter.

1945

Gabriela Mistral

(1889-1957)

In 1933, she was appointed ambassador-at-large for Latin American Culture and representative to the League of Nations. She received Nobel Prize in Literature for lyric poetry in 1945. She is symbol of the idealistic aspirations of the entire Latin American world. In addition, she was a guiding force in education in Chile and Mexico.

1950

Ana Figuero Gjardo

In 1950, she was appointed Ambassador to the United Nations and in 1952 became Member of the Security Council.

1951

Inez Enriquez Frodden

In 1951, she became the first woman congressional representative in Chile.

1953

Violeta Parro (1917-1967)

A songwriter, she rescued Chile's authentic rural music and collected more than 3000 songs throughout the country. She was also a great rescuer of the natural culture, which she considered to be embedded in folk music. In 1953, she was awarded Caupolican for outstanding folklorist of the year.

1960

Ana Figueroa (1908-1970)

She was the first person to hold the position of Assistant Director-General of the International Labor Organization.

1977

Monica Madrige Gotierez

She was Minister of Justice form 1977-83 and Ambassador to the Organization of American States from 1983-85.

1990

Soledad Alvear Valenzuela

From 1990-94, she was Minister for the National Women Service, Minister of Justice from 1994-99 and Minister of Foreign Affairs in 2000.

2000
Wilma Kalsich Sanchez
She became Provincial
Governor of Tierra Del Fuego
in 2000.

COLUMBIA
1780
Manuela Beltran
In 1780, she led an uprising
against undue taxation by the
colonial government in her
country, the first woman to
organize a revolt against the
Spanish government in
Columbia.

1843
Maria Martinez de Nisser
In 1843, she published her
diary describing her
experiences as a soldier
during the revolution in
Antioquia.

1878
Soledad Acosta de Samper
(1833-1903)
She was editor of the
feminist journal *La Mujer*
that she founded in 1878.
She wrote historical fiction,
biographies and history and
dedicated her life to
feminist causes.

1940
Fanny Burtrago (1940-)
In 1969, she won the Cali
Theater Festival prize for
her play *El hombre de paja*.
The pattern of dysfunctional
families extends throughout
her writing even to her
children's literature.

1956
Josephine Valencia de Hubach
Former Governor of the
Province of Cavca, she was
Education Minister in 1956-
58, the first woman in the
Columbian cabinet.

1962
**Esmeralda Arboleda de Cuevas
Cancino**
A Columbian politician, she
was appointed Minister of
Transport from 1960-62, the
first woman in Columbia to
hold a cabinet-level
position. She was also the
first Columbian woman to be
elected to the Senate and
from 1966 to 1968, she became
her country's first female
ambassador to Austria and
Yugoslavia.

1982
Nohemi Sanin Posada de Rubio
From 1982-85, she was
Minister of Communication,
from 1991-94, Minister of
Exernal Relations and 1998
presidential candidate. She
was Ambassador to Venezuela
and Germany from 1985-91 and
to United Kingdom from 1994-
98.

1995
**Maria Emma Mejia Velez de
Caballero**
Former Ambassador to Spain,
she became Minister of
Education from 1995-96 and
Minister of External
Relations from 1996-98.

2000

Nancy Patricia Guitierrez Castaneda

Former Secretary General of Government of Cundinamarea, Acting Governor and Secretary of Environment, she became President of Camera de Representatives in 2000.

ECUADOR

1929

Alicia Yanex Cossio

(1920-)

Her first novel *Bruna soroche y los tios* published in 1973 distinguished her as one of Ecuador's principal novelists of the last 25 years. Most of her work focuses on live in Ecuador's central range of the Andes. Her second novel *Yo vendo unos ojos negros* published in 1979 reiterates her deep concern over women's place in modern society and the need to overcome the taboos and traditions which continue to stifle growth and development.

1956

Rosalia Arteaga Serrano de Cordova de Fernandez

She was a provincial governor in 1986, Vice-Minister of Culture from 1992-94, Vice President from 1996-98 and a presidential candidate in 1998.

1982

Fabiola Cuvi Ortiz

An economist at the Central University in Quito, she founded and is director of the Ecuadorian Institute for the Study and Training of Women. She is founder and director of National Office for Women. In 1982, she became the first Ecuadorian woman to graduate from the Interamerican College of Defense in Washington DC. She was named Ambassador of Peace at the European University for Peace in Austria in 1993.

1991

Ana Luisa Arijios

She was president of Banco Central del Ecuador from 1991-93. In 1999, she became Minister of Finance.

1994

Rosalia Arteaga Serrano de Fernandez de Cordova

A former minister, she was Vice President from 1994-98, Acting President in 1997 and a presidential candidate in 1998.

FALKLAND ISLANDS

1992

S. Cameron

She became the Government Representative in London in 1992.

1998

Sharon Halford

In 1998, she became Councilor of Public Works and Housing.

GUYANA

1964

Winifred Gasin

Between 1964-70, She was Minister of Education, Youth, Recreations and Social

Development and Ambassador to Barbados from 1973-79.

1967
Cecilene Cleef Baird
In 1967, she became Lord Mayor of Georgetown and Minister of Education from 1970-71.

1973
Edith Bynoe
Between 1973-78, she was Parliamentary Secretary of Trade and Parliamentary Secretary of Consumer Protection from 1978-82.

Winifred Gakin
She was appointed Ambassador to Barbados from 1973-79, the first woman ambassador of her country.

1983
Urima E. Johnson
She was Minister in Office of the Premier Minister and Minister of National Development (1983-85), Minister within the Ministry of National Mobilization and Deputy Minister of Regional Development (1985-90) and Minister of Regional Development (1990-92).

1984
Yvonne V. Harewood-Benn
From 1984-89, she was Minister of Information and Minister in the President's Office from 1989-91.

1992
Indranie Chandarpal
She was Minister of Social Development and Labor (1992-93), Minister in the Ministry of Labor, Human Services and Social Security with additional charge of Women's Affairs and Housing (1993-98) and Minister of Human Services and Social Security (1998).

1997
Janet Jagan
From 1973-97, she was Editor-in-Chief of The Mirror and Ambassador-at-Large. In 1993, she became Acting Permanent Representative of the United Nations. Upon President Jagan's death in 1997, his widow Janet Jagan became Prime Minister and then executive president.

PARAGUAY
1945
Isabel Arrua Vallejo
Former Director General for the Minister of Finance, she became attaché of the Embassy of Paraguay to Brazil in 1945, Paraguay's first woman with diplomatic rank. From 1949-50, she was Ambassador to United States.

1989
Maria Cyntia Prieto Conti de Alegre
She was Minister of Health and Social Affairs from 1989-93.

1993
Christina Munos
She was Ministerof Women's Affairs in Ministry of Health and Social Welfare (1993-97), Minister of Women's Affairs (1997-98) and Minister and Executive Secretary in the Secretariat of Women's Affairs in 1999.

1999
Elisa Ruiz Dia
In 1999, she became Minister in the Presidency for Press and Communication.

PERU

1852
Clorinda Matto de Turner
(1852-1909)
She was the first Peruvian novelist to command an international reputation and the first to dramatize the exploitation of indigenous Latin American people. A dedicated feminist, she wrote the first guide to literature for Peruvian women and worked on behalf of Andean Indians. *Aves sin nido* was the first major Spanish American novel to protest the plight of native peoples and important reading for all students of the indigenous cultures of South America. The novel *Torn from the Nest* explores the relationship between the landed gentry and the indigenous peoples of the Andean Mountain communities. *Birds without a Nest* was published in 1889 and portrays a vivid picture of Peruvian life and argues against the oppression of women and native Peruvians.

1900
Laura Esther Rodgriguez-Dulanto
In 1900, she became the first licensed woman physician in Peru.

1904
Irene Silva de Santolalla
(1904 -)
An internationally recognized expert on family education and school, she was an active suffragist and was invaluable in women getting the right to vote in 1955. She was elected to the Peruvian Senate in 1956, the first woman in the Senate.

1917
Maria Jesus Alvarado Rivera
Feminist, she founded Peru's first women's organization Evolucion Femenina in 1917.

1926
Blanca Varela (1926-)
Poet, she published her first volume of poetry *Ese puerto existe* in 1959. Her poetry has made her one of the most important points of reference regarding literature written by Peruvian women in the second half of the 20th century. She has also been director of the publishing house Fondo de Cultura Economica.

1927
Yma Symac (1927 -)
A Peruvian song stylist, she imitated birds, drums, etc. as she sang and revived interest in ancient South American music.

1988
Maria Salzar Castellanos
In 1998, she was appointed Ambassador to Poland, the first female ambassador of her country.

1992
Maria Hermina Drago Correa
She was Comptroller from 1992-93 and 1994-97.

1994
Maria Luisa Federica Soto
She was Minister of the Presidency from 1994-95 and Ambassador to France and UNESCO since 1996.

1996
Elisa Carrera Cabrere de Escalante
Between 1996-97, she was Minister of Transport, Communication, Housing and Construction.

1997
Edith Mella do Cespedes
In 1997, she became 1st Vice President and took over the leadership for most of the year because of the president's illness. She became Acting President of the Congreso de la Republica in 1998.

1999
Martha Hildebrant Perrez Trevino
She was 2nd Vice President from 1996-97 and became President of the Congreso de Republica in 1999.

SURINAME
1941
Yvonne Reine Antoniette Rawales-Resida (1941 -)
In 1996, she became Minister of Regional Development and in 1999 Minister of Justice and Police. Since 2000, she has been leader of the NDP 2000 Fraction in the Nationale Assemblee.

1987
Evelyn M.B. Alexander-Vanenburg
From 1987-90, she was Minister of the Interior, District Administration and People's Mobilization.

1996
Marijke Indra Kjawalapersad
In 1996, she co-founded and became vice-president of Basispartij voor Democratie en Vernieuwing. She was President of the National Assemblee From 1996-2000.

URAGUAY
1907
Delmira Agustini
(1886-1914)
She published her 3-volumne book of poems, The White Book, in 1907. Her poetry was noted for its sensuality, warmth and passion. In 1914, her husband murdered her.

1911
Clotilde Lursi
In 1911, she is the first woman to enter the diplomatic service in her country.

1950
Juana de Abarbourou
In 1950, she published *Perdida* and became President of the Uruguayan Society of Authors.

1968
Alba Roballo
A former President of Senado, she became Minister of Education and Social Welfare in 1968, her country's first female minister.

1970
Quintana Solari
In 1970, she was appointed Ambassador to Yugoslavia, the first female ambassador of her country.

1984
Adela Dias Sosa Reta
She was Minister of Culture and Education from 1984-89 and Acting Minister of Justice in 1985.

2000
Primavera Garbarino
In 2000, she became Minister of Industry, Energy and Mines.

VENEZUELA

1936
Carmen Clemente
In 1936, she was first woman journalist to begin printing cultural columns for women in several newspapers in Venezuela.

Lya Imber
In 1936, she received her degree and became Venezuela's first woman doctor.

1948
Ida Gramcko
She became Venezuela's Ambassador to the Soviet Union in 1948.

1950
Paulina Luisi
Feminist activist, she became the first woman physician in Uruguay in 1950 and worked to change the prostitution laws and to destroy while slavery and alcoholism. Later, she became a member of the Uruguayan diplomatic corps.

1969
Avra Celina Cassanova
When appointed in 1969, she was the first woman to serve her country as Minister of Development.

1992
Ruth de Krivoy
She was President of Banko Central de Venezuela from 1992-94.

Irene Saez (1952 -)
In 1992, she was elected Mayor of Chacao, the richest district of Venezuela's capital, Caracas. She was re-elected on an anti-corruption, efficient-government platform.

List of Countries

Bibliography

1. Chronology of Women's History by Kirstin Olsen, Green wood Press, 1994.
2. Encyclopedia of Latin American Literature by Verity Smith, Fitzroy Dearborn, 1997.
3. Famous First Facts, a record of first happenings, discoveries and inventions in American history by Joseph Nathan Kane, Steven Anzouin and Janet Podell, 5th ed., published H. W. Watson Co, 1997.
4. Lesser Known Women by Beverly E. Galenbu, Lynn Reenner Publications, 1992.
5. Maryland Biographical Sketches by George and Virginia Schaun, Maryland Historical Press, 1984.
6. Mothers of Invention by Ethlie Ann Vare and Greg Ptacek, William Morrow & Co, 1988.
7. Notable Maryland Women, edited by Winifred G. Helmes, Tidewater Publications, 1977.
8. The Timetables of Women's History by Karen Greenspan, published Simon & Schuster, 1994.
9. 1999 Women in World History Curriculum, http://www.womeninworldhistory.com/index/html
10. A Celebration of Women Writers, WRITERS FROM AUSTRALIA, http://www.cs.cmu.edu/~mmbt/women/generate/AUSTRALIA/html
11. Center for Digital Discourse and Culture at Virginia Tech University, http://www.cddc.vt.edu/feminism/
12. Congressional Biographies, http://www.glue.umd.edu
13. Connecticut Women's Hall of Fame, http://www.cwhf.org/
14. Czech Feminist Trailblazers: Women Trailblazers, http://www.pinn.net/~sunshine/czech/torzo.html
15. Dictionary of New Zealand Biography, http://www.nzhistory.net.nz
16. Famous 5 Foundation, http://www.canuck.com/famous5/html/
17. Famous Polish discoverers, travelers and scientists, http://www.hum.amu.edu.pl/~zbzw/ph/sci/distra.htm
18. Goldman Environmental Prize, 1999, http://www.goldmanprize.org
19. Inventions and Inventors of Latvia, http://inventions.lxa.lv
20. Latvian Scientists, http://www.lza.lv/scientists
21. Lemelson-MIT Program's Invention Dimension, http://www.mit.edu/invent/index.html
22. Notable Northern Women, http://www.yukoncollege.yk.ca/
23. Notable Women Ancestors, http://www.rootsweb/com
24. School of Mathematics and Statistics, University of St Andrews, Scotland, http://www-history.mcs.st-andrews.ac.uk

25. Spotlight on Chile – Women's Influence,
    http://www.localaccess.com/chappell/chile/women.html
26. Sunshine for Women,
    http://www.pinn.net/~sunshine/march99.html
27. The Australian Magazine, http://wisdom.psinet.net.au
28. The Australian Science Archives Project,
    http://www.asap.unimelb.edu.au/bsparcs/bsparcs.htm
29. The Canadian Encyclopedia,
    http://www.science.ca/reference/html
30. The Hashemite Royal Court of Jordan, edited on 22 June 99,
    http://www.go.com.jo/QNoorjo
31. The Hunger Project, http://www.igc.org.thp/prize
32. The International Archive of Women in Architecture, updated
    9/10/99, http://spec.lib.ut.edu/spec/iawa/
33. The National Women's Hall of Fame,
    http://www.greatwomen.org.
34. University of Western Australia, Department of French
    Studies, http://www.arts.uwa.edu.au
35. Voices from the Gaps, http://voices.cla.umn.edu
36. Worldwide Guide to Women in Leadership,
    http://hjem.get2net,dk/Womeningovernments/
37. Women Artists in History, http://home.webcom.se/art
38. Women of Achievement and Herstory, Women's Internet
    Information Network, http://www.undelete.org/index.html.
39. Women's History by Cowles History Group, 1996,
    http://www.thehistorynet.com/WomensHistory/
40. Women's International Center, http://www.wic.org

Printed in the United States
By Bookmasters